The Lost Lennon Tapes Project
An Unauthorized Guide To The Complete Radio Series 1988 - 1992

The Lost Lennon Tapes Project
An Unauthorized Guide To The Complete Radio Series 1988 - 1992

All 218 Episodes Listed In Detail With A Complete Index Of Unreleased Tracks, Bag Bootleg Tracks, And Commercially Released Tracks

Compiled By: Charles Iscove   ISBN:978-0-9699363-0-5   © Charles Iscove 2009
                                                              essentialrecords.ca

TABLE OF CONTENTS

Acknowledgements iii

Forward by Belmo iv

Historical Perspective vii

The Lost Lennon Tapes Project
    Introduction x
    The Methodology x
    The Episodes xiii
    Intros and Extros xiii
    Live At The BBC Tracks xiv
    The Unreleased Tracks xiv

The Lost Lennon Tapes
First Published In Beatlology Volume 3 No. 1 Sept./Oct. 2000 xiv

John's Residences xvii

The Episodes 1988 - 1992 1

Chronology of Lost Lennon Tapes Tracks 197

Unreleased Tracks Index In Song Title Order 210

Bag Records Bootlegs Tracks 234

Commercial Versions of Lost Lennon Tracks 251

Afterward 258

ACKNOWLEDGEMENTS

Whenever I read acknowledgments in books I am flabbergasted by the number of people listed. I often think to myself, "I don't think I've met that many people in my entire life!" So I will thank only three who had a direct connection to the completing of this book. All other family members, Beatle friends, and pets, past and present, I will leave as inferred.

I would like to thank Fred McKie, who helped me source all the shows and put up with my insistence on using only high-quality tape "back in the day." Without Fred I never would have had a copy of each show soon enough after it was aired to make notes, and without having done that at the time, it's unlikely that I would have tackled the task after 218 episodes were completed.

When I was working on *Compressed Belmo* in 2001, a compilation of years of *Belmo's Beatleg News* (which rated bootlegs and was an indispensable collector's resource), I mentioned to Belmo that I had started a Lost Lennon Tapes book back in 1992 and completed a first draft a few years later, but I had long since abandoned the idea. He asked me why and I told him it was because like the Beatles, I had been turned down by literally every publisher of Beatles' books in the world at that time, even though there was nothing of its kind in print. (L.R.E. King published books on the first two years, but covered only half of the series.) I was amazed because pretty picture books featuring common collectibles and rewrites of The Beatles' story were being cranked out at a remarkable pace, and they appeared to be no problem for the budding Beatles' author to publish. Belmo not only urged me to revive the book, he hounded me for years about it. Once I told him that I was transferring my cassettes to digital format (for my own collection, not for the book) he turned up the heat and insisted that I HAD to finish the book because nobody else would do it, and the world needed the documentation as part of The Beatles' history. So, we all have Belmo to thank for the existence of this book.

I must thank my partner in Beatles (and everything else) Janet Harrison who not only has one of the most wonderful last names in the history of the world, (I used to joke that I'm going to change MY name to hers), she is a great proof-reader, and because we met as Beatles' collectors (and married our collections) she never tired of hearing me blathering on and on about what I did last week with *The Lost Lennon Tapes*. It takes a genuine interest and a strong constitution to listen to a breakdown of the distinct differences between the nine versions of *Serve Yourself* over dinner.

And to every Beatles' book publisher in the world who turned down this book (and because I do not have an MBE to return in protest), all I can say is thank you. Had the book been published in 1995, it would not have been nearly as accurate as it is now. And thank you to the digital age, and to on-demand book publishing, without which this book would not have been printed.

Finally, I would also like to thank the following websites which were very helpful in confirming and cross-referencing much of my research. *JPGR* (http://www.jpgr.co.uk/), *The Beatles Archive - Between the Lines: Complete Home Recordings 1975-1980* (http://web.ncf.ca/fl512/beatles/releases/between_the_lines.htm) and *John Lennon's Homes* (http://homepage.ntlworld.com/carousel/pob40.html).

FOREWARD BY BELMO

The world was a much different place in 1988.

In 1988 there was no Internet. You couldn't download files or share the latest bootlegs with fellow collectors. The only way to get the newest releases was to purchase them from the local record store or via mail order. There were no iPods or MP3s. Compact discs were relatively new and digital recording was in its infancy. LPs (long playing vinyl albums) were the medium of choice for collectors. Cassette tapes were the only options for trading music.

My early collection of Beatles bootlegs ('Beatlegs') consisted of poor sounding vinyl records and cassettes sent to me by fellow fans. But by the early 1980s, Beatlegs took on a new dimension. Collectors were soon being treated to a higher level of rarities by the Fab Four. From about 1985 through 2001, the Beatlegs fans were hearing of some of the most amazing studio outtakes, demos, and live recordings ever made available. These years have since become known as "The Golden Age of Beatlegs."

I was lucky enough to be involved in the underworld of Beatleg collecting and trading during this time. I was so into it that in 1987 I edited and published an international newsletter (*Belmo's Beatleg News*) solely devoted to reviewing the plethora of new Beatlegs. BBN was a labor of love and lasted for a wonderful 15 years.

Who could forget the many groundbreaking titles to come our way: *Sessions*, *Abbey Road Studio Tour*, *At the BEEB* series on Transcription Records, *The Quarrymen at Home*, *Not For Sale*, *No. 3 Abbey Road N.W. 8*, *Nothing Is Real* and *Sweet Apple Trax* to name just a few. These Beatlegs blew our minds at the time. However, no one could have predicted what was yet to come or the impact that the compact disc would have on collecting.

In 1988 Swingin' Pig Records entered the bootleg arena with the jaw-dropping CD series, *Ultra Rare*, featuring studio outtakes in stereo! We couldn't believe our luck. These were followed by *Stars of '63*, Bulldog Records *Live* collections, *Songs From the Past* and so many more.

It was in this environment that Yoko Ono Lennon announced *The Lost Lennon Tapes* radio program to the world. Fans wondered just how much truly rare music we would hear and if the shows would be worthy of our time. They would be. Of course, Lennon and Beatles fans were thrilled at the prospect of hearing rare Lennon tunes. Anticipation was high when the three-hour premier aired in the United States on February 7, 1988. Needless to say, the program was greeted with enthusiasm by most all.

At the time of the airing, I was living in Anchorage, Alaska. Unfortunately, no local radio station played the radio show. My disappointment was palpable. Luckily for me, I had friends in the 'Lower 48' who sent me cassettes of the shows as they were aired. My heartfelt thanks go out to them.

John Lennon had made no secret of the fact that he would like to have his own radio show. On one occasion he actually did play DJ for a New York radio station. Yoko Ono knew this and she also knew that fans would appreciate hearing his unreleased music. In a radio interview promoting *The Lost Lennon Tapes*, Yoko said, "I think that the spirit of sharing is what we are all about. I have the choice of keeping these things locked up or to share them."

To this end Yoko enlisted the help of friend and confidante Elliot Mintz to help organize the tapes and produce them for Westwood One. Said Mintz at the time, "This is raw Lennon. Lennon without tears. It's not a tribute program but an audio portrait of a man's life and work. It is a weekly appointment with John Lennon where you can tune in and visit with him."

While *The Lost Lennon Tapes* shows would occasionally be bogged down by Elliot Mintz's ramblings, some poor editing and song repetition, most of the programs were quite satisfying and often revelatory. I was especially gratified to hear so many of Lennon's home demos and alternate takes.

It was inevitable that the music from the shows would find their way onto bootlegs. This task was taken up by Bag One Records out of Los Angeles. Each colored vinyl bootleg featured a color sleeve and adequate liner notes. There would eventually be 35 volumes of LPs and, later on, 22 CDs covering the same material but with a few extras added.

The Bag One *Lost Lennon Tapes* were a highlight for collectors from 1988 through 1997 - when the final LP was released. For many fans whose local radio stations didn't air the show, these bootlegs were their only chance to hear the songs from the shows.

During these 'Golden Years', we saw a number of other amazing Beatlegs come to the fore: *Artifacts* from Big Music, *The Complete BBC Sessions* on Great Dane, Yellow Dog's *Let It Be Rehearsals* and the *Day By Day* series, Vigotone's many releases such as *Imagine All The Outtakes, As Nature Intended, The John Barrett Tapes* and *Revolution*, Silent Sea's all inclusive album collections, and Dr. Ebbetts beautiful reissues of the original albums onto CD.

Still, there was more! This time fans would be able to purchase 'official bootlegs' from The Beatles and Yoko Ono. There is little doubt that The Beatles *Anthology* was inspired by the huge international success of "Artifacts" (three volumes); while many believe that numerous tracks on *Anthology* were actually sourced from Beatlegs.

Paul McCartney would also get into the act by producing his own radio show in the summer of 1995. It was called *Oobu Joobu* and was on Westwood One Radio. While interesting and mildly entertaining, Macca's shows were nowhere near as influential or groundbreaking as the Lennon programs.

Finally, in the fall of 2009, the remastered Beatles catalog was released amid a flurry of great reviews. Worldwide sales netted The Beatles' empire millions in revenue. Apple officials unofficially gave some of the credit to Dr. Ebbetts for the timing of the remasters.

One might wonder how much of the unreleased music we've been hearing from so many of the classic rock artists would still be gathering dust in the vaults if it hadn't been for the bootleggers. It was the wildly successful sales of bootlegs featuring outtakes, demos and live recordings that forced record executives to finally recognize the financial merit of including 'bonus' tracks on reissues and in box sets.

Bootleggers have always 'given fans what they want'. And what they wanted were rarities by their musical heroes. Yoko Ono Lennon also knew what John's fans wanted and provided the songs for all to hear. We should all commend her for that.

And, now, in this book, Charles Iscove has given us what we want; and that is a thorough and exhaustively researched compendium of John Lennon's official and unofficial musical output broadcast on *The Lost Lennon Tapes* radio show series. Charles' analysis of *The Lost Lennon Tapes* radio show is insightful and his attention to detail is remarkable.

The Lost Lennon Tapes Project is everything I hoped it would be - and more. True, I bugged Charles for years to complete this book. I knew he was the ideal person to take on such a daunting undertaking. He has not let us down. I believe Beatles and Lennon historians will, for years to come, refer to Charles' book as THE FINAL WORD on *The Lost Lennon Tapes*.

Finally, the book accomplishes something else here besides the obvious cataloging of information and program descriptions. It reveals the magnitude of John Lennon's musical genius and illustrates just how prolific a songwriter and musician he was. The "Lost Lennon Tapes" was a unique program in that nothing like it had ever been attempted before. No single artist has had such a treatment before or since. And I am certain there will never be another radio show as historic or influential because there will never be another John Lennon.

Belmo is the author of seven books on The Beatles: *BLACK MARKET BEATLES* (co-author Jim Birkenstadt), *THE BEATLES: NOT FOR SALE, THE BEATLES ARTIFACTS, THE MAKING OF SGT. PEPPER, GEORGE HARRISON: HIS WORDS, WIT AND WISDOM, THE BEATLES DISCOVERED,* and *THE BEATLES CHRISTMAS BOOK* (co-author Garry Marsh). Belmo occasionally writes articles for Beatles fanzines and was editor/publisher of *Belmo's Beatleg News* from 1987 through 2001. His favorite Beatle is John Lennon.

HISTORICAL PERSPECTIVE

In order to put John Lennon into perspective you have to start with the Beatles. And in order to understand why I would take on a project like this, I need to go back to 1964. I was born in Toronto in 1954, so I was 10 years old when the Beatles landed in New York and old enough to have a clear memory of watching the first Ed Sullivan show with my disapproving parents in the background. In that same year, my brother bought the Canadian *Twist And Shout* LP (Canada's version of *Please Please Me*) and I remember playing it endlessly while dancing around the living room. As with most kids my age, I had a hand-sized transistor radio which I carried everywhere with me; even to bed. I listened constantly to our local AM pop chart radio stations as these were the days before FM rock radio.

The excitement generated by the Beatles was enormous. In the early years, people didn't know the names of each Beatle, who sang lead, or who played which instrument; a far cry from today where there is a huge historical resource of Beatles' books and films for verification. They had such an ecstatic sound that when heard constantly on the radio it became contagious and spilled over into day-to-day life, making it fun and exciting. As a result, the release of each Beatles' record, whether single or album was an event comparable with the breaking of a major news story. The effect of such an enormous influence on society is difficult to imagine now that the ability of any band or musician to instigate that level of change has long gone. Literally, there is no comparison.

A key ingredient of the excitement that surrounded The Beatles was the idea that change for the better was not only possible, but inevitable, and that it was going to happen very quickly. The only thing in the way was the attitude of the "older" generation, but surely it wouldn't take long for them to change once they could see there was a better way or once they got too old and moved out of the way. The "generation gap" as they called it, between the kids and their parents was primarily blamed on materialism. In retrospect, it wasn't about that at all. Just look at all of the material wealth the "baby boomers" have accumulated since the '60s. Our parents had lived through the lean years of the Depression and World War II, and it was natural for them to now want material comforts that they couldn't have during those years. The generational gap was in music appreciation and morality - not a life experience gap. Most of our parents refused to listen to anything that resembled so-called "rock" music. Subsequently, it was banned in many households. And along with the music ban was a ban on any ideas that sprang from it. Bickering couples were common. Men were still the lord of the household and women were subservient. Today, we would call some of their "normal" behaviour towards each other abusive. Middle-class children were expected to become professionals, get married, and have their own children by their early twenties. If you were thirty and not married with children there was "something" wrong with you.

In the world I grew up in conformity meant short hair and no casual clothing. Blue jeans were not allowed in schools. Fathers still wore suits most of the time - even at home. It was the uniform that a man was expected to wear. Casual clothes were not meant to be worn once you were a "grownup". In 1969, I remember having the fight of my life to be allowed to grow my hair just over the top of my ears.

The Beatles didn't look or behave like our parents. They were more stable, had more fun, and had better values than the society we grew up in. Who you were inside was more important than appearances. And so kids began to follow The Beatles' values instead of their parents: the casual lifestyle, the long hair, the dropping out of school (the Beatles did it to form a band) and to some extent, the drugs. From my perspective, drugs were not nearly as widespread as history makes them out to be. Middle-class kids that

I grew up with were generally afraid of drugs if they had any common sense. By the late '60s, once it had been established that marijuana was pretty harmless, nearly everyone was trying it, including some of our parents. But the idea that it was addictive and would eventually lead to harder drugs was silly and untrue. That was society's scare tactic. The people that I knew who smoked dope back then went on to become professionals, not drug addicts.

Growing up in the '60s, we had the fear of nuclear war and the war in Viet Nam, but we never heard about environmental devastation, climate change, vanishing species, population explosion, terrorists, and financial meltdown. There is a sense today that many of the world's problems can never be solved. But in the '60s, it was genuinely felt that if we could change the world; we could end all wars and there would be nothing else to worry about. Give peace a chance! When John took up the peace crusade, it wasn't just the stuffy old press who thought he'd lost his way. His chosen path was widely considered naive and crazy by nearly everyone that I knew, young or old; even if it was thought a noble one. The problem with giving peace a chance is that even if there are no countries, no religion and only sky, there would still be turf wars because we are a tribal species. We are hard-wired and need to belong to a cohesive group, whether it's our own family or an extended family. And because most tribes are territorial, conflict over limited resources is inevitable. It is very difficult to fight the biological imperative so that, "the world live as one".

In 1970, The Beatles had broken up, gone out of fashion, and generally, music became heavier and slower. If you examine the hits of the early '70s you can't help but notice how slow they were, even the remakes of '60s songs were all slower than the originals - a reflection of the depressing feeling of the times. Nixon was in the White House and there was always a feeling of distrust with him. The Viet Nam war was still going on despite all the talk about peace and love. For music fans, overblown stadium rock shows were becoming common place and boring.

There weren't many Beatles fans who stuck with John during the post-Beatles' period. In fact there weren't many Beatles fans at all in the early 1970s. My continued interest in collecting Beatles' records made me unpopular with my peers and I was warned numerous times by friends and family, that I was crazy and I was throwing my money away. People like me needed to grow up and leave The Beatles back in their childhood where they belonged. Of course it was the very same people who phoned me immediately after John died to say, "Just think of how much your Beatles' collection is worth now!"

After the Beatles broke up, I used to believe, as did everyone back then, that the "next" Beatles was just around the corner because even the Beatles said so. Some new sound would come along to lift us out of the doldrums. Or the Beatles would come back one day and "save" us. But it never happened. After the Nixon years, there was plastic music called disco. What really made people hate disco was that it was an invention of improving technology. The art in music was taken away from the writer/performer and given over to studio production. It seemed to reflect a vacant, mindless society that just wanted to dance. And then punk arrived, and though it brought back the energy of the early Beatles, it was completely negative; anti-everything. This was understandable given the times, but British Rock no longer had the world-wide influence that it had in the '60s and its message of violence and anarchy was fortunately mostly irrelevant outside of Britain.

While Paul was consistently cranking out the light hits, John's music was for the eclectic purist collector. This is the way I perceived not just my own, but the public's reaction to John's major albums when they were released. *Plastic Ono Band* was brilliant, but stark and nakedly personal to the point of being uncomfortable to listen to unless you were a major fan. *Imagine* had some great tracks but was uneven moving from the bare sound of *Oh My Love*, to the excessive arrangement on *How Do You Sleep?*, to the wall-of-sound that is *Don't Wanna Be A Soldier*, to the embarrassing *Oh Yoko!*. While great material, as an album it seemed disconnected and wasn't considered a landmark Lennon piece as it is today. *Live In New York City* was a disappointment. It was actually what John wanted it to be - a collection of disposable news stories hastily composed and recorded. The live *Cold Turkey* and *Well (Baby Please Don't Go)* were the best tracks and the ones that I played the most. *Mind Games* was a great album but by then he had blown it in the public perception arena and it was pretty much overlooked. Thanks to the number one hit with Elton John, *Walls And Bridges* got the attention it deserved. The only question was when would he get rid of Phil Spector and stop drowning every new LP in increasing layers of echo? *Double Fantasy* was much maligned before his death because the great oracle Lennon was writing boring songs about domesticity. Wasn't he supposed to be saving the world instead? The echo was finally gone but Yoko was back big-time and that didn't sit well with the music world, or most fans, in those days. The chart positions tell a different story as people bought John Lennon's albums anyway - only because he was John Lennon. As with all solo Beatles' work, I have always felt that the best tracks are the hidden gems, like *Remember, Crippled Inside, Out The Blue* and *Scared*.

Part of the energetic drive of the '60s was built on anticipation - what was new and what was coming next was exciting. Nobody espoused that more than the Beatles. Looking back was for losers and old people. It was the present and the future that were important. In fact, John said in 1980, "I'm for the living, not the dead"; a quote rarely seen in these days of deifying John Lennon, the Beatles and the 1960s. What bothers me about retrospectives and anniversaries is that we have them at all. What I loved about the Beatles and their solo work, and still do was the music.

From John's point of view, he would have liked the fact that the end of his life meant the end of the cult of Beatles. He said that he had learned that following leaders doesn't work because the leaders aren't gods, they're the same as you and me, and that fans should stop looking to him for answers because he was only a pop star and didn't have any. In the end, the life lessons we all learned from The Beatles were that "the love you take is equal to the love you make" and that each of us should look inward instead of to others to solve our problems. You can't change the world by music or violence. It has to come from within each individual person.

THE LOST LENNON TAPES PROJECT

INTRODUCTION

From January 1988 to March 1992, the most remarkable Beatles-related radio series ever broadcast was heard each Monday evening in the United States for 218 consecutive weeks. *The Lost Lennon Tapes* featured a total of 814 John Lennon and Beatles' rarities of which 533 were unique, unreleased tracks and broadcast on the radio for the first and last time.

The series covered the story of John's life using in-depth interviews with intimates, friends and co-workers, as well as rare TV appearances, outtakes, rough mixes, studio dialogue, and home demos of nearly every solo John Lennon song and many of Lennon's Beatles' songs.

However, the series was a disappointment for fans and was considered "too American" in its rambling format to be aired in the U.K. The narration by host Elliot Mintz was annoyingly slow and plodding. The early segments lacked organization, jumping irrationally from one topic to another (while later shows were built around themes). To add to the confusion, many of the unreleased tracks were broadcast repeatedly throughout the four years, in varying lengths, edits and quality. In the end, each show consisted of only a few rarities.

For millions of fans like me, being a Beatles' collector meant possessing every Beatles' and solo album, single and snippet of dialogue, as well as any record with Beatle involvement, and anything unreleased. This was not idol worship - it was our unwavering assumption that everything they did was brilliant. It's impossible to imagine any contemporary musical artist having that much cultural importance today.

For collectors who already had everything they could get their hands on, the wealth of unreleased material that *The Lost Lennon Tapes* promised to air was like a glimpse at the Holy Grail. It required that the entire show be taped and dissected. However, the series rambled on every week for four years, often repeating content that had been previously broadcast. It was far longer than most fans had the patience for, and with each passing year fewer and fewer radio stations aired it. The majority of collectors resorted to buying the Bag One Records bootlegs which they assumed had everything. I was always leery of the content of bootlegs and sensed that if you didn't stick with taping the shows you weren't going to get the ultimate Lost Lennon tapes. My research for this book proved that I was right.

THE METHODOLOGY

The level of accuracy that I have achieved in writing and researching this book could not have been reached before the digital age. Here is a brief rundown of what it took to compile this information.

For the first two years of the series, *The Lost Lennon Tapes* was broadcast on Sunday in Toronto, initially at night. Then, it suddenly switched to early Sunday morning (see the article in *Beatlology* Volume 3, No. 1, Sept./Oct. 2000 for more information, reprinted here). I recorded every episode off the radio and onto individual high quality cassette tapes (TDK SA-X60) or video tape (Maxell UD 35-90) setup on timer, when I was away from home for the weekend. The last two years were not broadcast in Canada so I had to obtain copies of these shows from a friend in the U.S. Initially, I bought and mailed boxes of the same brand of cassette tape because they were unavailable where he lived. Later, when he could no longer get the show locally he sent me copies (on varying quality tapes) that he had obtained himself from other U.S. collectors.

I borrowed and later returned original vinyl LP copies of roughly two thirds of the first two years of shows, shortly after the series ended in 1992. I taped each of these over my originally-broadcast tapes. This proved to be immensely time consuming due to having to physically move the arm of the record player to each new segment because of the locked grooves in radio broadcast LPs (refer to the *Beatlology* article for more about this). It also proved to be a horrible mistake, because unbeknownst to me at the time, nearly all of these albums had tiny particles of dirt that were impossible to see or remove with standard cleaning. The dirt was so ingrained that nearly every segment of every show had multiple skips in them, making all of those tapes useless. I can't imagine that this set of discs was ever used for broadcast as it was too soon after the show had aired for that much dirt to have accumulated.

I didn't discover the extent of the skipping until 2006, when I took up the project again and began to slowly transfer every one of the 218 hour long episodes to digital files by recording them one by one onto my computer. Once this was done, I adjusted the overall volume level for each tape to the proper level and then burned them in order to 28 DVD discs.

I then began the arduous task of selecting and removing each of the 814 rarities. Having the advantage of digital software in which you can see the sound wave form, I was able to zoom in to the exact position where each track begins and ends and cut it exactly to the second. This would have been impossible using the old method of hitting the pause button on a tape recorder. Thus, in my notes on the *Bag One* bootlegs, you will see that most of the bootlegged tracks are missing the beginning, the end, or both by a number of seconds. I didn't document how long it took, but there was only so much Lost Lennon I could stand to listen through, even when following my notes to roughly pinpoint where to cut. This phase of the project took roughly two years to complete.

Once I had all of the rarities separated, I was able to compare them and correct several mistakes that I had made when originally I had only a cassette player for this task. Before that could happen, I needed to replace any rarity tracks that skipped. After issuing an appeal for more cassette copies of the original shows in 2007, I eventually came up with the "definitive" set of recordings. However, simply comparing demo A with demo B was not as easy as it sounded. I had to deal with several factors for proper comparison. As the tapes had come from many different sources, there were varying tape speeds, so length of take could not be compared until the version that was too slow or fast was digitally corrected. Again, this would have been impossible before the digital age. Tape quality was another problem because tape hiss or too many generations of copying could make two tracks that were identical sound different. And of course, everything had to be listened to with complete focus several times over to catch some nearly imperceptible skips that were missed, and then to replace those tracks. Lastly, the indiscriminate editing and re-ordering of some of the material made it extremely difficult to piece together what the original sound file contained. This occurred not only for the music but also for John's guest DJ radio appearances.

Once the "definitive" set was complete, midway through 2008, I converted each track to mp3 copies so they would be easier to sort and listen to for final comparisons. At that point I did more research to determine, as closely as possible, the chronological date order of the recordings (not release date). The table that I compiled is included in this book.

I never lost any data during the project, although I did have a hard drive crash early on in the days of burning the transferred tapes to DVD. Consequently, some of my early audio files are in folders called "recovery" on the DVDs, as I was able to retrieve everything using recovery software. Although, it wasn't a catastrophe since I still had the original tapes (and still do), having to transfer all of those episodes again would have been a considerable setback. After that, each week that I worked on the project I had what I called "backup Fridays", where I would force myself to stop all Lost Lennon work on Friday and use that time to back everything up. Each week I would burn six re-writeable DVDs to backup all of the wave files and text files and occasionally I would burn them on DVD-Rs as a permanent backup, just in case.

I used MP3 copies of the *Bag One* bootlegs to compare with the Lost Lennon tracks because I never bought the originals boots since I had all of the shows on tape. Since much of the Lost Lennon material had either been previously bootlegged or was suddenly available to the bootleggers in a longer version than what had been broadcast (hmm, I wonder why), I found that a lot of the material on the bootlegs was not what was broadcast on *The Lost Lennon Tapes* series. For example, how did a track from Part 134 end up with content from Part 86 on CD Number 14 when it hadn't been broadcast yet? Aside from that, there is terrible sibilance and really slow speech on the early CDs. Most tracks are cut off at the beginning and/or end due to fades and inaccuracy of cutting compared with digital editing. Time differences, e.g., 2 seconds, noted in my comparison table are estimated due to differing tape speeds. The worst case of an intro that is completely missing from the bootlegs is the early composing version of *Oh My Love*, which interestingly begins with "John my love for the first time in my life ...". The bootleg track begins after that. Several tracks are longer on *The Lost Lennon Tapes* by several minutes with an extreme example being *Mirror Mirror On The Wall*, which is six minutes longer.

The worst case of butchering that I found is the *How Do You Sleep?* rehearsals. I have determined that there are actually only two of these, but this is how they have been spread out and mangled in the broadcast and on the bootlegs:
LLT Broadcasts:
Part 87 - rehearsal 1 complete
Part 69 - rehearsal 2 incomplete intro fragments played
Part 118 - rehearsal 2 aired without intro
Part 197 - rehearsal 2 intro aired in two pieces but the second piece is incorrectly cut to dialogue at the end of the first run-through - followed by a brief Mintz comment - followed by the second run-through of rehearsal 1

Bootleg 18:
rehearsal 2 - as broadcast in Part 197 - with the second incorrect piece removed
rehearsal 2 - intro from Part 197 is cut too early, before the last line "where would we put 'em" to the second run-through of rehearsal 1

A similar mess could be found in the multiple airings of the single practice session for *Mucho Mungo* with Harry Nilsson.

Finally, I found an oddity, picked up when I compared my translation with L.R.E. Kings' books of the first two years of the series. Occasionally, King's book listed a complete, commercially-released track that was different from what I had in my notes. Upon closer examination, through careful listening, I determined that once in awhile radio stations padded out the shows with their own insertion of a Beatles' or Lennon track. In the handful of cases where this occurred, I have removed the titles.

THE EPISODES

Number One is the first show following the three-part preview, as printed on the original broadcast LP discs. Initially, some sources called this show Number Four, creating considerable confusion for collectors. In addition, each summary contains the original U.S. broadcast date and the title of the show when they were given.

Unreleased demos, outtakes and studio dialogue appear in bold and are underlined. Demos have been numbered in order of appearance on the program, unless a later broadcast contained an earlier-dated version. A demo listed without a number indicates that there was only one demo of that song broadcast.

When a commercially-released song is played in its entirety, the title is capitalized and the source is listed, using U.K. albums and Past Masters for singles. Any song broadcast with narration over part of it is listed as "under dialogue." John Lennon interviews from an unknown source are listed as "interview re:".

Demos and live performances have been cross-referenced to all other episodes in which they occur in complete form. An episode number underlined at the end of an unreleased track indicates the location of the best version of that track (such as "also #114"). If there is no underlined number, the best version is in the episode in which you are looking.

As the same demos were frequently repeated, the following priority was used to select the best one: the longest version, the best quality, the first broadcast. There was a considerable amount of repetition throughout the series. The quality of demos was generally better during the last year of the show, and as a result, the best sound quality is nearly always the last version broadcast. However, this is offset by the fact that so few original LPs of the last two years were made that the sound quality from existing sources of those years is worse than the first two years.

INTROS AND EXTROS

Beef Jerky was used as the intro and extro of every show until Part 130. Thereafter, it was used sporadically until the end of the series - *What You Got* having taken over as the series theme. Two outtake versions of *Beef Jerky* were used throughout the extro broadcasts, one with a prominent piano and one with a prominent guitar. Because there were so many repetitions, they have been omitted from the Unreleased Tracks table, except Part 64, which contained a piano outtake with a count-in as an extro.

LIVE AT THE BBC TRACKS

Several episodes contained tracks that were performed live by the Beatles for BBC Radio. The sound quality of these tracks was vastly improved from previous radio specials about the Beatles at the Beeb. However, today all of the tracks have been released in better quality than those aired in this series (some commercially on *Beatles Live At The BBC* in November 1994).

THE UNRELEASED TRACKS

Unreleased Tracks are listed in a separate table, sorted by song title and type - the type being a demo, outtake, BBC or live cut.

The Lost Lennon Tapes
(First Published in Beatlology Volume 3 No. 1 Sept./Oct. 2000)

In late 1987, one of the most exciting and incredible events in the history of radio was announced. Yoko Ono had agreed to allow access to a reported 300 hours of unreleased recordings of John's material to be used in a year-long, weekly radio show. Although, much of the material consisted of interviews, there were also hours of rare TV appearances, outtakes, rough mixes, studio dialogue, and home demos. In fact, the sessions for both the *Imagine* and *Double Fantasy* albums, including control room playbacks, had been recorded in their entirety. There was an estimated 100 hours of material from the *Double Fantasy* sessions alone.

Long-time broadcaster and friend of the Lennon's, Elliot Mintz, was appointed by Yoko to host the series. He admitted in television interviews, at the time, to be "terrified" by the enormity of the responsibility.

Production of the series was licensed to Westwood One, which already had a history of excellent documentary and live concert broadcasts. Westwood One does not own radio stations but sells their shows to licensed broadcasters. *The Lost Lennon Tapes* were scheduled for one-hour time slots and actually ran from 45 to 50 minutes, without the commercial breaks.

Each show was pressed on to two vinyl albums since CDs were still in their infancy in 1988. Most often, the first segment ran uninterrupted for 10 to 15 minutes. The other three sides each contained one or two segments. When two segments were included on a single side they were separated by a "locked groove." At the end of each segment was a run-out groove, like the one at the end of a record's side, and the tone arm had to be lifted and placed into the next segment. Pressed into the end of each segment were two or three commercials that were to be broadcast before stations aired their local ads. Several shows contained recruitment ads for the U.S. army. My, how John would have loved that!

An interesting aside for Canadians was that because the ads on the records were for U.S. companies, Canadian stations could not play them, so they were sent copies of the shows on tape with the commercials edited out. This resulted in the airing of tapes with bad dropouts and several shows being broadcast entirely in mono! When I complained to Westwood One, their explanation was that many of John's demos were recorded in mono, despite my pointing out that most of the shows contained stereo album tracks and stereo outtakes.

On Monday night, January 25th 1988, (Sunday the 24th in Canada) the first 3-hour Lost Lennon Preview episode began with an introduction by Yoko followed by two tracks from the Quarry Men rehearsal tapes. Coincidentally, a bootleg album of these previously unheard rehearsals had been released in 1987 and was well known among collectors. There was a slim possibility that these tracks had come from the Dakota archives, but it was more likely that the producers of the series were using the bootleg to fill up time between the real Lost Lennon tapes. This was later confirmed when other popular bootlegs, like *Ultra Rare Trax*, were interspersed throughout the shows.

The Preview show featured complete songs from Beatles' albums, fragments of common interview material, and lots of commentary by Elliot Mintz. The only unreleased track played in the first hour was a fragment of a *Strawberry Fields Forever* demo. The second hour contained an acoustic *Peggy Sue* from the 1971 *Clock* film soundtrack. The third hour had some studio dialogue and fragments of rehearsals and demos from *Double Fantasy*, none of which were played in their entirety.

When the series started, using the same format as the Preview, it was given bad reviews by the press and the running joke among collectors, "if this is the Lost Lennon tapes - then they're still lost!" Particularly annoying was the obnoxious *Dakota Mind Movie*, which consisted of snippets of John doing impersonations, surrounded by circus music, sound effects, and fake audience noises - fun for engineers who fancied themselves as little Sgt. Peppers, but a dreadful waste of air time. Westwood One eventually reacted to the bad publicity and half way through the first season the *Mind Movie* blessedly disappeared and most shows began to have titles and themes such as, "Lennon At Large In Hollywood".

In the early shows, the most you could hope for was two or three genuine, uninterrupted rarities per show. And, as is typical in North American radio, most songs retained an overlapping fraction of dialogue at the beginning, the end or both. Some unreleased tracks were buried under an interview or were maddeningly cut short after one or two verses by Elliot Mintz's commentary. Eventually, all of these songs would be played in their entirety. But at the time, who knew? There were plans in the first year and a half to rework the series for British radio, but Westwood One insisted that oversees stations buy the series intact. In July 1989, the U.K. magazine, *Record Collector*, reported that, "All attempts to tie up the rights for U.K. exposure of the shows have ended in failure." The format was obviously too commercial for the BBC and *The Lost Lennon Tapes* were never aired in England.

In Canada, the audience was declining, and the Toronto radio station which had been broadcasting the show suddenly - and with no prior warning - dropped it in July of the first year. A competing station picked it up, after much confusion (they played previously broadcast episodes and new ones out of order until they straightened it out). The new station moved the broadcast time from Sunday night to Sunday morning (9 a.m. and later changed to 8 a.m.); not peak times in radio, I'm sure. By the start of the second year, Toronto was the only Canadian city that still carried the *The Lost Lennon Tapes*. The official explanation for extending the show into its second year was that the researchers had suddenly found more tapes! You could almost imagine some poor troll in the basement of the Dakota wading through endless cabinets of tapes when suddenly, one day, he turned around, and to his delight, discovered another hundred cabinets he'd never seen before.

The series was extended for two more years (did they find even more tapes?) When it finally ended quietly with Part 218 on March 23, 1992, *The Lost Lennon Tapes* had been airing every week for four years and two months. For those who stuck with it, the rewards were well worth the wait. The studio chat and outtakes from *Double Fantasy* were fairly interesting, but the first-ever broadcast of composing demos of unreleased songs like *Dear John*, outtakes from every solo Lennon album, and John's solo vocals on *Goodnight Vienna* and *Whatever Gets You Through The Night*, were an incredible listening experience.

When it was all over, most of the unreleased material had been repeated more than once throughout the series. The same track was played up to three times in some cases, with each rebroadcast being of a different length. The tendency was to play a little bit more with each new airing, but that was not always the case. Also, in the third and fourth year many of the home demos from the first two years were rebroadcast in much better quality than originally broadcast. Obviously, there had been time to clean them up in the interim. Multiple versions of most songs were spread out over the four years. For example, in the case of Beautiful Boy from the Double Fantasy album, we heard six home demos, one alternate take, one studio runthrough, and two rough mixes, throughout the series. The award for most variations of any song in the series went to the nine different demos of *Serve Yourself*, a sarcastic attack on Bob Dylan's hit song of the time, *Gotta Serve Somebody*.

John told reporters, during his 1980 interviews, that he was unable to write until the end of his "house-husband" years. However, *The Lost Lennon Tapes* proves that he invented that story. Several demos dating from 1975 through 1979 were broadcast throughout the series. In fact, it is now well known that John and Yoko were planning to produce a Broadway play about their lives. From the lyrics of these demos, you can hear that many of these songs were being developed for that project.

Despite its failings, *The Lost Lennon Tapes* is still the most comprehensive documentary ever produced about John Lennon. Aside from the songs, the series included segments of John's live radio appearance with Tom Donahue, and hundreds of illuminating anecdotes and interviews with insiders such as Pete Shotton, Alan Williams, Alistair Taylor, engineer Ken Scott, George Martin, John's Aunt Mimi, Ray Coleman, Jim Keltner, Eric Clapton, Pete Best, Billy Preston, Harry Nilsson, Julian and Sean Lennon, the other Beatles, and many, many others. The depth of coverage of a single topic was often amazing, even if the shows were light on unreleased material. A two-part special on the "Live Peace" concert in Toronto included interviews with concert promoter, John Brower and others, which put the listener there with stories about rehearsing on the plane, poor ticket sales, trying to convince local media that John really was coming, and John with Little Richard backstage.

Realizing that I would never have time to listen to the entire production again, I took extensive notes as I listened to and taped each show. Elliot Mintz acknowledged the inevitability of collectors taping in an interview in *Musician* magazine. "Let's just play it on the radio and let everybody enjoy it. And let those who want to tape it off the air, tape it off the air." When the series suddenly went off the air in Toronto, on July 1, 1991, I completed the task with the help of my friend, Fred McKie, in the U.S. It was virtually impossible to continue marathon taping, every week for years, when taking into account, electrical storms, power failures, holidays, and human error. So Fred and I traded the bits and pieces we were each missing, and thanks to him I was able to finish my notes.

I spent the next three years slowly wading through the tapes, comparing every version of every demo and outtake to determine which ones were the same, and if they were which one was of better quality and/or ran longer. After countless hours of headphone ache, surrounded by boxes of tapes, and computer printouts, I compiled the results into a detailed account of every show, plus a spreadsheet containing a cross-reference to the best quality airing of each of the unique unreleased tracks. Over the next year, I sent the manuscript to every Beatles' book publisher in the world and to my astonishment, was turned down by every one of them.

Back in March of 1989, an official CD boxed set of *The Lost Lennon Tapes* was in the works. Historian, Mark Lewisohn, a consultant on the series, compiled a track listing in the early 1990s. Nothing came of the proposed release, most likely due to the poor sales of *Live in New York City*, *Imagine: John Lennon* soundtrack, and *Menlove Avenue*, which failed to chart in the top 100 in either the U.S. or the U.K. Rumours of an October release continued every year as John's birthday approached, until November 2, 1998, when the 4 CD boxed set *The John Lennon Anthology* finally appeared in the stores. By that time, a series of 35 bootleg albums of material from the shows had already been circulating. *The John Lennon Anthology* contained a few tracks not broadcast during *The Lost Lennon Tapes*. However, unlike Lewisohn's proposal, the CDs included live concerts, TV appearances, and nothing prior to the *Plastic Ono Band* album. A single album compilation called *Wonsaponatime* followed in December. No singles were released to accompany the box or the album.

JOHN'S RESIDENCES

Below is a list of John's residences and whereabouts during the years covered by the series.

1940-1942	9 Newcastle Road Liverpool L15
1942-1943	Dairy Cottage, High Street, Woolton Village, Liverpool
1943-1946	9 Newcastle Road Liverpool L15
1946	Blackpool , Gateacre flat, Liverpool
1946-1963	Mendips, 251 Menlove Avenue, Liverpool L25
1948-1958	1 Blomfield Road, Springwood Council Estate Garston, Liverpool L19 (Mother's house)
1959-1960	Flat 3 Hillary Mansions, Gambier Terrace, Liverpool L1
1960	Bambi-Filmkunsttheater, 33 Paul-Roosen Strasse, Hamburg, West Germany
1960-1961	The Top Ten, 136 Reeperbahn, Hamburg, West Germany
1962	Grosse Freiheit 30, Hamburg, West Germany
19??-1962	93 Garmoyle Road, Liverpool L15
1962-1963	36 Falkner Street, Liverpool L8
1963	57 Green Street, Flat L, 4th floor. Mayfair, London W1
1963-1964	13 Emperors Gate, Brompton, Knightsbridge, London SW7
1964-1968	Kenwood, Wood Lane, St George's Hill Estate, Weybridge, Surrey
1964-7-15	buys "Weybridge" in Kenwood
1968	Rishikesh, India
1967-1968	25 Hanover Gate Mansions, Park Road (Regent's Park), Lisson Grove, Marylebone, London NW1 (Yoko's home)
1968	7 Cavendish Avenue, St John's Wood, London NW8 , (briefly lived with Yoko at Paul's house)
1968	34 Montagu Square, Marylebone, London W1 (Ringo's house)

1969-5	buys Titenhurst Park
1969	The Inn On The Park, Hamilton Place, Park Lane, London W1 (stayed at hotel while Titenhurst Park was being renovated)
1969-8-11 to 1971	"Titenhurst Park", Ascot
1971-8-31	left england
September 3	New York - West Bank Street, Greenwhich Village, apartment studio
1971	St Regis Hotel, 5th Avenue, East 55th Street, New York City
1971-72	105 Bank Street, Greenwich Village, New York City
1973	The Dakota, 1 West 72nd Street, New York City
October	separation and L.A. - Bel Air, L.A. to early 1974
1973-75	various home L.A. & New York City
1975-1	return to The Dakota
1977	
June to October 4	"Hotel Okura" Tokyo, Japan
1978	
Summer	"Hotel Okura" Tokyo, Japan
1979	
March	"El Solano" villa in Palm Beach Florida - Dakota for a few weeks
Summer	"Hotel Okura" Tokyo, Japan
September	The Dakota
Thanksgiving (Nov.)	"Cannon Hill" Cold Spring Harbor, Long Island
1980	
February	"El Solano" villa, Palm Beach Florida - for Yoko's birthday
March 20	"El Solano" villa, Palm Beach Florida - their 11th wedding anniversary
April 9 to June 3	"Cannon Hill" Cold Spring Harbor, Long Island
June 4 to 11	cruise, Newport to Bermuda on "Megan Jaye" lands at St. George
June 11	house in Knapton Hill, Bermuda
June 18 to July 29	moves to "Villa Undercliff" Fairylands, Bermuda
August 2	"Double Fantasy" rehearsals start at the Dakota
August 7	"Double Fantasy" rehearsals start at the Hit Factory
September 5	"Double Fantasy" horn players' overdub session
September 7	"Hard Times Are Over" choir session
September 26	"Starting Over" mixed at the Record Plant
September 29	"Double Fantasy" sound effects added
September 30	"Double Fantasy" mixing moved back to the Hit Factory
October 20	"Double Fantasy" completed

The Lost Lennon Tapes Record Cover Art
Every episode was pressed onto a promotional only double album and housed in this sleeve.

THE EPISODES
1988 - 1992

The Lost Lennon Tapes Preview Part 1
Broadcast the Week of January 24, 1988 - Episode 00 - Three Hour Special

STRAWBERRY FIELDS FOREVER cover version intro
Yoko introduction to The Lost Lennon Tapes
HALLELUJAH I LOVE HER SO The Quarry Men, fragment
MOOVIN' AND GROOVIN' The Quarry Men, fragment
'62 first Beatles radio interview
LOVE ME DO Ringo version, single 1962
'76 Mintz John interview re: Please Please Me LP
TWIST AND SHOUT Please Please Me LP
SWEET LITTLE SIXTEEN BBC, 23 July 1963, fragment, into
Melbourne Australia Beatles arrival, 14 June 1964
A HARD DAY'S NIGHT single 1964
interview continued re: touring
TOMORROW NEVER KNOWS Revolver LP
'66 Chicago press conference re: Christ remark
'66 Doug Layton & Tommy Charles Beatle boycott Birmingham
NOWHERE MAN Rubber Soul LP
'65 interview John & Paul re: songwriting
LUCY IN THE SKY WITH DIAMONDS Sgt. Pepper's LP
STRAWBERRY FIELDS FOREVER demo 2, fragment
STRAWBERRY FIELDS FOREVER, Magical Mystery Tour LP
'80 Peebles John interview re: John meets Yoko
HELP! Help! LP
interview re: point of bed-ins
GIVE PEACE A CHANCE under dialogue

The Lost Lennon Tapes Preview Part 2

BEEF JERKY intro
'71 Mintz first John interview re: growing old
INSTANT KARMA single 1970
interview continued re: the draft
POWER TO THE PEOPLE single 1971
interview continued re: anything to say
IMAGINE Imagine LP
'73 Mintz John interview re: Beatles reunion
How Do You Sleep? under dialogue
interview continued re: relationship with Paul
MIND GAMES Mind Games LP
interview continued re: chauvinism and romance
WOMAN IS THE NIGGER OF THE WORLD Sometime In NYC LP
PEGGY SUE St. Regis Hotel, Clock film soundtrack, also #26
'76 Mintz John interview re: separation

WHATEVER GETS YOU THROUGH THE NIGHT Walls And Bridges LP
interview continued re: fame
STAND BY ME Rock 'N' Roll LP
interview continued re: Beatles reunion
#9 DREAM Walls And Bridges LP
interview continued re: happy new year
AS TIME GOES BY improv, John only, also #49

The Lost Lennon Tapes Preview Part 3

BEEF JERKY intro
WOMAN guitar overdub, under dialogue
'80 Peebles John interview re: writing in Bermuda
WATCHING THE WHEELS demo 1, fragment
WATCHING THE WHEELS demo 3, fragment, also #29
Watching The Wheels studio dialogue "better with the rythm...he's not driving the damn truck"
WATCHING THE WHEELS Double Fantasy LP
BE-BOP-A-LULA Jam, Double Fantasy
interview continued re: Starting Over as first single
STARTING OVER Double Fantasy LP
I'M LOSING YOU demo, fragment
I'M LOSING YOU rehearsal, fragment
I'M LOSING YOU Double Fantasy LP
BEAUTIFUL BOY demo 2, fragment, also #37
Beautiful Boy studio dialogue "only one rythm place where this works...we can do it in one take"
BEAUTIFUL BOY Double Fantasy LP
interview continued re: Woman
WOMAN Double Fantasy LP
CLEANUP TIME dialogue starts before 86 "you & me together" "all those holes" also #86, #179
CLEANUP TIME runthrough, "you can go Slick"
CLEANUP TIME Double Fantasy LP
interview continued re: Lennon on Lennon
Beatles & Lennon medley under dialogue extro

The Lost Lennon Tapes Part 1
Show #88-05, Broadcast the Week of January 25, 1988

STRAWBERRY FIELDS FOREVER cover version intro
Yoko interview re: circulating John's spirit
INSTANT KARMA under dialogue
'80 Peebles John interview re: recording Instant Karma
INSTANT KARMA One To One rehearsals, under dialogue
INSTANT KARMA Live In New York City LP fragment
SAVE THE LAST DANCE Nilsson, under dialogue

NOBODY LOVES YOU (WHEN YOU'RE DOWN AND OUT) under dialogue
'75 Old Grey Whistle Test John interview re: the Troubadour incident
MUCHO MUNGO Nilsson, under dialogue
MUCHO MUNGO demo 1
REMEMBER under dialogue
'70 Wenner John interview highlights
WORKING CLASS HERO Plastic Ono Band LP
THE BALLAD OF JOHN AND YOKO single 1969
IN MY LIFE under dialogue
DON'T LET ME DOWN Get Back LP, fragment
ONE AFTER 909 Quarry Men, fragment
ONE AFTER 909 Let It Be LP
'76 Mintz John interview re: end of the Beatles
GET BACK Let It Be LP
I FOUND OUT under dialogue
interview re: primal scream
WELL WELL WELL under dialogue
'76 Mintz John interview re: John's father
ISOLATION under dialogue
MY MUMMY'S DEAD Plastic Ono Band LP
GOD demo 2, coda cut to cv below, also #**99**
GOD coda, Plastic Ono Band LP
BEEF JERKY extro

The Lost Lennon Tapes Part 2
Show #88-06, Broadcast the Week of February 1, 1988

BEEF JERKY intro
SHE LOVES YOU under dialogue
'64 Kennedy Airport press conference Paul & George
'70 Wenner John interview re: 1964 invasion
I WANT TO HOLD YOUR HAND single 1964
BIRTHDAY under dialogue
YELLOW SUBMARINE under dialogue
'87 Mintz Sean interview re: Yellow Submarine story
BEAUTIFUL BOY under dialogue
interview continued re: did you resent parents going back to work
LIFE BEGINS AT 40 demo, also #185, #213, #**204**
'70 Wenner John interview fragment re: Plastic Ono Band LP
MOTHER Plastic Ono Band LP
WITHIN YOU WITHOUT YOU under dialogue
interview continued re: Epstein's death
interview continued re: feelings at that time
interview continued re: Paul taking over after
I AM THE WALRUS Rarities U.S. LP

interview continued re: I Am The Walrus
A DAY IN THE LIFE under dialogue
BLUE SUEDE SHOES Live Peace In Toronto LP, under dialogue
'80 Peebles John interview re: Live Peace
COLD TURKEY Live Peace In Toronto LP
GIVE PEACE A CHANCE Live Peace LP
POWER TO THE PEOPLE intro, under dialogue
POWER TO THE PEOPLE alternate mix
CLEANUP TIME under dialogue
CLEANUP TIME demo 2, also #69
TWO VIRGINS LP under dialogue
'80 Peebles John interview re: Two Virgins LP
'70 Wenner Yoko interview re: Two Virgins photo
IMAGINE Attica State benefit
'80 Peebles John interview re: Imagine
BEEF JERKY extro

The Lost Lennon Tapes Part 3
Show #88-07, Broadcast the Week of February 8, 1988

BEEF JERKY intro
PLEASE PLEASE ME under dialogue
PLEASE PLEASE ME BBC, 3 June 1963
ALL MY LOVING Ed Sullivan 1964, also #57, #133, #160
SHE LOVES YOU Ed Sullivan 1964, also #57, #160
CRY FOR A SHADOW under dialogue
ROLL OVER BEETHOVEN Star Club LP, under dialogue
'70 Wenner John interview re: Hamburg days
TWIST AND SHOUT Star Club LP
BEAUTIFUL BOYS under dialogue
John interviews Sean December 1975
FLYING under dialogue
Mintz Sean int re: John looking after him
BEAUTIFUL BOY demo 4, also #69, #217
Double Fantasy studio dialogue everyone yells "goodnight Sean"
Sean interview re: Beautiful Boy
BEAUTIFUL BOY backing tracks, under dialogue
interview continued re: Bermuda with John
REAL LOVE - GIRLS AND BOYS demo 1, Imagine: John Lennon Soundtrack LP, also #37, #215
ROCK AND ROLL MUSIC under dialogue
BE-BOP-A-LULA Rock 'N' Roll LP, under dialogue
'75 Old Grey Whistle Test John interview re: Rock 'N' Roll LP songs
BE MY BABY, Roots LP, under dialogue
May Pang interview re: Rock 'N' Roll LP
interview continued re: sessions for Rock 'N' Roll LP

unknown instrumental under dialogue
Sean interview re: trip to Japan
MEAT CITY under dialogue
interview continued re: eating meat
Mintz Sean interview re: favourite Beatles song or LP
Sean sings & asks John about A LITTLE HELP FROM MY FRIENDS
A LITTLE HELP FROM MY FRIENDS Sgt. Pepper's LP
Sean interview fragment re: his favourite post Beatles song
WOMAN demo 2
Sean interview continued re: relationship with Julian
REAL LIFE under dialogue
VALOTTE Valotte LP
BEEF JERKY extro

The Lost Lennon Tapes Part 4
Show #88-08, Broadcast the Week of February 15, 1988

BEEF JERKY intro
STARTING OVER under dialogue
NORWEGION WOOD under dialogue
DRIVE MY CAR under dialouge
'80 Sheff John interview re: Indica Gallery meeting
SHE SAID SHE SAID under dialogue
TOMORROW NEVER KNOWS under dialogue
GIRL Rubber Soul LP
sitar music under dialogue
'74 Tom Donahue KSAN John guest DJ appearance
interview continued re: Maharishi in India
interview continued re: meditating in India
interview continued re: Mia Farrow incident
THE FOOL ON THE HILL under dialogue
YER BLUES The Beatles LP
'74 Tom Donahue KSAN John guest DJ appearance
interview continued re: Yer Blues
I'M SO TIRED The Beatles LP
interview fragment continued re: I'm So Tired
SEXY SADIE The Beatles LP
interview continued re: Sexy Sadie
'73 Mintz John interview re: God
GOD under dialogue
THE HAPPY RISHIKESH SONG demo
PAPERBACK WRITER under dialogue
'64 Swedish TV appearance Good Dog Nigel reading by John
I'M ONLY SLEEPING under dialogue
'64 Murray The K I Sat Belonely reading by John

- 6 -

GOOD MORNING, GOOD MORNING under dialogue
'65 BBC **The National Health Cow reading by John**
THE CONTINUING STORY OF BUNGALOW BILL under dialogue
'80 Sheff Yoko interview re: Beatles reaction to her
REVOLUTION 1 under dialogue
'80 Sheff John interview re: Yoko controlling John
EVERYBODY'S GOT SOMETHNG TO HIDE EXCEPT FOR ME AND MY MONKEY under dialogue
interview continued re: someone impressing John
I WANT YOU (SHE'S SO HEAVY) Abbey Road LP
interview continued re: John's relationship with Yoko
STRAWBERRY FIELDS FOREVER demo 1, also #49, #131, #180
BEEF JERKY extro

The Lost Lennon Tapes Part 5
Show #88-09, Broadcast the Week of February 22, 1988

BEEF JERKY intro
WHATEVER GETS YOU THROUGH THE NIGHT rehearsal, under dialogue
May Pang interview fragment re: writing song
WHATEVER GETS YOU THRU THE NIGHT under dialogue
'80 Peebles John interview re: Whatever Gets You Thru The Night
interview continued re: Whatever Gets You Thru The Night, time to paydues
WHATEVER GETS YOU THROUGH THE NIGHT Madison Square Garden, single 1981
'88 Mintz Elton John interview re: John playing that night
LUCY IN THE SKY WITH DIAMONDS Madison Square Garden single, 1981
DON'T LET ME DOWN Get Back LP, under dialogue
THE WORD under dialogue
'80 Peebles John interview re: bed-ins
'69 Donald Zec John bed-in interview re: Peace
GOODBYE AMSTERDAM Wedding LP
COME TOGETHER under dialogue
'69 Vienna John press conference in bag re: why in bag
'80 Peebles John interview re: bag and bagism
THE BALLAD OF JOHN AND YOKO under dialogue
'69 John interview re: protesting peacfully, Wedding LP
ALL YOU NEED IS LOVE under dialogue
'80 Peebles John interview re: bed-ins political message
interview continued re: Give Peace A Chance
Tommy Smothers interview re: recording single
GIVE PEACE A CHANCE single 1969
RIP IT UP under dialogue
ROCK ISLAND LINE Lonnie Donegan, under dialogue
acoustic guitar under dialogue
ROCK ISLAND LINE demo 2, also #148
JOHN HENRY demo 1

WELL WELL WELL Live In New York City LP
SURPRISE SURPRISE demo 1, also #35
SURPRISE SURPRISE under dialogue
'80 Peebles John interview re: reunion with Yoko
I SAW HER STANDING THERE Madison Square Garden, single 1975
interview fragment continued re: singing I Saw Her Standing There
blues instrumental, under dialogue
TENNESSEE demo 1, take 1, fragment
TENNESSEE demo 2, take 4
BEEF JERKY extro

The Lost Lennon Tapes Part 6
Show #88-10, Broadcast the Week of February 29, 1988

BEEF JERKY intro
REVOLUTION demo, also #85
WHAT YOU GOT under dialogue
'74 Dennis Elsas WNEW John guest DJ appearance
intro to John's as guest host
MAKE ME SMILE Chicago, under dialogue
John introduced how Dennis met John
intro to
WHATEVER GETS YOU THROUGH THE NIGHT Walls And Bridges LP
interview continued re: Walls And Bridges
John reads weather
#9 DREAM Walls And Bridges LP
interview continued re: cover, musicians
OH MY LOVE under dialogue
CHILD OF NATURE demo
JEALOUS GUY Imagine LP
I'M ONLY SLEEPING under dialogue
74 Dennis Elsas WNEW John guest DJ appearance
interview continued re: John co-hosting
John comments on commercials
John reads weather
intro to
SOME OTHER GUY Richie Barrett
WHAT'D I SAY Ray Charles, under dialogue
John comments on What'd I Say
interview continued re: Beatles and Stones in the 1960s
I WANNA BE YOUR MAN Rolling Stones, single 1963
I WANNA BE YOUR MAN With The Beatles LP
interview continued re: Stones, clubs, dancing to
DADDY ROLLIN' STONE Derek Martin 1963
BEEF JERKY piano outake, extro

The Lost Lennon Tapes Part 7
Show #88-11, Broadcast the Week of March 7, 1988

BEEF JERKY intro
POWER TO THE PEOPLE under dialogue
THE LUCK OF THE IRISH demo 1, takes 1 & 2
DIZZY MISS LIZZY under dialogue
'64 Murray The K Epstein interview re: Christ comment
THE WORD under dialogue
'66 press conference re: Christ comment
THE NIGHT BEFORE under dialogue
I'M LOOKING THROUGH YOU under dialogue
IT'S ONLY LOVE under dialogue
I'M LOOKING THROUGH YOU under dialogue
'80 Sheff John interview fragment re: Christ comment
STARTING OVER backing tracks, under dialogue
'69 David Wigg John interview fragment re: Yoko
Yoko interview re: Everyman Has A Woman Who Loves Him LP
EVERYMAN HAS A WOMAN WHO LOVES HIM Everyman Has A Woman Who Loves Him LP
EVERYMAN HAS A WOMAN rough mix, John & Yoko vocal
interview continued re: Everyman has a woman lyric
interview continued re: Eddie Money connection to LP
I'M MOVING ON Eddie Money, fragment
interview continued re: I'm Moving On
DR. ROBERT under dialogue
'80 Sheff John interview re: She Said She Said
TOMORROW NEVER KNOWS under dialogue
HE SAID HE SAID demo 1, fragment, also #127
SHE SAID SHE SAID demo fragment, also #127
SHE SAID SHE SAID Revolver LP
EVERYMAN HAS A WOMAN WHO LOVES HIM under dialogue
Yoko interview re: Nilsson on Everyman Has A Woman Who Loves Him LP
DREAM LOVE Harry Nilsson, Everyman Has A Woman Who Loves Him LP
Yoko interview re: It's Alright by Sean
IT'S ALRIGHT Sean, Everyman Has A Woman Who Loves Him LP
GROW OLD WITH ME demo, end under dialogue, also #213
Yoko interview re: growing old with John
BEEF JERKY extro

Lost Lennon Tapes Part 8
Show #88-12, Broadcast the Week of March 14, 1988

BEEF JERKY intro
Daddy's Little Sunshine Boy, ad lib with Ringo
I'M THE GREATEST under dialogue
I'M THE GREATEST demo 1, John vocal, also #201
I'M THE GREATEST studio demo 1, John vocal
#9 DREAM under dialogue
May Pang interview re: Goodnight Vienna
GOODNIGHT VIENNA rough mix, John vocal, also #201
SUN KING demo, under dialogue
'74 Mintz Ringo interview re: Abbey Road
'70 Wenner John interview re: Abbey Road
George Martin interview re: Abbey Road
SUN KING under dialogue
'70 Wenner John interview re: releasing Get Back
'80 Sheff John interview re: doing Abbey Road
interview continued re: Abbey Road
MEAN MR. MUSTARD demo
POLYTHENE PAM under dialogue
interview fragment continued re: Mean Mr. Mustard
interview continued re: Polythene Pam
CARRY THAT WEIGHT under dialogue
interview continued re: John's guitar playing
CARRY THAT WEIGHT/THE END Abbey Road LP
MAKE LOVE NOT WAR demo, Mind Games, also #93, #150, #209
I PROMISE demo, also #150, #209
MIND GAMES Mind Games LP
'80 Sheff John interview re: Beatles love songs
IN MY LIFE under dialogue
STRAWBERRY FIELDS FOREVER under dialogue
interview continued re: Paul's contribution
IN MY LIFE Rubber Soul LP
SOMETHING under dialogue
GIVE PEACE A CHANCE under dialouge
Timothy Leary interview re: asking John to write Come Together
'80 Sheff John interview re: Come Together campaign song
Timothy Leary interview continued re: Come Together
COME TOGETHER Abbey Road LP
'80 Sheff John interview re: not giving song to Leary
interview continued re: one of his favourite songs
YOU CAN'T CATCH ME Chuck Berry, under dialogue
'70 Wenner John interview re: being sued
YOU CAN'T CATCH ME Rock 'N' Roll LP
BEEF JERKY extro

The Lost Lennon Tapes Part 9
Show #88-13, Broadcast the Week of March 21, 1988

BEEF JERKY intro
THE CHASE under dialogue
'80 Sheff John interview re: Help! song
HELP! home 1970, fragment cut to
HELP! Help LP
SUE ME SUE YOU BLUES under dialogue
TOO MANY PEOPLE Ram LP
How Do You Sleep? alternate take
How Do You Sleep? under dialogue
Paul interview re: How Do You Sleep?
'73 Mintz John interview fragment re: How Do You Sleep?
interview continued re: How Do You Sleep?
IMAGINE under dialogue
REVOLUTION 9 under dialogue
DOWN IN E AUSTRALIA I MET HER home improv
'65 BBC TV: We Must Not Forget The General Erection and
The Wumberlog Or The Magic Dog
YOU KNOW MY NAME demo, fragment cut to
YOU KNOW MY NAME single 1970
A LITTLE HELP FROM MY FRIENDS under dialogue
'75 Mal interview re: being accepted as a songwriter
Mal interview re: producing Two Sides Of The Moon
DON'T WORRY BABY Keith Moon, under dialogue
MOVE OVER MS. L Keith Moon, under dialogue
Mal interview re: Keith Moon's In My Life
IN MY LIFE Keith Moon
ROLL OVER BEETHOVEN Chuck Berry, under dialogue
JOHNNY B. GOODE Chuck Berry, under dialogue
YOU CAN'T CATCH ME Chuck Berry, under dialogue
John intro to Chuck Berry on Mike Douglas
MEMPHIS TENNESSEE Mike Douglas Show 1972, also #148
Mike Douglas interview fragment with John and Chuck
JOHNNY B. GOODE Mike Douglas Show 1972
BEEF JERKY extro

The Lost Lennon Tapes Part 10
Show #88-14, Broadcast the Week of March 28, 1988

BEEF JERKY intro
MONEY Pop '63, Sweden
SHE LOVES YOU Pop '63, Sweden, also #56 #89
TWIST AND SHOUT Pop '63, Sweden
SCHOOL DAYS Chuck Berry, under dialogue
Pete Shotton interview re: John at school
THAT'LL BE THE DAY Buddy Holly, under dialogue
Cynthia Lennon interview re: John at school
interview continued re: Helen Anderson & jealousy
DON'T BE CRUEL Elvis Presley, under dialogue
interview continued re: John's influence
HEARTBREAK Elvis Presley, under dialogue
interview continued re: common bond with Cynthia
interview continued re: attraction to John
WILL YOU LOVE ME TOMORROW The Shirelles, under dialogue
Pete Shotton interview re: John & Cynthia's relationship
HE'S A REBEL The Crystals, under dialogue
interview continued re: John challenging rules
Cynthia interview continued re: John as a rebel
STARTING OVER under dialogue
STARTING OVER demo 2, also #180 #21
STARTING OVER under dialogue
'80 Peebles John interview re: Starting Over as 1st single
WATCHING THE WHEELS Double Fantasy LP
WATCHING THE WHEELS under dialogue
YELLOW SUBMARINE under dialogue
'80 Sheff John interview re: John's sailing trip
SEA DITTIES MEDLEY improv, also #185
FLYING under dialogue
interview continued re: birth of I Am The Walrus
Pete Shotton interview re: yellow matter custard
sitar under dialogue
I AM THE WALRUS basic tracks
'80 Sheff John interview re: the walrus & the carpenter
sitar under dialogue
interview continued re: Krishna put-down
interview continued re: overdubs on I Am The Walrus
I AM THE WALRUS Magical Mystery Tour LP
BEEF JERKY extro

The Lost Lennon Tapes Part 11
Show #88-15, Broadcast the Week of April 4, 1988

BEEF JERKY intro
WHATEVER HAPPENED TO demo, take 1, under dialogue
WHATEVER HAPPENED TO demo, take 2, also #213
STRING OF PEARLS Glen Miller, under dialogue
Pete Shotton interview re: Wolton and John
PENNY LANE under dialogue
STRAWBERRY FIELDS FOREVER Magical Mystery Tour LP
interview continued re: John's upbringing
'80 Sheff John interview re: John's upbringing
solo guitar under dialogue
cut with comments from Aunt Mimi
Pete Shotton interview re: Aunt Mimi
ROCK ISLAND LINE Lonnie Donegan, under dialogue
'80 Sheff John interview re: The Quarry Men and Quarrybank school
Pete Shotton interview re: The Quarry Men
CUMBERLAND GAP Lonnie Donegan, under dialogue
Pete Shotton interview re: Ivan, Paul & village fete
BE-BOP-A-LULA Gene Vincent, under dialogue
'65 John and Paul interview re: first meeting
Pete Shotton interview re: John meeting Paul
TWENTY FLIGHT ROCK Eddie Cochran, under dialogue
interview continued re: asking Paul to join band
RAUNCHY Bill Justis, under dialogue
'70 Wenner John interview re: letting Paul & George into the band
instrumental under dialogue
Paul interview fragment re: knowing each other a long time
ONE AFTER 909 The Quarry Men
SHE SAID SHE SAID under dialogue
STRAWBERRY FIELDS FOREVER demo 2, also #113
JULIA under dialogue
JULIA backing tracks with count-in, under dialogue
Pete Shotton interview re: Julia
'80 Sheff John interview re: John's future & parents
WORRIED MAN BLUES Lonnie Donegan, under dialogue
BLUE SUEDE SHOES Carl Perkins, under dialogue
cut with comments from Aunt Mimi
interview continued re: parents
Pete Shotton interview re: Julia
JULIA demo 2, also #105
'80 Sheff John interview re: Julia's death
MY MUMMY'S DEAD Plastic Ono Band LP
Pete Shotton interview re: Julia's death
MOTHER Plastic Ono Band LP

'80 Sheff John interview re: losing his mother twice
Pete Shotton interview re: John at school
JULIA backing tracks, under dialogue
interview continued re: bitterness
Pete Shotton interview re: inner strength
BEEF JERKY extro

The Lost Lennon Tapes Part 12
Show #88-16, Broadcast the Week of April 11, 1988

BEEF JERKY intro
WHATEVER GETS YOU THROUGH THE NIGHT demo 1, intro longer, also #165, #216
HALLELUJAH, I LOVE HER SO The Quarry Men, under dialogue
SURE TO FALL Decca Sessions LP, under dialogue
interview re: drummers hard to come by
Pete Best interview re: joining the Beatles
I'LL BE ON MY WAY BBC, under dialogue
Pete Best interview re: conditions in Hamburg
Paul interview re: Hamburg experience
I'M GONNA SIT RIGHT DOWN AND CRY OVER YOU BBC, under dialogue
Tony Sheridan interview re: Jürgen Vollmer
TO KNOW HER IS TO LOVE HER Tony Sheridan
Vollmer interview re: first trip to Kaiserkeller
Klaus Voorman interview re: excitement of Rock N Roll
interview continued re: Beatles destined for success
Vollmer interview re: Stu and Astrid
LEND ME YOUR COMB BBC, under dialogue
'76 Mintz Ringo interview re: meeting Beatles in Hamburg
MONEY live at the Kaiserkeller, under dialogue
George interview fragment re: being underage
interview continued re: vice control police raids
TOO MUCH MONKEY BUSINESS BBC, under dialogue
Pete Best interview re: torching theatre incident
interview continued re: deportation
interview continued re: time in jail
SO HOW COME BBC, under dialogue
SEARCHIN' Decca Sessions LP, under dialogue
'76 Mintz John interview fragment re: staying in Hamburg alone
interview continued re: end of Hamburg experience
interview continued re: sneaking back to Liverpool
BORROWED TIME Milk and Honey LP
DEAR JOHN demo, last song, also #165 longest end, #213
CRY FOR A SHADOW under dialogue
Tony Sheridan interview re: playing with the Beatles
interview continued re: Top Ten Club

BE-BOP-A-LULA Star Club LP, under dialogue
THREE COOL CATS Decca Sessions LP, under dialogue
interview continued re: Astrid & image change
interview continued re: Polydor recordings
MY BONNIE Tony Sheridan, with slow English intro
interview continued re: The Saints
THE SAINTS Tony Sheridan, The Beatles First LP
FROM ME TO YOU U.S. single 1964
HOLD ME TIGHT With The Beatles LP
I SAW HER STANDING THERE Star Club LP, under dialogue
Sheridan interview re: girls in Hamburg
ROLL OVER BEETHOVEN Star Club LP, under dialogue
1976 Mintz John interview re: carrying on after Hamburg
BEEF JERKY extro

The Lost Lennon Tapes Part 13
Show #88-17, Broadcast the Week of April 18, 1988

BEEF JERKY intro
interview re: inspiration for Across The Universe
ACROSS THE UNIVERSE No One's Gonna Change Our World LP, under dialogue
'80 Sheff John interview continued re: others not interested in it
interview continued re: song never done properly
ACROSS THE UNIVERSE alternate mix
NEW YORK CITY under dialogue
'74 Dennis Elsas WNEW John guest DJ appearance
interview re: celebrity & immigration
SCARED Walls And Bridges LP
'74 Tom Donahue KSAN John extro to Scared
CRY FOR A SHADOW under dialogue
MY BONNIE Tony Sheridan, under dialogue
'64 BBC Epstein interview re: first trip to the cavern
ROLL OVER BEETHOVEN Star Club LP, under dialogue
Bob Wooler interview re: announcing groups at the Cavern
interview continued re: Beatles being most popular
interview continued re: announcing the Beatles
HIPPY HIPPY SHAKE Star Club LP, under dialogue
Paul interview re: lunchtime sessions
Wooler interview re: Beatles at the Cavern
RED SAILS IN THE SUNSET Star Club LP, under dialogue
interview continued re: watching the Beatles on stage
Pete Best interview re: Beatles getting Cavern job
SWEET LITTLE SIXTEEN Star Club LP, under dialogue
Pete Best interview continued re: Cavern atmosphere
I REMEMBER YOU Star Club LP, under dialogue

'70 Wenner John interview re: harmonica as a gimic
Pete Best interview re: on stage antics
TWIST AND SHOUT Star Club LP, under dialogue
'70 Wenner John interview re: early work was best
Pete Best interview re: on stage attitude
MATCHBOX under dialogue
'74 Mintz Ringo interview re: Rory Storm first Cavern group
George interview re: getting Ringo into the group
'74 Mintz Ringo interview re: 1st session with the Beatles
SOME OTHER GUY Cavern Club, live
LEND ME YOUR COMB Star Club LP, under dialogue
'74 Mintz John interview re: throwing Pete Best out
CRY FOR A SHADOW under dialogue
Tony Sheridan interview re: Polydor giving up Beatles
YOU KNOW MY NAME under dialogue
'76 Mintz John interview re: songs with Paul & Mary Jane
WHAT'S THE NEW MARY JANE? Kinfauns demo, also #113
COOKIN' Ringo Star, under dialogue
'80 Sheff John interview re: Cookin'
COOKIN' demo 1, take 8
BEEF JERKY extro

The Lost Lennon Tapes Part 14
Show #88-18, Broadcast the Week of April 25, 1988

BEEF JERKY intro
Ray Coleman interview re: John's power to communicate
LOVE ME DO original version, under dialogue
BLOWIN' IN THE WIND Bob Dylan, under dialogue
**'74 Tom Donahue KSAN John guest DJ appearance
interview re: first hearing Dylan**
CORRINA CORRINA Bob Dylan, under dialogue
A HARD RAIN'S A-GONNA FALL Bob Dylan
interview re: New York and meeting Dylan
I WANT TO HOLD YOUR HAND under dialogue
'68 Release John interview re: writing a story versus song
BABY'S IN BLACK under dialogue
I'M A LOSER under dialogue
'80 Sheff John interview re: I'm A Loser
YOU'VE GOT TO HIDE YOUR LOVE AWAY Help! LP
interview continued re: You've Got To Hide Your Love Away
IN MY LIFE under dialogue
interview continued re: In My Life
'70 Wenner John interview re: relationship with Dylan
COLD TURKEY Live Peace in Toronto LP, under dialogue

interview continued re: the last time he saw Dylan
interview continued re: Eat The Document appearance
WORKING CLASS HERO under dialogue
interview fragment re: Dylan's mythical status
'70 Wenner John interview re: Working Class Hero
GOD coda, Plastic Ono Band LP
interview fragment continued re: Zimmerman in God
'80 Sheff John interview re: songwriting about yourself
interview continued re: influence on John's writing
KNOCKIN' ON HEAVEN'S DOOR Bob Dylan, under dialogue
KNOCKIN' ON HEAVEN'S DOOR parody, also #172
THE NEWS OF THE DAY FROM REUTERS parody, also #49, #172
I BELIEVE IN YOU Bob Dylan, under dialogue
interview continued re: Dylan's Slow Train phase
CONVERSION Bob Dylan, under dialogue
'80 Sheff John interview cont'd re: pushing a point of view
SUBTERRANEAN HOMESICK BLUES Bob Dylan, under dialogue
interview continued re: Dylan for the message
GOTTA SERVE SOMEBODY Bob Dylan, Slow Train Coming LP
SERVE YOURSELF demo 1
BEEF JERKY extro

The Lost Lennon Tapes Part 15
Show #88-19, Broadcast the Week of May 2, 1988

BEEF JERKY intro
WITHIN YOU WITHOUT YOU under dialogue
GOOD MORNING, GOOD MORNING demo, also #175, cut to
GOOD MORNING, GOOD MORNING Sgt. Pepper's LP
'80 Sheff John interview re: Good Morning, Good Morning
SGT. PEPPER'S REPRISE under dialogue
NOBODY TOLD ME under dialogue
MARCH OF THE MEANIES under dialogue
'80 Peebles John interview fragment re: getting busted
DR. ROBERT Revolver LP
'80 Sheff John intinterview fragment re: not being busted earlier
A HARD DAY'S NIGHT George Martin, under dialogue
interview continued re: marijuana during Help! years
'68 interview fragment re: being busted
EVERYONE HAD A HARD YEAR demo, also #114
DRAGNET THEME under dialogue
'80 Peebles John interview fragment re: pic on Life With The Lions
EVERYBODY'S GOT SOMETHING TO HIDE EXCEPT FOR ME AND MY MONKEY demo
CRY BABY CRY under dialogue
interview continued re: copping plea

interview continued re: having a record for life
CLEANUP TIME alternate mix
NOBODY TOLD ME under dialogue
'80 Peebles Yoko interview re: drugs a thing of the past
'80 Peebles John interview re: getting rid of record
acoustic guitar under dialogue
interview re: early musical influences
interview continued re: discovering the blues
interview continued re: Liverpool sailors & blues
'70 Wenner John interview re: the blues
I'M A MAN improv
BROWN EYED HANDSOME MAN/GET BACK improv, also #148
REAL LOVE under dialogue
JULIA intro under dialogue
Mimi interview re: family history
interview continued re: Alfred Freddie Lennon
MOTHER under dialogue
I'LL CRY INSTEAD under dialogue
'80 Sheff John interview fragment re: Freddie washing dishes
interview continued re: sending Freddie 12 pounds a week
I SHOULD HAVE KNOWN BETTER George Martin, under dialogue
Mimi interview continued re: John accepting his father
THAT'S MY LIFE (MY LOVE & MY HOME) Freddie Lennon
interview continued re: Freddie remarrying
REAL LOVE under dialogue
'76 Mintz John interview re: throwing Freddie out
YELLOW SUBMARINE George Martin, under dialogue
TWAS A NIGHT LIKE ETHEL MERMAN poetry
LA MER/BLUE MOON/YOUNG LOVE French parody, also #150
thank you thank you exto
BEEF JERKY extro

The Lost Lennon Tapes Part 16
Show #88-20, Broadcast the Week of May 9, 1988

BEEF JERKY intro
IMAGINE under dialogue
'80 Peebles John interview re: couldn't go out in London
interview continued re: living in Greenwich Village
interview continued re: Yoko encouraging him to go out
WORKING CLASS HERO under dialogue
interview re: meeting Jerry Rubin
Abbie Hoffman interview re: living back then
POWER TO THE PEOPLE alternate take
THE LUCK OF THE IRISH under dialogue

'72 NYC John interview at pro Irish protest at BOAC building
JEALOUS GUY Imagine LP
KICK OUT THE JAMS MC5 under dialogue
BRING ON THE LUCIE under dialogue
David Sinclair interview fragment re: 15,000 at rally
David Sinclair Ten For Two speech
POWER TO THE PEOPLE under dialogue
Bob Rudnick intro to performance
'80 Jon Wiener Bobby Seale interview re: rally
Geraldo Rivera John Sinclair Benefit: "this is like a dream", also #193
ATTICA STATE John Sinclair Benefit
THE LUCK OF THE IRISH John Sinclair Benefit, also #193
JOHN SINCLAIR John Sinclair Benefit, also #76, #168
JOHN SINCLAIR under dialogue
John Sinclair interview when freed
EVERYBODY'S SMOKING MARIJUANA John Peel, under dialogue
'71 phone conversation between Sinclair & John & Yoko
interview fragment re: David Peel
THE POPE SMOKES DOPE Peel, under dialogue
interview fragment re: New York city
THE BALLAD OF NEW YORK CITY John Peel, under dialogue
GOING TO SAN DIEGO Bob Dylan and Allen Ginsberg, originally from unreleased Apple LP
GIVE PEACE A CHANCE single under dialogue
'80 Sheff John interview re: going to Republican convention
REVOLUTION single alternate mix
CRIPPLED INSIDE under dialogue
interview continued re: proposed tour
interview continued re: tour info being leaked
interview continued re: John perceived dangerous
JOHNNY B. GOODE Mike Douglas, under dialogue
GIVE ME SOME TRUTH under dialogue
Bobby Seale interview fragment re: Mike Douglas Show appearance
Jerry Rubin interview on Mike Douglas Show
REVOLUTION 1 under dialogue
BEEF JERKY extro

The Lost Lennon Tapes Part 17
Show #88-21, Broadcast the Week of May 16, 1988

BEEF JERKY intro
ROCK 'N' ROll PEOPLE Johnny Winter, under dialogue
ROCK 'N' ROLL PEOPLE demo 1, also #216
ROCK 'N' ROLL PEOPLE alternate take
DO YOU WANT TO KNOW A SECRET under dialogue
THE LONELY BULL Herb Alpert, under dialogue

'80 Sheff John interview re: Spanish holiday with Epstein
Spanish song under dialogue
BAD TO ME demo
BAD TO ME Billy J. Kramer, under dialogue
interview continued re: Bad To Me
YOU'VE GOT TO HIDE YOUR LOVE AWAY under dialogue
interview cont'd re: John's 1st experience with a homosexual
'80 Peebles John interview re: Bob Wooler beat up at party
instrumental under dialogue
'80 Sheff John interview re: Brian in love with Paul
Tony Barrow interview re: Brian with Peter Brown
LET IT BE under dialogue
Paul interview re: Brown's book & Spain incident
I'M STEPPING OUT under dialogue
REAL LIFE demo 1 fragment
REAL LIFE demo 2, take 3, fragment, also #215
REAL LIFE demo 3 fragment
REAL LIFE demo 4 fragment, middle 8
I'M STEPPING OUT demo 1
ROCK 'N' ROLL PEOPLE under dialogue
'74 Tom Donahue KSAN John guest DJ appearance
interview re: next two records
RIVER DEEP MOUNTAIN HIGH Ike & Tina Turner, under dialogue
BLUE SUEDE SHOES Carl Perkins
interview continued re: Sam Phillips
RIVER DEEP MOUNTAIN HIGH Tina Turner, under dialogue
interview continued re: River Deep Mountain High fiasco
TIGHT A$ under dialgoue
MIND GAMES under dialogue
call re: request for Tight A$
TIGHT A$ demo
Beef Jerky intro from '74 Tom Donahue KSAN guest DJ appearance
BEEF JERKY under dialogue
interview re: writing Beef Jerky
interview re: other instrumentals
BEEF JERKY continued extro

The Lost Lennon Tapes Part 18
Show #88-22, Broadcast the Week of May 23, 1988

BEEF JERKY intro
ROCK ISLAND LINE improv 1
SCHOOL DAYS Chuck Berry, under dialogue
'70 Wenner John interview re: talent at school
BAD BOY under dialogue

MOVIN' & GROOVIN' The Quarry Men, under dialogue
'69 Man Of The Decade interview re: school versus music
rock 'n' roll guitar under dialogue
'70 Wenner John interview re: school
interview fragment re: continued re: Aunt Mimi
THAT'LL BE THE DAY Buddy Holly, under dialogue
Pete Shotton interview re: Aunt Mimi
Aunt Mimi interview re: John's adolescence
'70 Wenner John interview re: Mimi throwing stuff out
LOOK AT ME under dialogue
interview continued re: John's genius
GETTING BETTER under dialogue
interview continued re: John's interests
IMAGINE under dialogue
How Do You Sleep? under dialogue
interview continued re: John's work
A HARD DAY'S NIGHT George Martin, under dialogue
'63 Doncaster Neville Club reading by John, also #179
'63 The Clinic read by Cynthia
'68 Christmas record: Jock & Yono
'87 Sean tape, radio station EXP
EXP Jimi Hendrix
LITTLE WING Jimi Hendrix, under dialogue
Sean interview re: who he listens to
ARE YOU EXPERIENCED? Jimi Hendrix, under dialogue
Sean interview continued re: liking Hendrix
A LITTLE HELP FROM MY FRIENDS under dialogue
'88 Sean Rock 'N' Roll Hall Of Fame speech
A LITTLE STORY Sean, Season Of Glass LP
SPEC OF DUST Yoko Ono, under dialogue
IT'S ALRIGHT Yoko Ono, under dialogue
Sean interview re: recording early material
SPEC OF DUST Yoko Ono, under dialogue
Sean extro to Never Say Goodbye
interview continued re: It's Alright
IT'S ALRIGHT Sean, under dialogue
BEAUTIFUL BOY under dialogue
interview continued re: video for It's Alright
Sean intro to It's Alright
interview continued re: Star Peace LP contribution
STAR PEACE Yoko Ono, under dialogue
WHY Yoko Ono, under dialogue
MRS. LENNON Yoko Ono, under dialogue
Sean on guitar with John talking to him
interview continued re: John teaching Sean guitar
Sean on guitar continued, John briefly yodelling

I FEEL FINE Ed Sullivan 1965
TICKET TO RIDE Ed Sullivan 1965
HELP! Ed Sullivan 1965, also #80
BEEF JERKY extro

The Lost Lennon Tapes Part 19
Show #88-23, Broadcast the Week of May 30, 1988

BEEF JERKY intro
POWER TO THE PEOPLE under dialogue
GOD SAVE US under dialogue
GOD SAVE US demo, - longer intro here - also #186
GOD SAVE US John vocal
DO THE OZ Bill Elliot & The Elastic Oz Band, under dialogue
NEW YORK CITY under dialogue
Yoko interview re: doing concerts for needy
interview continued re: John playing for a cause
interview continued re: Elephant's Memory
INSTANT KARMA One To One rehearsals, also #186
Jam One To One rehearsals, under dialogue
Yoko interview re: Geraldo Rivera
Jon Wiener Rivera interview re: meeting John & Yoko
interview continued re: reason he got close to them
interview continued re: Willowbrook Hospital
interview continued re: community concern
interview continued re: asking John to do concert
Rivera John interview re: reason for concert
Rivera interview continued re: filming John for news
interview continued re: concert preparations
NEW YORK CITY One To One rehearsals 1, "pissed" third verse cut, has proper ending, also #213
Jam One To One rehearsals, under dialogue
One To One radio promo "Wings and Fred Astaire"
One To One radio promo "quiet backing" Geraldo Rivera into **NEW YORK CITY**, also #186
GIVE PEACE A CHANCE One To One rehearsals, fragment
Rivera interview re: deinstitutionalization
interview continued re: retarded kids seeing show
interview continued re: emceeing and John's performance
ROCK AND ROLL MUSIC Candlestick Park, under dialogue
RUN FOR YOUR LIFE under dialogue
interview re: end of touring
HELP! Help! LP
THE BITTER END under dialogue
'80 Sheff John interview re: How I Won The War
HOW I WON THE WAR single 1967, fragment with John
interview continued fragment re: How I Won The War

STRAWBERRY FIELDS FOREVER under dialogue
interview continued re: writing Strawberry Fields Forever
interview continued re: the real Strawberry Fields
STRAWBERRY FIELDS FOREVER backing tracks, under dialogue
interview continued fragment re: original version
STRAWBERRY FIELDS FOREVER version 1, take 1
BEEF JERKY extro

The Lost Lennon Tapes Part 20
Show #88-24, Broadcast the Week of June 6, 1988

BEEF JERKY intro
Japanese instrumental under dialogue
JENNY JENNY Samurai Lounge Lizzard
JEALOUS GUY under dialogue
JEALOUS GUY alternate take
MIRROR MIRROR ON THE WALL demo 3, take 1, also #212
MIRROR MIRROR ON THE WALL demo 1, take 5
DEAR PRUDENCE under dialogue
'70 Wenner John interview re: writing Dear Prudence in Rishikesh
DEAR PRUDENCE demo 2
interview continued re: the problems with Prudence
DEAR PRUDENCE alternate mix
Japanese insturmental under dialogue
PINK PANTHER THEME under dialogue
Maurice Dupont Part 1, mind movie
PEPPERLAND LAID WASTE under dialogue
Jam One To One rehearsals, under dialogue
Geraldo Rivera interview re: success of One To One
COLD TURKEY One To One rehearsals
Yoko interview re: documenting event
Jam One To One rehearsals, under dialogue
interview continued re: not releasing show
interview continued re: 1986 release
interview continued re: energy of John at concert
Power To The People audience chant under dialogue
NEW YORK CITY Live In New York City LP
IMAGINE Live In New York City LP
GIVE PEACE A CHANCE Live In New York City LP, under dialogue
Yoko interview re: crowd reaction
Rivera interview re: affect of show
BEEF JERKY extro

The Lost Lennon Tapes Part 21
Show #88-25, Broadcast the Week of June 13, 1988

BEEF JERKY intro
AIN'T THAT A SHAME under dialogue
'80 Sheff John interview re: Walls And Bridges
interview continued re: change in 1975
WATCHING THE WHEELS demo 2
COMING IN FROM THE COLD reggae, under dialogue
ROCK LOBSTER B-52'S, under dialogue
LIFE BEGINS AT 40 demo, under dialogue
interview re: Double Fantasy songs
BEAUTIFUL BOY Double Fantasy LP
reggae song under dialogue
'80 Sheff John interview re: theme of Double Fantasy
I'M STEPPING OUT Milk And Honey LP
EVERYMAN HAS A WOMAN WHO LOVES HIM Yoko, under dialogue
interview re: collaborating with Yoko
DEAR YOKO demo 1
STARTING OVER under dialogue
STARTING OVER - MY LIFE demo 1, take 2
STARTING OVER - MY LIFE demo 2, take 3
STARTING OVER - DON'T BE CRAZY demo 1, fragment, also #180
STARTING OVER - THE WORST IS OVER demo 2, also #180
STARTING OVER backing tracks, under dialogue
STARTING OVER demo 2, take 3, fragment, also #10 #180
STARTING OVER studio rehearsal
Starting Over dialogue, under dialogue
STARTING OVER sound from booth
STARTING OVER rough mix
BEEF JERKY extro

The Lost Lennon Tapes Part 22
Show #88-26, Broadcast the Week of June 20, 1988

BEEF JERKY intro
THAT'LL BE THE DAY Buddy Holly, under dialogue
WORDS OF LOVE Beatles For Sale LP
HEARTBEAT Buddy Holly, under dialogue
HELLO LITTLE GIRL Fourmost single 1963
interview fragment in middle re: 1st song
MAYBE BABY St. Regis Hotel, CLOCK film soundtrack
RAVE ON St. Regis Hotel, CLOCK film soundtrack
NOT FADE AWAY St. Regis Hotel, CLOCK film soundtrack
Jam Not Fade Away, Sometime In NYC LP sessions

THAT'LL BE THE DAY outake, Rock 'N' Roll LP
STARTING OVER backing tracks, under dialogue
'80 Sheff John interview re: forthcoming Double Fantasy LP
interview continued re: peoples expectations
WOMAN demo 3
WOMAN demo 3, under dialogue
'80 Peebles John interview re: inspiration for Woman
WOMAN demo 4
interview continued re: Woman
<u>Woman</u> studio dialogue, "guitar in my ears", "Motown Beatles", "female race"
WOMAN vocal overdub - starts with guitar intro, "sounded good", "not worried about singing"
studio dialogue - "double tracking", also #160, #<u>189</u>
studio dialogue - "I know your underpants", "still in the fucking Beatles",
"turn into GIRL", GIRL comment also #<u>160</u>
overdub test starts "Yeah Yeah", "an ex-Beatle you fucking", "supposed to be Smokey Robinson"
interview continued re: Beatle sound of Woman
MAGGIE MAE studio improv, fragment
WOMAN rough mix basic track and reference vocal
<u>Maurice Dupont Part 2</u>, mind movie, also #218
RAVE ON Buddy Holly, under dialogue
BLUE SUEDE SHOES Carl Perkins, under dialogue
EVERYBODY'S TRYING TO BE MY BABY under dialogue
Carl Perkins interview re: meeting the Beatles
<u>Jam</u> Honey Don't/Don't Be Cruel/Matchbox, POB session, also #49, #187
Plastic Ono Band LP sessions
BEEF JERKY extro

The Lost Lennon Tapes Part 23
Show #88-27, Broadcast the Week of June 27, 1988

BEEF JERKY intro
HERE WE GO AGAIN demo, under dialogue
HERE WE GO AGAIN demo, also #<u>201</u>
HERE WE GO AGAIN Menlove Ave LP
COLD TURKEY Live Peace In Toronto, under dialogue
'80 Peebles John interview re: always expressing feelings
interview re: writing Cold Turkey
'69 Toronto press conference interview re: rise in drug use
HEROIN Lou Reed, under dialogue
'70 Wenner John interview re: reason for taking heroin
COLD TURKEY demo 2, also #146
SISTER MORPHINE The Rolling Stones, under dialogue
'80 Peebles John interview re: banning Cold Turkey
interview continued re: Cold Turkey a new sound
COLD TURKEY alternate take

CLEANUP TIME under dialogue
'73 Mintz John interview re: being off drugs
CLEAN UP TIME demo 1, also #179
ALL YOU NEED IS LOVE under dialogue
'73 Mintz Yoko interview re: getting off drugs
Comedy Theatre, mind movie
'66 Christmas record: Podgey & Jasper to Get A Free One
BEING FOR THE BENEFIT OF MR. KITE under dialogue
'68 Christmas record: Jock & Yono
'68 Christmas record: NOWHERE MAN Tiny Tim
'65 Christmas record: Johnny Rythm goodnight
HERE WE GO AGAIN under dialogue
SWEET LITTLE SIXTEEN outake
YOU CAN'T CATCH ME outake
BEEF JERKY extro

The Lost Lennon Tapes Part 24
Show #88-28, Broadcast the Week of July 4, 1988

BEEF JERKY intro
ONE OF THE BOYS demo 1, take 2
CRY FOR A SHADOW under dialogue
MONEY Decca Sessions LP, under dialogue
'80 Clive Epstein interview re: Brian
TO KNOW HER IS TO LOVE HER Decca Sessions LP
CRYING, WAITING HOPING Decca Sesssions LP, under dialogue
SEARCHIN' Decca Sessions LP, under dialogue
MEMPHIS Decca Sessions LP
Mind Games queen advertisement
MIND GAMES under dialogues
'80 Sheff John interview re: origin of title
MAKE LOVE NOT WAR demo, under dialogue
'80 Sheff John interview re: original version and meaning
MIND GAMES early mix
'80 Peebles John interview re: Mind Games a fun track
MAKE LOVE NOT WAR demo, under dialogue
THE SAINTS Tony Sheridan, under dialogue
'62 Clive Epstein interview re: Brian & Decca rejection
ONE AFTER 909 The Quarry Men, under dialogue
TILL THERE WAS YOU Decca Sessions LP, under dialogue
George Martin interview re: first meeting with Brian
TILL THERE WAS YOU Star Club LP, under dialogue
interview continued re: first Parlophone session
BESAME MUCHO The Beatles, first Parlophone session
P.S. I LOVE YOU under dialogue

George Martin interview re: Pete Best
Paul interview re: How Do You Do It
George Martin interview fragment re: How Do You Do It
Paul interview continued re: How Do You Do It
HOW DO YOU DO IT outake, also #137
interview continued re: doing their own songs
LOVE ME DO Ringo version, single 1963
I DON'T WANNA FACE IT under dialogue
'80 Peebles John interview re: contract for Double Fantasy
interview continued Yoko re: men and women switching roles
I DON'T WANNA FACE IT demo 2
DON'T BE SCARED Yoko Ono, under dialogue
interview continued re: Geffen and signing contracts
HARD TIMES ARE OVER Yoko Ono, alternate mix, fragment
BEEF JERKY extro

The Lost Lennon Tapes Part 25
On The Air With Dr. Winston O'Boogie, September 1974
Show #88-29, Broadcast the Week of July 11, 1988

BEEF JERKY intro
'74 Tom Donahue KSAN John guest DJ appearance
Donahue comment re: Revolver being changing point
John talks about trends
GIRL Rubber Soul LP
intro to Watch Your Step
WATCH YOUR STEP Bobby Parker
DAY TRIPPER Yesterday And Today LP
interview continued re: Yesterday And Today covers
interview continued re: extra LPs in the U.S.
interview continued re: stereo versus mono
interview continued re: VJ and Capitol
intro to I Call Your Name
I CALL YOUR NAME Beatles Second Album LP
intro to Surprise Surprise
SURPRISE SURPRISE Walls And Bridges LP
interview continued re: Elton John on Surprise Surprise
interview continued re: Record Plant East
intro to Bless You
BLESS YOU Walls And Bridges LP
WHAT YOU GOT under dialogue
'74 Dennis Elsas WNEW John guest DJ appearance
John reads burger chain tag
interview re: John's importance to people
interview continued re: being a radio guest

interview continued re: Beatles phoning every station
interview continued re: Beatles only part of the 60s
intro to
I AM THE WALRUS Magical Mystery Tour LP
interview continued re: mixing I Am The Walrus
interview continued re: making Revolution 9
intro to Beef Jerky
intro to 6 o'clock news
BEEF JERKY under dialogue
LUCY IN THE SKY WITH DIAMONDS under dialogue
'74 Tom Donahue KSAN John guest DJ appearance
interview re: most expensive Beatles LP on Pepper
interview continued re: number of tracks
A DAY IN THE LIFE Sgt. Pepper's LP
Tom thanks to John for appearing
BEEF JERKY extro

The Lost Lennon Tapes Part 26
Show #88-30, Broadcast the Week of July 18, 1988

BEEF JERKY intro
MR. MOONLIGHT Star Club LP
ASK ME WHY Star Club LP
MATCHBOX Star Club LP
PAPERBACK WRITER, count-in from We Can Work It Out, under dialogue
'80 Sheff John interview fragment re: Paperback Writer
interview continued fragment re: first backwards song
interview continued re: playing Rain backwards
SHE SAID SHE SAID under dialogue
George Martin interview re: producing Rain
RAIN The Beatles 62-66 LP
interview continued re: fade & singing backwards
I'M ONLY SLEEPING Revolver LP
interview continued fragment re: I'm Only Sleeping
RAIN backwards ending, under dialogue
MAYBE BABY St. Regis Hotel, Clock film soundtrack, under dialogue
HEARTBEAT St. Regis Hotel, Clock film soundtrack
PEGGY SUE GOT MARRIED St. Regis Hotel, Clock film soundtrack
PEGGY SUE St. Regis Hotel, Clock film soundtrack, also Part #2
John answers the phone
PEGGY SUE continued
ACROSS THE UNIVERSE alternate mix, under dialogue
TOMORROW NEVER KNOWS under dialogue
interview continued re: Tomorrow Never Knows
George Martin interview fragment re: Tomorrow sound picture

interview continued re: John's voice on Tomorrow Never Knows
'68 Kenny Everett interview re: creating sound effects
TOMORROW NEVER KNOWS reference mix, also #111
STRAWBERRY FIELDS FOREVER backing tracks, under dialogue
George Martin interview fragment re: Revolver to Pepper
John backwards speak for overdub session
STRAWBERRY FIELDS FOREVER backwards ending
Mintz says backwards: "Yeah Ringo take it easy, you might blow a gasket or something."
STRAWBERRY FIELDS FOREVER version 2, take 26, overdubs, rough mix, also #<u>88</u>
WHAT YOU GOT backing tracks, under dialogue
STEEL AND GLASS Walls And Bridges rehearsals
MOVE OVER MS. L Walls And Bridges rehearsals
BEEF JERKY extro

The Lost Lennon Tapes Part 27
Show #88-31, Broadcast the Week of July 25, 1988

BEEF JERKY intro
Jam Roll Over Beethoven, Sometime In NYC LP session
Jam Whole Lotta Shakin' Going On/It'll Be Me, Sometime In NYC LP session
CORRINA CORRINA Bob Dylan, under dialogue
CORRINA CORRINA improv, also #170
SERVE YOURSELF demo 2
THE BEST THINGS IN LIFE ARE FREE improv, fragment
circus music, Flying Trapeze
Jam, Rock 'N' Roll Circus
YER BLUES R 'N' R Circus, fragment, also #127, #<u>156</u>
'80 Peebles John interview fragment re: Yer Blues at R 'N' R Circus
HER BLUES Rock 'N' Roll Circus end, under dialogue
interview continued re: it was instantly creative
interview continued fragment re: film not coming out
Ethan Russell interview re: the Rolling Stones performance
Jesse Ed Davis song, under dialogue
AIN'T THAT A LOT OF LOVE Taj Mahal, under dialogue
'87 Davis interview re: meeting John
MYSTERY TRAIN Scotty Moore, under dialogue
FARTHER ON DOWN THE ROAD Jesse Ed Davis, Ululu LP
BONIE MARONIE under dialogue
interview continued re: having fun with John
interview continued re: Mucho Jesse
MUCHO MUNGO demo 2, take 3
MUCHO MUNGO Jesse Ed Davis, demo
WATCHING THE RIVER FLOW Bob Dylan, under dialogue
Davis interview re: John Trudel
GOD HELP HIM Jesse Ed Davis and John Trudel, fragment

interview continued re: Mark Chapman
JUST LIKE TOM THUMB'S BLUES Bob Dylan, under dialogue
interview continued re: drugs
interview continued re: reality beyond this life
BEEF JERKY extro

The Lost Lennon Tapes Part 28
Show #88-32, Broadcast the Week of August 1, 1988

BEEF JERKY intro
CATSWALK The Quarrymen, under dialogue
LOVE ME DO Ringo version, under dialogue
'62 Paul interview re: who writes the songs
'80 Sheff John interview re: deal to use both names
P.S. I LOVE YOU single 1962
P.S. I LOVE YOU under dialogue
interview re: P.S. I Love You, Paul's song
'62 John interview continued re: Please Please Me
PLEASE PLEASE ME single 1963
'80 Sheff John interview re: Please Please Me
ASK ME WHY under dialogue
George Martin interview re: issuing song in U.S.
ANNA (GO TO HIM) under dialogue
'80 Sheff John interview re: From Me To You
FROM ME TO YOU with count-in, single 1963
THANK YOU GIRL under dialogue
interview continued re: Thank You Girl
George Martin interview re: From Me To You & Capitol
FROM ME TO YOU Del Shannon, under dialogue
MISERY under dialogue
interview continued re: Misery and Do You Want To Know A Secret
DO YOU WANT TO KNOW A SECRET alternate mix, also #97
TWIST AND SHOUT under dialogue
THERE'S A PLACE Please Please Me LP
ASK ME WHY under dialogue
interview continued re: collaborating
Paul interview re: collaborating
BOYS under dialogue
interview continued re: friendly rivalry
I SAW HER STANDING THERE Please Please Me LP
BABY IT'S YOU under dialogue
interview continued re: inspired songs
interview fragment continued re: I'll Get You
interview continued re: She Loves You
interview continued re: oos and yeah yeah yeah

SHE LOVES YOU single 1963
I'LL GET YOU under dialogue
George Martin interview re: U.S. market
I WANNA BE YOUR MAN With The Beatles LP
interview fragment re: Tip Of My Tongue
interview continued re: I Wanna Be Your Man
I WANNA BE YOUR MAN Rolling Stones, under dialogue
I'M IN LOVE The Fourmost, singles 1963
LITTLE CHILD under dialogue
interview continued re: It Won't Be Long
IT WON'T BE LONG With The Beatles LP
ALL I'VE GOT TO DO under dialogue
interview continued re: I Want To Hold Your Hand
I WANT TO HOLD YOUR HAND The Beatles 62-66 LP
THIS BOY under dialogue
BEEF JERKY extro

The Lost Lennon Tapes Part 29
Show #88-33, Broadcast the Week of August 8, 1988

BEEF JERKY intro
WITHIN YOU WITHOUT YOU under dialogue
George Martin interview re: All You Need Is Love broadcast
All You Need Is Love dialogue intro
ALL YOU NEED IS LOVE broadcast, also #73
WATCHING THE WHEELS demo 2, under dialogue
WATCHING THE WHEELS demo 3, also #Preview 3
BANANA SONG improv
KHJ DJ apperance, John reads Tobias commercial, Jeans Revolution - shouting version
Maurice Dupont Part 3, mind movie
PEPPERLAND LAID WASTE under dialogue
MARCH OF THE MEANIES under dialogue
SHE LOVES YOU Ed Sullivan, under dialogue
Ed Sullivan intro to 3rd 1964 show
TWIST AND SHOUT Ed Sullivan 1964, also #115
PLEASE PLEASE ME Ed Sullivan 1964
I WANT TO HOLD YOUR HAND Ed Sullivan 1964, also #107, #129
JEALOUS GUY under dialogue
How Do You Sleep? alternate take, under dialogue
Alan White interview re: recording Imagine LP
interview continued re: How Do You Sleep?
interview continued re: rift with Paul and song
CRIPPLED INSIDE alternate take
OH MY LOVE under dialogue
interview continued re: John in the studio

interview continued re: John as one of the lads
OH YOKO! under dialogue
interview continued re: John relentless in studio
interview continued re: Imagine
IMAGINE alternate take
BEEF JERKY extro

The Lost Lennon Tapes Part 30
Show #88-34, Broadcast the Week of August 15, 1988

BEEF JERKY intro
SALLY AND BILLY demo 2, fragment, also #201
SALLY AND BILLY demo 1
I CAN'T GET NO NOOKIE The Masked Marauders, under dialogue
SATURDAY NIGHT AT THE COW PALACE The Masked Marauders, under dialogue
HAVE YOU HEARD THE WORD The Fut, under dialogue
radio question re: Have You Heard The Word
LULLABY (FOR A LAZY DAY) Grapefruit, demo fragment
LULLABY (FOR A LAZY DAY) Grapefruit 1968
I'M A MAN improv, under dialogue
A CASE OF THE BLUES demo, also #204
IT'S SO HARD alternate take, also #91
SEND ME SOME LOVIN' improv
John intro to NOBODY LOVES YOU (WHEN YOU'RE DOWN AND OUT)
NOBODY LOVES YOU (WHEN YOU'RE DOWN AND OUT) Menlove Ave LP, fragment
Mintz John interview re: being down and out in Hollywood
NOBODY LOVES YOU (WHEN YOU'RE DOWN AND OUT) Menlove Ave LP, continued
I'M LOSING YOU - STRANGER'S ROOM demo 2, fragment
'80 Sheff John interview re: I'm Losing You
I'M LOSING YOU demo 3
I'M LOSING YOU Double Fantasy LP
NEW YORK CITY under dialogue
NEW YORK CITY demo 1, incorrectly attributed to St. Regis Hotel, Clock film soundtrack
NEW YORK CITY demo 2, also #170
BEEF JERKY extro

The Lost Lennon Tapes Part 31
Show #88-35, Broadcast the Week of August 22, 1988

BEEF JERKY intro
I WANT TO HOLD YOUR HAND under dialogue
I SAW HER STANDING THERE Pop '63, Sweden, also #100
FROM ME TO YOU Pop '63, Sweden
ROLL OVER BEETHOVEN Pop '63, Sweden

YOU'VE REALLY GOT A HOLD ON ME Pop '63, Sweden
Jam One To One rehearsals, under dialogue
'80 Sheff John interview re: Woman Is The Nigger Of The World
WOMAN IS THE NIGGER OF THE WORLD demo 1
interview continued re: dissatisfied with lyrics
AIN'T THAT A SHAME outake, under dialogue
interview continued re: idea getting across
'72 Dick Gregory interview re: song not being played
WOMAN IS THE NIGGER OF THE WORLD Live In NYC LP
intro, mind movie
A HARD DAY'S NIGHT Peter Sellers single 1965
SHE LOVES YOU Peter Sellers single 1965
GET BACK under dialogue
'74 Tom Donahue KSAN John guest DJ appearance
interview re: Walls And Bridges title
What You Got intro
WHAT YOU GOT Walls And Bridges LP
interview continued re: eleven songs on LP
interview continued re: The Wailers
GET UP STAND UP The Wailers
I SHOT THE SHERRIFF Eric Clapton, under dialogue
BORROWED TIME demo 1, also #119, #173
BEEF JERKY extro

The Lost Lennon Tapes Part 32
Show #88-36, Broadcast the Week of August 29, 1988

BEEF JERKY intro
TAXMAN Revolver LP
THE WORD under dialogue
interview re: wealth
GETTING BETTER under dialogue
interview re: aim of Apple
Alistair Taylor interview re: basic Apple outline
ALL YOU NEED IS LOVE broadcast, under dialogue
BABY YOU'RE A RICH MAN under dialogue
WITHIN YOU WITHOUT YOU under dialogue
MAGICAL MYSTERY TOUR Magical Mystery Tour LP
FLYING under dialogue
Alistair Taylor interview re: Apple concept
Mal Evans interview re: Magical Mystery Tour idea
'70 Wenner John interview re: Magical Mystery Tour film
I AM THE WALRUS under dialogue
YOUR MOTHER SHOULD KNOW under dialogue
AERIAL TOUR INSTRUMENTAL, Flying, first mix

FLYING ending under dialogue
HELLO GOODBYE under dialogue
STRAWBERRY FIELDS FOREVER backing tracks, under dialogue
Alistair Taylor intreview re: in-jokes in Magical Mystery Tour
Paul interview re: film's response
interview continued re: film looks better now
I AM THE WALRUS Magical Mystery Tour LP
I Am The Walrus intrumental under dialogue
Alistair Taylor interview re: General Manager of Apple
Derek Taylor interview re: Apple concept
A LITTLE HELP FROM MY FRIENDS Sgt. Pepper's LP
GOT TO GET YOU INTO MY LIFE under dialogue
Pete Shotton interview re: joining Apple
interview continued re: John & Paul making decision for him
interview continued re: trapped into merchandising division
TOMORROW NEVER KNOWS under dialogue
interview continued re: confronting John about it
IT'S ALL TOO MUCH under dialogue
Alister Taylor interview re: blaming everyone
OB-LA-DI OB-LA-DA under dialogue
interview re: people wanting Apple to fail
BEEF JERKY extro

The Lost Lennon Tapes Part 33
Lennon At Large In Hollywood, Part 1: The Spector Sessions
Show #88-37, Broadcast the Week of September 5, 1988

BEEF JERKY intro
BE-BOP-A-LULA under dialogue
'80 Sheff John interview re: remembering old rock songs
'75 Whistle Test John interview re: Rock 'N' Roll LP idea
DO YOU WANT TO DANCE Rock 'N' Roll LP
BE MY BABY, Roots LP, intro under dialogue
'80 Peebles John interview re: working with Spector on Rock 'N' Roll LP
SWEET LITTLE SIXTEEN under dialogue
Jim Keltner interview re: Rock 'N' Roll sessions
JUST BECAUSE alternate take
Jim Keltner interview re: drinking on L.A. portion of LP
YA YA under dialogue
'88 Elton John interview fragment re: meeting John
Jim Keltner interview fragment re: not knowing who showed up
STAND BY ME alternate take
THAT'LL BE THE DAY rehearsal, under dialogue
Jim Keltner interview re: John drinking on sessions
interview continued re: painful period for John

AIN'T THAT A SHAME under dialogue
interview continued re: John pulling Jim's hair out
BRING IT ON HOME TO ME/SEND ME SOME LOVIN' alternate take
Mintz Keltner interview re: keeping up with John
BONIE MARONIE under dialogue
PEGGY SUE rehearsal, under dialogue
Keltner interview re: Spector shooting the studio
RIP IT UP/READY TEDDY alternate take
BE-BOP-A-LULA under dialogue
Jim Keltner interview fragment re: crazed sessions
'80 Peebles John interview re: Spector ran off with the tapes
YOU CAN'T CATCH ME under dialogue
'74 Tom Donahue KSAN John guest DJ appearance
interview fragment re: fight to stay in the country, also <u>Part 91</u>
30 DAYS rehearsal, under dialogue
SLIPPIN' AND SLIDIN' alternate take
thanks to Jim Keltner
BEEF JERKY extro

The Lost Lennon Tapes Part 34
Lennon At Large In Hollywood, Part 2: The Nilsson Phase
Show #88-38, Broadcast the Week of September 12, 1988

BEEF JERKY intro
YA YA alternate take
SWEET LITTLE SIXTEEN Rock 'N' Roll LP
'75 Old Grey Whistle interview re: hanging with L.A. musicians
I CAN'T STAND THE RAIN Anne Peebles, under dialogue
'88 Mintz Jim Keltner interview re: Kotex on forehead incident
AIN'T THAT A SHAME Rock 'N' Roll LP
RIP IT UP/READY TEDDY under dialogue
Nilsson intro to Everybody's Talkin'
EVERYBODY'S TALKIN' under dialogue
Nilsson interview re: first conversation with John
interview continued re: John & Harry kindred spirits
1941 Harry Nilsson, under dialogue
ROCK 'N' ROLL PEOPLE Menlove Ave. LP
THE LAST GREAT WALTZ Smothers Brothers do Nilsson, under dialogue
Nilsson interview re: Troubadour incident
Smothers Brothers interview re: Troubadour incident
'75 Old Grey Whistle Test interview re: hitting a photographer
interview continued re: idea to do a project with Harry
WITHOUT YOU Harry Nilsson, under dialogue
interview re: producing Pussy Cats LP
LOOP DE LOOP Pussy Cats LP

Don't Forget Me Harry Nilsson, under dialogue
Jim Keltner interview re: Pussy Cats LP
'75 Old Grey Whistle Test interview re: Harry losing his voice
ROCK AROUND THE CLOCK Pussy Cats LP
SAVE THE LAST DANCE FOR ME under dialogue
Mucho Mungo rehearsal dialogue
MUCHO MUNGO rehearsal, Harry and John, intro different to #173, also #<u>173</u>
MT. ELGA rehearsal, Harry and John
MUCHO MUNGO/MT. ELGA Pussy Cats LP
MANY RIVERS TO CROSS Jimmy Cliff, under dialogue
MANY RIVERS TO CROSS rough mix
OLD FORGOTTEN SOLDIER Pussy Cats, under dialogue
'80 Peebles John interview re: mixing Pussy Cats
BEEF JERKY extro

The Lost Lennon Tapes Part 35
Lennon At Large: Coast To Coast
Show #88-39, Broadcast the Week of September 19, 1988

BEEF JERKY intro
NEW YORK CITY under dialogue
'74 Tom Donahue KSAN John guest DJ appearance
interview re: working with Harry, first night, "spot the edit", "spot the edit" also #173
SUBTERRANEAN HOMESICK BLUES Pussy Cats LP
interview continued re: single
DON'T FORGET ME Pussy Cats LP, under dialogue
Harry Nilsson interview re: Pussy Cats LP a flop
MANY RIVERS TO CROSS under dialgoue
SURPRISE SURPRISE demo 1
May Pang interview re: Walls And Bridges fastest LP John made
STEEL AND GLASS under dialogue
WHATEVER GETS YOU THROUGH THE NIGHT rehearsal
WHATEVER GETS YOU THROUGH THE NIGHT under dialogue
SURPRISE SURPRISE Walls And Bridges LP
TWILIGHT ZONE THEME under dialogue
May Pang interview re: UFO sighting
MOVE OVER MS. L single 1974
GOODNIGHT VIENNA Ringo, under dialogue
May Pang interview re: giving Only You to Ringo
ONLY YOU John vocal
MIND GAMES under dialogue
GIVE ME SOME TRUTH Imagine LP
BRING ON THE LUCIE under dialogue
'74 interview re: living in New York
LUCY IN THE SKY WITH DIAMONDS under dialogue

LUCY IN THE SKY WITH DIAMONDS Elton single 1974
BEEF JERKY extro

                The Lost Lennon Tapes Part 36
            Dr. Winston O'Boogie On The Air: Part 2
   Show #88-40, Broadcast the Week of September 26, 1988

BEEF JERKY intro
'74 Dennis Elsas WNEW John guest DJ appearance
interview re: Pussy Cats LP
SAVE THE LAST DANCE FOR ME Pussy Cats LP
John reads the weather
'74 Tom Donahue KSAN John guest DJ appearance
introduction
GIVE ME LOVE Rosie & The Originals, under dialogue
interview re: Angel Baby
ANGEL BABY Rosie & The Originals
interview continued re: Roy Wood
BRONTOSAURUS STOMP The Move (Roy Wood)
NEW YORK CITY under dialogue
'74 Dennis Elsas WNEW John guest DJ appearance
John reads commercial for The Joffre Ballet
intro to
SHOWDOWN ELO
I HEARD IT THROUGH THE GRAPEVINE Marvin Gaye
extro to above two songs
FLYING under dialogue
interview continued re: Beatles reunion
GRAVY TRAIN The Place I Love LP, Splinter
I'M THE GREATEST Ringo LP
WHAT YOU GOT Walls And Bridges LP
John reads station I.D.
'74 Tom Donahue KSAN John guest DJ appearance
interview continued re: Old Dirt Road
OLD DIRT ROAD Walls And Bridges LP
BEEF JERKY extro

                The Lost Lennon Tapes Part 37
   Show #88-41, Broadcast the Week of October 3, 1988

BEEF JERKY intro
STAND BY ME under dialogue
'76 Mintz John & Yoko interview re: having a child
CHILD OF NATURE demo, under dialogue

BEAUTIFUL BOY take 1, demo 2, also #3
CLEANUP TIME under dialogue
interview continued re: child being healthy
MOTHER NATURE'S SON under dialogue
interview continued re: Sean's birth
CRY BABY CRY demo, under dialogue
HOLD ON Plastic Ono Band LP
BLESS YOU under dialogue
interview continued re: Sean's appearance
BEAUTIFUL BOY early mix
Sean's Goodnight, Double Fantasy session
interview continued re: Sean's name
interview continued re: telling Mimi the name on the phone
John interview's Sean re: New York's fiscal crisis
BEAUTIFUL BOY end instrumental under dialogue
'79 John talks with Sean about wanting to be 4
IT'S JOHNNY'S BIRTHDAY George, also #91
HERE COME THE THREES Donovan, John birthday song, also #91
HAPPY TRAILS Janis Joplin, John birthday song, also #91
HAPPY BIRTHDAY JOHN Ringo, John birthday song, also #91
WHAT'D I SAY John's Birthday Party 1971
YELLOW SUBMARINE Ringo improv, with crowd 1971 birthday
HAPPY BIRTHDAY improv, with crowd 1971 birthday
IMAGINE under dialogue
A DAY IN THE LIFE under dialogue
'88 Andrew Solt interview re: making of Imagine film
interview continued re: toughest part of making film
REAL LOVE - GIRLS AND BOYS demo 1, Imagine: John Lennon Soundtrack LP, also #3, #215
IN MY LIFE under dialogue
interview continued re: the music in Imagine film
IMAGINE (REHEARSAL) Imagine Soundtrack LP
GOODNIGHT IRENE John's Birthday Party 1971
BEEF JERKY extro

The Lost Lennon Tapes Part 38
Imagine: John Lennon Spotlight Part 2/Julian Lennon Part 1
Show #88-42, Broadcast the Week of October 10, 1988

BEEF JERKY intro
IMAGINE under dialogue
Yoko interview re: sharing tapes and films
interview continued re: why she didn't do documentary
DON'T LET ME DOWN under dialogue
Andrew Solt interview re: having creative control
A DAY IN THE LIFE Imagine: John Lennon Soundtrack LP

STRAWBERRY FIELDS FOREVER under dialogue
interview continued re: George Martin mixing songs
HOW? under dialogue
interview continued re: Imagaine sessions on film
CHILD OF NATURE demo, under dialogue
'88 Jim Keltner interview re: gearing up for I Don't Wanna Be A Soldier
'88 Alan White interview re: playing vibes
Jim Keltner interview re: fantastic experience
JEALOUS GUY Imagine LP
IN MY LIFE under dialogue
Andrew Solt interview re: the story of Imagine
P.S. I LOVE YOU under dialogue
Cynthia interview re: being pregnant with Julian
PLEASE PLEASE ME single 1963
BABY IT'S YOU under dialogue
interview fragment continued re: being separated from John
'63 Cynthia & Julian dialogue
VALOTTE under dialogue
GOOD DAY SUNSHINE under dialogue
'88 Mintz Julian interview re: living in Weybridge
YELLOW SUBMARINE under dialogue
Cynthia interview re: parties at Weybridge
LUCY IN THE SKY WITH DIAMONDS Sgt. Pepper's LP
LUCY IN THE SKY WITH DIAMONDS instrumental under dialogue
'88 Mintz Julian interview re: Lucy
interview continued re: painting
GOT TO GET YOU INTO MY LIFE under dialogue
interview continued re: incompetent father
WHAT GOES ON under dialogue
interview continued re: arguments at home
interview continued re: Paul visiting at Weybridge
interview continued re: Hey Jude
HEY JUDE The Beatles 1967-1970
interview continued re: relating to Lucy In The Sky With Diamonds and Hey Jude
interview continued re: first meeting Yoko
interview continued re: being locked in the attic
YOU'VE GOT TO HIDE YOUR LOVE AWAY under dialogue
interview continued re: nightmares and tantrums
Cynthia interview re: losing John
BEEF JERKY extro

The Lost Lennon Tapes Part 39
Imagine: John Lennon Spotlight Part III/Julian Lennon Part II
Show #88-43, Broadcast the Week of October 17, 1988

BEEF JERKY intro
TWIST AND SHOUT under dialogue
'80 Sheff John interview re: toppermost of the poppermost
'88 Andrew Solt interview re: Paul's reaction to Imagine film
interview continued re: Paul's reaction to the film
interview continued re: Paul not liking original ending
LET IT BE under dialogue
interview continued re: Paul remarkably at ease
interview continued re: George & Ringo's reactions
THE BALLAD OF JOHN AND YOKO Imagine: John Lennon Soundtrack LP
DON'T LET ME DOWN under dialogue
interview continued re: Sean and home footage
interview continued re: fascination with John
interview continued re: John speaking through his music
HEY JUDE under dialogue
'88 Mintz Julian interview re: Titenhurst Park
interview continued re: one scary night
PEPPERLAND LAID WASTE under dialogue
I WANT YOU (SHE'S SO HEAVY) under dialogue
'69 David Wigg John interview re: Julian's education
GETTING BETTER under dialogue
'88 Julian interview re: schools Julian attended
HOW? alternate take
CRIPPLED INSIDE under dialogue
'88 Cynthia interview re: John moving to New York
ISOLATION Plastic Ono Band LP
BIRTHDAY under dialogue
Julian birthday thank you to John & Yoko
LOVE ME DO under dialogue
Mintz Julian interview re: guitar John gave him
intro, mind movie
SHE LOVES YOU Peter Sellers
HELP! single 1965
MEAT CITY under dialogue
Cynthia interview re: bringing Julian to L.A. to see John
Julian interview re: L.A. apartment John stayed in
BONIE MARONIE Rock 'N' Roll LP
YA YA under dialogue
interview continued re: visiting Jim Keltner and his son
interview continued re: recording Ya Ya
YA YA Walls And Bridges LP
SLIPPIN' AND SLIDIN' under dialogue

STAND BY ME Old Grey Whistle Test, also #216
Julian goodbye dad tape to John
Julian birthday goodbye to John
BEEF JERKY extro

The Lost Lennon Tapes Part 40
Lennon's Star On The Hollywood Walk Of Fame - September 30, 1988
Show #88-44, Broadcast the Week of October 24, 1988

BEEF JERKY intro
POWER TO THE PEOPLE under dialogue
Yoko interview re: honour of receiving award
interview continued re: project started by fans
interview continued re: people helped get project going
interview continued re: John would have loved it
interview continued re: we'd still be working
COME TOGETHER under dialogue
CELLULOID HEROES The Kinks, under dialogue
Jim Ladd interview re: location of star
Jeff Pollack interview re: listener's did it
TWIST AND SHOUT under dialogue
Mike Reynolds Joe Smith interview re: interest in John
IMAGINE (REHEARSAL) Imagine: John Lennon Soundtrack LP
INSTANT KARMA under dialogue
Mike Reynolds Wolper interview re: not being a fan of John
interview continued re: ambivalent towards John
IN MY LIFE under dialogue
interview continued re: amount of material on John
interview continued re: no approval rights
Ladd Solt interview re: responsibility of doing film
A DAY IN THE LIFE under dialogue
interview continued re: interview with guy in garden
interview continued re: format for film
interview continued re: Lennon as narrator
interview continued re: Aunt Mimi
interview continued re: how much of film unreleased
interview continued re: what people come away with
NODBODY TOLD ME under dialogue
medley of John's songs
Jim Ladd Yoko interview re: special day
DEAR YOKO under dialogue
interview continued re: would have pleased John
interview continued re: reaction to The Lost Lennon Tapes
interview continued re: giving up editorial control
interview continued re: film fair and accurate

interview continued re: album and book
interview continued re: changes in Soviet Union
WOMAN under dialogue
interview continued re: peace message was theatre
interview continued re: renewed interest in the 60s
interview continued re: how Sean is
Jim Ladd Elliot Mintz interview re: movie
interview continued re: candor in movie
ALL YOU NEED IS LOVE under dialogue
Yoko Ladd interview re: facing truth
interview continued re: her optimism
interview continued re: keepers of the wishing well
THE BALLAD OF JOHN AND YOKO under dialogue
Jim Ladd reporting induction ceremony
Johnny Grant dedication
Jim Ladd J.J. Jackson interview re: his thoughts
Mike Reynolds interview Martin from Iowa re: attending
Johnny Grant dedication continued
Yoko introduced and presentation of scroll
David Wolper speech re: Imagine: John Lennon film
Yoko thank you speech
Jim Ladd reports on unveiling of star
Jim Ladd Jeff Pollock interview re: Yoko's acceptance speech
Jim Ladd J.J. Jackson interview re: Yoko's reaction
Jim Ladd Jeff Pollock interview re: Goldman book not discussed
interview continued re: everything coming off as planned
Johnny Grant sign off
Jim Ladd re: fans very warm to Yoko
Mike Reynolds interview fragment re: guys up in the trees
IMAGINE under dialogue extro
BEEF JERKY extro

The Lost Lennon Tapes Part 41
Rock And Roll, Part II
Show #88-45, Broadcast the Week of October 31, 1988

BEEF JERKY intro
CLEANUP TIME under dialogue
interview re: difference between Phil Spector & John
SWEET LITTLE SIXTEEN under dialogue
'75 Old Grey Whistle Test John interview re: getting tapes back
ANGEL BABY Menlove Ave LP
BRING IT ON HOME TO ME under dialogue
interview re: finishing Rock 'N' Roll LP
SINCE MY BABY LEFT ME Menlove Ave LP

BE MY BABY, Roots LP, under dialogue
COME TOGETHER under dialogue
YOU CAN'T CATCH ME under dialogue
TO KNOW HER IS TO LOVE HER Menlove Ave LP
BONIE MARONIE under dialogue
interview continued re: New York tracks on Rock 'N' Roll LP
BE-BOP-A-LULA Rock 'N' Roll LP
DO YOU WANNA DANCE under dialogue
'88 Jim Keltner interview re: rehearsal at Moriss Levi's
Jam Rumble/Whole Lotta Love, R 'N' R LP rehearsal, fragment
interview continued re: Rip It Up/Ready Teddy
RIP IT UP/READY TEDDY Rock 'N' Roll LP
PEGGY SUE Rock 'N' Roll LP
SLIPPIN' AND SLIDIN' under dialogue
'75 Old Grey Whistle Test interview re: playing LP to Capitol
YA YA under dialogue
JUST BECAUSE Walls And Bridges LP
'80 Peebles John interview re: John's farewell in Just Because
STAND BY ME under dialogue
'80 Sheff John interview re: reception of Rock 'N' Roll LP
AIN'T THAT A SHAME Rock 'N' Roll LP
NOBODY TOLD ME - EVERYBODY'S TALKING, NOBODY'S TALKING demo 2, also #200
'80 Peebles John interview re: not making records
WATCHING THE WHEELS backing tracks, under dialogue
NOBODY TOLD ME rough mix
BEEF JERKY extro

The Lost Lennon Tapes Part 42
Show #88-46, Broadcast the Week of November 7, 1988

BEEF JERKY intro
BBC intro to
DREAM BABY BBC, fragment, also #70, #106, #161
POP GO THE BEATLES BBC, under dialogue
BBC intro to
CAROL BBC, 16 July 1963, also #136
BBC intro to
SOLDIER OF LOVE BBC, 16 July 1963, also #136
BBC intro to
LEND ME YOUR COMB BBC, 16 July 1963
I AM THE WALRUS under dialogue
'88 Mark Lewisohn interview re: EMI asking him to do book
ASK ME WHY under dialogue
interview continued re: How Do You Do It
HOW DO YOU DO IT outake

CATSWALK The Quarry Men, under dialogue
interview continued re: hearing tapes
A HARD DAY'S NIGHT under dialogue
interview continued re: astonishing output
interview continued re: Kansas City
KANSAS CITY Beatles For Sale LP
ROCK AND ROLL MUSIC Beatles For Sale LP
NEW YORK CITY under dialogue
Jam Send Me Some Lovin', One To One rehearsals
Jam Don't Be Cruel/Houndog, One To One rehearsals
REVOLUTION under dialogue
Mark Lewisohn interview re: studio technique
interview continued re: George Martin's role
HAPPINESS IS A WARM GUN The Beatles LP
JULIA under dialogue
interview continued re: number of takes in later songs
interview continued re: unreleased songs
LEAVE MY KITTEN ALONE take 5
POWER TO THE PEOPLE under dialogue
JOHN LENNON FOR PRESIDENT David Peel, under dialogue
interview fragment re: recent administration
BEEF JERKY extro

The Lost Lennon Tapes Part 43
Show #88-47, Broadcast the Week of November 14, 1988

BEEF JERKY intro
BIRTHDAY under dialogue
'80 Sheff John interview re: The Continuing Story of Bungalow Bill
THE CONTINUING STORY OF BUNGALOW BILL demo
A TASTE OF HONEY under dialogue
George Martin interview re: double tracking
interview re: double tracking
NOT A SECOND TIME With The Beatles LP
12 BAR ORIGINAL under dialogue
'88 Mark Lewisohn interview re: double tracking
George Martin interview re: ADT and Ken Townshend
interview continued re: ADT machine
Mark Lewisohn interview re: first use of ADT
TOMORROW NEVER KNOWS Revolver LP
WORKING CLASS HERO under dialogue
'75 interview re: John's favourite album, Plastic Ono Band
I FOUND OUT alternate mix, Gone Gone, also #84, #187 beginning cut
WELL WELL WELL under dialogue
'70 Wenner John interview re: precision or feeling

interview continued re: singing better on Plastic Ono Band
LOVE Plastic Ono Band LP
insert interview fragment re: Love
POLYTHEN PAM under dialogue
REVOLUTION 1 under dialogue
Lewisohn interview re: John wanting to record instantly
YER BLUES The Beatles LP
interview fragment re: Yer Blues
MAXWELL'S SILVER HAMMER under dialogue
interview re: Maxwell's Silver Hammer
'88 Mark Lewisohn interview re: Paul's recordings
'80 Sheff John interview re: Abbey Road
'88 Mark Lewisohn interview re: medley on side 2 of Abbey Road
MEAN MR. MUSTARD/POLYTHENE PAM/SHE CAME IN THROUGH THE BATHROOM WINDOW
I'M A LOSER Paris 1965
A HARD DAY'S NIGHT Paris 1965
BEEF JERKY extro

The Lost Lennon Tapes Part 44
Show #88-48, Broadcast the Week of November 21, 1988

BEEF JERKY intro
John's Nowhere Man intro
SHE SAID SHE SAID under dialogue
'88 Julia Baird interview re: loving family life
interview continued re: John's childhood
JULIA backing tracks, under dialogue
JULIA demo 3, also #113
THINGS WE SAID TODAY under dialogue
THERE'S A PLACE Please Please Me LP
BAD BOY under dialogue
Julia Baird interview re: playing with John
ROCK AROUND THE CLOCK Bill Haley, under dialogue
interview re: Rock Around The Clock
Baird interview re: Julia encouraging John
'80 Sheff John interview fragment re: Ain't That A Shame
AIN'T THAT A SHAME Rock 'N' Roll LP
I'LL ALWAYS BE IN LOVE WITH YOU Quarry Men, under dialogue
Baird interview re: Paul always at house
interview continued re: John the Beatle
HELP! Live At The Hollywood Bowl LP
Mel Torment, mind movie intro
Ringo intro
John Tommy Cartwright line
SAILOR, COME BACK TO ME Ringo, fragment

EL TANGO TERRIBLE John as Woody Woodbine
Tobias Sportswear commercial, '74 KSAN appearance, "stiff suit and a dopey tie" - Scottish accent
Ringo intro
COOCHIE FROM BRAZIL/DOWN BY THE SEA John & Ringo ad lib
MOTHER backing tracks, under dialogue
'80 Sheff John interview re: John's childhood
MOTHER alternate take
ANY TIME AT ALL under dialogue
Julia Baird interview re: last time she saw John in 1968
ROCK AND ROLL MUSIC under dialogue
interview fragment continued re: missing his family
interview re: favourite LP, Rock 'N' Roll
BE-BOP-A-LULA Rock 'N' Roll LP
'75 Old Grey Whistle Test interview re: visiting England
We'll Meet Again, fragment in interview
TOMORROW NEVER KNOWS under dialogue
RAIN under dialogue
Mark Lewisohn interview re: backwards end of Rain
RAIN basic tracks
BEEF JERKY extro

The Lost Lennon Tapes Part 45
Show #88-49, Broadcast the Week of November 28, 1988

BEEF JERKY intro
IT'S SO HARD under dialogue
John tells John Sinclair story on The David Frost Show
JOHN SINCLAIR The David Frost Show
IT'S SO HARD The Mike Douglas Show, incorrectly attributed to The David Frost Show, also #108
THE LUCK OF THE IRISH The Mike Douglas Show, incorrectly attributed to The David Frost Show
French instrumental under dialogue
'80 Sheff John interview re: first trip to Paris
'76 Mintz John interview re: Paris holiday with Paul
MY BONNIE Tony Sheridan, The Beatles First LP
CRY FOR A SHADOW under dialogue
Jürgen Vollmer interview re: John & Paul in Paris
interview continued re: they were never serious
DA DOO RON RON in French, under dialogue
interview continued re: trying to book the Beatles
MONEY Decca Sessions LP
LEND ME YOUR COMB BBC, under dialogue
Vollmer interview re: showing off girl to John & Paul
I'LL BE BACK under dialogue
interview continued re: meeting same girl years later
SATISFACTION live, under dialogue

CAN'T BUY ME LOVE Paris 1965
ROCK AND ROLL MUSIC Paris 1965
IN MY LIFE under dialogue
WE CAN WORK IT OUT under dialogue
'80 Sheff John interview re: We Can Work It Out
WE CAN WORK IT OUT Paul demo, fragment
cut to John speke
WE CAN WORK IT OUT early mix, take 2
WATCH YOUR STEP Bobby Parker, under dialogue
'80 Sheff John interview re: words to Day Tripper
DAY TRIPPER rough mix, takes 1, 3
TENNESSEE take 4, under dialogue
HOWLING AT THE MOON demo
MEMORIES demo 1
BEEF JERKY extro

The Lost Lennon Tapes Part 46
Show #88-50, Broadcast the Week of December 5, 1988

BEEF JERKY intro
STRAWBERRY FIELDS FOREVER demo, under dialogue
'80 Sheff John interview re: scope of John's infleunce
STRAWBERRY FIELDS FOREVER backing tracks, under dialogue
THERE'S A PLACE outakes, takes 3, 4
DO YOU WANT TO KNOW A SECRET under dialogue
interview continued re: realism is reality
JAILHOUSE ROCK Elvis Presley, under dialogue
MISERY Please Please Me LP
BAD TO ME demo, fragment
interview continued re: holiday in Spain with Brian
I'LL CRY INSTEAD under dialogue
interview continued re: being a rebel
A HARD DAY'S NIGHT under dialogue
interview continued re: being on pills & other drugs
HELP! U.S. Help! LP
interview continued re: emotional extremes
FROM ME TO YOU FANTASY under dialogue
YOU'VE GOT TO HIDE YOUR LOVE AWAY Help! LP
interview continued re: You've Got To Hide Your Love Away
THE WORD Rubber Soul LP
interview fragment over re: putting out messages
interview continued re: first experience with acid
TOMORROW NEVER KNOWS under dialogue
YELLOW SUBMARINE under dialogue
interview continued re: second acid trip in L.A.

EIGHT MILES HIGH The Byrds, under dialogue
SHE SAID SHE SAID Revolver LP
THINK FOR YOURSELF under dialogue
'66 Chicago Jesus controversy press conference fragment
August 28/'66 L.A. press conference fragment
STRAWBERRY FIELDS FOREVER single 1967
'80 Sheff John interview re: being crazy or a genius
IT'S ALL TOO MUCH under dialogue
'70 Wenner John interview fragment re: thousands of trips
'67 Maharishi interview re: meditation and the Beatles
ALL YOU NEED IS LOVE under dialogue
WITHIN YOU WITHOUT YOU under dialogue
Beatles Bangor Wales interview re: Brian's death
SEXY SADIE under dialogue
'68 Crowse John & Paul interview re: Maharishi & meditation
SEXY SADIE demo, also #85
'70 Wenner John interview fragment re: end of the first lesson
BEEF JERKY extro

The Lost Lennon Tapes Part 47
Show #88-51, Broadcast the Week of December 12, 1988

BEEF JERKY intro
ACROSS THE UNIVERSE No One's Gonna Change Our World LP, under dialogue
'68 Mitchell Crowse John interview re: drugs
'70 Wenner John interview re: taking acid in 1968
REVOLUTION promo film
interview re: Revolution
REVOLUTION 1 under dialogue
REVOLUTION 9 under dialogue
I'VE GOT A FEELING under dialogue
THE BALLAD OF JOHN AND YOKO under dialogue
WEDDING LP interview re: peace through peaceful means
GIVE PEACE A CHANCE single 1969
'80 Sheff John interview re: writing Give Peace A Chance
COLD TURKEY Live Peace in Toronto LP under dialogue
'70 Wenner John interview re: misperception of drug abuse
COME TOGETHER under dialogue
COLD TURKEY Sometime In New York City LP
HAPPY XMAS (WAR IS OVER) under dialogue
interview re: War Is Over poster
interview continued re: poster concept
BLUE SUEDE SHOES Live in Toronto LP, under dialogue
'69 Toronto press conference interview re: believing in God
INSTANT KARMA single 1970

'80 Sheff John interview re: Instant Karma
INSTANT KARMA live, under dialogue
POWER TO THE PEOPLE under dialogue
interview continued re: Power To The People
MOTHER backing tracks, under dialogue
interview continued re: therapy with Janov
interview continued re: Primal Scream
interview continued re: father figures
I FOUND OUT demo 1, take 1, also #126
GOD under dialogue
'73 Mintz John interview re: God
GOD demo 3, also #142
'80 Sheff Yoko & John interview fragment re: God
BEEF JERKY extro

The Lost Lennon Tapes Part 48
Show #88-52, Broadcast the Week of December 19, 1988

BEEF JERKY intro
MOTHER under dialogue
'80 Sheff John interview re: Mother
IMAGINE Mark Knopfler and Chet Atkins, under dialogue
interview continued re: Imagine
IMAGINE alternate take
HAPPY XMAS (WAR IS OVER) under dialogue
'80 Peebles John interview re: Happy Xmas
HAPPY XMAS (WAR IS OVER) demo
Happy Xmas John and Yoko Xmas message
SISTERS O SISTERS under dialogue
'73 Danny Schechter John interview re: feminist movement
WOMAN IS THE NIGGER OF THE WORLD Sometime In NYC LP
interview over re: women are oppressed
MIND GAMES Mind Games LP
OUT THE BLUE rough mix
SINCE MY BABY LEFT ME under dialogue
NOBODY LOVES YOU (WHEN YOU'RE DOWN AND OUT) Walls And Bridges LP
WATCHING THE WHEELS backing tracks, under dialogue
'76 Mintz John interview re: separation & reunion decisions
'80 Sheff John interview re: why things go bad
SERVE YOURSELF demo 2, under dialogue
'80 Sheff John interview re: agnostics essence of Christianity
SERVE YOURSELF demo 3
BORROWED TIME rough mix
interview continued fragment re: God came to the session
GONE FROM THIS PLACE demo 1

'76 Mintz John interview over re: magic is so subtle
BEEF JERKY extro

The Lost Lennon Tapes Part 49
Best Of The Lost Lennon Tapes - Year One
Show #89-01, Broadcast the Week of December 26, 1988

BEEF JERKY intro
TWIST AND SHOUT live, Stockholm 1963
WHATEVER GETS YOU THROUGH THE NIGHT Madison Square Garden, single 1981
Elton John interview fragment re: crowd went bananas
'80 Sheff John interview re: crowd was fantastic
HONEY DON'T/MATCHBOX/DON'T BE CRUEL POB session, also #22, #187
BAD BOY under dialogue
MOOVIN' AND GROOVIN' The Quarry Men, under dialogue
guitar under dialogue
'70 Wenner John interview re: art school
interview continued fragment re: guitar's all right for a hobby
THAT'LL BE THE DAY Buddy Holly, under dialogue
Pete Shotton interview re: Aunt Mimi
Aunt Mimi interview re: being hard on John in his teens
'70 Wenner John interview re: Mimi throwing his poetry out
LOOK AT ME under dialogue
How Do You Sleep? under dialogue
interview continued re: assessing his work
ANOTHER HARD DAY'S NIGHT under dialogue
'63 Doncaster Neville Club reading by John
'68 Christmas record: Jock & Yono
'63 Cynthia interviews Julian
'79 John interviews Sean
A LITTLE HELP FROM MY FRIENDS under dialogue
blues instrumental, under dialogue
STRAWBERRY FIELDS FOREVER demo 1, also #4, #131, #<u>180</u>
THE NEWS OF THE DAY FROM REUTERS parody, also #<u>14</u>, #172
WHATEVER HAPPENED TO take 2
ACROSS THE UNIVERSE alternate mono mix
How Do You Sleep? **alternate mix**, fragment
How Do You Sleep? under dialogue
Great WOK 1978 New Year's resolution, fragment, also #<u>50</u>, #185, #217
AS TIME GOES BY improv, John only, also #Preview 2
BEEF JERKY extro

The Lost Lennon Tapes Part 50
The Year Two Preview
Show #89-02, Broadcast the Week of January 2, 1989

BEEF JERKY intro
Great WOK 1978 New Year's resolution, also #49, #185, #217
ROCKER - INSTRUMENTAL 42 Get Back LP
SAN FRANCISCO BAY BLUES studio improv, fragment, also #53
Jam One To One rehearsals, fragment, Tequila
WHATEVER GETS YOU THROUGH THE NIGHT 1st take, fragment, also #104
RIP IT UP rehearsal, fragment
A HARD DAY'S NIGHT Paris 1964, under dialogue
I SAW HER STANDING THERE, Star Club LP, fragment
TOO MUCH MONKEY BUSINESS BBC, fragment
YER BLUES Rock 'N' Roll Circus rehearsal #1, fragment
YOU CAN'T DO THAT Melbourne 1964, fragment
COME TOGETHER Live In New York City LP
IT'S ALL TOO MUCH under dialogue
Aunt Mimi interview fragment re: Socialist gov't
'80 Sheff John interview fragment re: Paul adding lightness
Paul interview fragment re: his relationship with John
Cynthia interview fragment re: her book
'88 Mintz Julian interview fragment re: John
THE BALLAD OF JOHN AND YOKO under dialogue
John and Yoko Wedding Album radio ad
JOHN AND YOKO Wedding Album LP, excerpt
interview fragment re: battle for Kyoko
interview fragment re: finding Kyoko
Sean interview fragment re: John & Yoko's love
I WANT YOU (SHE'S SO HEAVY) Abbey Road LP
JOHN AND YOKO under dialogue
interview re: what have you written lately
interview fragment re: Apple going broke
Paul interview fragment re: the breakup
interview fragment re: the breakup
GOD under dialogue
'71 Mintz John interview fragment re: reunion
'76 Mintz John interview fragment re: reunion
'80 Sheff John interview fragment re: reunion
KHJ guest DJ appearance continued
'76 KHJ John interview re: I Am The Walrus
'76 Mintz John interview fragment re: immigration
'70 Wenner John interview fragment re: tours
NORWEGIAN WOOD under dialogue
A DAY IN THE LIFE alternate take, fragment
DIG IT Get Back rehearsals, fragment

ROCK 'N' ROLL PEOPLE alternate take, fragment
Dear Yoko studio dialogue, sings "oh my god damn dear, dear Yoko ... OK what are waiting for?"
DEAR YOKO basic tracks
#9 DREAM under dialogue
#9 DREAM - SO LONG demo 1, fragment
MIRROR MIRROR demo 2, take 4, fragment
JOHN HENRY demo 2, fragment
SHE'S A FRIEND OF DOROTHYS demo 2, also #201
BEEF JERKY extro

The Lost Lennon Tapes Part 51
Show #89-03, Broadcast the Week of January 9, 1989

BEEF JERKY intro
WHAT YOU GOT backing tracks, under dialogue
IMAGINE under dialogue
KHJ John guest DJ appearance
introduction, John says good morning
COME TOGETHER Abbey Road LP
intro to
SUBTERRANEAN HOMESICK BLUES Harry Nilsson, edited
call Mike re: will Beatles get back together, also #185
call Dana re: request for Mind Games, also #185
MIND GAMES Mind Games LP
THINK FOR YOURSELF under dialogue
'70 Wenner John interview re: Rubber Soul LP
I'M DOWN under dialogue
interview fragment continued re: Rubber Soul title
interview continued re: nothing mysterious
DRIVE MY CAR Rubber Soul LP
THE CHASE under dialogue
'80 Sheff John interview re: Nowegian Wood
interview continued re: use of sitar
NORWEGIAN WOOD alternate take, under dialogue
ANOTHER HARD DAY'S NIGHT under dialogue
interview continued re: doing Norwegian Wood himself
interview continued re: showing guitar lick to George
NORWEGIAN WOOD take 4, LP version with intro & extro
KHJ John guest DJ appearance
KHJ station I.D.
Mark Howard Lennon introduction
intro to
SUPERSTITION Stevie Wonder, edited
call re: request for Cold Turkey
COLD TURKEY edited

- 52 -

John reads Tobias commercial, "stiff suit... stiff suit and a dopey tie"
call Ed re: request for Be Yourself by Graham Nash also #185
call Peter re: request for Beep Beep or Hold On John, also #185
HOLD ON JOHN Plastic Ono Band LP
WHAT YOU GOT under dialogue
intro to, also #187
GET UP, STAND UP The Wailers, edited
John: listen for regular DJ next week, also #187
Walls and Bridges radio ad with Ringo, "listen to this radio spot", also #185
John: LP available this afternoon, also #187
I'M THE GREATEST Ringo
call Lance re: request for It's Only Love, also #187
call John re: thank you for all you've done for music, also #187
call Louise re: request for something off the new album, also #187
WHAT YOU GOT under dialogue
Jam One To One rehearsals, under dialogue
HOUND DOG/LONG TALL SALLY One To One rehearsals
BEEF JERKY extro

The Lost Lennon Tapes Part 52
Show #89-04, Broadcast the Week of January 16, 1989

BEEF JERKY intro
Jam New York City, One To One rehearsals, under dialogue
IT'S SO HARD One To One rehearsals, also #186
IMAGINE under dialogue
'75 Scott Muni John interview re: Imagine LP his best
'71 Mintz John interview re: Imagine LP
OH YOKO! demo 2, fragment, also #182
OH YOKO! Imagine LP
'80 Sheff John interview re: stopping Oh Yoko! single
OH YOKO! rough mix
WHAT YOU GOT under dialogue
KHJ John guest DJ appearance
call Donna re: request for a cut from your new album, also #187
#9 DREAM Walls And Bridges LP
John reads Tobias commercial - Jeans Revolution - "I'm getting tired of the Jeans Revolution"
news interview clips re: reaction to John as guest, also #187
call Mark re: Walrus and where do your insane lyrics come from, also #187
I AM THE WALRUS The Beatles 1967-1970 LP
call Kid re: can you play a song off your new album
WHAT YOU GOT under dialogue
TWIST AND SHOUT Live At The Hollywood Bowl LP, under dialogue
IF I FELL Philadelphia 1964
I WANT TO HOLD YOUR HAND Philadelphia 1964

A HARD DAY'S NIGHT Philadelphia 1964
GIVE ME SOME TRUTH under dialogue
'80 Sheff John interview re: Give Me Some Truth
GIVE ME SOME TRUTH Get Back rehearsals, fragment
GIVE ME SOME TRUTH alternate take, also #76
BEEF JERKY extro

The Lost Lennon Tapes Part 53
Show #89-05, Broadcast the Week of January 23, 1989

BEEF JERKY intro
HOW? under dialogue
HOW? demo 1, under dialogue
HOW? alternate take
GIVE ME SOME TRUTH Imagine LP
'71 Mintz first interview with John
May Pang directs operator
REMEMBER under dialogue
interview re: good piece you did with Yoko
interview continued re: concept of age
I DON'T WANNA BE A SOLDIER under dialogue
interview continued re: draft in U.S., would you go
interview continued re: any cause worth dying for
interview continued re: defensive violence
interview continued re: taking someone's life
THE LUCK OF THE IRISH Sometime In New York City LP
inteview continued re: any regrets
OH YOKO! under dialogue
IMAGINE end fragment
IMAGINE under dialogue
'80 Sheff John interview fragment re: Oh My Love
OH MY LOVE alternate take
SAN FRANCISCO BAY BLUES studio improv, also #50
How Do You Sleep? alternate take, take 2
DR. ROBERT under dialogue
'80 Sheff John interview re: Dr. Robert
PILL only take
COLD TURKEY One To One rehearsals, under dialogue
One To One radio promo re: addition of 2nd show "hold it hold it"
One To One radio promo re: addition of 2nd show, take 2, group reading
WOMAN IS THE NIGGER OF THE WORLD One To One rehearsals
BEEF JERKY piano outake, extro

The Lost Lennon Tapes Part 54
Grapefruit: Can You Dig It?
Show #89-06, Broadcast the Week of January 30, 1989

BEEF JERKY intro
YOU CAN'T DO THAT Philadelphia 1964
SHE LOVES YOU Philadelphia 1964
THINGS WE SAID TODAY Philadelphia 1964
LONG TALL SALLY Philadelphia 1964
IMAGINE under dialogue
'80 Peebles John interview re: Imagine and Grapefruit
Grapefruit excerpts read by John and Yoko:
Yoko: A Piece For Orchestra
Yoko: Building Piece For Orchestra
John: Water Piece
John: Wall Piece I
John: Tunafish Sandwich Piece
Yoko: Drinking Piece For Orchestra
IMAGINE Mark Knopfler and Chet Atkins, under dialogue
Yoko: Tape Piece III Snow Piece
John: Stone Piece
John: Wood Piece
Yoko: Tape Piece II Room Piece
Yoko: Fish Piece
John: Snow Piece
John: 3 More Snow Pieces For Solo Or Orchestra
DIG IT under dialogue
'80 Sheff John interview fragment re: Dig It
GET BACK under dialogue
DIG IT complete, 8 minutes 8 seconds
YOU NEVER GIVE ME YOUR MONEY under dialogue
'71 Mintz John interview re: John's wealth
I FOUND OUT under dialogue
MONEY Live Peace In Toronto LP
NEW YORK CITY under dialogue
interview continued re: living in NY, Kyoko, dreams
FLYING under dialogue
IMAGINE (REHEARSAL) under dialogue
Grapefruit excerpts:
Yoko: Clock Piece
Yoko: Collecting Piece
John: Snow Piece For Solo Or Trio
John: Wind Piece
Yoko: Bell Piece
Yoko: Bicycle Piece For Orchestra
John: City Piece

John: City Piece
Yoko: Earth Piece
Yoko: Water Piece
John: Walking Piece
John: Hide And Seek Piece
Yoko: Breathe Piece
Yoko: Pulse Piece
John: Concert Piece
John: Line Piece
John: Line Piece
John: Water Piece
Yoko: Dawn Piece
John reads U.S. and U.K. publishers
IMAGINE alternate take
John's Tape Piece over extro
BEEF JERKY extro

The Lost Lennon Tapes Part 55
The Beatles: Coming To America, Part 1
Show #89-07, Broadcast the Week of February 6, 1989

BEEF JERKY intro
BABY IT'S YOU under dialogue
'74 interview fragment re: making it in America
'64 Larry Kane John interview re: first time in America
LOVE ME DO original version, single 1962
ASK ME WHY under dialogue
'64 Epstein interview re: preplanning for American trip
'80 Musician Paul interview re: developing the act
FROM ME TO YOU take 2
AMERICA Simon and Garfunkel, under dialogue
interview continued re: working out better than they imagined
ALL I'VE GOT TO DO With The Beatles LP
'80 Sheff John interview fragment re: All I've Got To Do
SOLDIER OF LOVE BBC, under dialogue
'64 Larry Kane John interview re: early American influences
BABY LET'S PLAY HOUSE Elvis Presley, under dialogue
'70 Wenner John interview re: black music
SOME OTHER GUY Cavern Club, live, under dialogue
I SAW HER STANDING THERE take 2
MONEY under dialogue
LEND ME YOUR COMB BBC, under dialogue
'80 Musician Paul interview re: haircuts
interview continued re: the rest of their image
YOU REALLY GOT A HOLD ON ME With The Beatles LP

PLEASE MISTER POSTMAN under dialogue
'74 Howard Cosell John interview re: leading the '60s
ROLL OVER BEETHOVEN under dialogue
PLEASE PLEASE ME Please Please Me LP ST
CHAINS under dialogue
'89 Dr. Demento interview re: stiffs of '63 and VJ
FROM ME TO YOU Del Shannon, under dialogue
interview continued re: She Loves You and Swan
SHE LOVES YOU single 1963
DO YOU WANT TO KNOW A SECRET under dialogue
interview continued re: Capitol didn't want to know
THE JAMES BOND THEME under dialogue
'76 Mintz Ringo interview re: George checking out America
DON'T BOTHER ME under dialogue
IT WON'T BE LONG under dialogue
Sid Bernstein interview re: 1st booking the Beatles
TWIST AND SHOUT Pop '63, under dialogue
'63 BBC report of London Airport return from Sweden
RINGO'S THEME (THIS BOY) under dialogue
'76 Mintz Ringo interview re: Ed Sullivan being in the airport
I WANT TO HOLD YOUR HAND Beatles 62-66 LP
interview continued fragment re: just by luck over extro
BEEF JERKY extro

The Lost Lennon Tapes Part 56
The Beatles: Coming To America, Part 2
Show #89-08, Broadcast the Week of February 13, 1989

BEEF JERKY intro
MISERY take 1, also #78
TILL THERE WAS YOU Royal Variety, under dialogue
TWIST AND SHOUT Royal Variety
THIS BOY Love Songs LP, under dialogue
'64 Brian Epstein interview re: poor response in States
PLEASE PLEASE ME Please Please Me LP, under dialogue
Walter Cronkite interview re: 1st report on the news
SHE LOVES YOU Pop '63 Sweden, also #10 #89
I'M LEAVING IT ALL UP TO YOU Dayle & Grace, under dialogue
DOMINIQUE Sister Luke Gabriel, under dialogue
LOUIE LOUIE The Kingsmen, under dialogue
Phillip Norman interview re: Kennedy assasination & Beatles
NOT A SECOND TIME With The Beatles LP
I SAW HER STANDING THERE under dialogue
'80 Sheff John interview re: I Saw Her Standing There
'76 Mintz Ringo interview re: Capitol promised promotion

MONEY With The Beatles LP
COMBAT! under dialogue
IT WON'T BE LONG under dialogue
Phillip Norman interview re: BOA stewardess
interview continued re: Capitol pressing A HARD DAY'S Night
'63 Xmas Record excerpt - John speech at beginning
I'LL GET YOU single
RINGO'S THEME (THIS BOY) under dialogue
Jack Parr Victor Spinetti interview re: hair style
YOU REALLY GOT A HOLD ON ME under dialogue
John, Paul & George interview with French reporter re: likes
FROM ME TO YOU Paris 1964, under dialogue
Paul interview re: news I Want To Hold Your Hand #1 in U.S.
Mal Evans interview re: I Want To Hold Your Hand #1 in U.S.
I WANT TO HOLD YOUR HAND Paris 1964, also #109
THIS BOY Paris 1964, under dialogue
George Martin interview re: #1 in America
KOMM GIB MIR DEINE HAND under dialogue
Larry Kane John interivew re: German recordings
SIE LIEBT DICH U.S. Rarities LP
CAN'T BUY ME LOVE alternate take, under dialogue
MY BONNIE Tony Sheridan, under dialogue
I WANT TO HOLD YOUR HAND Beatles 62-66 LP, under dialogue
'64 Brian Epstein interview re: leaving at London Airport
interview fragment re: we knew we would wipe 'em out
'76 Ringo Mintz interview re: excitement going to New York
interview continued fragment re: The day we arrived were were #1
BEEF JERKY extro

The Lost Lennon Tapes Part 57
Show #89-09, Broadcast the Week of February 20, 1989

BEEF JERKY intro
'64 newsreel soundtrack: February 7, 1964 Beatles London departure
I WANT TO HOLD YOUR HAND under dialogue
PLEASE PLEASE ME under dialogue
'64 Tony Marvin Kennedy airport report
'64 Vic Rosse interviews fans at Kennedy Airport
interview continued re: Kennedy airport reception
BOYS under dialogue
'75 Mintz Ringo interview re: reception in New York
'64 Vic Rosse news report Kennedy airport
'89 Scott Muni interview fragment re: airport security
BABY IT'S YOU under dialogue
'64 press conference fragment: haircuts question

'64 Vic Rosse interview re: aggresive photographers
press conference excerpt: Murray the K, Elvis
'89 Scott Muni interview re: press conference
'64 press conference excerpt: George's haircut yesterday
THERE'S A PLACE take 1
TO KNOW HER IS TO LOVE HER Decca Sessions LP, under dialogue
'89 Scott Muni interview re: Phil Spector on the flight
P.S. I LOVE YOU under dialogue
'75 Mintz Ringo interview re: motorcade to Plaza Hotel
LOVE ME DO under dialogue
George Martin interview re: New York reception
'64 fan interview outside the Plaza Hotel
George Martin interview re: Ringo on phone in & saturation
TWIST AND SHOUT under dialogue
Fred Martin interview re: Plaza Hotel press conference
press conference excerpt: John, being a Beatle
THIS BOY Paris 1964
CHAINS under dialogue
'64 Larry Kane Paul interview re: going out to see NY
'70 Wenner John interview re: being professional by 1964
'75 Mintz Ringo interview re: press came to kill us
JAWS THEME under dialogue
SHOUT Around The Beatles, under dialogue
DO YOU WANT TO KNOW A SECRET under dialogue
'80 Sheff John interview re: reaction to press
ASK ME WHY under dialogue
Ed Sullivan Show debut intro to first set
ALL MY LOVING Ed Sullivan 1964, also #3, #133, #160
TILL THERE WAS YOU Ed Sullivan 1964
SHE LOVES YOU Ed Sullivan 1964, also #160
I SAW HER STANDING THERE under dialogue
'64 Bill Grundy Brian Epstein interview re: timing
LITTLE CHILD With The Beatles LP
I WANNA BE YOUR MAN under dialogue
'70 Wenner John interview re: no concept of fashion in U.S.
I WANNA BE YOUR MAN The Rolling Stones, under dialogue
interview continued re: U.S. critical reception
Fred Martin interview re: major talents
ALL I'VE GOT TO DO under dialogue
I SAW HER STANDING THERE Ed Sullivan 1964, also #110, #160
I WANT TO HOLD YOUR HAND Ed Sullivan 1964, also #29, #107, #129
Ed Sullivan Show debut extro
'74 Howard Cosell John interview re: changing the music
CRY FOR A SHADOW under dialogue
BEEF JERKY extro

The Lost Lennon Tapes Part 58
Toronto Rock & Roll Revival Spotlight, Part 1
Show #89-10, Broadcast the Week of February 27, 1989

BEEF JERKY intro
REAL LOVE demo 1, take 1
GIVE PEACE A CHANCE under dialogue
'70 Wenner John interview re: decision to leave Beatles
COME TOGETHER Abbey Road LP
YER BLUES Rock 'N' Roll Circus, under dialogue
John Brower interview re: Brower Walker
interview continued re: lineup of Toronto concert
interview continued re: lineup of others appearing
interview continued re: disinterest in ticket sales
I WANT YOU (SHE'S SO HEAVY) Abbey Road LP
interview continued re: Kim Fowley suggested John
interview continued re: phoning Apple, talking to John
YOU NEVER GIVE ME YOUR MONEY under dialogue
John Brower interview re: John not concerned about money
'88 Mintz Alan White interview re: John asking him to play
THE BALLAD OF JOHN AND YOKO under dialogue
John Brower interview re: convincing local media
MEAN MR. MUSTARD Abbey Road LP
POLYTHEN PAM under dialogue
interview continued re: radio confirmation in Detroit
SHE CAME IN THROUGH THE BATHROOM WINDOW under dialogue
'88 Mintz Alan White interview re: Plastic Ono Band concept
BECAUSE under dialogue
'80 Sheff John interview re: writing Because
MOONLIGHT SONATA under dialogue
BECAUSE early reference mix, fragment, begins under dialogue
BECAUSE vocals only
THE END under dialogue
Brower interview re: John & Yoko missing the plane
BLUE SUEDE SHOES Carl Perkins, under dialogue
Alan White interview re: rehearsing on the plane
Brower interview fragment re: explaining the delay to the press
SUN KING Abbey Road LP
BORN TO BE WILD Steppenwolf, under dialogue
Brower interview re: motorcycles at the airport
BEEF JERKY extro

The Lost Lennon Tapes Part 59
Live Peace In Toronto 1969 Spotlight, Part 2
Show #89-11, Broadcast the Week of March 6, 1989

BEEF JERKY intro
BORN TO BE WILD Steppenwolf, under dialogue
John Brower interview re: entourage arriving backstage
YER BLUES Rock 'N' Roll Circus rehearsal #2, under dialogue
BLUE SUEDE SHOES Get Back rehearsals
TOUCH ME The Doors, under dialogue
John Brower interview re: placement of John in the concert
RIP IT UP under dialogue
interview continued re: backstage fraternizing
interview continued re: John and Little Richard exchange
interview continued re: bad stage freight
RIP IT UP Little Richard, under dialogue
'88 Mintz Alan White interview re: Gene Vincent backstage
Plastic Ono Band introduction
John Brower interview re: John's choice of material
BLUE SUEDE SHOES Live Peace In Toronto LP
DO WHAT YOU LIKE Blind Faith, under dialogue
'88 Alan White interview re: drums on stage
John Brower interview re: Klein asking for more money
MONEY Live Peace In Toronto LP, under dialogue
DIZZY MISS LIZZY Live Peace In Toronto LP
COLD TURKEY demo, under dialogue
John Brower interview re: John asking for coke
YER BLUES Live Peace In Toronto LP, under dialogue
interview continued re: no heavy dope backstage
COLD TURKEY Live Peace In Toronto LP
'80 Sheff John interview re: throwing up backstage
GIVE PEACE A CHANCE Live Peace In Toronto LP
DON'T WORRY KYOKO Live Peace In Toronto LP, under dialogue
JOHN, JOHN (LET'S HOPE FOR PEACE) Live Peace in Toronto LP, under dialogue
John Brower interview re: crowd reaction to Yoko
interview continued re: Jim Morrison, The Doors and others
ROADHOUSE BLUES The Doors, under dialogue
interview continued re: concert a success financially
interview continued re: John and Yoko staying at Caledon
BECAUSE under dialogue
'70 Wenner John interview re: not wanting to release LP
John Brower interview re: film of concert not coming out
MOTHER backing tracks, under dialogue
I FOUND OUT demo 2, take 2
BEEF JERKY extro

The Lost Lennon Tapes Part 60
(Almost) Nothing But Beatles & Elvis
Show #89-12, Broadcast the Week of March 13, 1989

BEEF JERKY intro
HEARTBREAK HOTEL Elvis Presley, under dialogue
'68 Maurice Hindel John interview fragment re: Heartbreak Hotel
'80 Sheff John interview re: worshipped Elvis
Paul interview re: Elvis in the 50s
ALL SHOOK UP Elvis Presley, under dialogue
THAT'S ALL RIGHT, MAMA BBC, 16 July 1963, fragment
THAT'S ALL RIGHT, MAMA Elvis Presley, under dialogue
LOVE ME TENDER Elvis, under dialogue
Paul interview re: Love Me Tender film
HOUND DOG Elvis Presley, under dialogue
'74 Mintz Ringo interview re: influence of Elvis
'68 Hindel John interview re: Elvis got him hooked on rock n roll
Tony Sheridan interview re: influence of Elvis
RIP IT UP Elvis Presley, under dialogue
'70 Wenner John interview re: moving like Elvis
interview continued re: playing live in Hamburg
I GOT A WOMAN BBC, 4 April 1964
Jam Don't Be Cruel/Matchbox, under dialogue
interview continued re: wanting to be bigger than Elvis
Paul interview re: Elvis going commercial
'70 Wenner John interview re: expressing himself
BLUE SUEDE SHOES Live Peace in Toronto LP, under dialogue
MYSTERY TRAIN under dialogue
'71 Mintz John interview re: performing Blue Suede Shoes
WHAT YOU GOT under dialogue
KHJ John guest DJ appearance
call re: do you still have your black Rickenbaker, also #187
call Dennis: request for The Night Before - "ok" end edited on here - does not play it, also #187
THE NIGHT BEFORE under dialogue
call re: the meaning of gear and fab, also #187
YOU'RE GOING TO LOSE THAT GIRL Help! LP
ACT NATURALLY under dialogue
THE CHASE under dialogue
Mal interview re: Paul calling Elvis
THE TIMES THEY ARE A-CHANGIN' The Byrds, under dialogue
YOU'VE GOT TO HIDE YOUR LOVE AWAY Help! LP
TELL ME WHAT YOU SEE under dialogue
'71 Mintz John interview re: Elvis's house & jamming
DO THE CLAM Elvis Presley, under dialogue
'65 John and Paul interview re: meeting Elvis last night
BLUE MOON OF KENTUCKY Elvis Presley, under dialogue

interview continued re: Paul tells Elvis to make r'n'r records
SUCH A NIGHT Elvis Presley single 1964
ONE NIGHT WITH YOU Elvis Presley, under dialogue
'74 Mintz Ringo interview re: meeting Elvis
Mal interview re: Elvis and guitar picks
interview continued re: Beatles jamming with Elvis
'74 Mintz Ringo interview re: Colonel Tom Parker
DEVIL IN DISGUISE Elvis Presley, under dialogue
'74 Mintz Ringo interview re: Priscilla & meeting with Elvis
HOUND DOG Live In New York LP
I GOT STUNG Elvis Presley, under dialogue
interview continued re: never liked Elvis after Jailhouse Rock
JAILHOUSE ROCK under dialogue
Mal interview re: Elvis impressed by Mal
Jam That's All Right, Mama, P.O.B. LP session, under dialogue
'80 Sheff John interview re: could never be the King again
Jam Mystery Train, Double Fantasy LP session
BEEF JERKY piano outake, extro

The Lost Lennon Tapes Part 61
Lennon & The Beatles In The Studio & On The Set
Show #89-13, Broadcast the Week of March 20, 1989

BEEF JERKY intro
I'M THE GREATEST demo 2, John vocal, under dialogue
'80 Sheff John interview re: I'm The Greatest
I'M THE GREATEST studio demo 2, John vocal, also #218
TICKET TO RIDE under dialogue
interview conrinued re: Ticket To Ride
TICKET TO RIDE BBC, 7 June 1965, also #171
YES IT IS Love Songs LP
interview continued fragment re: Yes It Is
YES IT IS take 1, with reference vocal
I'M STEPPING OUT demo, under dialogue
I'M STEPPING OUT vocal overdub, under dialogue
I'm Stepping Out studio dialogue "check the tempo"
I'M STEPPING OUT runthrough 1, false start, "feels good", fragment
I'm Stepping Out studio dialogue, "it went faster ... silly to have that speed up crap at our age"
I'M STEPPING OUT unedited rough mix, control room playback
ANOTHER HARD DAY'S NIGHT under dialogue
Walter Shenson interview re: Beatles wanted to progress
interview continued re: Beatles quick studies
ACT NATURALLY Help! LP
THE CHASE under dialogue
'65 John, Ringo & George interview clips re: Help!

HELP! take 1
HELP! backing tracks, take 5
HELP! under dialogue
'80 Sheff John interview re: inspiration for Help!
interview continued re: Al Aronowitz and Help!
HELP! demo, under dialogue
'70 Wenner John interview re: his best songwriting
interview continued re: his favourites including Help!
STRAWBERRY FIELDS FOREVER backng trcaks version 1, under dialogue
interview continued re: Strawberry Fields Forever lyrics
STRAWBERRY FIELDS FOREVER version 1, take 4
STRAWBERRY FIELDS FOREVER under dialogue
Beatles goodbye
Michael Lindsay-Hogg Get Back fragment re: It's a wrap
BEEF JERKY piano outake, extro

The Lost Lennon Tapes Part 62
Show #89-14, Broadcast the Week of March 27, 1989

BEEF JERKY intro
ROCK AND ROLL MUSIC BBC, 26 December 1964, also #98
MEMPHIS TENNESSEE BBC, 8 March 1962, also #195
TOO MUCH MONKEY BUSINESS BBC, 10 September 1963
SWEET LITTLE SIXTEEN BBC, 23 July 1963
I'M THE GREATEST Ringo, under dialogue
'73 Mintz John interview re: only George Ringo & I in studio
Ringo interview re: making the Ringo LP
I'M THE GREATEST take 1, John vocal
SIX O'CLOCK Ringo, under dialogue
interview re: I'm The Greatest session
'76 Mintz Ringo interview re: how Paul fit in
interview continued re: still likes Ringo LP
BRING ON THE LUCIE under dialogue
'80 Sheff John interview re: Bring On The Lucie
BRING ON THE LUCIE demo fragment
BRING ON THE LUCIE rough mix
MIND GAMES under dialogue
John continued interview re: Mind Games cover art
MOVE ON FAST Yoko, under dialogue
'73 Mintz John interview re: reunion rumours
GOD Plastic Ono Band LP
A HARD DAY'S NIGHT under dialogue
THINGS WE SAID TODAY under dialogue
'64 John Edwards John and Paul interview at Darwin Airport
'64 John, Paul & Jimmy Sydney press conference excerpt

LONG TALL SALLY under dialogue
YOU CAN'T DO THAT under dialogue
I SAW HER STANDING THERE Adelaide 1964
BEEF JERKY piano outake, extro

The Lost Lennon Tapes Part 63
Show #89-15, Broadcast the Week of April 3, 1989

BEEF JERKY intro
A HARD DAY'S NIGHT under dialogue
'64 advance promo for Australia with Waltzing Matilda
'64 interview on plane re: weather, next release
ANOTHER HARD DAY'S NIGHT under dialogue
ALL MY LOVING Adelaide 1964
WHEN I GET HOME under dialogue
'64 Bob Rogers Jimmy Nicol interview re: Australia
interview continued with John & George re: Ringo, fish eye lenses
I'M HAPPY JUST TO DANCE WITH YOU under dialogue
Bob Francis live report - Beatles greet fans
George: what do you think of the reception
Jimmy: How do you feel
John: Are you happy with this reception
Paul: Did you have a good trip over from Sydney
TWIST AND SHOUT Adelaide 1964
YOU GET WHAT YOU WANT Julian Lennon, under dialogue
'89 Roger Scott Julian interview re: past albums
interview continued re: Now You're In Heaven
NOW YOU'RE IN HEAVEN Julian Lennon, Mr. Jordan LP
interview continued re: now involved in business & music
EVERYDAY Julian Lennon, under dialogue
WOMAN IS THE NIGGER OF THE WORLD under dialogue
THE LUCK OF THE IRISH demo 2, fragment
THE LUCK OF THE IRISH demo 3
LUCK OF THE IRISH Sometime in New York City LP
STICK AROUND Julian Lennon, under dialogue
'89 Roger Scott Julian interview re: Mr. Jordan LP
MOTHER MARY Julian Lennon, Mr. Jordan LP
WHATEVER GETS YOU THROUGH THE NIGHT under dialogue
SO LONG AGO demo 1, #9 Dream, also #203
'80 Sheff John interview re: #9 Dream
#9 DREAM Walls And Bridges LP
BEEF JERKY piano outake, extro

The Lost Lennon Tapes Part 64
Show #89-16, Broadcast the Week of April 10, 1989

BEEF JERKY intro
ROLL OVER BEETHOVEN BBC, 30 March 1964, also #109, 135, 160
JOHNNY B. GOODE BBC, 15 February 1964, also #171
I GOT TO FIND MY BABY BBC, 11 June 1963, also #161
NOW YOU'RE IN HEAVEN Julian Lennon, under dialogue
'89 Roger Scott Julian interview re: Now You're In Heaven
MOTHER MARY Julian Lennon, under dialogue
interview continued re: Mr. Jordan LP title
SECOND TIME Julian Lennon, Mr. Jordan LP
TIE ME KANGAROO DOWN, SPORT Rolf Harris, under dialogue
Adelaide Australia radio interview with John, Paul, & Mal
TELL ME WHY under dialogue
I WANT TO HOLD YOUR HAND Adelaide 1964
I SHOULD HAVE KNOWN BETTER under dialogue
'64 Larry Kane Derek Taylor interview re: Adelaide reception
'70 Wenner John interview re: tours were like Satyricon
MAKE IT UP TO YOU Julian Lennon, under dialogue
'89 Roger Scott Julian interview re: Make It Up To You
interview continued re: preproduction
interview continued re: John McCurry
interview continued re: singing low
YOU'RE THE ONE Julian Lennon, Mr. Jordan LP
interview continued re: playing LP to Bowie
OPEN YOUR EYES Julian Lennon, under dialogue
interview continued re: trying to sound like John
MOVE OVER MS. L rehearsal, take 1, under dialogue
MOVE OVER MS. L demo 1
MOVE OVER MS. L demo 2
MOVE OVER MS. L rehearsal, take 2
BEEF JERKY piano outake with count-in, extro

The Lost Lennon Tapes Part 65
Show #89-17, Broadcast the Week of April 17, 1989

BEEF JERKY intro
MEDLEY Around The Beatles, 1964, CAN'T BUY ME LOVE also #116
YOU'RE THE ONE Julian Lennon, under dialogue
'89 Roger Scott Julian interview re: playing with John McCurry
interview continued re: I Get Up
I GET UP Julian Lennon, Mr. Jordan LP
ANGILETTE Julian Lennon, under dialogue
interview continued re: Angillette

NOW YOU'RE IN HEAVEN Julian Lennon, under dialogue
interview continued re: having a home
RINGO'S THEME (THIS BOY) under dialogue
'64 Jimmy Nicol Adelaide interview re: after Ringo arrives
'64 Rutherford Ringo interview re: travelling, haircuts, noise
radio report re: Beatles greeting crowds on balcony
YOU CAN'T DO THAT Melbourne 1964
OPEN YOUR EYES Julian Lennon, Mr. Jordan LP
'89 Roger Scott Julian interview fragment re: Open Your Eyes
I AM THE WALRUS under dialogue
interview continued re: I Want You To Know
I WANT YOU TO KNOW Julian Lennon, Mr. Jordan LP
interview continued re: U.K. LP ending with Jules B. Goode
JOHNNY B. GOODE Chuck Berry, under dialogue
JULES B. GOODE Julian Lennon, Mr. Jordan LP
interview fragment continued re: big favourite with many people
JOHN SINCLAIR under dialogue
PEOPLE demo, Angela, also #186
ANGELA Sometime In New York City LP
BEEF JERKY extro

The Lost Lennon Tapes Part 66
Show #89-18, Broadcast the Week of April 24, 1989

BEEF JERKY intro
guitar under dialogue
A Midsummer Night's Scream Around The Beatles, 1964
ROLL OVER BEETHOVEN Around The Beatles
LOVE ME DO under dialogue
'64 Larry Kane interview re: John's role in the play
SHOUT Around The Beatles
I ME MINE under dialogue
'73 Mintz John interview re: firing Klein & business meetings
GIVE ME SOME TRUTH under dialogue
interview continued re: immigration problems
ONLY PEOPLE early mix
I'M THE GREATEST take 1, John vocal, coda under dialogue
I'M THE GREATEST take 2, John vocal
OH MY MY under dialogue
'73 Mintz John interview re: attending Hollywood party
ROCK 'N' ROLL PEOPLE outake
OUT THE BLUE under dialogue
Yoko and John interview continued re: their relationship
ONE DAY AT A TIME Mind Games LP
Mind Games ad

MIND GAMES Mind Games LP
YOU CAN'T DO THAT Melbourne 1964, under dialogue
'64 radio John interview re: USSR, book, army, mods, haircut
ALL MY LOVING Melbourne 1964, under dialogue
SHE LOVES YOU Melbourne 1964
TWIST AND SHOUT Melbourne 1964
LONG TALL SALLY Melbourne 1964
BEEF JERKY extro

The Lost Lennon Tapes Part 67
Show #89-19, Broadcast the Week of May 1, 1989

BEEF JERKY intro
Jam Ain't That A Shame Sometime in NYC LP
NOW WE BE SAILIN' ON THE CARRIBEAN improv
FLOWER PRINCESS under dialogue
MY LITTLE FLOWER PRINCESS demo, take 3
WHAT YOU GOT under dialogue
'74 Dennis Elsas WNEW John guest DJ appearance
KHJ Superstar Week and John Lennon ad
INSTANT KARMA single 1970
call re: will you do any concerts
John reads Tower Records ad
intro to
SCARED Walls And Bridges LP
intro to
Listen To This Radio Spot
call re: request for Intuition
INTUITION Mind Games LP
intro to
SURPRISE SURPRISE Walls And Bridges LP
call re: play a slow song off your new LP
John reads Tobias Sportswear commercial, "tell your friends by what they were taking"
LONG TALL SALLY Little Richard, edited
intro to
NOBODY LOVES YOU (WHEN YOU'RE DOWN AND OUT) Walls And Bridges LP
extro to Nobody Loves You
DIZZY MISS LIZZY Larry Williams, under dialogue
DIZZY MISS LIZZY BBC, 7 June 1965
My Little Flower Princess studio dialogue, "does it sound latin to you?"
My Little Flower Princess studio dialogue, "relax...I have to rewrite everything...little club"
MY LITTLE FLOWER PRINCESS alternate take 3
BEEF JERKY piano outake, extro

The Lost Lennon Tapes Part 68
Lennon Remembers - The January '69 Get Back Sessions
Show #89-20, Broadcast the Week of May 8, 1989

BEEF JERKY intro
GET BACK under dialogue
'70 Wenner John interview re: Get Back project
interview continued re: Paul wanting to rehearse
TWO OF US under dialogue
film dialogue: Let It Be intro
interview continued re: playing early in the morning
interview continued re: Paul yawns in Across The Universe
ACROSS THE UNIVERSE/ROCK AND ROLL MUSIC Get Back rehearsals
DIG A PONY under dialogue
interview continued re: George & Paul insulting Yoko
'74 Ringo interview re: Yoko was a stranger
ACROSS THE UNIVERSE alternate mono mix, under dialogue
ACROSS THE UNIVERSE Get Back rehearsals
I'VE GOT A FEELING under dialogue
Ringo interview re: George walking off the set
GET BACK under dialogue
'70 Wenner John interview fragment re: playing the solo on Get Back
GET BACK Get Back rehearsals
SHAKIN' IN THE 60'S Get Back rehearsals
I DON'T WANNA BE A SOLDIER under dialogue
'69 Wigg John interview re: bed, attacking & defending, peace
'69 Toronto press conference excerpt re: war against war naive
I DON'T WANNA BE A SOLDIER take 1
DON'T LET ME DOWN under dialogue
Magic Alex Dan Richter test tape
ROCK AND ROLL MEDLEY Get Back rehearsals
LET IT BE Let It Be LP under dialogue
'70 Wenner John interview re: nobody could face looking at it
interview continued re: the Get Back LP
ONE AFTER 909 Get Back LP, also #96
THE LONG AND WINDING ROAD under dialogue
interview continued re: giving Spector the tapes
interview continued re: the Let It Be movie
Lindsay-Hogg Get Back sessions It's A Wrap, over extro
BEEF JERKY extro

The Lost Lennon Tapes Part 69
Show #89-21, Broadcast the Week of May 15, 1989

BEEF JERKY intro
GOD SAVE US demo, under dialogue
RADIO FREE LONDON OZ MAGAZINE MESSAGE '71 Oz flexi disc John & Yoko
DO THE OZ Bill Elliot & The Elastic Oz Band, under dialogue
KEEP RIGHT ON TO THE END OF THE ROAD OZ benefit flexi, 1971
DO THE OZ Bill Elloit & The Elastic Oz Band, under dialogue
John and Yoko intro to
GOD SAVE US single 1971
STRAWBERRY FIELDS FOREVER version 1, takes 5, 6
LONG TALL SALLY Litte Richard, under dialogue
'86 Little Richard interview re: teaching John and Paul woo
LONG TALL SALLY BBC, 16 July 1964, also #166
KANSAS CITY Little Richard, under dialogue
interview continued re: percentage of the Beatles
interview continued re: didn't think group worth it
RIP IT UP Little Richard, under dialogue
RIP IT UP/READY TEDDY rough mix
How Do You Sleep? rehearsal, under dialogue
How Do You Sleep? studio dialogue, "hello mine are working"
How Do You Sleep? rehearsal 1, also #118
WELL, (BABY PLEASE DON'T GO) rehearsal
WATCHING THE WHEELS backing tracks, under dialogue
WATCHING THE WHEELS - I'M CRAZY demo 4, take 1
BEAUTIFUL BOY demo 4, also #3, #217
CLEANUP TIME demo 2, also #2
BEEF JERKY piano outake, extro

The Lost Lennon Tapes Part 70
Show #89-22, Broadcast the Week of May 22, 1989

BEEF JERKY intro
MOTHER demo, also #154
'80 Jonathan Cott John interview John re: lifetime of work
STARTING OVER under dialogue
interview continued re: what's reality
CLEANUP TIME under dialogue
I'M STEPPIN' OUT demo 2
ONLY THE LONELY - CRYING - GONE FROM THIS PLACE improv, fragments, also #74, #213
Starting Over studio dialogue, "another beer for me please, while I'm working"
ONLY THE LONELY Roy Orbison, under dialogue
PLEASE PLEASE ME Please Please Me LP
DREAM BABY Roy Orbison, under dialogue

Orbison interview re: performing on Beatles tour
interview continued re: letting them close the show
interview continued re: telling them to do Ed Sullivan
RUNNING SCARED Roy Orbison, under dialogue
interview continued re: British invasion
DREAM BABY BBC, fragment, also #42, #106, #161
WHATEVER GETS YOU THROUGH THE NIGHT Madison Square Garden, under dialogue
ONE DAY AT A TIME Elton John, single 1974
I SAW HER STANDING THERE Madison Square Garden rehearsal, also #216
WOMAN backing tracks, under dialogue
'80 Cott John interview re: choosing only two people to work with with, Paul & Yoko
WOMAN demo 5
WOMAN backing tracks, under dialogue
interview continued re: Woman
BEEF JERKY piano outake, extro

The Lost Lennon Tapes Part 71
Show #89-23, Broadcast the Week of May 29, 1989

BEEF JERKY intro
THAT'LL BE THE DAY The Quarry Men, fragment
THAT'LL BE THE DAY Buddy Holly, under dialogue
HELLO LITTLE GIRL The Quarry Men, under dialogue
'80 Sheff John interview re: Hello Little Girl
HELLO LITTLE GIRL Decca audition
WORDS OF LOVE Buddy Holly, under dialogue
CRYING, WAITING, HOPING BBC, 6 August 1963
REMINISCING Buddy Holly, under dialogue
'64 Australian interview re: Buddy Holly influence
THAT'LL BE THE DAY Get Back rehearsals, under dialogue
MAYBE BABY Get Back rehearsals
CRYIN' WAITIN' HOPIN' Get Back rehearsals
MAILMAN, BRING ME NO MORE BLUES Get Back rehearsals
RAVE ON Holly Days LP, under dialogue
Paul interview re: buying Buddy Holly catalogue
STARTING OVER under dialogue
Jonathan Cott John interview re: what he's wearing
interview continued re: description of Dakota apartment
BEAUTIFUL BOY backing tracks, under dialogue
I'M LOSING YOU - STRANGER'S ROOM demo 5, also #125, #175
DIG IT outake, under dialogue
CAN YOU DIG IT Get Back rehearsals, take 1
I'M LOSING YOU demo 1, under dialogue
'80 Peebles John interview re: I'm Losing You
I'M LOSING YOU rough mix, , also #218

MAILMAN, BRING ME NO MORE BLUES Buddy Holly, under dialogue
MAILMAN, BRING ME NO MORE BLUES St. Regis Hotel, Clock film soundtrack
PEGGY SUE rough mix
BEEF JERKY piano outake, extro

The Lost Lennon Tapes Part 72
Show #89-24, Broadcast the Week of June 5, 1989

BEEF JERKY intro
I'LL FOLLOW THE SUN BBC, 21 December 1963, under dialogue
I'M A LOSER BBC, 26 November 1964
SHE'S A WOMAN BBC, 26 November 1964, also #146
I FEEL FINE BBC, 26 November 1964, also #146
COLD TURKEY Live Peace LP, under dialogue
'80 Sheff John interview fragment re: Cold Turkey
'69 Toronto press conference re: the drug problem
COLD TURKEY demo 1, also #217
COLD TURKEY alternate take, under dialogue
'80 Sheff John interview re: solution to drug problem
I AM THE WALRUS under dialogue
BEAUTIFUL BOY backing tracks, under dialogue
'80 Sheff John interview re: direct lyrics on Double Fantasy
DEAR YOKO demo 2, takes 2, 3, also #183
WOMAN under dialogue
'80 Sheff Yoko interview re: Fushia original LP title
BLESS YOU Menlove Avenue LP, under dialogue
BLESS YOU rehearsal
MOVE OVER MS. L rehearsal, take 2, under dialogue
MOVE OVER MS. L rough mix, take 3
STAND BY ME single 1974
BORROWED TIME under dialogue
BORROWED TIME demo 2, also #210
BEEF JERKY piano outake, extro

The Lost Lennon Tapes Part 73
Lost Lennon Love Songs, Part One
Show #89-25, Broadcast the Week of June 12, 1989

BEEF JERKY intro
JULIA backing tracks, under dialolgue
THIS BOY BBC, 21 December 1963, also #100, #171
SHE LOVES YOU Paris 1964, also #110
THE HONEYMOON SONG BBC, 6 August 1963, also #166
IF I FELL Hollywood Bowl 1964

I WANT TO HOLD YOUR HAND Hollywood Bowl 1964
I FEEL FINE single 1965
YOU'VE GOT TO HIDE YOUR LOVE AWAY under dialogue
NORWEGIAN WOOD outake, take 2
GIRL Rubber Soul LP
WITHIN YOU WITHOUT YOU under dialogue
THE WORD Rubber Soul LP
ALL YOU NEED IS LOVE broadcast, also #29
WHEN I'M 64 Sgt. Pepper's Lonely Hearts Club Band LP
JULIA demo 1, also #89, #141
DON'T LET ME DOWN demo 1, also #139
JULIA backing tracks, under dialogue
HOLD ON JOHN Plastic Ono Band LP
OH MY LOVE rough mix
JEALOUS GUY rough mix
LOVE extro

The Lost Lennon Tapes Part 74
Show #89-26, Broadcast the Week of June 19, 1989

BEEF JERKY intro
Surprise Surpirse John intro
SURPRISE SURPRISE under dialogue
SURPRISE SURPRISE demo 2
SURPRISE SURPRISE alternate take
DIG IT, under dialogue
CAN YOU DIG IT Get Back rehearsals, take 2
HELP!/PLEASE PLEASE ME Get Back rehearsals
BORROWED TIME under dialogue
Borrowed Time studio dialogue, "give me a little echo on the voice"
Borrowed Time studio dialogue, "weird in here cause voices come from everywhere"
Borrowed Time studio dialogue, "give me a little echo on the voice"
Borrowed Time studio dialogue, "OK is everybody in their places"
Borrowed Time studio dialogue, "let's not be so German about this"
BORROWED TIME alternate take, take 3, clucks intro
I'M A LOSER Paris, 20 June 1965
CAN'T BUY ME LOVE Paris, 20 June 1965
I WANNA BE YOUR MAN Paris, 20 June 1965
A HARD DAY'S NIGHT Paris, 20 June 1965
ROCK AND ROLL MUSIC Paris, 20 June 1965
BORROWED TIME acoustic guitar overdub, under dialogue
GONE FROM THIS PLACE improv, fragment, ONLY THE LONELY - CRYING missing, also #70, #213
GONE FROM THIS PLACE demo 2, take 4, also #213
BEEF JERKY guitar outake, extro

The Lost Lennon Tapes Part 75
Show #89-27, Broadcast the Week of June 26, 1989

BEEF JERKY intro
film comment fragment re: camera and runout
film comment fragment re: quiet please
'68 Rock 'N' Roll Circus Michael Lindsay-Hogg John interview re: backup band
YER BLUES improv, John and Mick Jagger
YER BLUES Rock 'N' Roll Circus rehearsal #2
DON'T LET ME DOWN demo 1, under dialogue
DON'T LET ME DOWN demo 2
DON'T LET ME DOWN Get Back rehearsals
MEAT CITY under dialogue
'73 Mintz John interview re: rumours of split
YOU ARE HERE under dialogue
I KNOW (I KNOW) demo 1, take 2
I KNOW (I KNOW) rough mix
MEAT CITY - JUST GOTTA GIVE ME SOME RNR demo 1
SIX O'CLOCK under dialogue
'73 Mintz John interview re: Ringo and Hollywood parties
I'M THE GREATEST studio demo 3, John vocal
HAPPY TRAILS Roy Rogers, under dialogue
TOO MANY PEOPLE Paul, under dialogue
'72 press conference interview re: How Do You Sleep?
interview continued re: meeting with Paul and Linda
How Do You Sleep? outake, take 3
BEEF JERKY guitar outake, extro

The Lost Lennon Tapes Part 76
John & Yoko w/Jerry Rubin On Mike Douglas
Show #89-28, Broadcast the Week of July 3, 1989

BEEF JERKY intro
POWER TO THE PEOPLE under dialogue
'80 Sheff John interview re: writing Power To The People
POWER TO THE PEOPLE outake, take 2, reggae take, also #118
With A Little Help From My Friends Mike Douglas, under dialogue
Mike Douglas Show excerpt: intro to
OH MY LOVE Imagine: John Lennon Soundtrack LP
NEW YORK CITY under dialogue
Mike Douglas Show excerpt: intro to Jerry Rubin
WORKING CLASS HERO under dialogue
John Jerry Rubin interview re: difference in the movement
IMAGINE Mike Douglas Show 1972
CRIPPLED INSIDE under dialogue

Mike Douglas Show excerpt
John Jerry Rubin interview re: voting
I DON'T WANNA BE A SOLDIER Imagine LP
I FOUND OUT under dialogue
Mike Jerry interview re: honesty and the system
GIVE ME SOME TRUTH alternate take, also #52
IT'S SO HARD under dialogue
interview continued re: Jerry's home life and people
POWER TO THE PEOPLE outake
THE LUCK OF THE IRISH under dialogue
interview continued re: trust and the future
JOHN SINCLAIR John Sinclair Benefit, also #16, #168
BEEF JERKY extro

The Lost Lennon Tapes Part 77
Lost Lennon Love Songs, Part Two
Show #89-29, Broadcast the Week of July 10, 1989

LOVE intro
LOVE demo, also #154
OH YOKO! rough mix
I KNOW (I KNOW) under dialogue
OUT THE BLUE rough mix
SWEET LITTLE SIXTEEN under dialogue
BONIE MARONIE rough mix
BE MY BABY rough mix, ROOTS LP mix, also #158, #216
WHAT YOU GOT under dialogue
WHAT YOU GOT demo
GOING DOWN ON LOVE rehearsal
WATCHING THE WHEELS backing tracks, under dialogue
WOMAN early mix
GROW OLD WITH ME Milk & Honey LP
REAL LOVE - GIRLS AND BOYS demo 2, take 4
LOVE extro

The Lost Lennon Tapes Part 78
Show #89-30, Broadcast the Week of July 17, 1989

BEEF JERKY intro
PLEASE PLEASE ME under dialogue
'76 Mintz John interview re: LP recorded in 12 hour session
ANNA under dialogue
George Martin interview re: Please Please Me LP
MISERY take 1, also #56

DO YOU WANT TO KNOW A SECRET under dialogue
'88 Mark Lewisohn interview re: session wasn't rushed
interview continued re: Lennon had a heavy cold
Norman Smith interview re: throat lozenges on piano
MISERY takes 2, 3, 4, 5, 6
HOUNDOG One To One concert, under dialogue
WELL WELL WELL One To One rehearsals
NEW YORK CITY under dialogue
One To One radio promo "Hi this is Geraldo Ono"
HOLD ME TIGHT under dialogue
BABY IT'S YOU Please Please Me LP
TWIST AND SHOUT The Isley Brothers, under dialogue
Norman Smith interview re: taping Twist and Shout
'76 Mintz John interview re: Twist and Shout
Beatles studio dialogue, under dialogue
interview continued re: ashamed of Twist And Shout
TWIST AND SHOUT Please Please Me LP
I SAW HER STANDING THERE under dialogue
'88 Mark Lewisohn interview re: take 2 of Twist and Shout
'76 Mintz John interview re: LP was near to live
COME TOGETHER One To One concert, under dialogue
Come Together rehearsal and dialogue fragment re: Paul's piano part, also #186
COME TOGETHER One To One rehearsals, take 1, also #186
COOKIN' Ringo, under dialogue
COOKIN' demo 2, take 1
FREE AS A BIRD demo 1, take 1, also #213
BEEF JERKY piano outake, extro

The Lost Lennon Tapes Part 79
Show #89-31, Broadcast the Week of July 24, 1989

BEEF JERKY intro
STRAWBERRY FIELDS FOREVER under dialogue
George Martin interview re: 1st time hearing song
interview continued re: first version different than expected
STRAWBERRY FIELDS FOREVER version 1, take 7
STRAWBERRY FIELDS FOREVER backing tracks, under dialogue
interview continued re: making version 2
STRAWBERRY FIELDS FOREVER version 2, take 25
INTUITION under dialogue
'80 Sheff John interview re: Intuition
INTUITION demo 1, take 3, also #123
INTUITION rough mix
COME TOGETHER under dialogue
I WANT YOU Get Back rehearsals, under dialogue

- 76 -

I WANT YOU (SHE'S SO HEAVY) Get Back rehearsals, Paul vocal
I WANT YOU (SHE'S SO HEAVY) under dialogue
I WANT YOU (SHE'S SO HEAVY) Amsterdam 1969, Israeli radio
JOHN HENRY demo under dialogue
JOHN HENRY demo 2
I AIN'T GOT TIME improv
OLD DIRT ROAD Menlove Avenue LP
I WANT YOU (SHE'S SO HEAVY) under dialogue
(SHE'S SO HEAVY) Abbey Road LP, fragment
(SHE'S SO HEAVY) continued under dialogue
'80 Sheff John interview re: I Want You (She's So Heavy)
Alan Parsons interview re: cut at end of song
I Want You improv goodnight, Get Back rehearsals
BEEF JERKY extro

The Lost Lennon Tapes Part 80
M.B.E. Spotlight, Part One
Show #89-32, Broadcast the Week of July 31, 1989

BEEF JERKY intro
Royal Variety Show John intro to
TWIST AND SHOUT Royal Variety Show, under dialogue
EVERYBODY'S TRYING TO BE MY BABY under dialogue
I FEEL FINE backing tracks, take 6
PLEASE MR. POSTMAN under dialogue
'69 Ken Zelig John interview re: not wanting MBE
I DON'T WANT TO SPOIL THE PARTY Beatles For Sale LP
THE CHASE under dialogue
'65 Hugh Moran BBC Beatles interview re: feelings about MBE
ANOTHER HARD DAY'S NIGHT under dialogue
ACT NATURALLY Help! LP
TICKET TO RIDE under dialogue
'65 Twickenham Beatles newsreel interview re: reaction to MBE
HELP! Ed Sullivan Show 1965, also #18
AISUMASEN under dialogue
'80 Sheff John interview re: Aisumasen
CALL MY NAME demo 1
CALL MY NAME demo 2
AISUMASEN rough mix
12 BAR ORIGINAL, under dialogue
ROCK AND ROLL MUSIC Beatles For Sale LP
NOWHERE MAN under dialogue
'65 Richard Baker BBC John interview re: returning MBE
TELL ME WHAT YOU SEE under dialogue
'69 Ken Zelig John interview re: defence of receiving MBE
BEEF JERKY guitar outake, extro

The Lost Lennon Tapes Part 81
Show #89-33, Broadcast the Week of August 7, 1989

BEEF JERKY intro
SHAZAM! 1971 St. Regis Hotel, Clock film soundtrack
HONEY DON'T St. Regis Hotel, Clock film soundtrack
GLAD ALL OVER St. Regis Hotel, Clock film soundtrack
LEND ME YOUR COMB St. Regis Hotel, Clock film soundtrack
MUCHO MUNGO Harry Nilsson, under dialogue
MUCHO MUNGO demos 3, 4, takes 1, 2
MANY RIVERS TO CROSS Harry Nilsson, under dialogue
SO LONG demo 2, take 2, #9 Dream
SHE'S A FRIEND OF DOROTHY'S demo 2, under dialogue
SHE'S A FRIEND OF DOROTHY'S demo 1, also #201
ONE OF THE BOYS demo 2, take 1, also #211
I'M A MAN improv, under dialogue
A SHOT OF RHYTHM AND BLUES BBC, 18 June 1963, also #161
12 BAR ORIGINAL take 2, fragment
HE GOT THE BLUES demo
I'M A MAN improv, under dialogue
LET'S GO SURFING Jim Waller, under dialogue
SO LONG rough mix, #9 Dream
'74 Tom Donahue KSAN John guest DJ appearance
interview re: appearing live again
KSAN Hallelujah
John intro to
#9 DREAM Walls And Bridges LP, fragment
BEEF JERKY guitar outake, extro

The Lost Lennon Tapes Part 82
Show #89-34, Broadcast the Week of August 14, 1989

BEEF JERKY intro
GOD SAVE THE QUEEN instrumental, under dialogue
THE LONELY BULL Herb Alpert, under dialogue
'65 Graham Webb John & George interview re: MBEs returned
guitar under dialogue
HELP! backing tracks, take 5, under dialogue
YOU'RE GONNA LOSE THAT GIRL rough mix
WHAT YOU'RE DOING under dialogue
'69 David Wigg Paul interview re: reaction to MBE
interview continued re: what it was like getting award
YOU CAN'T DO THAT under dialogue
BAD BOY Past Masters Volume 2 LP
REMEMBER under dialogue

LOOK AT ME demo, also #187, #204
'70 Wenner John interview re: initial reaction to P.O.B. LP
interview continued re: Look At Me dating back to 1968
MY MUMMY'S DEAD take 2, also #187
REVOLUTION 1 under dialogue
interview re: myth we were protected by the MBE
'68 Maurice Hindel interview re: subversion and revolution
REVOLUTION Past Masters Volume 2 LP
WELL WELL WELL under dialogue
'70 Wenner John interview re: Primal Scream therapy
WELL WELL WELL demo
WELL WELL WELL outake, take 4
MOTHER backing tracks, under dialogue
'71 Kenny Everett interview re: do you like Yoko's singing
'70 Wenner John interview re: P.O.B. light on imagry
interview continued re: instrumental bcking sparse
GIVE PEACE A CHANCE under dialogue
COLD TURKEY demo 3, take 3
COLD TURKEY under dialogue
interview continued fragment re: returning MBE
'69 Zelig John interview re: returning MBE
HER MAJESTY with end chord
BEEF JERKY piano outake, extro

The Lost Lennon Tapes Part 83
Show #89-35, Broadcast the Week of August 21, 1989

BEEF JERKY intro
WOMAN IS THE NIGGER OF THE WORLD under dialogue
'73 Mintz John interview re: racism and chauvanism
WOMAN IS THE NIGGER OF THE WORLD demo 2
guitar instrumental under dialogue
'79 kitchen John Sean interview re: monster drawing
interview continued re: sign your name & monster name
interview continued re: the smoke in the drawing
REAL LIFE demo 7 also #215
I'M STEPPING OUT outake, take 1
I DON'T WANNA FACE IT under dialogue
I DON'T WANNA FACE IT demo 1
I WATCH YOUR FACE demo
STARTING OVER - MY LIFE demo 3, take 1
SISTERS, O SISTERS under dialogue
'73 Mintz Yoko interview re: what she learned from John
WOMAN IS THE NIGGER OF THE WORLD outake
AISUMASEN under dialogue

interview continued with John re: male pig conspiracy
guitar and drum machine instrumental under dialogue
'79 kitchen Sean John interview re: family portrait
interview continued re: Cold Springs Harbour
interview continued re: Sean signing drawing
interview continued re: Sean shows drawing to Yoko
BEAUTIFUL BOY rough mix
BEEF JERKY piano outake, extro

The Lost Lennon Tapes Part 84
Mike Douglas #4, Part 1, More P.O.B. & D.F.
Show #89-36, Broadcast the Week of August 28, 1989

BEEF JERKY intro
'72 Mike Douglas show intro John & Yoko over intro
John & Yoko introduce guests & Mike, day 4
Mike Douglas Yoko interview re: china cup mending
OH YOKO! under dialogue
interview continued re: a box of smiles
IMAGINE rough mix
MOTHER under dialogue
Mike Douglas John interview re: father, mother, & Mimi
interview continued re: attraction between John & Yoko
REMEMBER under dialogue
'70 Wenner John interview re: his guitar playing
interview continued re: I Found Out an example
I FOUND OUT alternate mix, Gone Gone, also #43, #187 beginning cut
WELL WELL WELL under dialogue
'70 Wenner John interview re: being an artist
ISOLATION under dialogue
'80 Johnathan Cott John interview re: Isolation and Watching The Wheels
WATCHING THE WHEELS demo 5
interview continued fragment re: what are these wheels
POWER TO THE PEOPLE under dialogue
Mike Douglas John interview re: Bobby Seale
I DON'T WANNA BE A SOLDIER under dialogue
ATTICA STATE demo 1, takes 2, 3
ANGELA under dialogue
Mike Douglas show guest host appearance
Mike and John introduce Bobby Seale
Bobby Seale interview re: new Black Panther programs
J.J. demo 1, take 1
BORN IN A PRISON under dialogue
'82 John Wienner Seale interview re: originally scheduled first guest
WATCHING THE WHEELS rough mix

WATCHING THE WHEELS/YES, I'M YOUR ANGEL link track
YES, I'M YOUR ANGEL under dialogue
'80 Jonathan Cott interview re: link effect before Yes, I'm Your Angel
BEEF JERKY piano outake, extro

The Lost Lennon Tapes Part 85
Lennon's Spiritual Development Revisited, Part 1
Show #89-37, Broadcast the Week of September 4, 1989

BEEF JERKY intro
FLYING Magical Mystery Tour soundtrack fragment
ACROSS THE UNIVERSE mono mix, under dialogue
Mike Love interview re: John's outlook
I'M SO TIRED demo
JULIA demo, under dialogue
interview continued re: meditation teaching course
interview continued re: Maharishi's concepts
EVERYBODY'S GOT SOMETHING TO HIDE EXCEPT FOR ME AND MY MONKEY under dialogue
SEXY SADIE demo, also #46
THE CHASE under dialogue
THE MAHARISHI SONG demo
NOT GUILTY demo, under dialogue
interview continued re: we all make mistakes
THE INNER LIGHT under dialogue
'68 Mitchell Crowse John & P. interview fragment re: your success
John and Paul interview re: channelling power for good
CHILD OF NATURE demo, under dialogue
BABY, YOU'RE A RICH MAN single 1967
ALL YOU NEED IS LOVE under dialogue
interview continued re: we don't have all the answers
REVOLUTION demo, also #6
IT'S ALL TOO MUCH under dialogue
'68 Maurice Hindel John interview re: it's all in your head
interview continued re: reincarnation
interview continued re: meditation
interview continued re: I haven't changed & spiritual influences
SAVOY TRUFFLE under dialogue
interview continued re: macro biotic diet
GOD demo 1
GOD under dialogue
'70 Wenner John interview re: writing God
interview continued re: I don't believe in Beatles line
WELL WELL WELL under dialogue
interview continued re: Yoko and Phil and performing
HOW demo 2
BEEF JERKY extro

The Lost Lennon Tapes Part 86
Lennon's Spiritual Development Revisited, Part 2
Show #89-38, Broadcast the Week of September 11, 1989

BEEF JERKY intro
BRING IT ON HOME TO ME under dialogue
MANY RIVERS TO CROSS improv, also #201
STARTING OVER backing tracks, under dialogue
'80 Peebles John interview re: how good a cook are you
COOKIN' demo 3
BEAUTIFUL BOY backing tracks, under dialogue
interview continued re: staying home & Yoko running the business
GOTTA SERVE SOMEBODY Bob Dylan, under dialogue
'80 Sheff John interview re: Dylan's spiritual shift
SERVE YOURSELF demo 4
interview continued re: Buddhists & no one answer
CLEANUP TIME under dialogue
CLEANUP TIME dialogue starts after #86 "the gods" "you can have all those holes", also #Prv 3, #179
CLEANUP TIME take 1
HAPPINESS IS A WARM GUN under dialogue
'80 Jonathan Cott John interview re: calling Yoko mother
DEAR YOKO rough mix
YOU SAVED MY SOUL demo 2, also #183, #213
Pop Is The Name Of The Game, vocal improv, also #213
SERVE YOURSELF, demo 9, coda, also #213
WATCHING THE WHEELS under dialogue
interview continued fragment re: perfecting the art of life
interview continued re: problems and solutions
interview continued fragment re: end of sermon
interview continued fragment re: fun to be on cover of Rolling Stone
BEEF JERKY piano outake, extro

The Lost Lennon Tapes Part 87
Show #89-39, Broadcast the Week of September 18, 1989

BEEF JERKY intro
Beautiful Boy/Memories/Howling At The Moon/Across The River demo/improv
WE LOVE YOU The Rolling Stones, under dialogue
REVOLUTION under dialogue
Nicky Hopkins interview re: sessions after Revolution single
YOU CAN'T ALWAYS GET WHAT YOU WANT Stones, under dialogue
OH YOKO! under dialogue
interview continued re: first home studio I'd seen
interview continued re: doing 2 Imagine LP songs per day

CRIPPLED INSIDE Imagine LP
How Do You Sleep? under dialogue
interview continued re: How Do You Sleep? lyrics
interview continued re: George's reaction to How Do You Sleep?
MIND GAMES under dialogue
'73 Saul Marx announces I.N.S. deportation ruling
continued re: reason application denied
continued re: appeal
Leon Wildes interview re: his feelings on the case
interview continued re: procedure of case
BRING ON THE LUCIE under dialogue
'73 John and Yoko read Nutopia declaration
'73 Mintz John interview re: will fight to stay
I'M THE GREATEST take 4, John vocal
Nicky Hopkins interview re: complimentary live track
How Do You Sleep? rehearsal 1, also #197
interview continued re: How Do You Sleep? & Oh My Love
interview continued re: interesting piano duet
OH MY LOVE rough mix
Jam, fragment
interview continued re: John's high energy level
I DON'T WANNA BE A SOLDIER under dialogue
interview continued re: didn't interfere with musicians
interview continued re: first time John played them Imagine
IMAGINE RUNTHROUGH longer than on Imagine: John Lennon Soundtrack LP
BEEF JERKY piano outake, extro

The Lost Lennon Tapes Part 88
The John & Sean Birthday Show, Part 1
Show #89-40, Broadcast the Week of September 25, 1989

BEEF JERKY intro
MIND TRAIN under dialogue
'71 Takahiro Imura J/Y interview re: John, r'n'r, avant guarde
avant guarde music under dialogue
TUTTI FRUTTI Little Richard, under dialogue
GOD under dialogue
interview continued re: being emperor of the world
LOOK AT ME rough mix
WORKING CLASS HERO under dialogue
interview continued re: Yoko middle class square avant guarde
interview continued re: no idea what people were like
STRAWBERRY FIELDS FOREVER backing tracks, under dialogue
STRAWBERRY FIELDS FOREVER version 2, take 26, overdubs, rough mix, also #26
THE PILE Yoko 1962, under dialouge

BE-BOP-A-LULA Star Club LP, under dialogue
'71 Takahiro Imura J/Y interview re: Hamburg stage happenings
SWEET LITTLE SIXTEEN Star Club LP
I WANNA BE YOUR MAN The Rolling Stones, under dialogue
interview continued re: deliberate art vs unconscious art
MY GENERATION The Who, under dialogue
interview continued re: going further than just music
TWIST AND SHOUT Star Club LP
MAGICAL MYSTERY TOUR under dialogue
Mark Lapidos interview re: Beatlefest
interview continued re: idea for Beatlefest
WITHIN YOU WITHOUT YOU under dialogue
interview continued re: telling John about Beatlefest
FROM US TO YOU BBC, various dates, also #166
SO HOW COME BBC, 23 July 1963, also #166
FLYING under dialogue
interview continued re: activities at Beatlefest
interview continued re: interest is growing
interview continued re: toll free # is 1-800-Beatles
I AM THE WALRUS under dialogue
GLASS ONION The Beatles LP
WHOLE LOTTA SHAKIN' GOIN' ON Jerry Lee Lewis, under dialogue
'71 Takahiro Imura J/Y interview re: history of bizarre things
LONG TALL SALLY Star Club LP
WE CAN WORK IT OUT under dialogue
interview continued re: smashing things not new to modern times
BEEF JERKY piano outake, extro

The Lost Lennon Tapes Part 89
The John & Sean Birthday Show, Part 2
Show #89-41, Broadcast the Week of October 2, 1989

BEEF JERKY intro
20 FLIGHT ROCK Eddie Cochran, under dialogue
rockabilly instrumental under dialogue
JULIA backing tracks, under dialogue
JULIA demo 1, also #73 #141
SOME OTHER GUY Cavern Club, live, under dialogue
ONE AFTER 909 rehearsal 1960, under dialogue
STAND BY ME under dialogue
I AM THE WALRUS under dialogue
'76 Mintz John & Yoko interview re: drugs & a child
CLEANUP TIME rough mix
HARD TIMES ARE OVER under dialogue
interview continued re: 9 months carrying Sean

CRY FOR A SHADOW under dialogue
WHY Tony Sheridan, fragment
LOVE ME DO original version, under dialogue
'76 Ringo interview re: 1st record the most important
PLEASE PLEASE ME under dialogue
HAPPY BIRTHDAY SATURDAY CLUB BBC, 5 October 1963, also #<u>161</u>
SHE LOVES YOU Pop '63, Sweden, also #56 #<u>10</u>
TWIST AND SHOUT Hollywood Bowl 1964
HERE COMES THE SUN under dialogue
'76 Mintz John & Yoko interview re: Sean's birth
BEAUTIFUL BOY demo 3
OUT THE BLUE under dialogue
interview continued re: 1st few hours after birth
NORWEGIAN WOOD under dialogue
'80 Sheff John interview re: Run For Your Life
RUN FOR YOUR LIFE take 5, rough mix, fragment
RUN FOR YOUR LIFE Rubber Soul LP
GOODNIGHT IRENE John's Birthday Party, fragment
Sean says Happy Birthday
BEEF JERKY piano outake, extro

The Lost Lennon Tapes Part 90
The John & Sean Birthday Show, Part 3
Show #89-42, Broadcast the Week of October 9, 1989

BEEF JERKY intro
RUN FOR YOUR LIFE under dialogue
IN MY LIFE Rubber Soul LP
STRAWBERRY FIELDS FOREVER demo 1, under dialogue
ALL YOU NEED IS LOVE under dialogue
DRIVE MY CAR under dialogue
AFTERMATH Musketeer Gripweed & The Third Troop, single 1966
GIVE ME SOME TRUTH alternate mix, under dialogue
'76 Mintz John interview re: reapplying for visa
SIME TWIST OF FATE Bob Dylan, under dialogue
interview continued re: reason for rejection
STARTING OVER - THE WORST IS OVER demo 1
STARTING OVER backing tracks, under dialogue
interview continued re: the best event
I'M SO TIRED under dialogue
THE CONTINUING STORY OF BUNGALOW BILL The Beatles LP
BIRTHDAY The Beatles LP
LITTLE CHILD instrumental under dialogue
'76 John Sean interview re: NY, the group, John & Yoko
FOREVER YOUNG Bob Dylan, under dialogue

NEW YORK NEW YORK Frank Sinatra, fragment
interview continued re: Sammy Davis, Sinatra etc.
TINY DANCER Elton John, under dialogue
interview continued re: Elton famous Godfather
BRING ON THE LUCIE under dialogue
Japanese music under dialogue
BEAUTIFUL BOY demo 1
SHE'S SO HEAVY under dialogue
HOLD ON under dialogue
WHEN A BOY MEETS A GIRL demo, also #182
BEEF JERKY piano outake, extro

The Lost Lennon Tapes Part 91
The John & Sean Birthday Show, Part 4
Show #89-43, Broadcast the Week of October 16, 1989

BEEF JERKY intro
HERE COME THE THREES Donovan, under dialogue, also #37
IT'S JOHNNY'S BIRTHDAY George, also #37
HAPPY TRAILS Janis Joplin, under dialogue, also #37
HAPPY BIRTHDAY JOHN Ringo, under dialogue, also #37
HEY JOHN Blossom Dearie
IMAGINE under dialogue
BLUE SUEDE SHOES John's Birthday Party 1971
HAPPY BIRTHDAY John's Birthday Party 1971
IT'S SO HARD alternate take, also #30
IT'S SO HARD One To One concert, under dialogue
I KNOW I KNOW under dialogue
interview fragment re: couldn't have affected convention
SWEET LITTLE SIXTEEN alternate mix
YOU CAN'T CATCH ME under dialogue
ROCK AROUND THE CLOCK Harry Nilsson, under dialogue
WHATEVER GETS YOU THROUGH THE NIGHT single 1974
'74 Tom Donahue KSAN John guest DJ appearance
interview fragment re: fight to stay in the country, also Part 33
BLESS YOU alternate mix
guitar and drum machine Bless You instrumental under dialogue
Sean's happy birthday by Cecil the puppet
BEAUTIFUL BOYS Double Fantasy LP
John talks to Sean re: age and being 4
interview continued re: dying & the spirit world
WITHIN YOU WITHOUT YOU fragment
REAL LOVE - GIRLS AND BOYS demo 3, take 5
BEEF JERKY guitar outake, extro

The Lost Lennon Tapes Part 92
The John & Sean Birthday Show, Part 5
Show #89-44, Broadcast the Week of October 23, 1989

BEEF JERKY intro
THE WORD under dialogue
'71 Mintz John interview re: word association
MY MUMMY'S DEAD rough mix
interview continued re: songs he likes
I AM THE WALRUS alternate mix
Sean comment: oh, okay
LIFE BEGINS AT 40 demo, under dialogue
Double Fantasy session, "I don't care where I am just lead me to the mic"
'80 Peebles John interview re: Beautiful Boy
Double Fantasy session, "anybody got any problems"
BEAUTIFUL BOY runthrough, "just take it easy" runthrough "smells good in here"
Double Fantasy session, "we can do it in one take..let's get a take before I have to go for a pee"
Double Fantasy session, "Hugh, put your fucking headphones on"
BEAUTIFUL BOY alternate take, take 1,
I DON'T WANNA BE A SOLDIER under dialogue
This Is Not Here press conference
interview continued re: why do an art show
GIVE PEACE A CHANCE John's Birthday Party 1971, fragment
GIVE PEACE A CHANCE under dialogue
interview continued re: communication
interview continued re: titles of their films
OH YOKO! Demo 1
I DON'T WANNA BE A SOLDIER under dialogue
interview continued re: artist is a frame of mind
interview continued re: any plans to play music
interview continued re: happy birthday John
interview continued re: thank you Everson Museum
MRS. LENNON under dialogue
CRIPPLED INSIDE John's Birthday Party 1971, fragment
interview continued re: John's ultimate goal in life
WE'RE ALL WATER under dialogue
'71 Mintz John interview re: idea for water event
OH MY LOVE under dialogue
interview continued re: Imagine LP cover
IMAGINE, OH YOKO! John's Birthday Party 1971, fragments
BEAUTIFUL BOY under dialogue
studio dialogue, Double Fantasy session, "hello Sean I can see you...funny place like a space ship"
SERVE YOURSELF, BE-BOP-A-LULA Sean, vocal only
John teaching Sean to play guitar "wiggle the volume knobs"
HOUND DOG Big Mama Thornton, under dialogue
'80 Peebles John interview re: Sean's interest in music

BEAUTIFUL BOY fragment
Double Fantasy session, "goodnight Sean wherever you are, fill in your own child's name"
AS TIME GOES BY improv, fragment, John and Yoko Earth News radio
Elliot Mintz sign off from Earth News radio
BEEF JERKY piano outake, extro

The Lost Lennon Tapes Part 93
Montreal Revisited Part 1 w/Roger Scott
Show #89-45, Broadcast the Week of October 30, 1989

BEEF JERKY intro
THE BALLAD OF JOHN AND YOKO vocal improv
THE BALLAD OF JOHN AND YOKO under dialogue
LIVE WITH ME The Rolling Stones, underdialogue
BECAUSE demo, fragment, Montreal bed-in
'69 Derek Taylor John, Yoko & Kyoko customs fragment Toronto
BECAUSE under dialogue
Roger Scott interview re: CFOX Montreal hotel room broadcast
LEGEND OF A MIND The Moody Blues, under dialogue
'69 Roger Scott John & Timothy Leary interview re: life outlooks
COME TOGETHER Abbey Road LP
'69 Roger Scott John & Yoko interview re: company you formed
I'VE GOT A FEELING under dialogue
interview continued re: do something for peace
HAPPINESS IS A WARM GUN demo, fragment
interview continued re: bed sores and jokes
HARE KRISHNA MANTRA under dialogue
'69 Chucky Chandler CFOX radio sign on in hotel room
'69 Roger Scott interview re: procession of journalists
'69 Montreal John & Yoko bed-in interview re: violence
'69 Derek Taylor interview re: organization
'69 Capitol Radio executive interview re: his role
'69 Montreal Kyoko interview fragment re: daddy, daddy
HELTER SKELTER fragment
'69 Montreal Yoko bed-in interview re: not here to preach
HELTER SKELTER coda
STREET FIGHTING MAN The Rolling Stones, under dialogue
'69 Montreal John & Y. bed-in interview re: change people 1st
REVOLUTION 1 The Beatles LP
ALL YOU NEED IS LOVE under dialogue
interview continued re: ADC and draft resisters
interview continued re: Gandhi's approach
interview continued re: people don't give love enough
I AIN'T MARCHIN' ANYMORE Phil Ochs, under dialogue
interview continued re: nobody's tried peace

WE CAN BE TOGETHER Jefferson Airplane, under dialogue
KPFA radio John interview re: people's park protesters
interview continued re: strategy for getting park
MAKE LOVE NOT WAR demo, Mind Games, also #8, #150, #209
HELLO GOODBYE backing tracks, under dialogue
interview continued re: call us anytime
VOLUNTEERS Jefferson Airplane, under dialogue
interview continued re: you have to wait a year or two
THE WORD under dialogue
STUDENT DEMONSTRATION TIME Beach Boys, under dialogue
'69 Montreal John & Yoko bed-in interview re: non-violent demonstration
GIVE PEACE A CHANCE rehearsal 1, Montreal bed-in
BEEF JERKY piano outake, extro

The Lost Lennon Tapes Part 94
Montreal Revisited Part 2 w/Roger Scott
Show #89-46, Broadcast the Week of November 6, 1989

BEEF JERKY intro
ROCKER - INSTRUMENTAL 42 Get Back LP, under dialogue
LET IT BE Get Back LP
FLYING under dialogue
'69 John & Yoko bed-in interview re: set up for Roger
bed-in excerpt re: set up for Roger Scott
Roger Scott interview re: the Mt. Royal march for peace
'69 Chucky Chandler John & Yoko interview re: peace march
Roger Scott interview re: listeners were into it
interview continued re: trying to get John & Yoko to perform
THE INNER LIGHT under dialogue
ACROSS THE UNIVERSE No One's Gonna Change Our World LP
GET TOGETHER The Youngbloods, under dialogue
Roger Scott interview re: phoning radio stations for John
interview continued re: KYA phone call
KYA interview re: planning to come back to U.S.
GIVE PEACE A CHANCE rehearsal 2, Montreal bed-in
THE BALLAD OF JOHN AND YOKO single 1969
'69 Tom Campbell John interview re: message in Ballad Of John & Yoko
GETTING BETTER Sgt. Pepper's LP, fragment
interview continued re: will you perform again
NO TIME OR SPACE Electronic Sound LP, fragment, under dialogue
CAMBRIDGE 1969 Life With The Lions LP fragment, under dialogue
interview continued re: Get Back project
DON'T LET ME DOWN under dialogue
GET BACK Get Back LP
GET BACK REPRISE Get Back LP

THE FOOL ON THE HILL under dialogue
Roger Scott interview re: disgusting Al Capp
NOWHERE MAN Rubber Soul LP
I'M ONLY SLEEPING under dialogue
'69 Al Capp John and Yoko bed-in interview re: bed-in
THINK FOR YOURSELF under dialogue
interview continued re: what is the next step
I'M SO TIRED under dialogue
'69 John & Yoko bed-in interview re: walking from Toronto
MONEY under dialogue
'69 John & Yoko bed-in interview re: photographer and photo
interview continued re: contract to sell photo
YOU NEVER GIVE ME YOUR MONEY alternate take
GOOD NIGHT under dialogue
BEEF JERKY piano outake, extro

The Lost Lennon Tapes Part 95
Montreal Revisited Part 3 w/Roger Scott
Show #89-47, Broadcast the Week of November 13, 1989

BEEF JERKY intro
SEA OF MONSTERS under dialogue
Yoko comment re: certain people rescueable
'69 Al Capp John & Yoko bed-in interview re: Hitler
MEAN MR. MUSTARD Get Back rehearsals, fragment
TWO VIRGINS under dialogue
interview continued re: being shy people
EVERYDAY PEOPLE Sly & The Family Stone, under dialogue
'69 Yoko & John bed-in interview re: criticising establishment
THE WORLD IS A GHETTO War, under dialogue
DIG A PONY Get Back LP
sitar under dialogue
bed-in re: yoga swami wants to do a demo of chanting and breathing
bed-in continued re: yoga demonstration
Murray the K mic check
THE BALLAD OF JOHN AND YOKO and OLD BROWN SHOE under dialogue
Al Capp John & Yoko bed-in interview re: The Ballad Of John and Yoko
I'VE GOT A FEELING Get Back LP
BAD MOON RISING Creedence Clearwater Revival, under dialogue
'69 Roger Scott interview re: Derek Talyor losing temper
interview continued re: everybody's connected
interview continued re: why you want peace
interview continued re: the other 3 guys are English
CRUCIFY CAPP improv, fragment, vocal only
ALL YOU NEED IS LOVE under dialogue

'69 Tom Campbell KYA phone call from bed-in
interview re: being readily available
interview continued re: peace
interview continued re: new songs
GIVE PEACE A CHANCE demo, under dialogue
REMEMBER LOVE rough mix
THE BALLAD OF JOHN AND YOKO fragment, under dialogue
LEGEND OF A MIND The Moody Blues, under dialogue
Timothy Leary interview re: crisis
STRAIGHT AHEAD Jimi Hendrix, under dialogue
'69 Dick Gregory bed-in interview re: organize
REVOLUTION promo film, intro under dialogue
NOW'S THE TIME TO FALL IN LOVE Smothers Brothers, fragment
Tom and John bed-in discussion re: authorities
interview continued re: turning off moderates
THE IMPOSSIBLE DREAM Smothers Brothers, under dialogue
TOMMY'S SONG Smothers Brothers, fragment
GOOD NIGHT under dialogue
BEEF JERKY piano outake, extro

The Lost Lennon Tapes Part 96
Montreal Revisited Part 4
Show #89-48, Broadcast the Week of November 20, 1989

BEEF JERKY intro
GIVE PEACE A CHANCE King Edward Hotel Toronto, 1969
DOWNTOWN Petula Clark, under dialogue
'69 Roger Scott interview re: only 2 DJs in Montreal hotel room
HARE KRISHNA MANTRA under dialogue
'69 John & Yoko bed-in interview fragment re: the flaming red rabbi
Tommy Smothers interview re: we're all Beatles groupies
interview continued re: playing guitar on Give Peace A Chance
Roger Scott interview re: Dylan showing up
GIVE PEACE A CHANCE rehearsal 1, under dialogue
interview continued re: lyrics on cardboard
interview continued re: call for recording equipment
interview continued re: 4 track in corner of room
GIVE PEACE A CHANCE alternate mix from LET'S HEAR IT FOR PEACE bed-in film
SUNDAY MORNING COMING DOWN Kris Kristofferson, under dialogue
'69 Fred Peabody John interview re: reaction on the whole
I WANT YOU (SHE'S SO HEAVY) under dialogue
interview continued re: offending everyone
interview continued re: people's ideals are right
YOU WIN AGAIN Get Back rehearsals
WE CAN WORK IT OUT backing tracks, under dialogue

interview continued re: being square
interview continued re: we have to go for peace
GET BACK under dialogue
'69 KYA radio John interview re: Billy Preston on Get Back
Billy Preston interview re: blending in
interview continued re: playing on Get Back
GET BACK Get Back rehearsals
ONE AFTER 909 Get Back LP, also #68
I DON'T WANNA BE A SOLDIER alternate take, under dialogue
'69 Fred Peabody John interview re: influencing someone else
interview continued re: would you go to war
interview continued re: world government and anarchy
HEY BULLDOG Yellow Submarine LP
interview continued re: what can average guy do
REMEMBER LOVE Yoko, under dialogue
interview continued re: we're all together
A DAY IN THE LIFE under dialogue
John and Yoko fragment re: affect on the world
Ottawa press conference fragment re: we love you, peace
TWO OF US under dialogue
'69 Roger Scott John interview re: people's reaction
GIVE PEACE A CHANCE under dialogue
interview continued re: Ringo overubbed later
interview continued re: original recording rough
interview re: beat on the on beat on recording
Roger Scott interview re: reaction to record
John and Yoko interview re: masturbation lyric
GIVE PEACE A CHANCE alternate take
'69 Chandler and Scott broadcast re: the last night
GIVE PEACE A CHANCE under dialogue
TOMMORROW NEVER KNOWS under dialogue
'69 Chucky Chandler and Roger Scott sign-off
John fragment re: it ain't easy
BEEF JERKY piano outake, extro

The Lost Lennon Tapes Part 97
Coleman On Eppy, Johnny & The Fabs, Part 1
Show #89-49, Broadcast the Week of November 27, 1989

BEEF JERKY intro
I'VE GOT ANTS IN MY PANTS improv, Double Fantassy LP session
I'M STEPPIN' OUT outake, take 2
PAPERBACK WRITER under dialogue
I'LL BE ON MY WAY Billy J. Kramer, under dialogue
'89 Ray Coleman interview re: why a book on Epstein

interview continued re: an interesting study
MY BONNIE Tony Sheridan, under dialogue
interview continued re: Brian a frustrated actor
THE SAINTS Tony Sheridan, under dialogue
BAD BOY Oldies But Goldies LP
CATSWALK under dialogue
interview continued re: knew Brian in early years
CRY FOR A SHADOW under dialogue
interview continued re: people he interviewed
interview continued re: Beatles would not cooperate
CHAINS under dialogue
interview continued re: relationship btwn John & Brian
interview continued re: John gave Brian a hard time
THINGS WE SAID TODAY under dialogue
BAD TO ME Billy J. Kramer
I'LL KEEP YOU SATISFIED Billy J. Kramer, under dialogue
interview continued re: being gay in the 60s
DO YOU WANT TO KNOW A SECRET alternate mix, also #28
DON'T LET ME DOWN under dialogue
SAVE THE LAST DANCE FOR ME Get Back LP
DON'T LET ME DOWN Get Back LP
SUN KING Get Back rehearsals, fragment
SUN KING/MEAN MR. MUSTARD Abbey Road LP
BABY YOU'RE A RICH MAN under dialogue
interview continued re: different from other managers
THE FOOL ON THE HILL under dialogue
interview continued re: Brian's biggest weakness
I CALL YOUR NAME Billy J. Kramer, under dialogue
TAXMAN Revolver LP
FLYING under dialogue
interview continued re: Brian to be Apple director
BEEF JERKY piano outake, extro

The Lost Lennon Tapes Part 98
Lennon's Spiritual Development Revisited, Part 3
Show #89-50, Broadcast the Week of December 4, 1989

BEEF JERKY intro
STRAWBERRY FIELDS FOREVER backing tracks, under dialogue
'80 Johnathan Cott John interview re: childhood and looking tough
THERE'S A PLACE rough mix, take 11
FERRY 'CROSS THE MERSEY Gerry & The Pacemakers, under dialogue
'70 Wenner John interview re: Liverpool
MY OLD MAN'S A DUSTMAN Lonnie Donegan, under dialogue
interview continued re: Beatles wit and Liverpool

DIGGIN' MY POTATOES Washboard Sam, under dialogue
interview continued re: country & western in Liverpool
TUTTI FRUTTI Litte Richard, under dialogue
interview continued re: why John chose rock 'n' roll
ROCK AND ROLL MUSIC BBC, 26 December 1964, also #62
JOHNNY B. GOODE BBC, under dialogue
interview continued re: money, power & rock 'n' roll
A HARD DAY'S NIGHT outake
CRY FOR A SHADOW under dialogue
'71 Takahiro Imura J/Y interview re: I made them and killed them
BAD BOY under dialogue
interview continued re: getting more quiet & being good
interview continued re: behaviour on stage
I FEEL FINE outake, take 9
I DON'T WANT TO SPOIL THE PARTY under dialogue
'70 Wenner John interview re: an artistic scene
interview continued re: copping out
YOU'VE GOT TO HIDE YOUR LOVE AWAY under dialogue
interview continued re: they could never keep me down
interview continued re: I don't have everything I need
CAN'T BUY ME LOVE outake
I FEEL FINE Paris 1965, afternoon show
TICKET TO RIDE Paris 1965, afternoon show
LONG TALL SALLY Paris 1965, afternoon show
TOMORROW NEVER KNOWS under dialogue
Timothy Leary interview re: drug use as a phenomena
LOVE YOU TO under dialogue
'69 Man of The Decade John interview re: an LSD trip
Timothy Leary interview re: why musicians use LSD
SHE SAID SHE SAID Revolver LP
FLYING under dialogue
dialogue intro to Magical Mystery Tour film
electronic music under dialogue
sitar music under dialogue
WEAR YOUR LOVE LIKE HEAVEN Donovan, under dialogue
'70 Wenner John interview re: taking LSD in L.A.
'69 Man of The Decade John interview re: drug use
interview over extro re: what does life mean to you
BEEF JERKY piano outake, extro

The Lost Lennon Tapes Part 99
Lennon's Spiritual Development Revisited, Part 4
Show #89-51, Broadcast the Week of December 11, 1989

BEEF JERKY intro
HELP! intro cut to
HELP! backing tracks, under dialogue
'71 Takahiro Imura J/Y interview re: believing in God
THE INNER LIGHT under dialogue
interview continued re: eastern philosophy
INSTANT KARMA single 1969
interview re: being anti-establishment
LOOK AT ME under dialogue
OH MY LOVE under dialogue
'70 Wenner John interview re: profile in '69
HOLD ON JOHN under dialogue
interview continued re: Hold On John
ART OF DYING George, under dialogue
GOD demo 2
GOD under dialogue
interview continued re: not believing in Beatles
interview continued re: opening line of song
interview continued re: I just felt it
I FOUND OUT under dialogue
interview continued re: won't sacrifice love
I FOUND OUT demo, under dialogue
interview continued re: kids on the phone line
SERVE YOURSELF demo 5
WHAT'S SO FUNNY 'BOUT, PEACE LOVE AND UNDERSTANDING Elvis Costello, under dialogue
'80 J. Cott John interview continued re: I don't claim divinity
WATCHING THE WHEELS demo 6, take 1
interview continued re: what is real
WATCHING THE WHEELS backing tracks, under dialogue
BORROWED TIME under dialogue
WOMAN demo 1
WOMAN backing tracks, under dialogue
interview continued re: not being yourself
YOU SAVED MY SOUL demo 1, also #213, #217
interview continued re: be yourself and death
GROW OLD WITH ME under dialogue
IMAGINE under dialogue
Maurice Dupont, mind movie fragment re: we did it
BEEF JERKY extro

The Lost Lennon Tapes Part 100
Xmas w/John & Yoko and The Beatles, Part 1
Show #89-52, Broadcast the Week of December 18, 1989

BEEF JERKY intro
CHESTNUTS ROASTING ON AN OPEN FIRE under dialogue
blues song under dialogue
'69 Ken Zelig John interview re: first harmonica
'69 Ken Zelig Yoko interview re: lava lamp
CUMBERLAND GAP Lonnie Donegan, under dialogue
'76 Ringo interview re: getting first drum kit
Paul interview re: cigar smoke at Christmas
TELL ME WHAT YOU SEE under dialogue
Paul interview re: shortsighted John story
I SAW HER STANDING THERE Pop '63, Sweden, also #31
BEATLES CRIMBLE MEDLEY XMAS FLEXI-DISC 1963
'63 Christmas record: John GOOD KING WENCESLAS, under dialogue
'63 Christmas record: John GOOD KING WENCESLAS
'63 Christmas record: John GOOD KING WENCESLAS, under dialogue
interview re: Christmas music
PLEASE MISTER POSTMAN under dialogue
Tony Barrow interview re: Xmas record idea
'63 Christmas record: John speaking
Tony Barrow interview continued re: ad libs best
'63 Christmas record: John and Paul
I WANT TO HOLD YOUR HAND under dialogue
'63 Christmas record: Paul continued
I WANT TO HOLD YOUR HAND It's The Beatles, Liverpool 1963
FROM ME TO YOU It's The Beatles 1963, under dialogue
'63 Christmas record: Paul continued sign-off
'63 Christmas record: Ringo, George, and end
THIS BOY under dialogue
THIS BOY BBC 21 December 1963, also #73, #171
RINGO'S THEME under dialogue
A HARD DAY'S NIGHT under dialogue
'64 Christmas record: George segment
HONEY DON'T excerpt
'64 Christmas record: Ringo segment
WHEN I GET HOME A Hard Day's Night LP
'64 Christmas record: Can You Wash Your Father's Shirt to end
ROCK AND ROLL MUSIC under dialogue
SHE LOVES YOU under dialogue
Jimmy Saville interview re: joke at Xmas show
WE CAN WORK IT OUT backing tracks, under dialogue
IN MY LIFE Rubber Soul LP
'65 Christmas record: Yesterday to end
BEEF JERKY piano outake, extro

The Lost Lennon Tapes Part 101
Xmas w/John & Yoko and The Beatles, Part Two
Show #89-53, Broadcast the Week of December 25, 1989

HAPPY XMAS (WAR IS OVER) intro
Surprise Surprise John intro
STRAWBERRY FIELDS FOREVER take 1, under dialogue
Tony Barrow interview re: 1966 Christmas record
'66 Christmas record: side one
'66 Christmas record: side two
FLYING under dialogue
'67 Christmas record: to Plenty of Jam Jars
'67 Christmas record: side two
HELLO GOODBYE backing tracks, under dialogue
CHRISTMAS TIME IS HERE AGAIN
OB-LA-DI OB-LA-DA under dialogue
THOSE WERE THE DAYS Mary Hopkin, under dialogue
Kenny Everett interview re: making the '68 Xmas record
'68 Christmas record: side one, original Jock & Yono
'68 Christmas record: side two, original Once Upon A Pool Table
Tiny Tim interview re: meeting George, making Xmas record
'68 Christmas record: side two continued
COLD TURKEY Live In New York City LP, under dialogue
THE END under dialogue
'69 Christmas record: side one
'69 Christmas record: side two
HAPPY XMAS (WAR IS OVER) extro

The Lost Lennon Tapes Part 102
Xmas w/ John & Yoko and The Beatles, Part 2
Best Of Year Two, Part One
Show #90-01, Broadcast the Week of January 1, 1990

BEEF JERKY intro
I'M STEPPING OUT demo, under dialogue, from #61
I'M STEPPING OUT take 1, under dialogue, from #61
I'm Stepping Out studio dialogue re: check tempo with Bermuda tape fragment, from #61
I'M STEPPING OUT take 2, fragment, from #61
I'm Stepping Out studio dialogue "dubbled up ... crazy to have that speed up crap" from #61
I'M STEPPING OUT unedited rough mix, from #61
HOW alternate take, from #53
PILL only take, from #53
GONE FROM THIS PLACE demo, from #48
interview over re: magic is so subtle, from #48
THE CHASE under dialogue, from #61

'65 John, Ringo & George interview clips re: Help!, from #61
HELP! take 1, from #61
HELP! backing tracks, take 5, from #61
How Do You Sleep? alternate take, take 2, from #53
GIVE PEACE A CHANCE single 1969
I'M A LOSER Paris 1965, from #43
A HARD DAY'S NIGHT Paris 1965, from #43
TOO MUCH MONKEY BUSINESS BBC, 10 September 1963, from #62
GIVE ME SOME TRUTH under dialogue, from #52
'80 Sheff John interview re: Give Me Some Truth, from #52
GIVE ME SOME TRUTH Get Back rehrsals, fragment, from #52
GIVE ME SOME TRUTH alternate take, from #52
BEEF JERKY piano outake, extro

The Lost Lennon Tapes Part 103
Best Of Year 2, Part 2
Show #90-02, Broadcast the Week of January 8, 1990

BEEF JERKY intro
I'M THE GREATEST studio demo 3, John vocal, from #75
GET BACK Get Back rehearsals, from #68
ROCK AND ROLL MEDLEY Get Back rehearsals, from #68
SWEET LITTLE SIXTEEN alternate mix, from #91
JOHNNY B. GOODE BBC, 15 February 1964, from #64
YOU CAN'T DO THAT Melbourne 1964, from #65
'70 Wenner John interview re: tours were like Satyricon, from #64
ALL MY LOVING Adelaide 1964, from #63, under dialogue
WATCHING THE WHEELS demo 4, from #84
BEAUTIFUL BOY under dialogue, from #92
Double Fantasy studio dialogue "Sean is here ...hello I can see you...like a space ship", from #92
SERVE YOURSELF, BE-BOP-A-LULA Sean, vocal only, from #92
John teaching Sean to play guitar, from #92
STARTING OVER Double Fantasy LP
MOVE OVER MS. L rehearsal, take 1, under dialogue, from #64
MOVE OVER MS. L demo 1, from #64
MOVE OVER MS. L demo 2, from #64
MOVE OVER MS. L rehearsal, take 2, from #64
I DON'T WANNA BE A SOLDIER under dialogue, from #87
interview continued re: didn't interfere with musicians, from #87
interview continued re: 1st time J. played them Imagine, from #87
IMAGINE Imagine LP cut to
IMAGINE RUNTHROUGH Imagine: John Lennon Soundtrack LP, from #87
BEEF JERKY piano outake, extro

The Lost Lennon Tapes Part 104
Year 3 Premiere
Show #90-03, Broadcast the Week of January 15, 1990

BEEF JERKY intro
COME TOGETHER One To One rehearsals, take 2
One To One radio promo, also #186 Geraldo Rivera into **NEW YORK CITY**, also #186
I KNOW (I KNOW) demo 2, take 3
WHATEVER GETS YOU THROUGH THE NIGHT under dialogue
'80 Sheff John interview re: Whatever Gets You Through The Night
WHATEVER GETS YOU THROUGH THE NIGHT demo 2
WHATEVER GETS YOU THROUGH THE NIGHT 1st studio rehearsal, fragment also #50
I AM THE WALRUS By George LP, George Martin, under dialogue
interview continued re: Glass Onion
I AM THE WALRUS under dialogue
Paul interview re: Glass Onion
GLASS ONION The Beatles LP
interview continued re: looking for the Glass Onion
HELTER SKELTER under dialogue
'70 Wenner John interview re: Paul is dead
interview continued re: Charles Manson
interview continued re: reading mysticism into Beatles songs
interview continued re: people having nothing better to do
PIGGIES demo
Cleanup Time studio dialogue, "how're we starting, bass, drums, wha?"
CLEANUP TIME take 1 "sneak in like the old days", under dialogue
CLEANUP TIME take 7, basic track no vocals
OH MY LOVE under dialogue
'80 John Cott John interview re: does Yoko produce records
CLEANUP TIME fragment
interview continued re: Yoko's magic edit
STRAWBERRY FIELDS FOREVER demo, under dialogue
George Martin interview re: Strawberry Fields Forever edit
STRAWBERRY FIELDS FOREVER version 1, fragment
STRAWBERRY FIELDS FOREVER version 2, fragment
interview continued re: altering speeds
interview continued re: see if you can find the edit
STRAWBERRY FIELDS FOREVER single 1967
BEEF JERKY piano outake, extro

The Lost Lennon Tapes Part 105
Show #90-04, Broadcast the Week of January 22, 1990

BEEF JERKY intro
TICKET TO RIDE rough mix, take 2
YES IT IS outake, take 1, under dialogue
YES IT IS outake, take 2
YES IT IS rough mix, take 14
ACROSS THE UNIVERSE No One's Gonna Change Our World LP
'70 Wenner John interview re: loafing at Weybridge in '68
TWO VIRGINS under dialogue
THE FOOL ON THE HILL under dialogue
Pete Shotton interview re: John believed he was Christ
I AM THE WALRUS take 9, no vocals
MAGICAL MYSTERY TOUR under dialogue
interview continued re: 1st night with Yoko at Weybridge
JULIA demo 2, also #11
I DON'T WANNA FACE IT demo 3
EVERYBODY'S TALKING, NOBODY'S TALKING demo, under dialogue
NOBODY TOLD ME demo 2
EVERYBODY'S GOT SOMETHING TO HIDE EXCEPT FOR ME AND MY MONKEY under dialogue
'70 Wenner John interview fragment re: Cynthia's reaction to Yoko
Cynthia interview re: seeing John & Yoko at Weybridge
CRY BABY CRY demo, Kinfauns 1968, also #179
JULIA backing tracks, under dialogue
Shotton interview re: John's life completely devoted to Yoko
interview continued re: Christ complex disappeared
BACK IN THE U.S.S.R. under dialogue
BACK IN THE U.S.S.R. Paul demo
BRING IT ON HOME TO ME Chobba B CCP LP, Paul, under dialogue
Paul interview re: the Russian album
KANSAS CITY Paul, Chobba B CCCP LP
BEEF JERKY piano outake, extro

The Lost Lennon Tapes Part 106
The Men Who Gave The Beatles Away
Show #90-05, Broadcast the Week of January 29, 1990

BEEF JERKY intro
studio dialogue - "whoever's here lets play it then ... goodnight Sean"
NOBODY TOLD ME outake, take 1
FAME & FORTUNE Elvis Presley, under dialogue
WHEN YOUR HEARTACHES BEGIN 1960 rehearsal, under dialogue
Alan Williams interview re: the Jacaranda
ONE AFTER 909 rehearsal 1960, under dialogue

interview continued re: John and Stu painting
WHITE LIGHTNING Big Bopper, under dialogue
BE-BOP-A-LULA Gene Vincent, under dialogue
interview continued re: managing the Beatles
interview continued re: Larry Parnes and Scotland
I SAW HER STANDING THERE Star Club LP
REMINISCING Star Club LP, under dialogue
interview continued re: the Beatles personalities
interview continued re: Williams's commission
EVERYBODY'S TRYING TO BE MY BABY Star Club LP, under dialogue
interview continued re: threatening letter
'62 Paul interview re: getting German engagements
Alan Williams interview re: Brian discovered them
MR. MOONLIGHT Star Club LP
MY BONNIE Tony Sheridan, under dialogue
Alistair Taylor interview re: Mr. Fixit
interview continued re: the Cavern a jazz club
SOME OTHER GUY Cavern Club, live, under dialogue
interview continued re: first encounter with the Beatles
interview continued re: Beatles didn't know they were there
HELLO LITTLE GIRL The Fourmost, under dialogue
interview continued re: going to lunch after the meeting
MONEY Decca Sessions LP
WHY Tony Sheridan, under dialogue
interview continued re: turning down 2 1/2% of the Beatles
AIN'T SHE SWEET Tony Sheridan, under dialogue
SURE TO FALL Decca Sessions LP, under dialogue
Pete Best interview re: Decca audition
MEMPHIS TENNESSEE Decca Sessions LP
interview continued re: Mike Smith said no problem
DREAM BABY, BBC, fragment, also #42 #<u>70</u>, #161
interview continued re: not getting the contract
interview continued re: the group's reaction
SEARCHIN' Decca Sessions LP
SHEIK OF ARABY Decca Sessions LP, under dialogue
Alistair Taylor interview re: defending Dick Rowe
CRY FOR A SHADOW Tony Sheridan, under dialogue
'62 Paul interview re: Polydor recordings
Tony Sheridan interview re: Polydor giving up contract
TO KNOW HER IS TO TO LOVE HER Decca Sessions LP, under dialogue
Alistair Taylor interview re: Geo Martin didn't want to know
CRYING, WAITING, HOPING, Decca Sessions LP
BEEF JERKY piano outake, extro

The Lost Lennon Tapes Part 107
The Fab Four In D.C.
Show #90-06, Broadcast the Week of February 5, 1990

BEEF JERKY intro
IT WON'T BE LONG under dialogue
I WANT TO HOLD YOUR HAND Ed Sullivan, 1964, also #29, #57, #129
THIS BOY under dialogue
Paul interview re: Beatles act
interview continued re: laying it on the Americans
MYSTERY TRAIN Scotty Moore, under dialogue
Ringo interview re: press out to destroy them
Fred Martin interview re: Washington concert
FROM ME TO YOU Washington D.C. 1964
ASK ME WHY under dialogue
'80 Sheff John interview re: first trip to America
Ringo interview re: their American shows
I WANT TO HOLD YOUR HAND under dialogue
'64 Carroll James Washington Beatles interview
SHE LOVES YOU Washington D.C. 1964
IT'S SO HARD under dialogue
YAKETY YAK The Coasters, under dialogue
REMINISCING Star Club LP under dialogue
Sounds Incorporated live at Shea Stadium, under dialogue
studio dialogue, King Curtis arrives, also #207
It's So Hard, intro playback for sax
It's So Hard, John acoustic demo for sax part
It's So Hard, King Curtis, studio dialogue
sax practice
IT'S SO HARD sax overdub on intro, cut to
IT'S SO HARD Imagine LP
studio dialogue re: solo for I Don't Wanna Be A Solider
I DON'T WANNA BE A SOLDIER sax solo
I WANNA BE YOUR MAN under dialogue
'64 Carol James Beatles interview continued
LITTLE CHILD under dialogue
THIS BOY Washington D.C. 1964
ROLL OVER BEETHOVEN under dialogue
interview continued re: career objectives
YOU REALLY GOT A HOLD ON ME under dialogue
Fred Martin interview re: Beatles great to work with
DON'T BOTHER ME under dialogue
'70 Wenner John interview re: being touched and pawed
Fred Martin interview re: woman cutting Ringo's hair
interview continued re: hotel party afterwards
PLEASE PLEASE Washington D.C. 1964

MONEY under dialogue
interview continued re: gettin private train car
interview continued re: train ride to New York
interview continued re: fans along the way
HOLD ME TIGHT under dialogue
interview continued re: Carnegie Hall concert
John says hi from Miami
BEEF JERKY piano outake, extro

The Lost Lennon Tapes Part 108
Show #90-07, Broadcast the Week of February 12, 1990

BEEF JERKY intro
MEMORIES demo 2, also #156
MEMPHIS TENNESSEE BBC, under dialogue
TO KNOW HER IS TO LOVE HER Decca Sessions LP
THREE COOL CATS Decca Sessions LP
LIKE DREAMERS DO Decca Sessions LP
LIKE DREAMERS DO The Applejacks, under dialogue
NEW YORK CITY One To One rehearsals, under dialogue
Mike Douglas excerpt
interview re: Elephant's Memory, R N R, Yoko & music
IT'S SO HARD Mike Douglas Show, also #45 ends with Douglas "we'll be right back" not on #45
NEW YORK CITY One To One rehearsals, under dialogue
interview continued re: people meeting you
HEY JUDE instrumental, under dialogue
'80 Sheff John interview re: Hey Jude
Paul interview re: Hey Jude and John's favourite line
interview continued re: who Hey Jude is really about
HEY JUDE outake, take 9
HEY JUDE under dialogue
'88 Julian interview re: Hey Jude (see part 38)
interview continued re: Paul was a lot of fun
interview continued re: hearing Hey Jude today
WE LOVE YOU The Rolling Stones, under dialogue
Nicky Hopkins interview re: We Love You
interview continued re: rumour of anamosity not true
ALL YOU NEED IS LOVE under dialogue
REVOLUTION demo, under dialogue
interview re: Revolution 1 as a single
Phil McDonald interview re: distorted guitar sound
Nicky Hopkins interview re: asked to do Revolution session
interview continued re: doing it in one take
REVOLUTION Past Masters LP
interview continued re: surprised at amount of distortion

REVOLUTION 1 under dialogue
'69 Fred Peabody interview re: meaning of Revolution
'80 Sheff John interview re: Revolution
BEEF JERKY piano outake, extro

The Lost Lennon Tapes Part 109
Epstein On Epstein, Part 1
Show #90-08, Broadcast the Week of February 19, 1990

BEEF JERKY intro
BAD TO ME Billy J. Kramer, under dialogue
Epstein interview re: did you think it would get this way
I SHOULD HAVE KNOWN BETTER under dialogue
A TASTE OF HONEY rough mix, take 7
I WANT TO HOLD YOUR HAND under dialogue
WHEN I GET HOME under dialogue
'64 Bill Grundy Epstein interview re: size of his empire
medley of Brian Epstein's artist's recordings
MONEY under dialogue
interview continued re: administration, staff, money, his 25%
I CALL YOUR NAME Past Masters LP
BEAUTIFUL DREAMER Billy J. Kramer, under dialogue
interview continued re: Brian's family and his past
instrumental under dialogue
BEETHOVEN'S FIFTH under dialogue
interview continued re: liking classical as much as pop
BBC intro
ROLL OVER BEETHOVEN BBC, 30 March 1964, also #64, #135, #160
BBC extro
MY BONNIE Tony Sheridan, under dialogue
interview continued re: Raymond Jones, Beatles at the Cavern
THE SAINTS Tony Sheridan, under dialogue
TILL THERE WAS YOU The Decca Sessions LP
BOYS under dialogue
interview continued re: liking their sound
BABY IT'S YOU under dialogue
interview continued re: changes in appearance
DREAM BABY BBC, under dialogue
BBC intro to
I WANNA BE YOUR MAN BBC, 30 March 1964, also #136
RINGO'S THEME under dialogue
interview continued re: acting and theatre
DO YOU WANT TO KNOW A SECRET Please Please Me LP
PLEASE PLEASE ME under dialogue
'64 Grundy Epstein interview re: knowing about hits

FROM ME TO YOU under dialogue
interview continued re: getting along well with people
IT'S FOR YOU Cilla Black, under dialogue
interview continued re: relatnship with artists, mngmt pleasures
I WANT TO HOLD YOUR HAND Paris 1964, also #56
BEEF JERKY piano outake, extro

The Lost Lennon Tapes Part 110
Epstein On Epstein, Part 2
Show #90-09, Broadcast the Week of February 26, 1990

BEEF JERKY intro
ONE AFTER 909 Quarry Men 1962, under dialogue
ONE AFTER 909 Quarry Men 1962
CATSWALK Quarry Men 1962
I'LL GET YOU single 1963
intrumental under dialogue
'64 Grundy Epstein interview re: preplanning America
I'LL BE BACK under dialogue
interview continued re: I Want To Hold Your Hand the right record
I WANT TO HOLD YOUR HAND intrumental under dialogue
interview continued re: trip to America timed right
I SAW HER STANDING THERE Ed Sullivan 1964, also #57, #160
SHE LOVES YOU Paris 1964, also # 73
I WANT TO HOLD YOUR HAND under dialogue
KOMM, GIB MIR DEINE HAND under dialogue
CAN'T BUY ME LOVE A Hard Day's Night LP
YOU CAN'T DO THAT under dialogue
ANYONE WHO HAD A HEART Cilla Black, under dialogue
interview continued re: softer sound coming
NEEDLES AND PINS The Searchers, under dialogue
FERRY CROSS THE MERSEY Gerry & The Pacemakers, under dialogue
interview continued re: moving to London
LOVE OF THE LOVED Cilla Black, single 1963
YOU'RE MY WORLD Cilla Black, under dialogue
interview continued re: move affecting talent scouting
interview continued re: sense of power, different style of life
WORLD WITHOUT LOVE Peter & Gordon, single 1964
NOBODY I KNOW Peter & Gordon, under dialogue
I'LL BE ON MY WAY BBC, 24 June 1963, also #161
THERE'S A PLACE under dialogue
A HARD DAY'S NIGHT unde dialogue
interview continued re: A Hard Day's Night film
SLOW DOWN Long Tall Sally EP
I'LL KEEP YOU SATISFIED Billy J. Kramer, under dialogue

interview continued re: timid of new areas, management
THINGS WE SAID TODAY under dialogue
BEEF JERKY piano outake, extro

The Lost Lennon Tapes Part 111
Show #90-10, Broadcast the Week of March 5, 1990

BEEF JERKY intro
ANOTHER HARD DAY'S NIGHT under dialogue
'67 Murray The K Epstein interview re: new direction
LOVE YOU TO under dialogue
GETTING BETTER Sgt. Pepper's LP
FROM ME TO YOU FANTASY under dialogue
interview continued re: appreciating music
WHAT GOES ON under dialogue
STRAWBERRY FIELDS FOREVER under dialogue
interview continued re: Beatles breakup, your relationship
I WANT TO TELL YOU Revolver LP
SHE SAID SHE SAID under dialogue
interview continued re: the last month or so
YESTERDAY Budokan 1966
interview continued re: tour different, not good on stage
THE FAMILY WAY soundtrack LP, under dialogue
MY GENERATION The Who, under dialogue
interview continued re: The Who and The Cream
Cream live under dialogue
interview continued re: smashing guitars
LAWDY MAMA BBC Cream
HEY JOE Jimi Hendrix, under dialogue
interview continued re: Jimi Hendrix
STONE FREE Jimi Hendrix, under dialogue
interview continued re: Hey Joe not representative of Jimi
DAY TRIPPER Budokan 1966
I'M ONLY SLEEPING under dialogue
interview continued re: people always wanting something
TOMORROW NEVER KNOWS reference mix, also #26
GOT TO GET YOU INTO MY LIFE under dialogue
interview continued re: life like a political circle
WHEN I'M SIXTY-FOUR Sgt. Pepper's LP, fragment
GOOD DAY SUNSHINE Revolver LP
STRAWBERRY FIELDS FOREVER backing tracks, under dialogue
interview continued re: Penny Lane
PENNY LANE Rarities LP
A DAY IN THE LIFE under dialogue
interview continued re: further musical expressions
BEEF JERKY piano outake, extro

The Lost Lennon Tapes Part 112
Show #90-11, Broadcast the Week of March 12, 1990

BEEF JERKY intro
YOU'VE GOT TO HIDE YOUR LOVE AWAY under dialogue
'67 Murray The K Epstein interview re: fusion of styles
Bob Dylan song under dialogue
interview continued re: not categorizing people
THINK FOR YOURSELF Rubber Soul LP
PAPERBACK WRITER Tokyo 1966
SHE LOVES YOU Candlestick Park 1966, under dialogue
interview continued re: not wanting to tour
THE BITTER END under dialogue
interview continued re: different to progress from those tours
TAXMAN under dialogue
interview continued re: appearing in public again
I'M DOWN Tokyo 1966, also # 117
WHEN I'M SIXTY-FOUR under dialogue
interview fragment continued re: they're working very hard
SGT. PEPPER'S REPRISE under dialogue
interview continued re: number of Pepper tracks finished
LUCY IN THE SKY WITH DIAMONDS Sgt. Pepper's LP
A DAY IN THE LIFE under dialogue
interview continued re: Beatles in the studio every night
STRAWBERRY FIELDS FOREVER take 1
STRAWBERRY FIELDS FOREVER backing tracks, under dialogue
interview continued re: meticulousness and perfection
Penny Lane horn rehearsals, several short clips with Mintz dialogue between
PENNY LANE rehearsal, Paul singing horn parts, while George Martin tries piano effects
PENNY LANE playback rehearsal, piano chords and singing in studio
George Martin rehearses brass section, brief fragment
George Martin studio dialogue and flute overdubs
heavily echoed flute riff
PENNY LANE rough mix
PENNY LANE coda under dialogue
STRAWBERRY FIELDS FOREVER under dialogue
'67 Murray The K Epstein interview re: single A side
SGT. PEPPER'S LONELY HEARTS CLUB BAND under dialogue
interview continued re: what's next for the Beatles
BEING FOR THE BENEFIT OF MR. KITE under dialogue
interview continued re: a show or new concept
SHE'S LEAVING HOME Sgt. Pepper's LP
A LITTLE HELP FROM MY FRIENDS under dialogue
interview continued re: everything is status quo
BEEF JERKY piano outake, extro

The Lost Lennon Tapes Part 113
Show #90-12, Broadcast the Week of March 19, 1990

BEEF JERKY intro
PAPERBACK WRITER under dialogue
NOWHERE MAN Munich 1966
'80 Peebles John interview re: were you happy
THINK FOR YOURSELF under dialogue
STRAWBERRY FIELDS FOREVER demo 2, also #11
Indian music under dialogue
interview continued re: meeting Yoko
DRIVE MY CAR under dialogue
interview continued re: going to gallery show
I'VE JUST SEEN A FACE Help! LP
GIRL under dialogue
interview continued re: hammer a nail in
interview continued re: Yoko's impression
GOT TO GET YOU INTO MY LIFE under dialogue
JULIA demo 3, also #44
TWO VIRGINS excerpt under dialogue
interview continued re: Two Virgins
MOTHER NATURE'S SON demo
NOT GUILTY demo, under dialogue
REVOLUTION 1 under dialogue
REVOLUTION 9 under dialogue
REVOLUTION 9 fragment
Paul interview re: John and Yoko affair
DON'T PASS ME BY under dialogue
'76 Mintz Ringo interview re: white LP sessions
'80 Peebles John interview re: how others felt
HAPPINESS IS A WARM GUN The Beatles LP
SEXY SADIE under dialogue
WHAT'S THE NEW MARY JANE? Kinfauns demo, also #13
WHAT'S THE NEW MARY JANE? under dialogue
THE CONTINUING STORY OF BUNGALOW BILL under dialogue
BABY'S HEARTBEAT under dialogue
OH MY LOVE demo 1, also #182
OH MY LOVE demo 2
OH MY LOVE Yoko, a cappella, also #182
OH MY LOVE under dialogue
BEEF JERKY piano outake, extro

The Lost Lennon Tapes Part 114
John & Yoko Anniversary Show: Wedding & Honeymoon
Show #90-13, Broadcast the Week of March 26, 1990

BEEF JERKY intro
YER BLUES under dialogue
YER BLUES Rock N Roll Circus, alternate take
YER BLUES Rock N Roll Circus, under dialogue
'68 Yoko interview re: genesis of the Plastic Ono Band
'68 Christmas record: Once Upon A Pool Table, under dialogue
EVERYONE HAD A HARD YEAR demo, also #15
Get Back rehearsals dialogue fragment
'80 Peebles John & Yoko interview re: going own way
JOHN, LET'S HOPE FOR PEACE Get Back rehearsals, fragment, also #127
interview continued re: Beatles like a job
I WILL under dialogue
THE HONEYMOON SONG Mary Hopkin, under dialogue
SEA OF MONSTERS under dialogue
IT'S ALL TOO MUCH Yellow Submarine film soundtrack edit
SEA OF MONSTERS under dialogue
JULIA backing tracks, under dialogue
interview continued re: getting married in Gibralter
I WANT YOU (SHE'S SO HEAVY) under dialogue
interview continued re: Gibralter
TWO OF US Get Back LP
DIG IT GET BACK LP, under dialogue
interview continued re: Amsterdam bed-in
WHY DON'T WE DO IT IN THE ROAD under dialogue
REVOLUTION 1 under dialogue
'69 Donald Zec John interview re: promoting peace
SEA OF TIME under dialogue
'69 Letramo interview re: having a talk-in
interview continued re: filming everything
interview continued re: next on the agenda
HEY BULLDOG Yellow Submarine LP
GOODBYE AMSTERDAM Wedding LP
PEPPERLAND LAID WASTE under dialogue
interview continued re: Rape film
PAPA'S GOT A BRAND NEW BAG James Brown, under dialogue
interview continued re: being in a bag
'69 Austrian John interview re: prove you're John
COME TOGETHER under dialogue
'80 Peebles John interview re: peaceful methods
'69 Today, interview fragment re: getting in a bag
GET BACK Get Back rehearsals, foreign languages
COME AND GET IT Badfinger, under dialogue

THE BALLAD OF JOHN AND YOKO alternate mix
'69 Peabody John interview re: The Ballad of John And Yoko
OLD BROWN SHOE under dialogue
BEEF JERKY piano outake, extro

The Lost Lennon Tapes Part 115
April '64 & More
Show #90-14, Broadcast the Week of April 2, 1990

BEEF JERKY intro
REAL LIFE demo 5
REAL LOVE - GIRLS AND BOYS demo 4
SHE LOVES YOU under dialogue
'64 Top 3 Billboard positions award presentation
ANOTHER HARD DAY'S NIGHT under dialogue
ALL MY LOVING BBC, 30 March 1964
MONEY under dialogue
CAN'T BUY ME LOVE BBC, 30 March 1964, also #136
FROM ME TO YOU backing tracks, under dialogue
CAN'T BUY ME LOVE (INSTRUMENTAL) under dialogue
WABC station I.D.
Scott Muni interview re: top 5 chart positions
Ed Sullivan intro to 3rd 1964 show
TWIST AND SHOUT Ed Sullivan 1964, also #29
I WANT TO HOLD YOUR HAND under dialogue
THIS BOY single 1964, fragment
AND I LOVE HER (INSTRUMENTAL) under dialogue
A HARD DAY'S NIGHT A Hard Day's Night LP
RINGO'S THEME under dialogue
I WANNA BE YOUR MAN Around The Beatles
DON'T BOTHER ME (INSTRUMENTAL) under dialogue
'64 BBC interview re: Foyle's literary luncheon
John's thank you acceptance speech
interview continued re: the scene afterwards
LONG TALL SALLY Around The Beatles
I SHOULD HAVE KNOWN BETTER (INSTRUMENTAL) under dialogue
interview continued re: asking John about writing
'64 BBC John interview re: writing books & his speech
THINGS WE SAID TODAY under dialogue
'64 Gene Loving George interview re: film's title
interview continued re: Wembley concert
I'M HAPPY JUST TO DANCE WITH YOU under dialogue
'64 Loving John interview re: film title, favourite song
'64 Loving Ringo interview re: all-star line up
I'LL BE BACK under dialogue

interview continued re: return to U.S.
interview continued re: eating regularly, police, fans
'64 Loving Wembley fan interview, intro to show
SHE LOVES YOU Wembley 1964
'64 Alan Freeman John BBC interview re: selling book
YOU CAN'T DO THAT under dialogue
BEEF JERKY piano outake, extro

The Lost Lennon Tapes Part 116
Show #90-15, Broadcast the Week of April 9, 1990

BEEF JERKY intro
TWIST AND SHOUT Around The Beatles
CAN'T BUY ME LOVE Around The Beatles, also #<u>65</u> last song of the medley
STARTING OVER - DON'T BE CRAZY demo 2
STARTING OVER backing tracks, under dialogue
'80 Peebles John interview re: inspirational songs
STARTING OVER demo 1
ROCK LOBSTER B-52'S, under dialogue
interview continued re: Bermuda disco
ROCK LOBSTER B-52'S, fragment
interview continued re: Yoko & the B-52'S
RAIN single 1966
PAPERBACK WRITER under dialogue
Paul interview re: Lewisohn's Beatles Live
HELP! live 1965, under dialogue
Lewisohn interview re: winding down live gigs
ROCK AND ROLL MUSIC Munich 1966
CRY FOR A SHADOW under dialogue
I FEEL FINE Munich 1966
THAT'S ALL RIGHT, MAMA BBC, 16 July 1963, fragment
BLUE SUEDE SHOES Elvis, Milton Berle 1956
'67 Paul interview re: fan of Elvis since 16
BLUE SUEDE SHOES Get Back rehearsals
ELVIS MEDLEY Get Back rehearsals
READY TEDDY Rock 'N' Roll LP
<u>Jam</u> That's All Right, Mama, P.O.B. LP session, fragment
WOMAN backing tracks, under dialogue
'80 Peebles Yoko interview re: making Double Fantasy
'80 Peebles John interview re: wanting to be a comedian
<u>Double Fantasy</u> studio dialogue, "I just better get down and smash a noise pretend I'm playing"
interview continued re: Starting Over single, tongue in cheek
STARTING OVER, vocal only, under dialogue
STARTING OVER rough mix
BEEF JERKY piano outake, extro

The Lost Lennon Tapes Part 117
The Fab Four's Far East Fiasco, 1966
Show #90-16, Broadcast the Week of April 16, 1990

BEEF JERKY intro
YESTERDAY Munich 1966
TICKET TO RIDE under dialogue
Japanese instrumental under dialogue
'66 Japanese Beatles interview re: security, hair
ROCK AND ROLL MUSIC Tokyo, 30 June 1966
Japanese instrumental under dialogue
SHE'S A WOMAN Tokyo, 30 June 1966
DAY TRIPPER under dialogue
TRIANGLE Janie Grant, under dialogue
YOU CAN'T DO THAT under dialogue
HELP! under dialogue
IF I NEEDED SOMEONE Tokyo, 30 June 1966
I'M ONLY SLEEPING under dialogue
BABY'S IN BLACK Tokyo, 30 June 1966
YOU WON'T SEE ME under dialogue
TAXMAN under dialogue
I WANNA BE YOUR MAN Tokyo, 30 June 1966
RUN FOR YOUR LIFE under dialogue
NOWHERE MAN Tokyo, 30 June 1966
WHAT GOES ON under dialogue
DRAGNET THEME fragment
FROM ME TO YOU FANTASY under dialogue
I FEEL FINE Tokyo, 30 June 1966
LOVE YOU TO under dialogue
I'M DOWN Tokyo, 30 June 1966, also #112
BEEF JERKY piano outake, extro

The Lost Lennon Tapes Part 118
Show #90-17, Broadcast the Week of April 23, 1990

BEEF JERKY intro
HONEY DON'T Carl Perkins, under dialogue
BBC Intro
EVERYBODY'S TRYING TO BE MY BABY BBC, 26 December 1964, also #134
HONEY DON'T BBC, 7 June 1965
GOOD MORNING, GOOD MORNING under dialogue
'75 Snider John interview re: people against rock 'n' roll
STAND UP Bob Marley, under dialogue
interview continued re: music you like
I CALL YOUR NAME under dialogue

'80 Peebles John interview re: ska and reggae
OB-LA-DI OB-LA-DA promo U.S. single 1976
Paul interview re: She's A Woman rhythm guitar
SHE'S A WOMAN Past Masters LP
interview continued re: one chord missing
TOMORROW NEVER KNOWS under dialogue
Snider John interview re: music and cycles
ROCK 'N' ROLL PEOPLE take 7, alternate mix, fragment
GIVE ME SOME TRUTH under dialogue
interview continued re: rock 'n' roll & drugs
EVERYBODY'S GOT SOMETHING TO HIDE EXCEPT FOR ME AND MY MONKEY under dialogue
reggae song under dialogue
POWER TO THE PEOPLE outake, take 2, reggae take, also #76
HOW DOW YOU SLEEP rehearsal 2, also #69, intro is in #197
LOVE IS STRANGE Paul, under dialogue
THE LONG AND WINDING ROAD under dialogue
Snider John interview re: Beatles breakup
INSTANT KARMA under dialogue
ACROSS THE UNIVERSE Let It Be LP, with intro
LET IT BE under dialogue
MAYBE I'M AMAZED under dialogue
BEEF JERKY piano outake, extro

The Lost Lennon Tapes Part 119
Show #90-18, Broadcast the Week of April 30, 1990

BEEF JERKY intro
TWIST AND SHOUT Hollywood Bowl 1965, fragment performed
SHE'S A WOMAN Hollywood Bowl 1965
DIZZY MISS LIZZY Hollywood Bowl 1965
THE ISRAELITES Desmond Dekker, under dialogue
'80 Peebles John interview re: Sisters O Sisters
SISTERS, O SISTERS under dialogue
interview continued re: reggae
LIVE AND LET DIE Paul, under dialogue
'73 Paul interview re: Live And Let Die
MIND GAMES under dialogue
interview re: Mind Games and reggae
MIND GAMES rough mix, basic tracks
STEEL AND GLASS Walls And Bridges LP
LUCY IN THE SKY WITH DIAMONDS Elton John, under dialogue
DO YOU WANNA DANCE alternate take
SEASIDE WOMAN Linda McCartney, under dialogue
BBC Paul and Linda interview re: Seaside Woman
FAMOUS GROUPIES McCartney, London Town LP

BORROWED TIME demo 1, also #31, #173
MADNESS reggae song, under dialogue
interview re: missing reggae
Jam, reggae, under dialogue
BORROWED TIME alternate mix
PAPER SHOES Yoko, under dialogue
'80 Peebles John interview re: we've done it all
I'M LOSING YOU under dialogue
BEEF JERKY piano outake, extro

The Lost Lennon Tapes Part 120
So, Who Did Break Up The Beatles?
Show #90-19, Broadcast the Week of May 7, 1990

BEEF JERKY intro
I'M STEPPING OUT demo 3, take 1
I'M STEPPING OUT demo 4, take 3
YOU ALWAYS HURT THE ONE YOU LOVE Ringo, under dialogue
'69 David Wigg Ringo interview re: Beatles relationship
FOR YOU BLUE under dialogue
I'VE GOT A FEELING Let It Be LP
HOW THE WEB WAS WOVEN Jackie Lomax, under dialogue
'83 Scott Muni Paul interview re: the breakup
GET BACK under dialogue
OO YOU Paul, under dialogue
interview continued re: McCartney LP press release
YOU NEVER GIVE ME YOUR MONEY fragment
YER BLUES Live Peace in Toronto LP, under dialogue
'70 Wenner John interview re: leaving the Beatles
MONEY Live Peace in Toronto LP, under dialogue
COLD TURKEY Live Peace In Toronto LP
COLD TURKEY demo, under dialogue
MOVE ON FAST Yoko, under dialogue
'80 Peebles John interview re: still an audience for John & Yoko
I'M STEPPING OUT outake, take 8
COLD TURKEY under dialogue
I WANT YOU (SHE'S SO HEAVY) under dialogue
COME TOGETHER under dialogue
'69 David Wigg Ringo interview re: permanent split
SOMETHING Abbey Road LP
'69 David Wigg George interview re: not wanting end of Beatles
LET IT BE under dialogue
'69 David Wigg John interview re: future of Beatles
BEEF JERKY piano outake, extro

The Lost Lennon Tapes Part 121
Show #90-20, Broadcast the Week of May 14, 1990

BEEF JERKY intro
TIGHT A$ rough mix
HEY JUDE under dialogue
'80 Garbarini Paul interview re: white LP most tense
interview continued re: George and Hey Jude
'70 Wenner John interview re: white album the breakup
'76 Ringo interview re: liking white album best
Ken Scott interview re: still Beatles on white LP
'80 Paul interview re: telling Ringo what to play
DON'T PASS ME BY The Beatles LP
WOMAN IS THE NIGGER OF THE WORLD Live In NYC LP, under dialogue
'73 Schechter Yoko interview re: women's conference
'73 Schechter John interview re: John's involvement
Yoko interview continued re: gathering seen as radical
ONLY PEOPLE early mix
I KNOW (I KNOW) demo 3, take 4, also #209
NUTOPIAN NATIONAL ANTHEM
I KNOW (I KNOW) under dialogue
'73 Schechter interview re: immigration and Nutopia
IMAGINE outake
I'M SO TIRED under dialogue
'76 Mintz Ringo interview re: why he left the Beatles
WHAT GOES ON under dialogue
Ken Scott interview re: Back In The USSR session
BACK IN THE U.S.S.R. The Beatles LP
DEAR PRUDENCE under dialogue
'76 Ringo interview re: flowers in the studio
REVOLUTION Past Masters LP
BEEF JERKY piano outake, extro

The Lost Lennon Tapes Part 122
Show #90-21, Broadcast the Week of May 21, 1990

BEEF JERKY intro
MATCHBOX BBC, 30 July 1963, also #166
HONEY DON'T BBC, 18 May 1964
HONEY DON'T Carl Perkins, under dialogue
Carl Perkins interview re: thanking them
DEAR YOKO under dialogue
WOMAN demo, new version, take 1, fragment
WOMAN demo, new version, take 7, John says "take 9"
EVERYMAN HAS A WOMAN Everyman Has A Woman Who Loves Him LP

NAME AND ADDRESS Paul, under dialogue
JUST BECAUSE Paul, Chobba B CCCP LP
THAT'S ALL RIGHT, MAMA Paul, Chobba B CCCP LP
BLUE MOON OF KENTUCKY Elvis Presley, under dialogue
THERE'S GOOD ROCKIN' TONIGHT Elvis Presley, under dialogue
Paul interview re: why does music affect you
IT'S NOW OR NEVER Elvis Presley, under dialogue
interview continued re: releasing his version
IT'S NOW OR NEVER Paul, The Last Temptation Of Elvis LP
MYSTERY TRAIN Scotty Moore, under dialogue
interview re: without Elvis no Beatles
I'M LOSING YOU under dialogue
I'M LOSING YOU - STRANGER'S ROOM demo 4
VALENTINE DAY Paul, under dialogue
'70 Wenner John interview re: Paul's reaction to breakup
interview continued re: fool not to do what Paul did
interview continued re: hurt not angry
ONLY A NORTHERN SONG under dialogue
interview continued re: I should have done it
LET IT BE Past Masters LP
BEEF JERKY piano outake, extro

The Lost Lennon Tapes Part 123
Show #90-22, Broadcast the Week of May 28, 1990

BEEF JERKY intro
REVOLUTION under dialogue
WHILE MY GUITAR GENTLY WEEPS French mono mix
MEAT CITY under dialogue
'73 Schechter Yoko interview re: men & sexism
MEAT CITY demo 2
WOMAN IS THE NIGGER OF THE WORLD under dialogue
'73 Schechter John interview re: liberation
ONE DAY AT A TIME early mix
BOYS under dialogue
interview re: I first met Ringo
'76 Mintz Ringo interview re: playing in Germany
MONEY Decca Sessions LP, under dialogue
'71 Takahiro Imura J/Y interview re: smashing the stage
MATCHBOX Star Club LP
MEMPHIS TENNESSEE Decca Sessions LP, under dialogue
interview continued re: stamping the beat on stage
ROLL OVER BEETHOVEN Star Club LP
IT'S SO HARD Live In New York City LP, under dialogue
'73 Schechter John interview re: musical projects

ROCK 'N' ROLL PEOPLE demo 2
I DON'T WANNA BE A SOLDIER under dialogue
interview continued re: current video projects
INTUITION demo 1, take 3, also #79
SIX O'CLOCK Ringo, under dialogue
interview continued re: Beatles session on others LPs
I'M THE GREATEST rough mix
GOD under dialogue
interview continued re: how a reunion would be
BEEF JERKY piano outake, extro

The Lost Lennon Tapes Part 124
Show #90-23, Broadcast the Week of June 4, 1990

WHAT YOU GOT intro
'74 Dennis Elsas WNEW John guest DJ appearance
interview re: clubs, early 60s and Stones
I WANNA BE YOUR MAN Stones 1963
I WANNA BE YOUR MAN With The Beatles LP
interview re: hanging around with the Stones
DADDY ROLLING STONE Derek Martin 1963
GET BACK under dialogue
'74 Tom Donahue KSAN John guest DJ appearance
interview re: change in Beatles
GIRL Rubber Soul LP
John deciding what to play
RIVER DEEP MOUNTAIN HIGH Turner, fragment
BLUE SUEDE SHOES Carl Perkins, fragment
interview continued re: Sam Phillips, Let It Be
interview continued re: Let It Be & Spector
WHAT YOU GOT under dialogue
'74 Tom Donahue KSAN John guest DJ appearance
KHJ station I.D.
call re: black Rickenbaker
call re: play The Night Before
THE NIGHT BEFORE under dialogue
call re: Beatles getting together
call re: gear and fab
YOU'RE GONNA LOSE THAT GIRL Help! LP
STAR TREK THEME under dialogue
interview continued re: Watch Your Step
WATCH YOUR STEP Bobby Parker
DAY TRIPPER Past Masters LP
interview continued re: butcher cover, tracks & LPs
interview continued re: number of tracks on LPs

I CALL YOUR NAME Past Masters LP
LUCY IN THE SKY WITH DIAMONDS under dialogue
'74 Tom Donahue KSAN John guest DJ appearance
interview re: Sgt. Pepper's LP
A DAY IN THE LIFE Sgt. Pepper's LP
thanks for comming on the show
WHAT YOU GOT extro

The Lost Lennon Tapes Part 125
Show #90-24, Broadcast the Week of June 11, 1990

BEEF JERKY intro
GET BACK under dialogue
George Martin interview re: Let It Be unhappiest time
interview continued re: John not liking production
interview re: so many takes of everything
George Martin interview re: album like a documentary
DON'T LET ME DOWN single 1969
JUST GOTTA GIVE ME SOME R N R demo 1, under dialogue
MEAT CITY demo 3, take 2, also #<u>209</u>
MEAT CITY rough mix
Kenneth Williams Mind Games ad
ONE AFTER 909 under dialogue
'70 Wenner John interview re: Glynn Johns mix
interview continued re: Glynn did a shity job
George Martin interview re: it lay in the can
CARRY THAT WEIGHT Abbey Road LP
THE END under dialogue
'70 Wenner John interview re: Get Back and Abbey Road
BECAUSE Abbey Road LP
I'M LOSING YOU under dialogue
I'M LOSING YOU - STRANGER'S ROOM demo 5, also #71, #<u>175</u>
LET IT BE under dialogue
'69 David Wigg John interview re: not recording with Beatles
YOU KNOW MY NAME single 1969
INSTANT KARMA under dialogue
interview re: getting Phil Spector in
I'VE GOT A FEELING under dialogue
George Martin interview re: Phil's overdubs
interview re: Phil worked like a pig on it
I ME MINE Let It Be LP
BEEF JERKY piano outake, extro

The Lost Lennon Tapes Part 126
Show #90-25, Broadcast the Week of June 18, 1990

BEEF JERKY intro
I ME MINE under dialogue
'70 BBC George interview re: I Me Mine
interview continued re: Dig A Pony
DIG A PONY Let It Be LP
GET BACK under dialogue
GET BACK Let It Be LP
MAGGIE MAE Let It Be LP
DIG IT Let It Be LP
FOR YOU BLUE under dialogue
interview continued re: For You Blue
THOSE WERE THE DAYS Mary Hopkin, under dialogue
LET IT BE Let It Be LP
TWO OF US Let It Be LP
ACROSS THE UNIVERSE Let It Be, under dialogue
'70 BBC George interview re: approach to Let It Be
George interview re: Let It Be LP like a demo record
'71 interview re: Across The Universe and other tracks
YOU'VE LOST THAT LOVIN' FEELING The Righteous Brothers, under dialogue
George Martin interview re: Spector's early work
interview continued re: didn't like what he did
Paul interview re: new phase Beatles album
George Martin interview re: overproduced by Spector
George interview fragment re: he's outvoted
RIVER DEEP MOUNTAIN HIGH Ike & Tina Turner, under dialogue
Roger Scott Paul interview re: not asked about production
interview re: Phil having fun on The Long And Winding Road
THE LONG AND WINDING ROAD Let It Be LP
ALL THINGS MUST PASS George
ISN'T IT A PITY George, under dialogue
I FOUND OUT demo 1, also #47
BEEF JERKY piano outake, extro

The Lost Lennon Tapes Part 127
Bondage, Liberation and Independence, Part One
Show #90-26, Broadcast the Week of June 25, 1990

BEEF JERKY intro
MISERY Rarities LP
JULIA backing tracks, under dialogue
Mimi interview re: determined to be with you
'70 Wenner John interview re: throwing his poetry out

interview continued re: trying to make him something else
JAILHOUSE ROCK Elvis Presley, under dialogue
DEVIL IN HER HEART under dialogue
interview fragment re: guitar's all right for a hobby
THERE'S A PLACE Rarities LP
TELL ME WHY under dialogue
Pete Shotton interview re: Mimi not liking rebel image
Mimi interview re: in your teens I was hard on you
HAIL HAIL ROCK 'N' ROLL Chuck Berry, under dialogue
interview re: school values didn't mean a thing
BAD BOY Oldies But Goldies LP
I'LL CRY INSTEAD under dialogue
SATISFACTION The Rolling Stones, under dialogue +
'65 press conference interview re: how do like being Beatles
HELP! Live At The Hollywood Bowl LP
DAY TRIPPER under dialogue
'70 Wenner John interview re: She Said She Said
HE SAID HE SAID demos takes 1 to 5, demo 1 also #7
SHE SAID SHE SAID demo, fragment, also #7
SHE SAID SHE SAID Revolver LP
ALL YOU NEED IS LOVE under dialogue
YER BLUES Rock 'N' Roll Circus, fragment, also #27, #156
JOHN LET'S HOPE FOR PEACE Get Back rehearsals, under dialogue, also #114
'70 Wenner John interview re: Yoko not accepted by group
INSTANT KARMA fragment
REMEMBER under dialogue
interview continued re: hooked lie a junk on Beatles
interview continued re: people beating me into being something
interview continued re: no one can recognize what I am
LOOK AT ME early mix
GOD under dialogue
interview continued re: creativity is torture
interview continued re: humiliating oneself
BEEF JERKY extro

The Lost Lennon Tapes Part 128
Bondage, Liberation and Independence, Part Two
Show #90-27, Broadcast the Week of July 2, 1990

BEEF JERKY intro
REVOLUTION 1 under dialogue
HAPPY XMAS rough mix
IMAGINE (REHEARSAL) under dialogue
interview re: war is over

COLD TURKEY Live In NYC LP, fraagment
YOU NEVER GIVE ME YOUR MONEY under dialogue
'73 Mintz John interview re: firing Alan Klein
YOU CAN'T CATCH ME outake
RIP IT UP under dialogue
interview re: Yoko allowing me back
BRING IT ON HOME TO ME under dialogue
interview re: being back with Yoko
NEW YORK CITY under dialogue
interview re: hanging out with the baddies
interview continued re: San Diego rally rumour
interview continued re: they were harassing me
GIVE ME SOME TRUTH alternate mix
CRIPPLED INSIDE under dialogue
interview re: who's sitting in the white house
interview continued re: it's a political decision
interview continued re: latest is I'm appealing
STAND BY ME fragment
WHATEVER GETS YOU THROUGH THE NIGHT under dialogue
#9 DREAM early mix
BEAUTIFUL BOY backing tracks, under dialogue
'76 Mintz John interview re: current immigration status
STARTING OVER backing tracks, under dialogue
interview outside court re: feelings about U.S.
WOMAN backing tracks, under dialogue
press conference interview re: what green card means to me
FREE AS A BIRD demo 2, take 3
SERVE YOURSELF demo 6
BEEF JERKY piano outake, extro

The Lost Lennon Tapes Part 129
Show #90-28, Broadcast the Week of July 9, 1990

BEEF JERKY intro
I WANT TO HOLD YOUR HAND Ed Sullivan, 1964, also #29, #57, #107
WHEN I GET HOME under dialogue
George interview re: a lot of film offers
MONEY under dialogue
Walter Shenson interview re: UA LP deal
interview continued re: choosing Richard Lester
interview continued re: Lester working with Goons
Goon show fragment
I SHOULD HAVE KNOWN BETTER A Hard Day's Night soundtrack
ACT NATURALLY under dialogue

interview continued re: using black and white
interview continued re: brilliant screenplay
THINGS WE SAID TODAY A Hard Day's Night LP
AND I LOVE HER (INSTRUMENTAL) under dialogue
'70 Wenner John interview re: illusion we were puppets
film press conference fragment
interview continued re: projection of us on tour
ANY TIME AT ALL A Hard Day's Night LP
I SHOULD HAVE KNOWN BETTER (INSTRUMENTAL) under dialogue
Shenson interview re: John and the title
Paul and Ringo interview re: the title song
A HARD DAY'S NIGHT A Hard Day's Night LP
George film soundtrack fragment: can you read
Shenson interview re: boys quick studies
YOU CAN'T DO THAT under dialogue
Paul interview re: people expect us to be bad
Ringo interview re: this one was fun
Paul interview re: breaking up giggling
interview continued re: singing If I Fell to Ringo
IF I FELL A Hard Day's Night LP
'70 Wenner John interview re: first attempt at a ballad
IN MY LIFE under dialogue
film fragment re: they're going potty
Shenson interview re: decoy camera and crew
CAN'T BUY ME LOVE A Hard Day's Night LP
RINGO'S THEME under dialogue
Spinetti interview re: Ringo and kids scene
interview continued re: clown's face
John film soundtrack fragment: Rule Britannia
Shenson interview re: expanding George's role
I'M HAPPY JUST TO DANCE WITH YOU (INSTRUMENTAL) under dialogue
John film soundtrack fragment: do the show here
I'M HAPPY JUST TO DANCE WITH YOU A Hard Day's Night LP
A HARD DAY'S NIGHT (INSTRUMENTAL) under dialogue
Spinetti film soundtrack fragment re: am I unsuitable
Spinetti interview re: playing the TV director scene
interview continued re: mixing final concert scene
SHE LOVES YOU under dialogue
I'LL BE BACK under dialogue
Shenson interview re: film legitimized the Beatles
TELL ME WHY A Hard Day's Night LP
AND I LOVE HER under dialogue
Spinetti interview re: classic cinema verité
Shenson interview re: Alun Owens dialogue
I'LL CRY INSTEAD A Hard Day's Night LP
BEEF JERKY extro

The Lost Lennon Tapes Part 130
Show #90-29, Broadcast the Week of July 16, 1990

BEEF JERKY intro
film soundtrack intro fragment: Kaili
HELP! under dialogue
interview fragment re: doesn't like Help! recording
Richard Lester interview re: likes Beatles
Walter Shenson interview re: Beatles unlike Elvis
YOU LIKE ME TOO MUCH under dialogue
YES IT IS Past Masters LP
THE BITTER END under dialogue
Ringo interview re: the plot of Help!
YOU'RE GONNA LOSE THAT GIRL Help! LP
John & Ringo film soundtrack fragment: ...on the floor
ANOTHER HARD DAY'S NIGHT under dialogue
Lester interview re: tailored to their performance
Beatles interview re: making the film
ANOTHER GIRL Help!
DIZZY MISS LIZZY live, under dialogue
Shenson interview re: Beatles were tired
'70 Wenner John interview re: skeptical about the plot
THE NIGHT BEFORE Help! LP
Ringo film soundtrack fragment: more than meets the eye
THE CHASE under dialogue
Paul interview re: we all enjoy it
Beatles interview re: problems with idol
I NEED YOU Help! LP
FROM ME TO YOU FANTASY under dialogue
Ringo interview re: ski scenes
Beatles film soundtrack fragment: fiendish thingy
FROM ME TO YOU FANTASY under dialogue
interview continued re: doing own stunts
TICKET TO RIDE Help! LP
interview re: Ticket To Ride first heavy metal record
YOU WON'T SEE ME under dialogue
Mal Evans film soundtrack fragment: white cliffs of Dover
Mal Evans interview re: his part in the film
I'VE JUST SEEN A FACE Help! LP
Beatles film soundtrack fragment: please say no more
THE BITTER END under dialogue
Spinetti film soundtrack fragment: we could rule the world
Victor Spinetti interview re: Beatles' personalities
ACT NATURALLY Help! LP
AND I LOVE HER under dialogue
Ringo interivew re: being married

YOU'VE GOT TO HIDE YOUR LOVE AWAY
interview re: I'm a chameleon
John and Paul film soundtrack fragment: filthy eastern ways
IN THE TYROL under dialogue
Beatles film soundtrack fragment: help
Beatles interview re: came from Dick Lester
interview re: only true songs were Help! and Strawberry Fields
'80 Sheff John interview re: Johnny is crying out for help
HELP Help! LP
reporter John interview re: critique of Help!
THE INNER LIGHT under dialogue
George intro to
YESTERDAY Ed Sullivan 1965
John intro to
HELP! Ed Sullivan 1965, extro

The Lost Lennon Tapes Part 131
Show #90-30, Broadcast the Week of July 23, 1990

BEEF JERKY intro
MAGICAL MYSTERY TOUR Magical Mystery Tour LP
SGT. PEPPER'S under dialogue
Alistair Taylor interview re: mystery tours
'80 Sheff John interview re: Paul working without him
LUCY IN THE SKY WITH DIAMONDS under dialogue
film soundtrack fragment: Jolly Jimmy Johnson
interview continued re: The Fool On The Hill
THE FOOL ON THE HILL Magical Mystery Tour LP
film soundtrack fragment: SHE LOVES YOU (INSTRUMENTAL) under dialogue
Victor Spinetti interview re: being courier
interview continued re: drill sergeant
Magical Mystery Tour soundtrack fragment: drill sergeant under dialogue
BLUE JAY WAY Magical Mystery Tour LP
film soundtrack fragment: magicians watching bus
BABY, YOU'RE A RICH MAN Past Masters LP
'80 Sheff John interview re: Baby, You're A Rich Man
piano under dialogue
George Martin interview re: Strawbbery Fields Forever/Penny Lane single
PENNY LANE Past Masters LP
IN MY LIFE under dialogue
interview re: the real Strawberry Fields
STRAWBERRY FIELDS FOREVER demo 1, also #4, #49, #180
'80 Sheff John interview re: subconscious sabotage
George Martin interview re: recording Strawberry Fields Forever
STRAWBERRY FIELDS FOREVER Past Masters LP

Magical Mystery Tour soundtrack fragment: look to your right
FLYING under dialogue
'70 Wenner John interview re: elevator dream sequence
interview continued re: I Am The Walrus
SEA OF TIME under dialogue
Mark Lewisohn interview re: King Lear on I Am The Walrus
I AM THE WALRUS Past Masters LP
MMT soundtrack fragment & ALL MY LOVING (INSTRUMENTAL) under dialogue
Paul interview re: BBC and scenes to be cut
YOUR MOTHER SHOULD KNOW Magical Mystery Tour LP
HELLO GOODBYE under dialogue
Paul interview re: panning of MMT by the media
MAGICAL MYSTERY TOUR coda
John film soundtrack frag: that was the Magical Mystery Tour
HELLO GOODBYE extro

The Lost Lennon Tapes Part 132
Show #90-31, Broadcast the Week of July 31, 1990

BEEF JERKY intro
ELEANOR RIGBY Revolver LP
HELP! live, under dialogue
Mal Evans interview re: tension in group
GOOD DAY SUNSHINE Revolver LP
I'M ONLY SLEEPING under dialogue
Lewisohn interview re: recording advancements
SHE SAID SHE SAID demo, fragment
experimental sounds under dialogue
'80 Sheff John interview re: She Said She Said
SHE SAID SHE SAID Revolver LP
interview continued re: interesting track
SHE LOVES YOU live, under dialogue
Lewisohn interview re: Tomorrow Never Knows
experimental sounds under dialogue
George Martin interview re: Tomorrow Never Knows
TOMORROW NEVER KNOWS Revolver LP
Indian music under dialogue
Paul interview re: using the sitar on Revolver
LOVE YOU TO Revolver LP
'70 Wenner John interview re: Got To Get You Into My Life
GOT TO GET YOU INTO MY LIFE Revolver LP
I'M LOOKING THROUGH YOU under dialogue
interview re: more popular than Jesus remark
THE WORD Rubber Soul LP
press conference interview re: what he meant

interview re: reaction to repriscussions
THINK FOR YOURSELF Revolver LP
press conference interview re: Christianity shrinking
interview re: not a practising Christian
L.A. press conference interview re: repeating Chicago remark
interview continued re: how much has tour grossed
TAXMAN Revolver LP
THINGS WE SAID TODAY live, under dialogue
interview re: I was scared and didn't want to tour
WHAT GOES ON Rubber Soul LP
A HARD DAY'S NIGHT live, under dialogue
Ray Coleman interview re: 1966 was the last tour
Brian Epstein interview re: hardest tour ever
HERE THERE AND EVERYWHERE Revolver LP
WHAT YOU GOT extro

The Lost Lennon Tapes Part 133
Show #90-32, Broadcast the Week of August 6, 1990

WHAT YOU GOT intro
IN MY LIFE under dialogue
Ray Coleman interview re: My Bonnie
MY BONNIE Tony Sheridan, with slow English intro
interview continued re: Brian heard of Beatles before
interview re: Brian told us to behave
READY TEDDY Little Richard, under dialogue
Ray Coleman interview re: Brian's strengths
MONEY BBC, under dialogue
George Martin interview re: meeting Brian
PLEASE PLEASE ME Past Masters LP
ROCK AND ROLL MUSIC under dialogue
Epstein interview re: knowing hit sounds
interview continued re: getting along with George Martin
George Martin interview re: #1 in America phone call
I WANT TO HOLD YOUR HAND Past Masters LP
ED SULLIVAN Bye Bye Birdie soundtrack LP
Ray Coleman interview re: getting them on Ed Sullivan
ALL MY LOVING Ed Sullivan 1964, also #3 #57 #160
CAN'T BUY ME LOVE live, under dialogue
Bob Ewbanks interview re: Brian not a great manager
SHE LOVES YOU Live At The Hollywood Bowl LP
Ray Coleman interview re: Brian and John's relationship
LITTLE CHILD under dialogue
interview re: Epstein not allowing war questions
CHAINS Please Please Me LP

YOU REALLY GOT A HOLD ON ME under dialogue
Philip Norman interview re: Brian looking after them
Ray Coleman interview re: Brian's homosexuality
IT WON'T BE LONG With The Beatles LP
interview re: being close to Brian
YOU'VE GOT TO HIDE YOUR LOVE AWAY under dialogue
interview re: trip to Spain with Brian
Paul interview re: John showing Brian who's boss
MISERY Please Please Me LP
CRY FOR A SHADOW under dialogue
Ray Coleman interview re: end of touring
Clive Epstein interview re: end of touring
WE CAN WORK IT OUT Past Masters LP
WITHIN YOU WITHOUT YOU under dialogue
Brian interview re: Beatles break-up rumours
A DAY IN THE LIFE under dialogue
Phillip Norman interview re: Brian's death
interview re: Brian knew what he was doing
Ray Coleman interview re: Brian lost potentially millions
interview continued re: Brian a very difficult man
Clive Epstein interview re: happiest moments for Brian
ALL YOU NEED IS LOVE Magical Mystery Tour LP
WHAT YOU GOT extro

The Lost Lennon Tapes Part 134
Show #90-33, Broadcast the Week of August 13, 1990

BEEF JERKY intro
BBC intro to
KANSAS CITY BBC, 26 December 1964, also #171
BBC intro to
EVERYBODY'S TRYING TO BE MY BABY BBC, 26 December 1964, also #118
Double Fantasy studio dialogue "you know I used to be pretty big in this business"
WATCHING THE WHEELS under dialogue
'80 Peebles John interview re: not writing
Watching The Wheels studio dialogue "we'll work out some harmony licks ... there's 2 rhythms"
WATCHING THE WHEELS rough mix
interview re: not writing and Bermuda
STARTING OVER - MY LIFE demo 4, fragment
STARTING OVER - DON'T BE CRAZY demo, fragment
STARTING OVER - THE WORST IS OVER demo, fragment
STARTING OVER demo, under dialogue
interview continued re: Starting Over
STARTING OVER Double Fantasy LP
THE LONG AND WINDING ROAD under dialogue

Julian interview re: fond memories of Paul
'80 Sheff John interview re: Hey Jude
HEY JUDE single 1968
Julian interview fragment re: warm feeling from song
interview re: exciting part of writing
REAL LOVE demo 2
WOMAN backing tracks, under dialogue
John and Yoko interview re: working together
interview continued re: sudden burst of creativity
interview continued re: Yoko never stops being creative
interview continued re: Yoko arriving in Bermuda & cow
DEAR YOKO Double Fantasy LP
WHAT YOU GOT extro

The Lost Lennon Tapes Part 135
Show #90-34, Broadcast the Week of August 20, 1990

WHAT YOU GOT intro
BBC intro to
ROLL OVER BEETHOVEN BBC, 30 March 1964, also #64, #109, #160
BBC intro to
TILL THERE WAS YOU BBC, 30 March 1964, also #171
WOMAN backing tracks, under dialogue
interview fragment re: it's a heartplay
interview re: who he's talking to
WOMAN rough mix
'80 Peebles Yoko interview re: Kiss Kiss Kiss
interview continued John & Yoko re: x-rated intro
KISS KISS KISS Double Fantasy LP
BEAUTIFUL BOY under dialogue
interview continued re: Beautiful Boy
interview re: Jimmy Nichols and better
Beautiful Boy studio dialogue re: pronunciation of better and Jimmy Nichols It's Getting Better
Beautiful Boy, vocal overdub of better
Beautiful Boy, last line, vocal overdub
BEAUTIFUL BOY Double Fantasy LP
REVOLUTION under dialogue
'70 Wenner John interview re: releasing Revolution as a single
interview continued re: mentioning Chairman Mao
REVOLUTION 1 The Beatles LP
REVOLUTION 9 fragment
GOTTA SERVE SOMEBODY Bob Dylan, under dialogue
Yoko interview re: John's reaction to Gotta Serve Somebody
SERVE YOURSELF demo 7
I'm Losing You studio dialogue intro "we just had guitars & amps ... and they just wanna dance"

I'M LOSING YOU Double Fantasy LP
WHAT YOU GOT extro

The Lost Lennon Tapes Part 136
Show #90-35, Broadcast the Week of August 27, 1990

WHAT YOU GOT intro
BBC intro to
I WANNA BE YOUR MAN BBC, 30 March 1964, also #109
BBC intro to
CAN'T BUY ME LOVE BBC, 30 March 1964, also #115
'80 Peebles John interview re: bell on Mother & Starting Over
STARTING OVER Double Fantasy LP
BEAUTIFUL BOYS Double Fantasy LP
Cleanup Time studio dialogue "uh, it's Bob Dylan ... started off as Dylan and turned into Jagger"
Cleanup Time studio dialogue "I hope I'm doing it on the overdub ... change in the vibe of the voice"
'80 Sheff John interview re: Yoko's edit in Cleanup Time
CLEANUP TIME Double Fantasy LP
EVERY MAN HAS A WOMAN WHO LOVES HIM Double Fantasy LP
I'm Moving On Yoko studio dialogue re: "I see through your jive" number of syllables
I'M MOVING ON Double Fantasy LP
BBC intro to
CAROL BBC, 16 July 1963, also #42
BBC intro
SOLDIER OF LOVE BBC, 16 July 1963, also #42
GIVE ME SOMETHING Double Fantasy LP
Yoko interview re: title of Double Fantasy
ONE LOVE Bob Marley, under dialogue
'80 Sheff John interview re: one world, one people
YES, I'M YOUR ANGEL Double Fantasy LP
interview continued re: selling a product
STARTING OVER backing tracks, under dialogue
interview continued re: how fans feel about the LP
interview continued re: praying at beginning of Hard Times Are Over
HARD TIMES ARE OVER Double Fantasy LP
WHAT YOU GOT extro

The Lost Lennon Tapes Part 137
Show #90-36, Broadcast the Week of September 3, 1990

BEEF JERKY intro
JOHNNY B. GOODE Chuck Berry, under dialogue
interview re: Toronto Rock 'N' Roll Revival
BLUE SUEDE SHOES Live Peace In Toronto LP

YOU KNOW MY NAME under dialogue
Alan White interview re: first time he met John
Eric Clapton interview re: John calling to do gig
White interview re: rehearsing set on the plane
MONEY Live Peace In Toronto LP
Jam That's All Right, Mama, under dialogue
Clapton interview re: being sick before going on
Alan White interview re: being nervous
DIZZY MISS LIZZY Live Peace In Toronto LP
YER BLUES Live Peace In Toronto LP under dialogue
White interview re: equipment problems
interview re: spontaneous show
White interview re: great learning experience
COLD TURKEY Live Peace In Toronto LP
ACROSS THE UNIVERSE David Bowie
interview re: his creative isolation
Bowie interview re: Fame session
FAME David Bowie
intro to Live Peace In Toronto LP under dialogue
'80 Peebles John interview re: being so nervous
DON'T WORRY KYOKO Live Peace in T.O. LP fragment under dialogue
Alan White interview re: philosophy of Plastic Ono Band
interview re: Capitol wouldn't put it out
interview continued re: went out as Plastic Ono Band
GIVE PEACE A CHANCE Live Peace In Toronto LP
I'M GONNA SIT RIGHT DOWN AND CRY OVER YOUE Star Club LP, under dialogue
Dezo Hoffman interview re: George's black eye
Ringo interview re: two chants going
interview continued re: George Martin didn't like his drumming
LOVE ME DO original version, Past Masters LP
George Martin interview re: main worry the material
HOW DO YOU DO IT outake, also #24
George Martin interview re: Please Please Me
PLEASE PLEASE ME single 1963
BEEF JERKY piano outake, extro

The Lost Lennon Tapes Part 138
Show #90-37, Broadcast the Week of September 10, 1990

WHAT YOU GOT intro
Walls And Bridges TV ad with Ringo, "listen to this television commer
WHAT YOU GOT intro
'74 Tom Donahue KSAN John guest DJ appearance
interview re: his favourite Walls & Bridge song
NOBODY LOVES YOU (WHEN YOU'RE DOWN AND OUT) Walls & Bridges LP

I'M SCARED fragment
interview continued re: who's on the album
OLD DIRT ROAD Walls & Bridges LP
GOING DOWN ON LOVE demo
interview continued re: title of album
'74 Dennis Elsas WNEW John guest DJ appearance
interview re: album cover
REVOLUTION 9 under dialogue
interview continued re: fascination with number 9
Jim Keltner interview re: pussy pussy
interview continued re: #9 Dream
#9 DREAM Walls & Bridges LP
'74 Tom Donahue KSAN John guest DJ appearance
interview re: Surprise Surprise
SURPRISE SURPRISE Walls & Bridges LP
interview fragment re: Elton on song
Keltner interview re: photo of John with glasses on
BLESS YOU Walls & Bridges LP
'74 Tom Donahue KSAN John guest DJ appearance
interview continued re: Ya Ya
Jim Keltner interview re: irritated he didn't play on Ya Ya
YA YA Walls & Bridges LP
Jim Keltner interview re: What You Got is a good riff
WHAT YOU GOT Walls & Bridges LP
WHATEVER GETS YOU THROUGH THE NIGHT demo, under dialogue
interview continued re: meeting Elton John
Keltner interview re: his mistake in Whatever Get You Through The Night
WHATEVER GETS YOU THROUGH THE NIGHT Walls And Bridges LP
interview continued re: his deal with Elton
I SAW HER STANDING THERE Madison Square Garden, under dialogue
John and Yoko interview re: reuniting at the concert
WHAT YOU GOT extro

The Lost Lennon Tapes Part 139
Spotlight On Abbey Road
Show #90-38, Broadcast the Week of September 17, 1990

WHAT YOU GOT intro
DON'T LET ME DOWN demo 1, also #73
LET IT BE LP under dialogue
George Martin interview re: Let It Be & Abbey Road
Let It Be LP intro to Two Of Us
'70 Wenner John interview re: putting out something else
TWO OF US under dialogue
YOU CAN'T CATCH ME Chuck Berry, under dialogue

'80 Sheff John interview re: Come Together
COME TOGETHER Abbe Road LP
THE LONG AND WINDING ROAD instrumental, under dialogue
Julian interview re: car accident in Scotland
Mark Lewisohn interview re: John's return to studio
'80 Sheff John interview re: Maxwell's Silver Hammer
MAXWELL'S SILVER HAMMER Abbey Road LP
George inteview re: his first A side
SOMETHING Abbey Road LP
interview re: we put everything we had into it
GET BACK Let It Be LP, under dialogue
'80 Sheff John interview re: montage of bits & pieces
George Martin interview re: classical form
SUN KING Abbey Road LP
ACT NATURALLY under dialogue
Ringo interview re: 2nd side of Abbey Road his favourite
George interview re: Octopus's Garden
OCTOPUS'S GARDEN Abbey Road LP
I WANT YOU (SHE'S SO HEAVY) Abbey Road LP
A DAY IN THE LIFE instrumental under dialogue
Mark Lewisohn interview re: Her Majesty
HER MAJESTY Abbey Road LP
WHAT YOU GOT extro

The Lost Lennon Tapes Part 140
Spotlight On Abbey Road Part Two
Show #90-39, Broadcast the Week of September 24, 1990

WHAT YOU GOT intro
WHAT'S THE NEW MARY JANE? outake, fragment
YES IT IS take 8
BECAUSE instrumental under dialogue
George interview re: Because his favourite song on LP
BECAUSE Abbey Road LP
Paul interview re: Because lyrics
interview re: Oh! Darling
OH! DARLING
YOU NEVER GIVE ME YOUR MONEY Abbey Road LP
George interview re: Here Comes The Sun
HERE COMES THE SUN Abbey Road LP
YESTERDAY instrumental under dialogue
George Martin interview re: good atmosphere on LP
Mark Lewisohn interview re: John contributed to medley
MEAN MR. MUSTARD demo, under dialogue
'80 Sheff John interview fragment re: Mean Mr. Mustard

MEAN MR. MUSTARD Abbey Road LP
interview continued re: Polythene Pam
POLYTHENE PAM Abbey Road LP
SHE CAME IN THROUGH THE BATHROOM WINDOW Abbey Road LP
interview fragment re: She Came In Through The Bathroom Window
Paul interview re: Golden Slumbers
GOLDEN SLUMBERS Abbey Road LP
I WANT YOU (SHE'S SO HEAVY) Abbey Road LP
COME TOGETHER under dialogue
interview re: his style of playing
CARRY THAT WEIGHT Abbey Road LP
THE END Abbey Road LP
George Martin interview re: love between John and Paul
THE END Abbey Road LP
COME TOGETHER instrumental extro

The Lost Lennon Tapes Part 141
Milestones
Show #90-40, Broadcast the Week of October 1, 1990

WHAT YOU GOT intro
John Lennon songs medley
'80 Sheff John interview re: toppermost of the poppermost
MOTHER backing tracks, under dialogue
interview continued re: his childhood
MOTHER Plastic Ono Band LP
REMEMBER under dialogue
Pete Shotton interview re: first meeting Mimi
JULIA demo 1, also #73 #**89**
interview continued re: John's relationship with Julia
MOTHER backing tracks, under dialogue
MOOVIN' AND GROOVIN' The Quarrymen 1960, under dialogue
interview continued re: researching date of fete
Beatles medley
Paul interview re: song writing collaboration
ONE AFTER 909 outake 1963
AIN'T SHE SWEET under dialogue
George Martin interview re: John & Cynthia getting married
Ray Coleman interview re: married because Cynthia pregnant
HELLO LITTLE GIRL The Beatles
Pete Shotton interview re: John & Cynthia's relationship
LOVE Plastic Ono Band LP
YOU ARE HERE under dialogue
'80 Sheff John and Yoko interview re: Indica gallery meeting
OH YOKO! under dialogue

'80 Peebles John interview re: divorce and marriage
THE BALLAD OF JOHN AND YOKO under dialogue
interview continued re: bed-in for peace idea
GIVE PEACE A CHANCE fragment
1st Mintz John interview re: Imagine, inspiration for people
IMAGINE Imagine LP
WHAT YOU GOT extro

The Lost Lennon Tapes Part 142
Milestones Part Two
Show #90-41, Broadcast the Week of October 8, 1990

WHAT YOU GOT intro
GOD demo 3, also #47
GOD coda, Plastic Ono Band LP
interview re: divorce
A HARD DAY'S NIGHT under dialogue
interview continued re: stages of relationship
DON'T LET ME DOWN Past masters LP
TICKET TO RIDE Live At The Hollywood Bowl LP
'73 Mintz John interview re: fed up with touring
WE CAN WORK IT OUT under dialogue
interview continued re: when he'd had it
I'M DOWN Past Masters LP
I'VE GOT A FEELING under dialogue
interview continued re: it was over at Let It Be
LET IT BE Past Masters LP
REVOLUTION 1 under dialogue
Immigration hearing excerpt
GIVE ME SOME TRUTH Imagine LP
Geraldo Rivera hearing statement
STAND BY ME fragment
NOWHERE MAN under dialogue
interview re: his father leaving and coming back
HEY JUDE under dialogue
interview re: Julian versus Sean
'88 Mintz Sean interview re: incompetent father
ISOLATION Plastic Ono Band LP
BEAUTIFUL BOY under dialogue
interview re: Yoko looking after business
interview continued re: mastering cooking
WATCHING THE WHEELS Double Fantasy LP
WHAT YOU GOT extro

The Lost Lennon Tapes Part 143
Show #90-42, Broadcast the Week of October 15, 1990

WHAT YOU GOT intro
1971 Dick Cavett show excerpt re:
playing Yesterday
Yoko dragon lady
married to one of the Beatles
the breakup
IT'S SO HARD Imagine LP
BACK IN THE USSR The Beatles LP
THE CHASE under dialogue
'80 Sheff John interview re: India and writing
interview continued re: Dear Prudence
DEAR PRUDENCE The Beatles LP
LONG LONG LONG under dialogue
interview continued re: Birthday
BIRTHDAY The Beatles LP
CRY BABY CRY under dialogue
Geoff Emerick interview re: arguments in studio
Ken Scott interview re: Revolution 9
REVOLUTION 9 fragment
Mintz Ringo interview re: quitting for two weeks
DON'T PASS ME BY The Beatles LP
'80 Sheff John interview re: Why Don't We Do It In The Road
WHY DON'T WE DO IT IN THE ROAD The Beatles LP
Ken Scott interview re: Savoy Truffle mix
SAVOY TRUFFLE The Beatles LP
interview continued re: each Beatle finishing his track
JULIA under dialogue
interview continued re: band only together for basic tracks
'80 Sheff John interview re: Everybody's Got Something To Hide Except For Me And My Monkey
EVERYBODY'S GOT SOMETHING TO HIDE EXCEPT FOR ME AND MY MONKEY The Beatles LP
LUCY IN THE SKY WITH DIAMONDS under dialogue
interview continued re: Happiness Is A Warm Gun
HAPPINESS IS A WARM GUN The Beatles LP
I AM THE WALRUS under dialogue
interview continued re: Glass Onion
Paul interview re: writing I Am The Walrus and Glass Onion
Ken Scott interview re: erasing snare drum
GLASS ONION The Beatles LP
WHAT YOU GOT extro

The Lost Lennon Tapes Part 144
Show #90-43, Broadcast the Week of October 22, 1990

WHAT YOU GOT intro
ROCKY RACCOON The Beatles LP
YER BLUES The Beatles LP
MOTHER NATURE'S SON under dialogue
interview re: knowing more about recording
'80 Sheff John interview re: Sexy Sadie
SEXY SADIE The Beatles LP
interview continued re: The Coninuing Story Of Bungalow Bill
THE CONTINUING STORY OF BUNGALOW BILL The Beatles LP
WHILE MY GUITAR GENTLY WEEPS The Beatles LP
OB-LA-DI OB-LA-DA The Beatles LP
'80 Sheff John interview re: I'm So Tired
HONEY PIE under dialogue
'69 Ken Zelig John interview re: returning MBE
REVOLUTION 1 The Beatles LP
interview re: Paul's Blackbird
BLACKBIRD The Beatles LP
Ken Scott interview re: nearly getting fired
PIGGIES The Beatles LP
'80 Sheff John interview re: Manson and Helter Skelter
HELTER SKELTER The Beatles LP
GOOD NIGHT The Beatles LP
WHAT YOU GOT extro

The Lost Lennon Tapes Part 145
Show #90-44, Broadcast the Week of October 29, 1990

WHAT YOU GOT intro
'63 Paul interview re: losing Liverpool speech
SHE LOVES YOU single 1963
Dezo Hoffman interview re: Royal Variety
intro to Royal Variety Show 1963
TWIST AND SHOUT Please Please Me LP
Paul interview re: turning down future shows
BABY YOU'RE A RICH MAN under dialogue
John and Paul interview re: the monarchy
TILL THERE WAS YOU Please Please Me LP
BE MY BABY The Ronnettes, under dialogue
Epstein interview re: breaking into the U.S.
I WANT TO HOLD YOUR HAND single 1964
REELIN' & ROCKIN' Chuck Berry, under dialogue
Bill Harry interview re: 1st impression of John

THREE COOL CATS Decca Sessions LP
Alan Williams interview re: painting toilets
MONEY Decca Sessions LP
ROCK AND ROLL MUSIC under dialogue
Klaus Voorman interview re: fights and Astrid
THANK YOU GIRL single 1963
Paul interview re: Stu quitting and bass
I SAW HER STANDING There Please Please Me LP
sitar under dialogue
'60s George interview re: sitar interest
'80 Sheff John interview re: Norwegian Wood sitar
NORWEGIAN WOOD Rubber Soul LP
CATHY'S CLOWN improv
YOU SEND ME improv
STAND BY ME Rock 'N' Roll LP
WHAT YOU GOT extro

The Lost Lennon Tapes Part 146
Censorship
Show #90-45, Broadcast the Week of November 5, 1990

WHAT YOU GOT intro
BBC Beatles edited intro to
SHE'S A WOMAN BBC, 26 November 1964, also #72
BBC intro to
I FEEL FINE BBC, 12 November 1964, also #72
BBC extro
A DAY IN THE LIFE Sgt. Pepper's LP
interview fragment re: knickers
I AM THE WALRUS Magical Mystery Tour LP
YOU CAN'T DO THAT under dialogue
interview fragment re: banning The Ballad Of John And Yoko
THE BALLAD OF JOHN AND YOKO single 1969
Paul interview re: banning Give Ireland Back To The Irish
GIVE IRELAND BACK TO THE IRISH Paul
Howard Cosell John interview re: words can't kill you
John and Yoko int re: mastication versus masturbation
GIVE PEACE A CHANCE fragment
interview re: Woman Is The Nigger Of The World on Dick Cavett
Dick Cavett Show intro to
WOMAN IS THE NIGGER OF THE WORLD Dick Cavett Show 1972
TWO VIRGINS under dialogue
'70 Wenner John interview re: interested in Yoko as an artist
interview continued re: making Two Virgins
interview re: releasing Two Virgins

'70 Wenner John interview re: taking cover photo
Paul interview re: banning Hi Hi Hi
HI HI HI single 1972
'80 Peebles John and Yoko interview re: Cold Turkey
COLD TURKEY demo 2, also #23
WHAT YOU GOT extro

The Lost Lennon Tapes Part 147
Show #90-46, Broadcast the Week of November 12, 1990

WHAT YOU GOT intro
'71 Dick Cavett appearance
interview re: ordering in a restaurant
IT'S SO HARD Imagine LP
Pete Best interview re: 1st trip to Hamburg
Alan Williams interview re: wild in Hamburg
HIPPY SHAKE Star Club LP
Ray Coleman interview re: honed their skills
Paul interview re: like circus barkers
ROLL OVER BEETHOVEN Star Club LP
Pete Best interview re: moving to Top Ten
SWEET LITTLE SIXTEEN Star Club LP
'76 Mintz John interview re: should I continue
TWIST AND SHOUT Star Club LP
'76 Mintz Ringo interview re: money & audience in Hamburg
LITTLE QUEENIE Star Club LP
Tony Sheridan interview re: needing a band & Hamburg
MY BONNIE Tony Sheridan, with intro
'71 Takahiro Imura J/Y intre: happenings on stage
Billy Preston interview re: playing in Hamburg
LONG TALL SALLY Past Masters LP
Little Richard interview re: meeting the Beatles & woo
interview re: he exagerates, we had down by then
LUCILLE Little Richard
interview continued re: Epstein brought him to Hamburg
KANSAS CITY Star Club LP
'80 interview re: hard to separate fact from fiction
George interview re: Hamburg like an apprenticeship
REMINISCING Star Club LP
WHAT YOU GOT extro

The Lost Lennon Tapes Part 148
The Musicians Who Influenced The Beatles
Show #90-47, Broadcast the Week of November 19, 1990

WHAT YOU GOT intro
TOO MUCH MONKEY BUSINESS improv
John intro to Chuck Berry on Mike Douglas
MEMPHIS TENNESSEE Mike Douglas Show 1972, also #9
BROWN EYED HANDSOME MAN/GET BACK improv, also #15
ROCK ISLAND LINE improv 2, also #5
Mike Douglas show interview re: American black music
ROLL OVER BEETHOVEN Chuck Berry, under dialogue
interview continued re: U.S. rock 'n' roll influences
BABY LET'S PLAY HOUSE Elvis Presley
Paul interview re: Elvis was really it
HEARTBREAK HOTEL Elvis Presley
NOT FADE AWAY Buddy Holly, under dialogue
Paul interview re: buying Buddy Holly's catalogue
THAT'LL BE THE DAY Buddy Holly
Paul interview re: I was just a fan of Buddy's
Beatles interview re: favourite groups, the Animals
I'M CRYING The Animals, under dialogue
HOUSE OF THE RISING SUN The Animals
medley of Phil Ochs songs
TWIST AND SHOUT Live At The Hollywood Bowl LP, under dialogue
I SHOULD HAVE KNOWN BETTER Phil Ochs and Eric Anderson
ATTICA STATE live, under dialogue
Ray Coleman interview re: John became a folk singer
Phil Ochs song, under dialogue
CHORDS OF FAME Phil Ochs Ann Arbor '71, John slide
EVERYBODY'S TRYING TO BE MY BABY Carl Perkins, under dialogue
Paul Beatles interview re: country and western influence
MATCHBOX Past Masters LP
Beatles interview re: influential artists like Sophie Tucker
I KNOW THERE'S AN ANSWER The Beach Boys, under dialogue
Paul interview re: influence of Pet Sounds
LOVELY RITA Sgt. Peppers LP
WHAT YOU GOT extro

The Lost Lennon Tapes Part 149
Fans
Show #90-48, Broadcast the Week of November 26, 1990

WHAT YOU GOT intro
'63 London airport fan interviews
fan interviews continued
YOU REALLY GOT A HOLD ON ME With The Beatles LP
George Martin interview re: saturation in New York
WABC, IT WON'T BE LONG station I.D.
interview continued re: Ringo on radio in NY
'64 New York radio clip of Ringo
George interview re: we're natural
DO YOU WANT TO KNOW A SECRET Please Please Me LP
'64 KLIF Beatles are coming excerpt
IT WON'T BE LONG With The Beatles LP
Mal Evans interview re: Texas airport
Paul interview re: Milwakee fans
YOU CAN'T DO THAT under dialogue
Derek Taylor interview re: Chicago news story
interview continued re: announcing arrivals
FROM ME TO YOU Past Masters LP
WABC Beatles I Saw Her Standing There station I.D.
Ringo interview re: girl throwing hook up to balcony
Paul interview re: fearing for fans safety
CAN'T BUY ME LOVE A Hard Day's Night LP
Paul interview re: being touched by fan
Mal Evans interview re: fans very inventive
CHAINS under dialogue
interview continued re: Beatles turned into caged animals
Paul interview re: laughing in an ambulance
interview continued re: dressing up as policemen
YOU WON'T SEE ME Rubber Soul LP
PLEASE MR. POSTMAN under dialogue
Cynthia & Dorothy Row read fan letters
P.S. I LOVE YOU Past Masters LP
John and Ringo interview re: genuine fans
BOYS under dialogue
Mrs. Harrison interview re: fans writing to her
Paul interview re: his Dad related to a Beatle
John & Ringo interview re: reporters conning families
NO REPLY Beatles For Sale LP
'64 WABC All My Loving station I.D.
George interview re: we don't have a private life anymore
Ringo interview re: fan on the beach
WHAT GOES ON Rubber Soul LP

I'LL GET YOU under dialogue
Paul interview re: girl sending secret messages
interview continued re: rich and famous get close to them
Ringo interview re: fan club secretaries appreciated
THANK YOU GIRL The Beatles Second Album LP
WHAT YOU GOT extro

The Lost Lennon Tapes Part 150
Show #90-49, Broadcast the Week of December 3, 1990

WHAT YOU GOT intro
LA MER/BLUE MOON/YOUNG LOVE French parody, also #15
THE BOAT SONG demo, also #185
HELP ME TO HELP MYSELF demo 1, takes 2, 3, also #180, #217
I PROMISE demo, also #8, #209
MAKE LOVE NOT WAR demo, Mnd Games, also #8, #93, #209, fragment
MIND GAMES Mind Games LP
CAN'T BUY ME LOVE Paul, Tripping The Live Fantastic LP, under dialogue
Paul interview re: singing Beatles songs again
SGT. PEPPER'S LONELY HEARTS CLUB BAND Paul, Tripping The Live Fantastic LP
interview continued re: hearing his first song on the radio
LOVE ME DO Past Masters LP
A DAY IN THE LIFE under dialogue
interview continued re: John's death and Paul bashing
THINGS WE SAID TODAY Paul, Tripping The Live Fantastic LP
interview continued re: John bad mouthing him
HEY JUDE Paul, Tripping The Live Fantastic LP
WHAT YOU GOT extro

The Lost Lennon Tapes Part 151
Show #90-50, Broadcast the Week of December 10, 1990

WHAT YOU GOT intro
YESTERDAY Help! LP
interview re: learning studio technique
George Martin interview re: couldn't relax till Rubber Soul
BABY LET'S PLAY HOUSE Elvis, under dialogue
'80 Sheff John interview re: Run For Your Life
RUN FOR YOUR LIFE Rubber Soul LP
RESPECT Otis Redding, under dialogue
DRIVE MY CAR Rubber Soul LP
interview continued re: Day Tripper
DAY TRIPPER Past Masters LP
interview continued re: Norwegian Wood

FOURTH TIME AROUND Bob Dylan, fragment
NORWEGIAN WOOD Rubber Soul LP
interview continued re: Rubber Soul title
Paul interview fragment re: Rubber Soul title
'80 Sheff John interview re: Nowhere Man
interview re: writing Nowhere Man
NOWHERE MAN Rubber Soul LP
IN MY LIFE fragment, solo at half speed
IN MY LIFE Rubber Soul LP
'80 Sheff John interview re: In My Life
Michelle guitar practice, fragment
interview continued re: Michelle
MICHELLE Rubber Soul LP
WHAT GOES ON Rubber Soul LP
THINK FOR YOURSELF Rubber Soul LP
WAIT Rubber Soul LP
interview continued re: Girl
GIRL Rubber Soul LP
THE WORD Rubber Soul LP
WHAT YOU GOT extro

The Lost Lennon Tapes Part 152
Show #90-51, Broadcast the Week of December 17, 1990

CHRISTMAS TIME IS HERE AGAIN intro
RUDOLPH THE RED-NOSED REGGAE Paul, under dialogue
Paul interview re: dad & cigars, John & nativity scene
WONDERFUL CHRISTMASTIME Paul
BE-BOP-A-LULA Star Club LP
EVERYWHERE IT'S CHRISTMAS 1966 Christmas record
'63 Christmas record: John & Paul speeches
I WANT TO HOLD YOUR HAND Past Masters LP
'64 Christmas record: Paul & John speeches
I FEEL FINE Past Masters LP
HELP! under dialogue
'65 Christmas record: what we've done to tried to please
'66 Christmas record: Podgey & Jasper
AND YOUR BIRD CAN SING Revolver LP
FLYING under dialogue
'67 Christmas record: BBC to gradually injured
I AM THE WALRUS Magical Mystery Tour EP
'68 Christmas record: Ringo to George segment
REVOLUTION Past Masters LP
'69 Christmas record: George happy Xmas to Ringo Merry Xmas
'69 Christmas record: John greeting to take two

'69 Christmas record continued under dialogue
'80 Peebles John interview re: War Is Over poster
HAPPY XMAS rough mix, no strings or choir
'65 Christmas record fragment: Johnny Rhythm goodnight
WHAT YOU GOT extro

The Lost Lennon Tapes Part 153
The Forces Behind The Beatles Break-Up
Show #90-52, Broadcast the Week of December 24, 1990

SEA OF TIME intro
COME TOGETHER under dialogue
'70 Wenner John interview re: collapsed after Brian died
interview continued re: disintegration on White album
OB-LA-DI OB-LA-DA The Beatles LP
interview continued re: choosing Beatles or Yoko
REAL LOVE Imagine: John Lennon Soundtrack LP
MONEY under dialogue
interview continued re: the Apple Boutique
THERE'S A PLACE Please Please Me LP
MAGICAL MYSTERY TOUR under dialogue
Pete Shotton interview re: managing Apple Boutique
YOU CAN'T DO THAT under dialogue
'70 Wenner John interview re: giving everything away
SHE CAME IN THROUGH THE BATHROOM WINDOW Abbey Road LP
WITHIN YOU WITHOUT YOU under dialogue
interview continued re: leaving the Maharishi's camp
SEXIE SADIE The Beatles LP
New York City press conference fragment announcing Apple
'70 Wenner John interview re: meeting Allen Klein
interview continued re: writing letter to EMI
YOU NEVER GIVE ME YOUR MONEY Abbey Road LP
TWO OF US under dialogue
Paul interview re: first meeting with Klein
WE CAN WORK IT OUT Past Masters LP
'70 Wenner John interview re: Eastman abusing Klein
Paul interview re: John breaking the group up
GET BACK Let It Be LP
interview continued re: suing the Beatles
IT'S ALL TOO MUCH Yellow Submarine LP
I ME MINE under dialogue
Paul interview re: bubble bursts question
HELLO GOODBYE Magical Mystery Tour LP
WHAT YOU GOT extro

The Lost Lennon Tapes Part 154
New Beginnings
Show #91-01, Broadcast the Week of December 31, 1990

WHAT YOU GOT intro
HOLD ON under dialogue
Mintz John interview re: reaction to breakup
LOVE IN THE OPEN AIR Paul, under dialogue
Paul interview re: McCartney LP
OO YOU Paul, under dialogue
MAYBE I'M AMAZED Paul
RED LADY TOO George, under dialogue
DREAM SCENE George, under dialogue
AWAITING ON YOU ALL George
interview re: stealing My Sweet Lord
MY SWEET LORD George
SENTIMENTAL JOURNEY Ringo, under dialogue
EARLY 1970 Ringo
TWO VIRGINS under dialogue
'70 Wenner John interview re: wanting entire album to himself
Smith John & Yoko interview re: playing and singing together
interview re: no overdubbing, bell before Mother
MOTHER demo, also #70
'80 Peebles John and Yoko interview re: P.O.B. LP reviews
interview continued re: remembering digs better than praise
GOD Plastic Ono Band LP
REMEMBER under dialogue
Tom Synder John interview re: not changing their accents
GIVE PEACE A CHANCE under dialogue
interview re: writing Give Peace A Chance
WORKING CLASS HERO Plastic Ono Band LP
interview re: favourite track on Plastic Ono Band LP
LOVE demo, also #77
interview re: being technical, cinema verité musician
I FOUND OUT Plastic Ono Band LP
INSTANT KARMA single 1970
WHAT YOU GOT extro

The Lost Lennon Tapes Part 155
Show #91-02, Broadcast the Week of January 7, 1991

WHAT YOU GOT intro
LOOK AT ME Plastic Ono Band LP
Paul and John interview re: meeting
I CALL YOUR NAME under dialogue

Paul interview re: writing with John
interview re: writing with Paul
I SAW HER STANDING THERE Please Please Me LP
Paul interview re: beauty queen line
Paul interview re: discovering next beat
PLEASE PLEASE ME Please Please Me LP
'65 Paul and John interview re: writing
ALL SHOOK UP Elvis Presley, under dialogue
interview re: yeah yeahs
SHE LOVES YOU Past Masters LP
interview re: writing more in early days
interview re: physical separation
Pete Shotton interview re: competition
ANY TIME AT ALL With The Beatles LP
'80 Sheff John interview re: writing Eleanor Rigby
Paul interview re: disputing John's claim
ELEANOR RIGBY Revolver LP
'80 Sheff John interview re: Getting Better
Paul interview re: Getting Bettery
GETTING BETTER Sgt. Pepper's LP
George Martin interview re: John and Paul arguments
MISERY Please Please Me LP
How Do You Sleep? backing tracks, under dialogue
'73 Mintz John interview re: rivalry with Paul
How Do You Sleep? Imagine LP
'80 Peebles John interview over re: used resentment against P.
Paul interview re: only a couple of months of bitterness
TOO MANY PEOPLE Paul
'76 Mintz John interview re: writing songs in ten minutes
TWIST AND SHOUT Please Please Me LP
WHAT YOU GOT extro

The Lost Lennon Tapes Part 156
The Beatles Versus The Rolling Stones
Show #91-03, Broadcast the Week of January 14, 1991

WHAT YOU GOT intro
'74 Dennis Elsas WNEW John guest DJ appearance
John reads weather report
John tells story of I Wanna Be Your Man
I WANNA BE YOUR MAN The Rolling Stones
I WANNA BE YOUR MAN With The Beatles LP
interview continued re: being close to the Stones
DIZZY MISS LIZZY Help LP!
Rolling Stones song under dialogue

interview continued re: hanging out together
'70 Wenner John interview re: disintegration of Brian Jones
SATISFACTION The Rolling Stones
interview continued re: Paul and Ringo underrated
SGT. PEPPER'S LONELY HEARTS CLUB BAND/A LITTLE HELP FROM MY FRIENDS Sgt. Pepper's LP
GOMPER The Rolling Stones, under dialogue
interview continued re: Stones copying Beatles
HONKY TONK WOMAN The Rolling Stones
'74 Dennis Elsas WNEW John guest DJ appearance
interview re: jamming with Mick in L.A.
TOO MANY COOKS John produced, also #173 released in 2007 on THE VERY BEST OF MICK JAGGER
Jam Nicky Hopkins piano, under dialogue
Nicky Hopkins interview re: We Love You sessions
WE LOVE YOU The Rolling Stones
YER BLUES Rock 'N' Roll Circus, fragment, also #27, #127
'76 Mintz John interview re: Beatle life
MEMORIES demo 2, also #108
WHAT YOU GOT extro

The Lost Lennon Tapes Part 157
Show #91-04, Broadcast the Week of January 21, 1991

WHAT YOU GOT intro
I WANT YOU improv, John and Yoko - not ABBEY ROAD version
BEING FOR THE BENEFIT OF MR. KITE! Sg. Pepper's LP
'76 Mal Evans interview re: getting close to the Beatles
interview continued re: no fans in sight when he arrived
A HARD DAY'S NIGHT Live At The Hollywood Bowl LP
interview continued re: contribution to Here, There And Everywhere
HERE THERE AND EVERYWHERE Revolver LP
interview continued re: contributing to Fixing A Hole
FIXING A HOLE Sgt. Pepper's LP
interview continued re: not giving him credit on songs
CARRY ON The Iveys, under dialogue
interview continued re: discovering The Iveys
NO MATTER WHAT Badfinger
'80 Peebles John interview re: remembering Saturday Club
THREE COOL CATS Decca Sessions LP
Mal Evans interview re: making a pick for Elvis
Help! soundtrack fragment: Mal and white cliffs of Dover
interview continued re: always included in the family
interview continued re: contribution to Let It Be
LET IT BE Past Masters LP
interview fragment continued re: wanting to be an entertainer
NOTHING FROM NOTHING Billy Preston, under dialogue

Billy Preston interview re: first meeting the Beatles
interview continued re: watching them from the wings
interview continued re: sitting in with the Beatles on Let It Be
DIG A PONY Let It Be LP
I'VE GOT A FEELING under dialogue
'76 Mintz John interview re: seeing Paul, any regrets
REMEMBER Plastic Ono Band LP
WHAT YOU GOT extro

The Lost Lennon Tapes Part 158
Show #91-05, Broadcast the Week of January 28, 1991

WHAT YOU GOT intro
ROCK AND ROLL MUSIC Beatles For Sale LP
interview re: thought we were the best
Paul interview re: stealing records at parties
ROCK AROUND THE CLOCK Bill Haley, under dialogue
interview re: not overwhelmed by Haley
JOHNNY B. GOODE Chuck Berry fades to
ROLL OVER BEETHOVEN With The Beatles
Paul interview re: physically moved by rock n roll
TWENTY FLIGHT ROCK Paul, Tripping The Live Fantastic LP
interview continued re: doing impressions
interview re: going along with music
BE-BOP-A-LULA Gene Vincent, under dialogue
'70 interview re: old songs avante guarde
'80 Peebles John interview re: being an old rocker
YOU CAN'T CATCH ME alternate take
Tony King interview re: sessions were wild
interview re: studio's burnt down
Jimmy Iovine interview re: Phil & Watergate tapes
PEGGY SUE under dialogue
'80 Sheff John interview re: salvaging the album
BE-BOP-A-LULA Rock 'N' Roll LP
BE MY BABY rough mix, ROOTS LP mix, also #<u>77</u>, #216
'80 Sheff John interview re: Ain't That A Shame, first song learned
AIN'T THAT A SHAME Rock 'N' Roll LP
Jimmy Iovine interview re: incredible working with John & Phil
READY TEDDY Little Richard, under dialogue
Jürgen Vollmer interview re: taking Rock 'N' Roll cover photo
interview continued re: leather jacket
SLIPPIN' AND SLIDIN' Rock 'N' Roll LP
interview re: saying farewell at end of album
JUST BECAUSE Rock 'N' Roll LP
STARTING OVER under dialogue

interview re: not listening to rock 'n' roll for years
I'M LOSING YOU alternate take, w/Cheap Trick's Rick Neilsen
WHAT YOU GOT extro

The Lost Lennon Tapes Part 159
The Beatles Conquer The Colonies Part One
Show #91-06, Broadcast the Week of February 4, 1991

WHAT YOU GOT intro
IT WON'T BE LONG With The Beatles LP
Murrary The K interview re: first playing Beatles
Sid Bernstein interview re: Kennedy death & Beatles
Phillip Norman interview re: release of I Want To Hold Your Hand
I WANT TO HOLD YOUR HAND Past Masters LP
Fred Martin interview re: putting out promo paper
ASK ME WHY Please Please Me LP
'76 Mintz Ringo interview re: New York like an octopus
'64 New York airport scene report
'64 New York reporter fan interview re: their style
BABY IT'S YOU Please Please Me LP
'64 NY press conference fragment re: shutup, sing something
MONEY under dialogue
New York reporter interview re: airport, hair question
'64 New York press conference fragment re: haircut question
reporter interview continued re: they were marvelous
BOYS With Please Please Me LP
Murray The K interview re: meeting George at the airport
interview continued re: getting in to meet them
'64 Murray The K Beatles record introduction
LOVE ME DO Past Masters LP
'76 Mintz Ringo interview re: meeting Ed Sullivan in 1963
press conference fragment re: the name Beatles, meeting fans
'64 Brian Mathews interview fragment re: America is wild
A TASTE OF HONEY Please Please Me LP
'64 Ed Sullivan Beatles introduction
ALL MY LOVING Ed Sullivan 1964, also #3, #57, #133
interview re: reads 1964 Newsweek review
SHE LOVES YOU Ed Sullivan 1964, also #57
Paul interview re: developed their act & waiting for number 1
'64 Ed Sullivan Beatles introduction
I SAW HER STANDING THERE Ed Sullivan 1964, also #57, #110
Ed Sullivan extro re: appreciation of police
Mintz Rinto interview re: press came to kill us
PLEASE PLEASE ME Please Please Me LP
interview re: being touched and pawed at British Embassy

Fred Martin interview re: train ride back to New York
P.S. I LOVE YOU Please Please Me LP
WHAT YOU GOT extro

The Lost Lennon Tapes Part 160
The Beatles Conquer The Colonies Part Two
Show #91-07, Broadcast the Week of February 11, 1991

WHAT YOU GOT intro
'64 George interview re: Sullivan shows & the press
BAD BOY under dialogue
Fred Martin interview re: antics on train
ROLL OVER BEETHOVEN BBC, 30 March 1964, also #64, #109, #135
Sid Bernstein interview re: Carnegie Hall show
Fred Martin interview re: couldn't get tickets
interview continued re: you could hear the show
TILL THERE WAS YOU Please Please Me LP
'64 Miami airport arrival radio report
HOLD ME TIGHT With The Beatles LP
fan interview re: touching the Beatles
'64 reporter interview re: hotel scene
LITTLE CHILD With The Beatles LP
George '64 Miami radio interview re: reception
DO YOU WANT TO KNOW A SECRET Please Please Me LP
interview continued re: name Beatles, special girl
DEVIL IN HER HEART With The Beatles LP
THIS BOY Ed Sullivan 1964
'64 George interview re: difference between U.S. and U.K.
THERE'S A PLACE Please Please Me LP
'64 Miami Beatles interview re: George, Paul & John thanks
SHE LOVES YOU Past Masters LP
interviews continued re: Ringo thanks
ALL MY LOVING With The Beatles LP
Epstein interview re: timing could not have been more right
Beatles interviews re: we'll be making a film
A HARD DAY'S NIGHT A Hard Day's Night LP
Woman vocal overdub rehearsal - starts "I know you understand...", also #189
studio dialogue re: double track certain words, also #189
Woman overdub - starts "tell you again", "GIRL", "Yeah Yeah", "double tracking", "dub my & your"
GIRL comment also #22
WOMAN dubbing over take
WHAT YOU GOT extro

The Lost Lennon Tapes Part 161
The Beatles Live On The BBC Part One
Show #91-08, Broadcast the Week of February 18, 1991

WHAT YOU GOT intro
Peter Pilbeam interview re: listening to groups
DREAM BABY BBC 8 March 1962, fragment, also #42, #70, #106,
SIDE BY SIDE BBC, various
TOO MUCH MONKEY BUSINESS BBC, 24 Jun 1963
THANK YOU GIRL BBC, 13 May 1963
FROM ME TO YOU BBC, April 1963
I'LL BE ON MY WAY BBC, 24 June 1963, also #110
Brian Matthew interview re: Saturday Club
I SAW HER STANDING THERE BBC, 5 October 1963
Bernie Andrews interview re: recording sessions
SOME OTHER GUY BBC, 23 June 1963
A TASTE OF HONEY BBC, 23 June 1963
Terry Henebery interview re: recording the series
POP GO THE BEATLES BBC, 18 June 1963
A SHOT OF RHYTHM AND BLUES BBC, 18 June 1963, also #81
I GOT TO FIND MY BABY BBC, 11 June 1963, also #64
HAPPY BIRTHDAY SATURDAY CLUB BBC, 5 October 1963, also #89
I'LL GET YOU BBC, 5 October 1963
Lee Peters intro to
YOUNG BLOOD BBC, 11 June 1963
SURE TO FALL BBC, 18 June 1963
BBC intro to
ANNA BBC, 25 June 1963
BBC intro to
TWIST AND SHOUT BBC, 25 June 1963
DEAR YOKO vocal overdub
DEAR YOKO rough mix
WHAT YOU GOT extro

The Lost Lennon Tapes Part 162
George Harrison's 48th Birthday
Show #91-09, Broadcast the Week of February 25, 1991

WHAT YOU GOT intro
ALL THOSE YEARS AGO under dialogue
George interview re: being kicked out of Germany
CRACKERBOX PALACE George
George speaks German
guitar improv
SIE LIEBT DICH single 1964

CRY FOR A SHADDOW under dialogue
George interview re: singing today versus old days
GOT MY MIND SET ON YOU George
INSTANT KARMA under dialogue
interview continued re: doing Instant Karma single
WHAT IS LIFE George
Alistair Taylor interview re: George deep and gentle
BANGLA DESH George
HERE COMES THE SUN under dialogue
George interview re: HandMade films arty
ALWAYS LOOK ON THE BRIGHT SIDE OF LIFE Monty Python, under dialogue
SMOKE ON THE WATER LIVE Deep Purple, under dialogue
interview continued re: playing with Deep Purple in Sydney
MATCHBOX Carl Perkins, under dialogue
interview continued re: doing Carl Perkins show
EVERYBODY'S TRYING TO BE MY BABY Beatles For Sale LP
George press conference interview re: kind of girl you like
SOMETHING Abbey Road LP
I AM THE WALRUS under dialogue
George interview re: favourite fab tunes and When We Was Fab
interview continued re: original Walrus cello players
interview continued re: using Ringo
WHEN WE WAS FAB George
interview continued re: George's original Gretsch
interview continued re: first meeting Eric Clapton
WHILE MY GUITAR GENTLY WEEPS The Beatles LP
interview continued re: doesn't see himself as a musician
BLOW AWAY George
WHAT YOU GOT extro

The Lost Lennon Tapes Part 163
Show #91-10, Broadcast the Week of March 4, 1991

WHAT YOU GOT intro
MEMORIES - WATCHING THE WHEELS demo 2, fades to
WATCHING THE WHEELS Double Fantasy LP
DOCTOR ROBERT Revolver LP
interview re: America always needed another cover
WE CAN WORK IT OUT under dialogue
interview re: butcher cover
AND YOUR BIRD CAN SING Revolver LP
interview re: 14 songs on the albums
ACT NATURALLY under dialogue
interview re: lyrics to Yesterday
YESTERDAY piano version, under dialogue

Paul interview re: Yesterday on planes
medley of Yesterday cover versions
Paul interview re: writing Yesterday
YESTERDAY Help! LP
Paul interview fragment re: Broad Street and Yesterday
'64 Murray The K I Sat Belonely reading by John
Thank you John's speech from Foyle's Literary Luncheon
CAN'T BUY ME LOVE A Hard Day's Night LP
'65 John interview re: Spaniard title
interview continued re: content of book
WHAT GOES ON Rubber Soul LP
'65 BBC The National Health Cow reading by John
THE WORD Rubber Soul LP
interview re: writing books
LUCY IN THE SKY WITH DIAMONDS Sgt. Pepper's LP
interview re: writing simply
LOVE Plastic Ono Band LP
interview re: likes Across The Universe
ACROSS THE UNIVERSE Past Masters LP
interview re: clarity of expression
CLEANUP TIME Double Fantasy LP
WHAT YOU GOT extro

The Lost Lennon Tapes Part 164
World Peace
Show #91-11, Broadcast the Week of March 11, 1991

WHAT YOU GOT intro
GIVE PEACE A CHANCE Peace Choir
ALL YOU NEED IS LOVE under dialogue
interview re: doing the bed-in
intererview re: press thinking we'd be naked in bed
THE BALLAD OF JOHN AND YOKO Past Masters LP
interview re: commercial for peace
interview continued re: the press loved it
#9 DREAM Walls And Bridges LP
'69 John & Yoko London New Year's peace message
GET IT TOGETHER demo, London, New Year's message 1969 - erroneously credited to Mont. bed-in
'80 Peebles John interview re: doing the bed-in in Montreal
GIVE PEACE A CHANCE fragment
interview continued re: not on front page, humour
'69 bed-in interview re: everybody's responsibility
I DON'T WANNA BE A SOLDIER Imagine LP
IMAGINE fragment
interview re: conceiving the idea first

IMAGINE (REHEARSAL) Imagine: John Lennon Soundtrack LP
IMAGINE: J.L. excerpt U.S. interview re: what do you know
BLESS YOU Walls And Bridges LP
'69 bed-in phone call re: we're only talking to press
xylophone under dialogue
POWER TO THE PEOPLE alternate take
'69 bed-in interview re: there are many ways of protesting
interview re: Mrs. Higgins staying in bed for peace
interview re: I'm as violent as the next man
ONLY PEOPLE alternate take
MAKE LOVE NOT WAR demo, under dialogue
interview re: Mind Games
MIND GAMES alternate version
WHAT YOU GOT extro

The Lost Lennon Tapes Part 165
Mind Games
Show #91-12, Broadcast the Week of March 18, 1991

WHAT YOU GOT intro
WHATEVER GETS YOU THROUGH THE NIGHT demo 1, intro longer, also #<u>12</u>, #216
TOMRROW NEVER KNOWS under dialogue
'73 Mintz John interview re: taking acid as a cure
SHE SAID SHE SAID Revolver LP
THE INNER LIGHT under dialogue
'67 Maharishi interview re: meditation & Beatles
GIVE ME SOME TRUTH Imagine LP
THE HAPPY RISHIKESH SONG demo, under dialogue
interview re: stunned by Brian's death
'67 interview re: Brian's death
'70 Wenner John interview re: he told us to smile
MAGICAL MYSTERY TOUR Magical Mystery Tour EP
SEXY SADIE under dialogue
'67 John and Paul interview re: maharishi
interview continued re: we reflect what we do
THE MAHARISHI SONG demo, fragment
interview continued re: writing in maharishi's camp
YER BLUES The Beatles LP
ISOLATION under dialogue
Mrs. Janov interview re: Primal Scream therapy
HOW under dialogue
interview re: Primal Scream book
LOOK AT ME Plastic Ono Band LP
interview re: going through the therapy
MOTHER Plastic Ono Band LP

'80 Sheff John interview re: answers are temporary escape
DEAR JOHN demo, last song, a few extra bars in fade out, also #12, #213
SHE RUNS THEM ROUND IN CIRCLES - BEAUTIFUL BOY demo
WHAT YOU GOT extro

The Lost Lennon Tapes Part 166
The Beatles Live On The BBC Part Two
Show #91-13, Broadcast the Week of March 25, 1991

WHAT YOU GOT intro
BBC intro to
NOTHIN' SHAKIN' BUT THE LEAVES ON THE TREES BBC, 23 July 1963
SO HOW COME BBC, 23 July 1963, also #88
THE HIPPY SHAKE BBC, 30 July 1963
TO KNOW HER IS TO LOVE HER BBC, 6 August 1963
BBC intro to
MATCHBOX BBC, 30 July 1963, also #122
BBC intro to
PLEASE MR. POSTMAN BBC, 30 July 1963
BBC intro to
DO YOU WANT TO KNOW A SECRET BBC, 30 July 1963
BBC intro to
THE HONEYMOON SONG BBC, 6 August 1963, also #73
PLEASE PLEASE ME BBC, 13 August 1963
BBC intro to
I GOT A WOMAN BBC, 13 August 1963
BBC intro to
CHAINS BBC, 17 September 1963
YOU REALLY GOT A HOLD ON ME BBC, 17 September 1963
NON STOP POP Beatles interview, August 1963
HONEY DON'T BBC, 3 September 1963, John vocal
Goodbye BBC extro
FROM US TO YOU BBC, various dates, also #88
WHIT MONDAY TO YOU BBC, 18 May 1964
BBC intro to
I FORGOT TO REMEMBER TO FORGET BBC, 18 May 1964
BBC extro
YOU CAN'T DO THAT BBC, 4 April 1964
1964 interview with Brian Matthew
SURE TO FALL BBC, April 4 1964
TOP GEAR promo
LONG TALL SALLY BBC, 16 July 1964, also #69
WHAT YOU GOT extro

The Lost Lennon Tapes Part 167
Beatles Rumours
Show #91-14, Broadcast the Week of April 1, 1991

DEVIL'S RADIO George/GLASS ONION intro
DO YOU WANT TO KNOW A SECRET Please Please Me LP
interview re: Bad To Me and holiday in Spain
BAD TO ME Billy J. Kramer
interview continued re: being close to Brian
'64 Larry Kane John interview fragment re: Cynthia
interview continued re: rumours
ACT NATURALLY Help! LP
'64 Larry Kane Ringo interview re: Ann Margaret
ANOTHER GIRL Help! LP
interview continued Ringo & John re: marriage rumours
I FEEL FINE Past Masters LP
interview re: why people gossip
'73 Mintz John interview re: Beatles reunion
GOD Plastic Ono Band LP
COME TOGETHER under dialogue
Paul interview re: Abbey Road cover and death rumour
GOLDEN SLUMBERS/CARRY THAT WEIGHT/THE END Abbey Rd LP
Number Nine played backwards
interview re: all bull shit
REVOLUTION 9 fragment
A DAY IN THE LIFE Sgt. Pepper's LP
STRAWBERRY FIELDS FOREVER end fragment
interview fragment re: cranberry sauce
STRAWBERRY FIELDS FOREVER end fragment
STRAWBERRY FIELDS FOREVER Past Masters LP
interview fragment re: it's just meaningless
GLASS ONION The Beatles LP
SHE'LL BE COMING ROUND THE MOUNTAIN improv
WHAT YOU GOT extro

The Lost Lennon Tapes Part 168
John Lennon's Political Awakening
Show #91-15, Broadcast the Week of April 8, 1991

WHAT YOU GOT intro
interview re: being more politically aware
REVOLUTION 1 The Beatles LP
EVERYBODY'S GOT SOMETHING EXCEPT FOR ME AND MY MONKEY under dialogue
interview re: communication and bag events
SCUMBAG under dialogue

interview re: doing acorns for peace
ONLY PEOPLE Mind Games LP
IMAGINE Imagine LP
HAIR Hair Soundtrack, under dialogue
Dick Gregory interview re: giving hair to Michael X
ATTICA STATE rehearsal, Elephephant's Memory, also #195
interview re: meeting Hoffman and Rubin
NEW YORK CITY fragment
interview re: John Sinclair benefit
JOHN SINCLAIR John Sinclair Benefit 1971, also #<u>16</u>, #76
phone call fragment John Sinclair re: being freed
New York City LP medley under review of album
ANGELA under dialogue
Jim Keltner interview re: loved Woman Is The Nigger Of The World
interview re: Jim Gregory and Woman Is The Nigger Of The World
WOMAN IS THE NIGGER OF THE WORLD Some Time In New York City LP
Keltner interview re: John & Yoko turning him on to feminism
interview re: where are all the women radicals
SISTERS O SISTERS Some Time In New York City LP
THE LUCK OF THE IRISH under dialogue
'80 Sheff John interview re: San Diego Republican convention
interview re: establishment turns pacifists violent
SUNDAY BLOODY SUNDAY Some Time In New York City LP
POWER TO THE PEOPLE under dialogue
interview re: do you have to be poor to be anti war
'80 Sheff John interview re: lyrics to Revolution stand today
REVOLUTION Past Masters LP
WHAT YOU GOT extro

The Lost Lennon Tapes Part 169
Show #91-16, Broadcast the Week of April 15, 1991

WHAT YOU GOT into
THE LUCK OF THE IRISH alternate take
Mimi interview re: John's family being Irish
PENNY LANE Past Masters LP
'80 Sheff John interview re: Penny Lane
Mimi interview re: looking after John
JULIA The Beatles LP
IN MY LIFE Rubber Soul LP
Mintz John interview re: his father leaving him
THAT'S MY LIFE (MY LOVE & MY HOME) Freddie Lennon, under dialogue
interview continued re: resolution with his Father
Mimi interview re: John couldn't stand her
REAL LOVE - GIRLS AND BOYS demo 5

NOWHERE MAN under dialogue
Ray Coleman interview re: John unable to be a father
GOOD NIGHT The Beatles LP
'80 Peebles John interview re: raising Sean vs Julian
BEAUTIFUL BOY Double Fantasy LP
TOMORROW NEVER KNOWS under dialogue
'80 Sheff John interview re: playing Rain backwards
THEY'RE COMING TO TAKE ME AWAY HA-HA Napoleon XIV, fragment
interview continued re: that was a gift of Ja
RAIN Past Masters LP
George Martin interview re: backwards ending
Basco commercial, Cascious and Sunny poem
KLIM Beatles station I.D.
I SAW HER STANDING THERE Please Please Me LP
Crackerjacks commercial
CAN'T BUY ME LOVE A Hard Day's Night LP
topless swimsuits, KLIM Beatles station I.D.
TWIST AND SHOUT Please Please Me LP
fed up negroes comment, Brylcreem commercial
SHE LOVES YOU Past Masters LP
civil rights act comment, Good and Plenty commercial
I WANT TO HOLD YOUR HAND
WHAT YOU GOT extro

The Lost Lennon Tapes Part 170
Lennon On Dylan
Show #91-17, Broadcast the Week of April 22, 1991

WHAT YOU GOT into
NEW YORK CITY demo, also #30
TALKIN' NEW YORK Bob Dylan
FROM ME TO YOU FANTASY under dialogue
Howard Cosell John interview re: Bob Dylan
'70 Wenner John interview re: Bob Dylan another poet
BLOWIN' IN THE WIND Bob Dylan
CORRINA CORRINA Bob Dylan, under dialogue
interview re: going through changes in public
CORRINA CORRINA improv, also #27
'80 Sheff John interview re: stopped listening to Dylan
RAINY DAY WOMAN NOS. 12 & 35 Bob Dylan
'80 Sheff John interview re: Help!
HELP! Help LP
I'M A LOSER Beatles For Sale LP
'80 Sheff John interview re: I'm A Loser
'70 Wenner John interview re: getting together with Dylan

SUBTERRANEAN HOMESICK BLUES Bob Dylan
interview re: Cold Turkey
YER BLUES under dialogue
'80 Sheff John interview re: Yer Blues
POSITIVELY 4TH STREET Bob Dylan
interview re: I don't believe in Dylan
interview re: New Morning
LIKE A ROLLING STONE Bob Dylan, fragment
'80 Sheff John interview re: religion and art
GOTTA SERVE SOMEBODY Bob Dylan, fragment
interview continued re: you don't have to listen
SERVE YOURSELF demo 8
WHAT YOU GOT extro

The Lost Lennon Tapes Part 171
The Beatles Live At The BBC Part III
Show #91-18, Broadcast the Week of April 29, 1991

WHAT YOU GOT into
BBC intro to
I SAW HER STANDING THERE BBC, 20 October 1963
BBC intro to
LOVE ME DO BBC, 20 October 1963
BBC interview re: Royal Variety Performance
SHE LOVES YOU BBC, 20 October 1963
BBC intro to
THIS BOY BBC, 21 December 1963, also #73, #100
BBC intro to
ROLL OVER BEETHOVEN - BEATLES CRIMBLE MEDLEY BBC, 21 December 1963
BBC carols medley and intro to
MEDLEY OF HITS BBC, 21 December 1963
BBC intro to
TIE ME KANGAROO DOWN SPORT BBC, 26 December 1963
'64 Malcolm Davis New York Beatlemania report
'64 Brian Matthew Paul interview re: reception
I WANT TO HOLD YOUR HAND BBC, 15 February 1964
Brian Matthew Ringo Miami interview re: reception
Brian Matthew George Miami interview re: Ed Sullivan
JOHNNY B. GOODE BBC, 15 February 1964, also #<u>64</u>
Alan Freeman interview re: From Us To You shows
BBC intro to
TILL THERE WAS YOU BBC, 30 March 1964, also #<u>135</u>
BBC Brian Mathew interview re: tired of being Beatles, riding on a bus, and She's A Woman
studio dialogue intro to
SHE'S A WOMAN BBC, 26 December 1964

KANSAS CITY BBC, 26 December 1964, also #134
TICKET TO RIDE BBC, 7 June 1965, also #61
'65 Beatles MBE interview
DIZZY MISS LIZZY BBC, 7 June 1965
WHAT YOU GOT extro

The Lost Lennon Tapes Part 172
Show #91-19, Broadcast the Week of May 6, 1991

LOVE ME DO barn yard version intro
KNOCKIN' ON HEAVEN'S DOOR parody, also #14
THE NEWS OF THE DAY FROM REUTERS parody, also #14, #49
Casey Kasem parody
OB-LA-DI OB-LA-DA barn yard version, under dialogue
press conference fragment
A HARD DAY'S NIGHT film soundtrack fragment
A HARD DAY'S NIGHT A Hard Day's Night LP
WE LOVE YOU BEATLES from broadcast
airport reception parody
POP HATES THE BEATLES Alan Sherman
WITHIN YOU WITHOUT YOU under dialogue
L.S. BUMBLE BEE Peter Cook & Dudley Moore
THE HISTORY OF ROCK 'N' ROLL Beatles parody
'70 Wenner John interview excerpts
MAGICAL MYSERY TOUR National Lampoon, fragment
GIVE BOOZE A CHANCE Bonzo Dog Band
GEORGE HARRISON album ad parody
MY SWEET LORD parody, Jonathan King
THE LATE PAUL McCARTNEY National Lampoon LP
GET UP AND GO The Rutles, under dialogue
Rutles dialogue a living legend
NUMBER ONE The Rutles, under dialogue
HOLD MY HAND The Rutles
Rutles dialogue Cavern Rutlands
WITH A GIRL LIKE YOU The Rutles, fragment
Rutles dialogue arrival in America
OUCH! The Rutles
God/Rod Stewart dialogue fragment
LOVE LIFE The Rutles
NEVERTHELESS The Rutles, under dialogue
Rutles dialogue taking tea
COME TOGETHER parody, under dialogue
PIGGY IN THE MIDDLE The Rutles
GET UP AND GO The Rutles
I WANT TO HOLD YOUR HAND barn yard version, extro

The Lost Lennon Tapes Part 173
Show #91-20, Broadcast the Week of May 13, 1991

BEEF JERKY intro
Mick Jagger song, under dialogue
Mick Jagger interview re: Sunday sessions
TOO MANY COOKS, John produced, also #156
YA YA under dialogue
CHUM FM John interview re: playing with friends
WHATEVER GETS YOU THROUGH THE NIGHT fragment
interview continued re: Harry on Whatever Gets You Through The Night
Harry Nilsson interview re: working with John
OLD DIRT ROAD rough mix
interview re: deciding to do Pussy Cats
Harry Nilsson interview re: John's first call
Harry Nilsson interview re: deciding to do Pussy Cats
LET THE GOOD TIMES ROLL Harry Nilsson, under dialogue
interview continued re: loaded all the time
MUCHO MUNGO rehearsal, Harry & John, also #34, longer here but intro #34 different
SUBTERRANEAN HOMESICK BLUES Harry Nilsson
'74 Tom Donahue KSAN John guest DJ appearance
interview continued re: "spot the edit", Harry lost his voice, "spot the edit" also #35
MANY RIVERS TO CROSS Harry Nilsson
interview continued re: Harry's voice gone
I'M STEPPING OUT rough mix, edited version
I DON'T WANT TO FACE IT demo, fragment
I DON'T WANT TO FACE IT rough mix
BORROWED TIME demo 1, also #31, #119
Borrowed Time studio rehearsal, "2, 3, 4" 2 chorus lines "what are we waiting for?"
Borrowed Time studio dialogue, "local 802, you want a basic acoustic"guitar overdub
BORROWED TIME rough mix
WHAT YOU GOT extro

The Lost Lennon Tapes Part 174
Show #91-21, Broadcast the Week of May 20, 1991

WHAT YOU GOT intro
WOUDLN'T IT BE NICE Beach Boys, under dialogue
Mike Love interview re: Pet Sounds influence on Pepper
SLOOP JOHN B The Beach Boys
LET'S GO AWAY FOR AWHILE The Beach Boys, under dialogue
Paul interview re: bass sound comming forward & Pet Sounds
George Martin interview re: Strawberry Fields single
PENNY LANE Past Masters LP
Paul interview re: pretending we're another group

interview re: separating the Beatles from the public
Paul interview continued re: Sgt. Pepper's
SGT. PEPPER'S LONELY HEARTS CLUB BAND/A LITTLE HELP FROM MY FRIENDS Sgt. Pepper's LP
George Martin interview re: A Little Help From My Friends and Ringo
interview re: not a concept album
Brian Adams interview re: first hearing Sgt. Pepper's
LUCY IN THE SKY WITH DIAMONDS Sgt. Pepper's LP
George Martin interview re: loved working on LP
Paul interview re: the original cover
GETTING BETTER Sgt. Pepper's LP
Paul interview continued re: not us, people heroes of the group
FIXING A HOLE Sgt. Pepper's LP
Dave Edmunds interview re: LSD, four track, drug references
George Martin interview re: smoking dope in the canteen
SHE'S LEAVING HOME Sgt. Pepper's LP
Alan Parsons interview re: first hearing Pepper
Chrissie Hind interview re: first hearing Pepper
George Martin interview re: Being For The Benefit of Mr. Kite
interview re: Mr. Kite poster
BEING FOR THE BENEFIT OF MR. KITE Sgt. Pepper's LP
NOBODY TOLD ME demo 1
NOBODY TOLD ME Milk And Honey LP
WHAT YOU GOT extro

The Lost Lennon Tapes Part 175
Show #91-22, Broadcast the Week of May 27, 1991

WHAT YOU GOT intro
SGT. PEPPER'S LP side one medley
Chrissie Hind interview re: music and its time
Paul interview re: the songs were good
WITHIN YOU WITHOUT YOU Sgt. Pepper's LP
Phil Collins interview re: first hearing Pepper
George Martin interview re: Penny/Strawb recorded first
WHEN I'M SIXTY-FOUR Sgt. Pepper's LP
interview re: Lovely Rita
LOVELY RITA Sgt. Pepper's LP
Ray Davies interview re: first time he heard Pepper
GOOD MORNING GOOD MORNING demo, also #15
interview re: Good Morning Good Morning
GOOD MORNING GOOD MORNING Sgt. Pepper's LP
interview re: reviews of Beatles albums
interview re: we were too big for reviews
Mike Rutherford interview re: first hearing Pepper
SGT. PEPPER'S REPRISE Sgt. Pepper's LP

A DAY IN THE LIFE instrumental under dialogue
interview re: writing A Day In The Life with Paul
Mark Lewisohn interview re: filming A Day In The Life
Paul interview re: conducting orchestra
A DAY IN THE LIFE with clean intro
George Martin interview re: runout groove and dog whistle
SGT. PEPPER'S RUNOUT GROOVE Sgt. Pepper's LP
I'M LOSING YOU - STRANGER'S ROOM demo 5 also #71, #125
I'M LOSING YOU Double Fantasy LP
WHAT YOU GOT extro

The Lost Lennon Tapes Part 176
Show #91-23, Broadcast the Week of June 3, 1991

WHAT YOU GOT intro
COME GO WITH ME Del Vikings, under dialogue
Paul interview re: meeting John at fete
TWENTY FLIGHT ROCK Elvis Presley, under dialogue
TWENTY FLIGHT ROCK Paul, Tripping The Live Fantastic LP
interview continued re: Lennon-McCartney credit
YESTERDAY Help! LP
IT WON'T BE LONG under dialogue
interview continued re: writing together
HERE THERE AND EVERYWHERE Revolver LP
interview continued re; writing Norwegian Wood
NORWEGIAN WOOD Rubber Soul LP
interview continued re: happy that they made up
ALL YOU NEED IS LOVE Magical Mystery Tour EP
interview continued re: still liked each other
TWO OF US Let It Be LP
THINK FOR YOURSELF under dialogue
John interview re: letting George in to the group
I NEED YOU Help! LP
George interview re: John and Paul were the stars
I WANT TO TELL YOU Revolver LP
interview continued re: toppermost of the poppermost
IT'S ALL TOO MUCH Yellow Submarine LP
interview continued re: John is brilliant
#9 DREAM Walls And Bridges LP
interview re: I couldn't sing I'm The Greatest
Richard Perry interview re: I'm The Greatest session
I'M THE GREATEST Ringo LP
WHAT YOU GOT extro

Lost Lennon Tapes Part 177
Paul McCartney's Birthday Part 1
Show #91-24, Broadcast the Week of June 10, 1991

WHAT YOU GOT intro
BIRTHDAY under dialogue
I LOST MY LITTLE GIRL Paul
Paul interview re: first gig with the Quarrymen
BALLROOM DANCING Paul, fragment
BALLROOM DANCING Paul, under dialogue
interview continued re: playing ballrooms
BE-BOP-A-LULA Paul
interview continued re: started with three guitars
RED SAILS IN THE SUNSET under dialogue
Paul interview re: best playing days
Paul interview re: didn't want a steady job
BABY, YOU'RE A RICH MAN Past Masters LP
THE LONG AND WINDING ROAD under dialogue
'84 Paul interview re: McCartney LP
EVERY NIGHT Paul, under dialogue
interview continued re: Ram LP
UNCLE ALBERT ADMIRAL HALSEY Paul, under dialogue
interview continued re: Wings Wildlife LP
DEAR FRIEND Paul, under dialogue
interview continued re: critics
LISTEN TO WHAT THE MAN SAID Paul
interview continued re: Give Ireland Back To The Irish
GIVE IRELAND BACK TO THE IRISH Paul
interview continued re: Hi Hi Hi
HI HI HI Paul, under dialogue
interview continued re: banning affects sales a bit
MARY HAD A LITTLE LAMB Paul, fragment
interview continued re: switching off music at end of day
BAND ON THE RUN Paul
MAMUNIA Paul, under dialogue
interview re: Carl Perkins and Gotta Get It
GET IT Paul
interview continued re: reminds me of western swing
interview continued re: Stevie Wonder and Ebony And Ivory
EBONY AND IVORY Paul, fragment
interview continued re: Live And Let Die
LIVE AND LET DIE Paul
THIS ONE Paul, under dialogue
interview continued re: Put It There
PUT IT THERE Paul
interview continued re: a bit of emotion

MY BRAVE FACE Paul
WHAT YOU GOT extro

The Lost Lennon Tapes Part 178
Paul McCartney's Birthday Part 2
Show #91-25, Broadcast the Week of June 17, 1991

WHAT YOU GOT intro
AIN'T THAT A SHAME Paul, Tripping The Live Fantastic LP
interview re: admired Paul playing small clubs
Paul interview re: I still get nervous
FIGURE OF EIGHT Paul, Tripping The Live Fantastic LP fragment
FIGURE OF EIGHT Paul, Tripping The Live Fantastic LP, continued under dialogue
interview continued re: relaxing after a gig and next day
ROLL OVER BEETHOVEN Star Club LP
PAPERBACK WRITER under dialogue
'84 Roger Scott Paul interview re: songs not as good
HERE THERE AND EVERYWHERE Paul, Unplugged LP
interview continued re: who do you bounce songs off now
JUNK Paul, Unplugged LP, under dialogue
WE CAN WORK IT OUT Paul, Unplugged LP
SGT. PEPPER'S Paul, Tripping The Live Fantastic LP
interview continued re: Beatles songs very fresh
HEY JUDE Paul, Tripping The Live Fantastic LP
I SAW HER STANDING THERE Paul, Trippling The Live Fantastic LP
interview continued re: writing another good song
YESTERDAY Paul, Tripping The Live Fantastic LP
SHE'S A WOMAN Beatles 65 LP
SHE'S A WOMAN Paul, Unplugged LP
She's A Woman studio dialogue re: Earl Slick plays riff "I hear ya ... enough of that, tea tea tea"
She's A Woman studio dialogue "What key do you keep playing...that in? ... I go back to the 50's"
SHE'S A WOMAN improv
BLACKBIRD improv fragment "Blackbird singing in a pile of shit"
WHAT YOU GOT extro

The Lost Lennon Tapes Part 179
Composing Part 1
Show #91-26, Broadcast the Week of June 24, 1991

WHAT YOU GOT intro
SEA OF HOLES under dialogue
Alice In Wonderland excerpt
interview re: Lewis Caroll influence
The Wumberlog Spaniard In The Works reading by John

'63 Doncaster **Neville Club** **reading by John**, also Part 18
PAPERBACK WRITER under dialogue
'65 journalist John interview re: Lewis Caroll
THE WALRUS AND THE CARPENTER excerpt
I AM THE WALRUS Magical Mystery Tour EP
'80 Sheff John interview re: I Am The Walrus
interview re: I still write
Yoko interview re: John recorded his writings
PEPPERLAND LAID WASTE under dialogue
improv dialogue watching television
GLASS ONION The Beatles LP
'80 Sheff John interview re: Glass Onion
'80 John interview re: who he related to as a child
CRY BABY CRY demo 2, fragment
CRY BABY CRY demo 3, fragment
CRY BABY CRY demo 4, fragment
CRY BABY CRY demo 1, Kinfauns 1968, also #105
CLEANUP TIME demo 1, also #23
CLEANUP TIME dialogue & runthrough "you can have all those holes Slick" also #Preview 3, #86
'80 Sheff John interview re: Yoko's edit
CLEANUP TIME Double Fantasy LP
ACROSS THE UNIVERSE melotron riff, fragment
interview continued re: Across The Universe
LADY MADONNA under dialogue
interview continued re: Paul subconsciously destroying great songs
ACROSS THE UNIVERSE No One's Gonna Change Our World LP, under dialogue
interview continued re: the song was never done properly
ACROSS THE UNIVERSE Let It Be LP
SHE CAN TALK TO ME demo, Hey Bulldog, fragment
YELLOW SUBMARINE IN PEPPERLAND under dialogue
interview continued re: stealing ideas for the film
interview continued re: good sounding song
HEY BULLDOG Yellow Submarine LP
WHAT YOU GOT extro

The Lost Lennon Tapes Part 180
Show #91-27, Broadcast the Week of July 1, 1991

WHAT YOU GOT intro
THE LORD LOVES THE ONE George, fragment
HELP ME TO HELP MYSELF demo 1, takes 2, 3, also #150, #217
HELP ME TO HELP MYSELF demo 2
melotron under dialogue
STRAWBERRY FIELDS FOREVER demo 1, also #4, #49, #131
STRAWBERRY FIELDS FOREVER melotron overdub

STRAWBERRY FIELDS FOREVER Past Masters LP
REAL LOVE - GIRLS AND BOYS demo fragments under dialogue
REAL LOVE - GIRLS AND BOYS demo 6, many early fragments with different titles
STARTING OVER - MY LIFE demo 5, fragment
STARTING OVER - MY LIFE demo 6, also #194
STARTING OVER - DON'T BE CRAZY demo 1, fragment, also #21
STARTING OVER - THE WORST IS OVER demo 2, also #21
Lewis Caroll Walrus excerpt
STARTING OVER demo 2, take 3, also #10 #21
STARTING OVER studio improv
STARTING OVER Double Fantasy LP
WHAT YOU GOT extro

The Lost Lennon Tapes Part 181
Ringo Starr's 51st Birthday
Show #91-28, Broadcast the Week of July 8, 1991

WHAT YOU GOT intro
RINGO Lorne Greene, excerpt
'76 Mintz Ringo interview re: first recollections of Liverpool
interview continued re: appendix and hospital
HAIL HAIL ROCK 'N' ROLL Chuck Berry, under dialogue
interview continued re: told my mother 3 times I'd be dead
interview continued re: not listed in school records
IT DON't COME EASY single 1970
interview continued re: being in a Liverpool gang
BACK OFF BOOGALOO Ringo, under dialogue
interview continued re: skiffle groups
interview continued re: practicing in his room, joining groups
interview continued re: love of drums
skiffle song under dialogue
interview continued re: favourite skiffle bands and Rory Storm
I'M THE GREATEST Ringo LP
'60 announcer: Ringo's mother doesn't have to work anymore
interview continued re: first introduction to the Beatles
LITTLE QUEENIE Star Club LP, under dialogue
interview continued re: first sitting in and joining the Beatles
RINGO I LOVE YOU Bonnie Jo Mason (Cher) excerpt
interview continued re: EMI not liking his drumming
interview continued re: freaking out George Martin on session
LOVE ME DO Past Masters LP
interview continued re: Love Me Do first number one and Liverpool
PLEASE PLEASE ME single 1963
'60s announcer re: feeling might let fans down
CAN'T BUY ME LOVE Live At The Hollywood Bowl LP, under dialogue

interview continued re: keeping themselves amused onstage
interview continued re: stayed up 3 days and 3 nights
A LITTLE HELP FROM MY FRIENDS Sgt. Pepper's LP
'60s announcer re: Ringo the odd ball Beatle
ACT NATURALLY Help! LP
'90 Ringo interview re: Shining Time Station
YELLOW SUBMARINE Revolver LP
The Lost Ringo Tapes - John Candy
SENTIMENTAL JOURNEY fragment
BEAUCOUPS OF BLUES fragment
PHOTOGRAPH Ringo LP
interview continued re: the All-Starr Tour 1991
interview continued re: getting down to the front of the stage
interview continued re: combination of musicians
interview continued re: it makes the show fun
YOU'RE SIXTEEN Ringo Starr And His All-Starr Band LP
WHAT YOU GOT extro

The Lost Lennon Tapes Part 182
John and Yoko's Love Part I
Show #91-29, Broadcast the Week of July 15, 1991

WHAT YOU GOT intro
WHEN A BOY MEETS A GIRL demo, also #90
GIRL under dialogue
interview fragment: she's me in drag
Yoko interview re: seeing his book in books shop
Grapefruit excerpts read by John and Yoko:
Yoko: A Piece For Orchestra
John: Water Piece
John: Wall Piece I
John: Tunafish Sandwich Piece
BECAUSE Abbey Road LP
John and Yoko hold one note as long as possible
BABY'S HEARTBEAT under dialogue
OH MY LOVE Yoko, a cappella, also #113
OH MY LOVE demo 1, also #113
OH MY LOVE IMAGINE LP
'68 Christmas record: Jock and Yono
THE BALLAD OF JOHN AND YOKO Past Masters LP
OH YOKO! demo 2, also #52
OH YOKO! demo 3
OH YOKO! Imagine LP
HAPPY GIRL Yoko, a cappella
I'LL MAKE YOU HAPPY demo 1

Yoko interview re: No One Sees Me Like You Do
NO ONE SEES ME LIKE YOU DO Yoko
Yoko interview re: separation could've gone either way
BLESS YOU Walls And Bridges LP
SOMEWHERE IN THE SKY Yoko, a cappella
ISOLATION Plastic Ono Band LP
WHAT YOU GOT extro

The Lost Lennon Tapes Part 183
John and Yoko's Love Part II
Show #91-30, Broadcast the Week of July 22, 1991

WHAT YOU GOT intro
LOVE Plastic Ono Band LP
WHATEVER GETS YOU THROUGH THE NIGHT under dialogue
'80 Peebles John & Yoko interview re: Madison Square Garden concert
I SAW HER STANDING THERE Madison Sq., single 1981
I'M HAVING A BABY Yoko
interview continued re: Yoko taking over business & house husband
BEAUTIFUL BOY Double Fantasy LP
WATCHING THE WHEELS Double Fantasy LP, fragment
I'M MOVING ON (fragment)/I'M LOSING YOU Double Fantasy LP
Dear Yoko studio dialogue, sings lyrics "OK what are we waiting for?"
'80 Peebles John interview re: all the material came to me
DEAR YOKO demo 2, takes 2, 3, also #72
I'M NOT AS STRONG AS YOU THINK Yoko, a cappella
interview re: writing Woman in Bermuda
Woman studio dialogue "I still feel like I'm in the fucking Beatles with this track ... Smokey Robinson"
WOMAN rough mix
YOKO ONO POEM GAME Yoko, a cappella 1970 fades to
WOMAN Double Fantasy LP
interview fragment re: Yoko' saved my life many times
YOU SAVED MY SOUL demo 2, also #86, #213
Yoko interview re: John's influence on her
YES, I'M YOUR ANGEL rough mix
WHAT YOU GOT extro

The Lost Lennon Tapes Part 184
John and Yoko's Love Part III
Show #91-31, Broadcast the Week of July 29, 1991

WHAT YOU GOT intro
'80 Peebles John interview re: Imagine and Yoko's influence
IMAGINE Imagine LP
Every Man Has A Woman Yoko double tracked vocals
Every Man Has A Woman studio playback, under dialogue
studio dialogue re: discussing photos of Yoko
studio dialogue re: pronunciation of "Every man"
Every Man Has A Woman Yoko double tracking middle 8 & dialogue
Every Man Has A Woman Yoko double tracking & dialogue continued
EVERY MAN HAS A WOMAN rough mix
interview re: Hard Times Are Over session
Hard Times Are Over choir practicing chorus
studio dialogue re: this song is a positive prayer
HARD TIMES ARE OVER runthrough
studio dialogue re: adding hand claps
HARD TIMES ARE OVER rough mix
WALKING ON THIN ICE rehearsal, Yoko vocal
studio dialogue re: weak now instead of dirty and nice
studio dialogue re: photos for Double Fantasy cover
WALKING ON THIN ICE vocal overdub, Yoko
WALKING ON THIN ICE single 1980
studio dialogue fragment re: your first number one
Mintz John interview fragment re: off the coast of Ireland
Yoko interview re: hoped to live a long time together
interview re: not believing in death
GROW OLD WITH ME rough mix
interview continued re: how Yoko remembers John
REMEMBER LOVE single 1969
interview continued re: his spirit is still around
OUT THE BLUE Mind Games LP
WHAT YOU GOT extro

The Lost Lennon Tapes Part 185
Show #91-32, Broadcast the Week of August 5, 1991

WHAT YOU GOT intro
LIFE BEGINS AT FORTY demo, also #2, #204, #213
'80 Sheff interview re: sailing from Newport to Bermuda
SEA DITTIES MEDLEY improv, also #10
interview continued re: taking over sailing cause everyone sick
PEDRO THE FISHERMAN improv

- 169 -

interview continued re: Hank the captain
THE BOAT SONG demo, also #150
Great WOK 1978 New Year's resolution, also #49, #50, #217
INSTRUMENTAL DIVERSION improv, continued under dialogue
John interviews Sean December 1975
BEAUTIFUL BOYS Double Fantasy LP
KHJ John guest DJ appearance
call Mike re: will Beatles get back together, also #51
GOODNIGHT VIENNA Ringo
call Dana re: request for Mind Games, also #51
MIND GAMES Mind Games LP
John reads station I.D. and weather - 6:19
call Cynthia re: request for Cold Turkey, also #51
COLD TURKEY single 1969
call Ed re: request for Be Yourself by Graham Nash, also #51
call Peter re: request for Beep Beep or Hold On John, also #51
HOLD ON JOHN Plastic Ono Band LP
Walls and Bridges radio ad with Ringo, "listen to this radio spot", also #51
SURPRISE SURPRISE Walls and Bridges LP
Surprise Surprise extro into Tobias commercial - Jeans Revolution - "dot dot" version
call Donna re: request for a cut from your new album, also #52
#9 DREAM Walls And Bridges LP
interview continued re: that's a cut from my new album
WHAT YOU GOT extro

The Lost Lennon Tapes Part 186
Show #91-33, Broadcast the Week of August 12, 1991

WHAT YOU GOT intro
'80 Sheff John interview re: Give Me Some Truth
GIVE ME SOME TRUTH Imagine Games LP
J.J. demo 2, take 1, Angela
PEOPLE demo, Angela, also #65
ANGELA Some Time In New York City LP
DO THE OZ Bill Elliot & The Elastic Oz Band, under dialogue
God Save Us radio promo, John and Yoko
GOD SAVE US demo, eq'd with ending - also #19
GOD SAVE US Bill Elliot & The Elastic Oz band, single 1971
One To One radio promos re: added show, "Hi this is John Lennon", "Geraldo - this is my business"
WELL WELL WELL John Lennon Live In NYC LP, under dialogue
Geraldo Rivera interview re: doing One To One concert
Geraldo John & Yoko interview re: why are you doing concert
COME TOGETHER One To One rehearsals, take 1, fragment, also #78
Come Together rehearsal and dialogue fragment re: Paul's piano part, also #78
IT'S SO HARD One To One rehearsals, also #52

Rivera interview continued re: John getting cold feet
Rivera interview continued re: giving tickets to retarded kids
NEW YORK CITY One To One rehearsals 2
One To One radio promo, John and Yoko reading
One To One radio promo, also #104 Geraldo Rivera into **NEW YORK CITY**, also #104
Jim Keltner interview re: doing the show
INSTANT KARMA One To One rehearsals, also #19
MOTHER One To One rehearsals
Rivera interview continued re: lineup of guests
IMAGINE John Lennon Live In NY LP
WHAT YOU GOT extro

The Lost Lennon Tapes Part 187
Show #91-34, Broadcast the Week of August 19, 1991

WHAT YOU GOT intro
Jam Honey Don't/Don't Be Cruel/Matchbox, POB session, also #22 #49
I FOUND OUT alternate mix, Gone Gone, beginning cut, also #43, #84
MY MUMMY'S DEAD take 2, also #82
LOOK AT ME demo, also #82, #204
LOOK AT ME Plastic Ono Band LP
KHJ John guest DJ appearance
call Chris re: will you play Mind Games
call Mark re: I Am The Walrus, also #52
call John re: thank you for all you've done for music, also #51
call Louise re: play something off your new album, also #51
BEEF JERKY Walls And Bridges LP
call Lance re: play It's Only Love, also #51
IT'S ONLY LOVE Rubber Soul LP
call Eloise re: play Tight A$
TIGHT A$ Mind Games LP
news interview clips re: reaction to John as guest
call re: meditation and play something by Led Zeppelin
call Dennis re: play The Night Before, also #60
THE NIGHT BEFORE Help! LP
call re: your Rickenbaker and strings in Walrus, also #60
call re: play You're Gonna Lose That Girl and gear fab, also #60
YOU'RE GONNA LOSE THAT GIRL Help! LP
call re: Have You Heard The Word and play God
GOD Plastic Ono Band LP
intro to, also #51
GET UP STAND UP The Wailers
call re: are you going to do any concerts
John reads Tower records ad
WHATEVER GETS YOU THROUGH THE NIGHT Walls And Bridges LP

interview continued re: It's 8:15 for Charlie Van Dyke
WHAT YOU GOT extro

The Lost Lennon Tapes Part 188
The Other Side Of The Glass - The Double Fantasy Sessions Part I
Show #91-35, Broadcast the Week of August 26, 1991

WHAT YOU GOT intro
I'M STEPPING OUT under dialogue
Lee DeCarlo interview re: why he hasn't spoken out till now
interview continued re: hearing from Jack Douglas about doing LP
interview continued re: taping everything
Double Fantasy studio dialogue "What's this one going round and round ... that's the slap" tuning up
I'M STEPPING OUT runthrough
interview continued re: he was just a regular guy & Lee's Hotel
interview continued re: laughter in the studio
NO ONE CAN SEE ME LIKE YOU DO runthrough
interview continued re: turning point in sessions
studio dialogue re: I'm sorry I was having fun...
LET'S GET PECULIAR improv, fragment
studio dialogue re: microphone sounds so violent
interview continued re: Orson Wells on log sheets and in studio
studio dialogue re: Orson likes it
interview continued re: John getting written up
studio dialogue re: Walrus parody
WATCHING THE WHEELS runthrough plus dialogue
interview continued re: he liked to record live words and ad libs
NOBODY TOLD ME runthrough
studio dialogue re: chocolate donuts
interview continued re: drinking espresso and sweets
studio dialogue re: espresso and marching around
WOMAN runthrough
WOMAN under dialogue
interview continued re: smuggling in food
studio dialogue re: breaking out of a diet
interview continued re: Cheap Trick on Losing You & John played Beatles songs, loved Hold Your Hand
I WANT TO HOLD YOUR HAND A Hard Day's Night LP
interview continued re: John's least favourite song
MAXWELL'S SILVER HAMMER fragment under dialogue
interview continued re: John's black and white Rickenbaker
INSTANT KARMA under dialogue
interview continued re: John always had music on
studio playback under dialogue
YESTERDAY fragment

interview continued re: John tuning his guitar
WOMAN guitar overdub
interview continued re: he knew what he wanted
interview continued re: writing Cleanup Time around bass riff
CLEANUP TIME runthrough
WHAT YOU GOT extro

The Lost Lennon Tapes Part 189
The Other Side Of The Glass - The Double Fantasy Sessions Part II
Show #91-36, Broadcast the Week of September 2, 1991

GIVE ME SOMETHING intro
WATCHING THE WHEELS backing tracks, under dialogue
studio dialogue re: remind producer to give him a copy of that mad stuff
Lee DeCarlo interview re: street musician playing Dulcimer
WATCHING THE WHEELS Double Fantasy LP
studio dialogue re: down in Zanzibar awwww
I'M LOSING YOU runthrough, under dialogue
interview continued re: macrobiotic diet
interview continued re: concern for everyone
ALL YOU NEED IS LOVE Past Masters LP
I'm Losing You brass overdubs
interview continued re: John getting the bill for horn track
I'M LOSING YOU Double Fantasy LP
STARTING OVER backing tracks, under dialogue
interview continued re: make me sound like John Lennon
interview continued re: he loved Elvis Presley
studio dialogue re: I want Elvis Vincent
studio dialogue re: Starting Over playback, fragment
interview continued re: bells drums and karma on Starting Over
studio dialogue re: right on its better
STARTING OVER Double Fantasy LP
Yoko studio dialogue re: amazed that Lee's not really fat
interview continued re: Yoko's really a very fair person
DEAR YOKO runthrough
DEAR YOKO Double Fantasy LP
WOMAN backing tracks, under dialogue
interview continued re: interlocking three 16 track tape machines
interview continued re: he visualised state of the art equipment
RAIN Past Masters LP
interview continued re: his technique for overdubbing vocals
Woman vocal overdub rehearsal - starts "I know you understand...", also #160
studio dialogue re: double track certain words, set of words in briefcase, love double tracking
studio dialogue re: yes sir, put me on on the intro, I can add it on Monday, adding intro
Woman vocal overdub - starts "other half of the sky" to 2nd verse "hand", "stop" at "short hand"

WOMAN Double Fantasy LP
studio dialogue re: - "Uh mother", "Did you get that message?", "I love her too yes."
studio dialogue fragment re: "I love that ending."
WHAT YOU GOT extro

The Lost Lennon Tapes Part 190
The Other Side Of The Glass - The Double Fantasy Sessions Part III
Show #91-37, Broadcast the Week of September 9, 1991

WHAT YOU GOT intro
Lee DeCarlo interview re: everything changed after John's LP
BORROWED TIME runthrough
interview continued re: first time I met John, hello face
I'VE JUST SEEN A FACE Help! LP
interview continued re: sound effects before Yes, I'm Your Angel
studio dialogue re: the sound of money dropping into a can
YES, I'M YOUR ANGEL Double Fantasy LP
studio dialogue fragment re: no guests, sorry
DO YOU WANT TO KNOW A SECRET under dialogue
interview continued re: the security was very high
I'M LOSING YOU runthrough, under dialogue
interview continued re: every record company after them to sign deal
interview continued re: moving through crowds of fans
I'M STEPPING OUT Milk And Honey LP
interview continued re: John would always ask why
studio dialogue re: Sean and Yoko in booth into
EVERYMAN HAS A WOMAN runthrough with Sean talking over
EVERYMAN HAS A WOMAN Everyman Has A Woman LP
interview continued re: absolutely devoted to Sean
studio dialogue re: Yoko says Sean is here
BEAUTIFUL BOY backing tracks, under dialogue
interview continued re: screwing up and quitting for five years
BEAUTIFUL BOY runthrough
interview continued re: Watching The Wheels stuck out for me
STARTING OVER backing tracks, under dialogue
interview continued re: feels good to talk about John
interview continued re: every day I pray for him and day go by
studio dialogue re: don't let another day go by
STARTING OVER studio playback
interview continued re: he was just a normal guy
WATCHING THE WHEELS Double Fantasy LP
interview continued re: Watching The Wheels was a phenomenal song
WHAT YOU GOT extro

The Lost Lennon Tapes Part 191
The Playboy Interview Part I
Show #91-38, Broadcast the Week of September 16, 1991

WHAT YOU GOT intro
'80 Sheff John int re: strange wanting to know about songs
interview continued re: Oo and Yeah
SHE LOVES YOU Past Masters LP
interview continued re: Misery
MISERY Please Please Me LP
interview continued re: I Call Your Name
I CALL YOUR NAME Past Masters LP
interview continued re: It Won't Be Long
IT WON'T BE LONG With The Beatles LP
interview continued re: All My Loving
ALL MY LOVING With The Beatles LP
interview continued re: I'll Be Back
I'LL BE BACK A Hard Day's Night LP
interview continued re: Things We Said Today
THINGS WE SAID TODAY A Hard Day's Night LP
interview continued re: This Boy
THIS BOY Past Masters LP
interview continued re: contributing to Paul's songs
interview continued re: Paul provided a lightness
interview continued re: Paul's a capable lyricist
IN MY LIFE Rubber Soul LP
interview continued re: Hey Jude
HEY JUDE Past Masters LP
interview continued re: Within You Without You
WITHIN YOU WITHOUT YOU Sgt. Pepper's LP
interview continued re: creativity changes with age
I WANT TO HOLD YOUR HAND Past Masters LP
interview continued re: Paul writes a story, I write about myself
interview continued re: blaming society for your problems
NOWHERE MAN Rubber Soul LP
WHAT YOU GOT extro

The Lost Lennon Tapes Part 192
The Playboy Interview Part II
Show #91-39, Broadcast the Week of September 23, 1991

WHAT YOU GOT intro
'80 Sheff John interview re: One After 909
ONE AFTER 909 Let It Be LP
interview continued re: Here There And Everywhere

HERE THERE AND EVERYWHERE Revolver LP
interview continued re: Doctor Robert
DOCTOR ROBERT Revolver LP
interview continued re: For No One
FOR NO ONE Revolver LP
interview continued re: Got To Get You Into My Life
GOT TO GET YOU INTO MY LIFE Revolver LP
interview continued re: There's A Place
THERE'S A PLACE Please Please Me LP
interview continued re: I Saw Her Standing There
I SAW HER STANDING THERE Please Please Me LP
interview continued re: You Can't Do That and Wilson Pickett
YOU CAN'T DO THAT A Hard Day's Night LP
interview continued re: If I Fell
IF IF FELL A Hard Day's Night LP
interview continued re: Tell Me Why
TELL ME WHY A Hard Day's Night LP
interview continued re: Ticket To Ride
TICKET TO RIDE Help! LP
interview continued re: I Want You
I WANT YOU (SHE'S SO HEAVY) Abbey Road LP
interview continued re: obvious who wrote what
interview continued re: Let It Be and S & G
LET IT BE Let It Be LP
interview continued re: Strawberry Fields
STRAWBERRY FIELDS FOREVER Past Masters LP
WHAT YOU GOT extro

The Lost Lennon Tapes Part 193
Show #91-40, Broadcast the Week of September 30, 1991

WHAT YOU GOT intro
EIGHT DAYS A WEEK Beatles For Sale LP
GOOD TIME MUSIC The Lovin' Spoonful, under dialogue
Joe Butler interview re: leaving gift at Shea Stadium
SUMMER IN THE CITY The Lovin' Spoonful, under dialogue
interview continued re: meeting them the next year
HELP Help! LP
DO YOU BELIEVE IN MAGIC The Lovin' Spoonful, under dialogue
interview continued re: renting Bank St apartment
MONEY under dialogue
interview continued re: John and Yoko being held up
I FOUND OUT Plastic Ono Band LP
interview continued re: the apartment
HAPPY XMAS (WAR IS OVER) under dialogue

interview continued re: John into the music business
interview continued re: John learning to type
OH YOKO! Imagine LP
interview continued re: John's karma and charisma
NEW YORK CITY under dialogue
David Peel interview re: John & Yoko showing up to see him play
JOHN LENNON YOKO ONO David Peel, under dialogue
interview re: meeting David Peel
Peel interview re: John asking about recording for Apple
interview continued re: recording the album
I AM A RUNAWAY David Peel, under dialogue
interview re: David Peel's a natural
Peel interview re: the album being a failure
THE POPE SMOKES DOPE The Pope Smokes Dope LP
Geraldo Rivera John Sinclair Benefit: "this is like a dream", also #16
THE LUCK OF THE IRISH John Sinclair Benefit 1971, also #16
interview continued re: putting his picture in John's FBI file
interview continued re: his musical and political plans
POWER TO THE PEOPLE single 1970
I'M LOSING YOU studio playbacks "bad stuff" edits
I'M LOSING YOU Double Fantasy LP
WHAT YOU GOT extro

The Lost Lennon Tapes Part 194
Show #91-41, Broadcast the Week of October 7, 1991

WHAT YOU GOT intro
SGT. PEPPER'S LONELY HEARTS CLUB BAND under dialogue
'71 Mintz John interview re: concept of age
STARTING OVER - MY LIFE demo 6, also #180
interview continued re: any regrets
BORROWED TIME Milk And Honey LP
STRAWBERRY FIELDS FOREVER under dialogue
Pete Shotton interview re: myth of John being poor
interview continued re: hearing Penny Lane playback
PENNY LANE Past Masters LP
MOTHER under dialogue
interview continued re: John's mother's death
JULIA The Beatles LP
television under dialogue
interview continued re: John's love of television
Bob Gruen interview continued re: John's love of television
studio dialogue fragment re: Nobody expects Bob Gruen
Gruen interview continued re: visiting Double Fantasy sessions
I DON'T WANNA FACE IT Milk And Honey LP

WELL WELL WELL Live In New York City LP, under dialogue
interview continued re: first seeing them at the Apollo
interview continued re: always being allowed to see them
IT'S SO HARD under dialogue
interview continued re: Statue Of Liberty photo
GIVE ME SOME TRUTH Imagine LP
interview continued re: telling John about Dylan concert
WATCHING THE RIVER FLOW Bob Dylan, edit, under dialogue
interview continued re: he was having a good time staying home
BEAUTIFUL BOY Double Fantasy LP
RAIN under dialogue
interview continued re: John's storm at sea
LOVE ME DO Past Masters LP
SUMMER IN THE CITY The Lovin' Spoonful, under dialogue
interview continued re: John shaving his head
WALKING ON THIN ICE under dialogue
interview continued re: Double Fantasy and the future
WHAT YOU GOT extro

The Lost Lennon Tapes Part 195
Show #91-42, Broadcast the Week of October 14, 1991

WHAT YOU GOT intro
John Wiener interview re: nobody telling Peace movement story
DRAGNET THEME under dialogue
interview continued re: FBI refusal reasons not good enough
POWER TO THE PEOPLE single 1970
interview continued re: FBI has one last chance
interview continued re: what could be so damaging in files
interview continued re: what triggered Nixon's interest
SURPRISE SURPRISE Walls And Bridges LP
interview continued re: FBI kept lyrics to John Sinclair secret
JOHN SINCLAIR Sometime In New York City LP
interview continued re: Beatles criticizing war in Viet Nam
MEMPHIS TENNESSEE Chuck Berry, under dialogue
interview continued re: Beatles not welcome in Memphis
interview continued re: how could they be not welcome
HEARTBREAK HOTEL Elvis Presley, fragment
MEMPHIS TENNESSEE BBC, 8 March 1962, also #62
interview continued re: Ku Klux Klan and cherry bomb
HELP! Live At The Hollywood Bowl LP, under dialogue
'70 Wenner John interview re: I was scared stiff and fire cracker
WHAT GOES ON Rubber Soul LP
interview continued re: May 1968 and revolution
REVOLUTION Past Masters LP

ALL TOGETHER The Rolling Stones, under dialogue
'70 Wenner John interview re: Mick knocking the Beatles
Weiner interview re: Stones defiant Beatles loveable
MISERY Please Please Me LP
interview continued re: Street Fighting Man an apology
STREET FIGHTING MAN The Rolling Stones
SYMPATHY FOR THE DEVIL The Rolling Stones, under dialogue
interview continued re: Attica State uprising
interview continued re: John and Yoko's new song Attica State
ATTICA STATE rehearsal, Elephephant's Memory, also #168
interview continued re: sentiments of audience on David Frost
'70 Wenner John interview re: wanted to speak about Revolution
REVOLUTION 1 The Beatles LP
WHAT YOU GOT extro

The Lost Lennon Tapes Part 196
The Playboy Interview Part III
Show #91-43, Broadcast the Week of October 21, 1991

WHAT YOU GOT intro
I'M SO TIRED under dialogue
'80 Sheff John interview re: talking about songs, P.S. I Love You
P.S. I LOVE YOU Please Please Me LP
interview continued re: Please Please Me
PLEASE PLEASE ME Please Please Me LP
FROM ME TO YOU Past Masters LP
interview continued re: It's Only Love
IT'S ONLY LOVE Help! LP
interview continued re: Do You Want To Know A Secret
DO YOU WANT TO KNOW A SECRET Please Please Me LP
interview continued re: Drive My Car
DRIVE MY CAR Rubber Soul LP
interview continued re: The Word
THE WORD Rubber Soul LP
interview continued re: Day Tripper
DAY TRIPPER Past Masters LP
interview continued re: Hey Bulldog
HEY BULLDOG Yellow Submarine LP
interview continued re: Maxwell's Silver Hammer
MAXWELL'S SILVER HAMMER Abbey Road LP
interview continued re: Dig A Pony
DIG A PONY Let It Be LP
interview continued re: I Got A Feeling
I GOT A FEELING Let It Be LP
interview continued re: Don't Let Me Down

DON'T LET ME DOWN Past Masters LP
interview continued re: The Long And Winding Road
THE LONG AND WINDING ROAD Let It Be LP
WHAT YOU GOT extro

The Lost Lennon Tapes Part 197
Show #91-44, Broadcast the Week of October 28, 1991

WHAT YOU GOT intro
PLEASE MR. POSTMAN under dialogue
AU under dialogue
Flo (Howard) interview re: Zappa and stars, working with John
Eddy (Mark) interview re: rehearsing beforehand
'80 Peebles John interview re: playing Well Baby Please Don't Go
WELL BABY PLEASE DON'T GO Sometime In New York City LP
Flo interview re: Yoko and bag on stage
SKUM BAG Sometime In New York City LP, fragment
Flo interview continued re: John using the jam on his album
Eddy interview continued re: litigation over some of the songs
instrumental under dialogue
Museum of Art John interview re: Frank Zappa was beautiful
Eddy interview continued re: John and Yoko were in love
Flo interview continued re: Frank didn't think it was very cute
REMEMBER Plastic Ono Band LP
How Do You Sleep? descending piano, rehearsal 2 intro, first piece of intro for #118
How Do You Sleep? rehearsal 2 intro, first segment is second piece of intro for #118
How Do You Sleep? rehearsal 1, also #87
How Do You Sleep? Imagine LP
'74 John Canada radio interview re: Walls And Bridges tracks
STEEL AND GLASS demo, fades to
STEEL AND GLASS rough mix
HURDY GURDY MAN Donovan, under dialogue
Donovan interview re: Hendrix the Hurdy Gurdy Man & Zeppelin
HURDY GURDY MAN Donovan, under dialogue
interview continued re: breakthrough record, George verse, on new CD
HURDY GURDY MAN Donovan, The Classics Live LP
Lost Lennon Tapes address
WHAT YOU GOT extro

The Lost Lennon Tapes Part 198
The Beatles In Hollywood - At The Bowl
Show #91-45, Broadcast the Week of November 4, 1991

WHAT YOU GOT intro
interview re: hated live recordings
TWIST AND SHOUT Live At The Hollywood Bowl LP
Bob Ewbanks interview re: borrowing money to put on concert
TICKET TO RIDE Live At The Hollywood Bowl LP
interview continued re: announcing it's our last song
LONG TALL SALLY Live At The Hollywood Bowl LP
interview continued re: riders: adequate sound, TV, towels and coke
A HARD DAY'S NIGHT Live At The Hollywood Bowl LP
press conference excerpt re: stars and Hollywood phoney
THINGS WE SAID TODAY Live At The Hollywood Bowl LP
press conference excerpt re: lip syncing
HELP! Live At The Hollywood Bowl LP
DIZZY MISS LIZZY Live At The Hollywood Bowl LP, under dialogue
'76 Mintz Ringo interview re: event around the concert & Elvis
I'M ALL SHOOK UP Elvis Presley
interview continued re: Elvis playing bass to his television
DON'T BE CRUEL Elvis Presley, under dialogue
interview continued re: Elvis's side of the meeting
GIVE ME SOME TRUTH under dialogue
'80 Sheff John interview re: Epstein biography irrelevant
CRIPPLED INSIDE Imagine LP
SHE'S A WOMAN Live At The Hollywood Bowl LP
Bob Ewbanks interview re: getting them out of Dodgers Stadium
SHE LOVES YOU Live At The Hollywood Bowl LP
NOBODY TOLD ME under dialogue
1973 Mintz John interview re: the Trubadour great moment
'80 Peebles John interview re: couldn't handle the separation
LOOK AT ME Plastic Ono Band LP
WHAT YOU GOT extro

The Lost Lennon Tapes Part 199
Show #91-46, Broadcast the Week of November 11, 1991

A HARD DAY'S NIGHT intro
Epstein interview re: George Martin
Mark Lewisohn interview re: George's early role
I'M GONNA SIT RIGHT DOWN AND CRY under dialogue
George Martin interview re: recording at the Cavern vs London
PLEASE PLEASE ME under dialogue
interview continued re: working very fast to get an album out

BABY IT'S YOU Please Please Me LP
LET IT BE under dialogue
interview continued re: idea of Let It Be
interview continued re: the unhappiest time of all
TWO OF US Let It Be LP
interview continued re: Can't Buy Me Love great
CAN'T BUY ME LOVE A Hard Day's Night LP
interview continued re: myth about John rocker and Paul softie
BECAUSE Abbey Road LP
interview continued re: technical not musical help
interview continued re: scoring background material
PEPPERLAND under dialogue
interview continued re: working quickly on Yellow Submarine
YELLOW SUBMARINE Revolver LP
REVOLUTION under dialogue
interview continued re: they were always anti-establishment
ALL TOGETHER NOW Yellow Submarine LP
interview continued re: somebody had to keep track in the chaos
SGT. PEPPER'S LONELY HEARTS CLUB BAND under dialogue
interview continued re: Sgt. Pepper's an inspirational time
interview continued re: like a collage, couldn't do it again
BEING FOR THE BENEFIT OF MR. KITE Sgt. Pepper's LP
'84 George Martin interview re: it wasn't the greatest
COME TOGETHER Abbey Road LP
SHE LOVES YOU under dialogue
Mark Lewisohn interview re: doing without George Martin
OB-LA-DI OB-LA-DA The Beatles LP
interview continued re: the white album much more fragmented
WHILE MY GUITAR GENTLY WEEPS The Beatles LP
LIVE AND LET DIE single 1973
Paul interview re: working with George Martin on Tug of War LP
George Martin interview continued re: working on Tug Of War LP
EBONY AND IVORY Tug Of War LP
WHAT YOU GOT extro

The Lost Lennon Tapes Part 200
Show #91-47, Broadcast the Week of November 18, 1991

WHAT YOU GOT intro
sampling of 1980 top 40 songs
'80 Peebles John interview re: disco in Bermuda and Rock Lobster
ROCK LOBSTER B-52'S, under dialogue
interview continued re: they're ready for Yoko
KISS KISS KISS Double Fantasy LP
interview continued re: reggae here with R&B in it

I CALL YOUR NAME Past Masters LP
'75 Tom Snyder, Tomorrow Show interview re: liking reggae
THE ISREALITES Desmond Decker, under dialogue
'80 Peebles John interview re: trying to teach musicians reggae
SISERS, O SISTERS Sometime In New York City LP
interview continued re: Mind Games
MIND GAMES Mind Games LP
interview continued re: trying to make Do You Want To Dance reggae
DO YOU WANT TO DANCE Rock 'N' Roll LP
I'M STEPPING OUT under dialogue
interview continued re: press misleading, going underground
Cleanup Time vocal overdub, under dialogue
studio dialogue re: listening to Barbara Graustark interview
STARTING OVER Double Fantasy LP
NOBODY TOLD ME - EVERYBODY'S TALKING, NOBODY'S TALKING demo 2, also #41
NOBODY TOLD ME - EVERYBODY'S TALKING, NOBODY'S TALKING demo 3
NOBODY TOLD ME Milk And Honey LP
sitar music under dialogue
Donovan interview re: being with other musicians for six weeks
interview re: teaching John claw hammer style of guitar
DEAR PRUDENCE The Beatles LP
WHAT YOU GOT extro

The Lost Lennon Tapes Part 201
Show #91-48, Broadcast the Week of November 25, 1991

WHAT YOU GOT intro
STAND BY ME Rock 'N' Roll LP
HERE WE GO AGAIN demo, also #23
I'M THE GREATEST demo 1, also #8
I'M THE GREATEST demo 2
I'M THE GREATEST Ringo LP
MANY RIVERS TO CROSS, Harry Nilsson, under dialogue
MANY RIVERS TO CROSS improv, also #86
GOODNIGHT VIENNA rough mix, John vocal, also #8
GOODNIGHT VIENNA, Ringo
SALLY AND BILLY demo 2, also #30
SALLY AND BILLY demo 3, take 2
SHE'S A FRIEND OF DOROTHY'S demo 2, also #50
SHE'S A FRIEND OF DOROTHY'S demo 1, also #81
TENNESSEE demo, under dialogue
TENNESSEE demo 3
MEMORIES demo 4
WHAT YOU GOT extro

The Lost Lennon Tapes Part 202
Fantasy Concert
Show #91-49, Broadcast the Week of December 2, 1991

crowd noise intro and throughout
COLD TURKEY single 1969
STARTING OVER rough mix
WHATEVER GETS YOU THROUGH THE NIGHT rough mix, no Elton vocal
I DON'T WANNA BE A SOLDIER rough mix
IMAGINE Imagine LP
WATCHING THE WHEELS Milk And Honey LP
YES, I'M YOUR ANGEL Double Fantasy LP
IT'S SO HARD Plastic Ono Band LP
JEALOUS GUY Imagine LP
WOMAN Double Fantasy LP
KISS KISS KISS rough mix
POWER TO THE PEOPLE Live In New York City LP
HAPPY XMAS (WAR IS OVER) rough mix, no choir
GIVE PEACE A CHANCE extro

The Lost Lennon Tapes Part 203
Show #91-50, Broadcast the Week of December 9, 1991

WHAT YOU GOT intro
THE TIMES ARE A-CHANGIN' Bob Dylan, under dialogue
Robert Christgau interview re: the term rock critic
interview continued re: first reading about the Beatles
interview continued re: buying She Loves You, his favourite
interview continued re: the song's incredible up spirit
SHE LOVES YOU Past Masters LP
interview continued re: didn't matter what age you were
RAINY DAY WOMAN NOS. 12 & 35, Bob Dylan, under dialogue
EVERY LITTLE THING Beatles For Sale LP
ROLL OVER BEETHOVEN Live At The Hollywood Bowl LP, under dialogue
interview continued re: they were rebellious
interview continued re: long hair was anti-social in 1965
BAD BOY A Collection of Beatles Oldies LP
NOWHERE MAN Rubber Soul LP
interview continued re: early work equal to later stuff
TWIST AND SHOUT Please Please Me LP
interview continued re: reproduced without imitating rock 'n' roll
ROCK AND ROLL MUSIC Beatles For Sale LP
PLEASE MR. POSTMAN The Marvelettes, under dialogue
interview continued re: the Beatles version is better
PLEASE MR. POSTMAN With The Beatles LP

interview continued re: writing different when writing for the band
GETTING BETTER Sgt. Pepper's LP
interview continued re: it's a shame musically that they broke up
interview continued re: Penny Lane and Strawberry Fields Forever equally good
PENNY LANE Past Masters LP
SO LONG AGO demo 1, #9 Dream, also #63
SO LONG AGO rough mix, #9 Dream
DON'T PASS ME BY under dialogue
interview continued re: Ringo and his simplicity
interview continued re: they knew their limits
NORWEGIAN WOOD Rubber Soul LP
interview continued re: Sgt. Pepper's LP
LUCY IN THE SKY WITH DIAMONDS Sgt. Pepper's LP
WHAT YOU GOT extro

The Lost Lennon Tapes Part 204
Show #91-51, Broadcast the Week of December 16, 1991

WHAT YOU GOT intro
BANGLA DESH George, The Concert For Bangla Desh LP, under dialogue
Cristgau interview re: collectivety giving way to the couple
interview continued re: we were in an age of individualism
ISOLATION Plastic Ono Band LP
interview continued re: writing something good about Yoko, Ringo and hotel
A LITTLE HELP FROM MY FRIENDS Sgt. Pepper's LP
interview continued re: Plastic Ono Band LP is stark yet powerful
MOTHER Plastic Ono Band LP
interview continued re: John had a bad period during middle '70s
I'M LOSING YOU Double Fantasy LP
A CASE OF THE BLUES demo, also #30
LIFE BEGINS AT FORTY demo, also #2, #185, #213
interview continued re: '80 article defense of unhealthy marriage
GOODBYE SADNESS Season Of Glass LP
interview continued re: Yoko's infantalizing of John
DEAR YOKO Double Fantasy LP
interview continued re: who was the controller in the marriage
interview continued re: John becoming a cult figure
WATCHING THE WHEELS Double Fantasy LP
LOOK AT ME demo, also #82, #187
LOOK AT ME rough mix
WHAT YOU GOT extro

The Lost Lennon Tapes Part 205
Christmas Edition
Show #91-52, Broadcast the Week of December 23, 1991

CHRISTMAS TIME IS HERE AGAIN intro
RUDLOPH THE RED-NOSED REGGAE Paul, under dialogue
Paul interview re: cigars, nativity scene and Christmas
WONDERFUL CHRISTMAS TIME Paul
BE-BOP-A-LULA Star Club LP
'63 Christmas record: EVERYWHERE IT'S CHRISTMAS
'63 Christmas record: John and Paul greetings
I WANT TO HOLD YOUR HAND Past Masters LP
'64 Christmas record: John and Paul greeting
I FEEL FINE Past Masters LP
HELP! under dialogue
'65 Christmas record: what have we done to Auld Lang Syne #2
'65 Christmas record: Podgy and Jasper
AND YOUR BIRD CAN SING Revolver LP
FLYING under dialogue
'68 Christmas record: BBC house to Jam Jars request
I AM THE WALRUS Magical Mystery Tour LP
'68 Christmas record: Ringo to George greeting
REVOLUTION Past Masters LP
'69 Christmas record fragment: Happy Xmas George to Ringo greeting
'69 Christmas record: John greeting to take 2, under dialogue
'80 Peebles John interview re: Happy Xmas posters
HAPPY XMAS (WAR IS OVER) rough mix
'65 Christmas record fragment: Johnny Rhythm goodnight
WHAT YOU GOT extro

The Lost Lennon Tapes Part 206
Show #92-01, Broadcast the Week of December 30, 1991

WHAT YOU GOT intro
Ray Coleman interview re: decision to report new music
jazz piece under dialogue
interview continued re: I liked it more than the staff
interview continued re: Brian Epstein calling and meeting Beatles
LOVE ME DO Past Masters LP
interview continued re: didn't go to the Cavern
interview continued re: their cheeky personalities
BESAME MUCHO The Decca Sessions LP, under dialogue
interview continued re: paper taking a broad minded attitude
I'LL FOLLOW THE SUN Beatles For Sale LP
BAD BOY under dialogue

interview continued re: John and Paul's different attitudes
MARTHA MY DEAR The Beatles LP
interview continued re: George always quiet
HERE COMES THE SUN Abbey Road LP
interview continued re: Ringo a clown in the nicest sense
ACT NATURALLY Help! LP
A HARD DAY'S NIGHT under dialogue
interview continued re: they created their own image
MAGICAL MYSTERY TOUR under dialogue
interview continued re: what would have happened if Brian had lived
THE LONG AND WINDING ROAD Let It Be LP
HELP! under dialogue
interview continued re: Hitler salute and making fun of Germans
HIPPY HIPPY SHAKE Live At The Star Club LP
interview continued re: what we love about John
HELLO GOODBYE under dialogue
interview continued re: John complaining his songs sabotaged
YESTERDAY Help! LP
OH YOKO! under dialogue
interview continued re: meeting Yoko and reverting to the artist
OUT THE BLUE rough mix
interview continued re: deifying John's life
WHATEVER GETS YOU THROUGH THE NIGHT Walls And Brdgs LP
FLYING under dialogue
interview continued re: John would be great had he died naturally
Lost Lennon Tapes address
WHAT YOU GOT extro

The Lost Lennon Tapes Part 207
Show #92-02, Broadcast the Week of January 6, 1992

WHAT YOU GOT intro
P.S. I LOVE YOU under dialogue
Mimi tape re: forget the genealogist
tape continued re: John's parents, birth & marriage dates
JULIA The Beatles LP
tape continued re: no such thing as a socialist government
MONEY under dialogue
tape continued re: people will exploit your idealism
GOD Plastic Ono Band LP
tape continued re: never having been loved
LOVE Plastic Ono Band LP
tape continued re: you didn't want anything to do with me
DON'T LET ME DOWN under dialogue
tape continued re: you couldn't bear the sight of me

Ray Coleman interview re: she was a substitute mother
Mimi tape continued re: in your teens I was hard to live with
AND I LOVE HER A Hard Day's Night LP
YAKETY YAK The Coasters & King Curtis
Imagine studio dialogue re: thanks for coming, also #107
studio dialogue continued re: playing on the intro
IT'S SO HARD guitar and vocal with sax runthrough
IT'S SO HARD partial runthrough
Curtis studio dialogue re: if there's anything you want, also #107
IT'S SO HARD rough mix playback with sax runthrough
studio dialogue re: let's hear it back
IT'S SO HARD Imagine LP
I DON'T WANT TO BE A SOLDIER under dialogue
studio dialogue re: where to come in
I DON'T WANNA BE A SOLDIER rough mix playback with sax runthrough
studio dialogue continued re: come in on the highest note
I DON'T WANNA BE A SOLDIER Imagine LP
HOW/CHILD OF NATURE/OH YOKO! demo
WHAT YOU GOT extro

The Lost Lennon Tapes Part 208
Show #92-03, Broadcast the Week of January 13, 1992

WHAT YOU GOT intro
TOMORROW NEVER KNOWS under dialogue
Kenny Everett interview re: touring with the Beatles in '66
interview continued re: couldn't hear themselves play
TICKET TO RIDE Live At The Hollywood Bowl LP
interview continued re: not knowing how to interview them
THINGS WE SAID TODAY A Hard Day's Night LP
interview continued re: fan getting into Weybridge
GIRL Rubber Soul LP
'68 Kenny Everett interview disc fragment: to good morning
GOOD MORNING GOOD MORNING Sgt. Pepper's LP
Kenny Everett interview re: recording Walrus
I AM THE WALRUS Magical Myster Tour LP
interview continued re: idea for I Am The Walrus
'71 Kenny Everett John interview re: new album about childhood
SHE SAID SHE SAID under dialogue
interview continued re: Mother
MOTHER Plastic Ono Band LP
interview continued re: I like people
interview continued re: being less popular, Isolation
ISOLATION Plastic Ono Band LP
LONG HAIRED LADY Paul, under dialogue

interview continued re: seeing others, Paul's music, writing
ALL TOGETHER NOW Yellow Submarine LP
interview continued re: primal therapy
HOLD ON Plastic Ono Band LP
interview continued re: Yoko's singing
WELL WELL WELL Plastic Ono Band LP
interview continued re: are you afraid of death
WHAT YOU GOT extro

The Lost Lennon Tapes Part 209
Show #92-04, Broadcast the Week of January 20, 1992

WHAT YOU GOT intro
'80 Sheff John interview re: Mind Games
MAKE LOVE NOT WAR demo, Mind Games, also #8, #93, #150
I PROMISE demo, also #8, #150
MIND GAMES Mind Games LP
'80 Peebles John interview re: Mind Games a fun track
'80 Sheff John interview re: Mind Games cover
ONE DAY AT A TIME rough mix
interview continued re: Yoko's idea to sing it false setto
INTUITION demo 2, take 4
INTUITION rough mix
TIGHT A$ rough mix, first half missing
interview continued re: Mind Games title from the book
interview continued re: Aisumasen
AISUMASEN rough mix
interview continued re: Only People a failure as a song
ONLY PEOPLE rough mix
YOU ARE HERE rough mix
I KNOW (I KNOW) demo 3, take 4, also #121
interview continued re: album had no clarity of vision
interview continued re: Meat City a piece of garbage
MEAT CITY demo 3, take 2, also #125
MEAT CITY rough mix
WHAT YOU GOT extro

The Lost Lennon Tapes Part 210
The Beatles B Sides, Part I
Show #92-05, Broadcast the Week of January 27, 1992

WHAT YOU GOT intro
MY BONNIE Tony Sheridan, slow english intro, under dialogue
PLEASE PLEASE ME under dialogue

ASK ME WHY Please Please Me single B side
FROM ME TO YOU under dialogue
THANK YOU GIRL From Me To You B side
SHE LOVES YOU under dialogue
I'LL GET YOU She Loves You B side
ROLL OVER BEETHOVEN under dialogue
PLEASE MR. POSTMAN Canadian Beethoven B side
I WANT TO HOLD YOUR HAND under dialogue
I SAW HER STANDING THERE I Want To Hold Your Hand B side
THIS BOY Canadian All My Loving B side
TWIST AND SHOUT under dialogue
THERE'S A PLACE Twist And Shout B side
CAN'T BUY ME LOVE under dialogue
YOU CAN'T DO THAT Can't Buy Me Love B side
A HARD DAY'S NIGHT under dialogue
I SHOULD HAVE KNOWN BETTER A Hard Day's Night B side
I'LL CRY INSTEAD under dialogue
I'M HAPPY JUST TO DANCE WITH YOU I'll Cry Instead B side
AND I LOVE HER under dialogue
IF I FELL And I Love Her B side
I FEEL FINE under dialogue
SHE'S A WOMAN I Feel Fine B side
EIGHT DAYS A WEEK under dialogue
I DON'T WANT TO SPOIL THE PARTY Eight Days A Week B side
TICKET TO RIDE under dialogue
YES IT IS Ticket To Ride B side
BORROWED TIME demo 2, also #72
WHAT YOU GOT extro

The Lost Lennon Tapes Part 211
The Beatles B Sides, Part II
Show #92-06, Broadcast the Week of February 3, 1992

WHAT YOU GOT intro
HELP! Help! LP
I'M DOWN Help! B side
YESTERDAY under dialogue
ACT NATURALLY Yesterday B side
WE CAN WORK IT OUT under dialogue
DAY TRIPPER We Can Work It Out B side
NOWHERE MAN under dialogue
WHAT GOES ON Nowhere Man B side
PAPERBACK WRITER under dialogue
RAIN Paperback Writer B side
YELLOW SUBMARINE under dialogue

ELEANOR RIGBY Yellow Submarine B side
PENNY LANE under dialogue
STRAWBERRY FIELDS FOREVER Penny Lane B side
ALL YOU NEED IS LOVE under dialogue
BABY, YOU'RE A RICH MAN All You Need Is Love B side
HELLO GOODBYE under dialogue
I AM THE WALRUS Hello Goodbye B side
LADY MADONNA under dialogue
THE INNER LIGHT Lady Madonna B side
ONE OF THE BOYS demo 2, take 1, also #81
WHAT YOU GOT extro

The Lost Lennon Tapes Part 212
The Beatles B Sides, Part III
Show #92-07, Broadcast the Week of February 10, 1992

WHAT YOU GOT intro
HEY JUDE Past Masters LP
REVOLUTION Hey Jude B side
GET BACK under dialogue
DON'T LET ME DOWN Get Back B side
THE BALLAD OF JOHN AND YOKO under dialogue
OLD BROWN SHOE The Ballad of John And Yoko B side
SOMETHING under dialogue
COME TOGETHER Something B side
LET IT BE under dialogue
YOU KNOW MY NAME Let It Be B side
FOR YOU BLUE The Long And Winding Road B side
THE LONG AND WINDING ROAD Past Masters LP
MIRROR MIRROR ON THE WALL demo 3, take 1, also #20
WIZZARD OF OZ fragment re: I am Oz, who are you
WHAT YOU GOT extro

The Lost Lennon Tapes Part 213
1980 Composing Tapes
Show #92-08, Broadcast the Week of February 17, 1992

WHAT YOU GOT intro
NEW YORK CITY under dialogue
'80 Sheff John interview re: hanging around in New York
NEW YORK CITY One To One Rehearsal 1, with third verse, faded different ending, also #19
FAME David Bowie, under dialogue
interview continued re: too shy to go back stage at theatre or on TV
WHATEVER HAPPENED TO demo, take 2, intro cut, also #11

Yoko interview re: we're just a normal couple
LET ME COUNT THE WAYS Milk And Honey LP
GROW OLD WITH ME under dialogue
MEMORIES demo, under dialogue
FREE AS A BIRD demo 1, also #<u>78</u>
GROW OLD WITH ME demo, also #7
I DON'T WANNA FACE IT Milk and Honey LP
YOU SAVED MY SOUL demo 1, also #<u>99</u>, #217
YOU SAVED MY SOUL demo 2, also #86, #183
Pop Is The Name Of The Game, vocal improv, also #86
SERVE YOURSELF demo 9, coda, also #86, #183
GONE FROM THIS PLACE improv, fragment, ONLY THE LONELY - CRYING missing, also #<u>70</u>, #74
GONE FROM THIS PLACE demo 2 take 4, also #<u>74</u>
HOLD ON JOHN under dialogue
'80 Sheff John interview re: feelings when Brian died
interview continued fragment re: Hold On John and death
'71 Mintz John interview re: remembered as two lovers
LIFE BEGINS AT FORTY demo, also #2, #185, #<u>204</u>
DEAR JOHN demo, edited from beginning and end of full take, also #<u>12</u>, #165
'80 Sheff John interview re: there's another 40 years to go
WHAT YOU GOT extro

The Lost Lennon Tapes Part 214
First Day Recording Double Fantasy - August 6, 1980
Show #92-09, Broadcast the Week of February 24, 1992

WHAT YOU GOT intro
I'M STEPPING OUT runthrough 1, first day
studio dialogue re: out of tune
'80 Peebles John interview re: musicians on Double Fantasy LP
I'M STEPPING OUT false runthrough start, fragment
studio dialogue re: still out of tune, It's Now Or Never
studio dialogue continued re: a little out of tune is nice
studio dialogue continued re: I'm stepping down
Little Jimmy Brown improv, fragment
I'M STEPPING OUT runthrough 2
RUN FOR YOUR LIFE under dialogue
interview continued re: changing roles to understand feminists
WORKING CLASS HERO Plastic Ono Band
interview continued re: motivation for being a house husband
DEAR YOKO Double Fantasy LP
interview continued re: making bread and working at home
studio dialogue re: food order for Yoko not me
I'M STEPPING OUT runthrough 3
studio dialogue re: band is speeding up

BEAUTIFUL BOY under dialogue
interview continued re: staying home with Sean compared to Julian
BEAUTIFUL BOY Double Fantasy LP
interview continued re: concerned I did it right
studio dialogue re: no echo on the voice
studio dialogue re: don't know if I'll get through a whole take
studio dialogue re: do it right away or the room changes
I'M STEPPING OUT runthrough 4, last take of the day
WHAT YOU GOT extro

The Lost Lennon Tapes Part 215
Show #92-10, Broadcast the Week of March 2, 1992

WHAT YOU GOT intro
I'M STEPPING OUT runthrough 4, fragment, last August 6, 1980, under dialogue
studio dialogue re: less, tight and sweet
studio dialogue re: Isley riff in Borrowed Time solo
BORROWED TIME runthrough, August 6, 1980
ENGLISHMAN IN NEW YORK Sting, under dialogue
'80 Peebles John interview re: NY becoming romantic like Paris
IF IF FELL A Hard Day's Night LP
interview continued re: Fawlty Towers, I'd love to be a comedian
WHEN I GET HOME A Hard Day's Night LP
interview continued re: do you get homesick
NEW YORK CITY Some Time In New York City
studio dialogue re: Get Up, Stand Up
studio dialogue continued re: listen to Get Up Stand Up
GET UP, STAND UP fragment Bob Marley, playback, talk over
studio dialolgue continued & tuning
BORROWED TIME runthrough
REAL LIFE demo 6, take 2
REAL LIFE demo 2, take 3, also #<u>17</u>
I'M STEPPING OUT Milk And Honey LP
REAL LIFE demo 7, also #83
REAL LOVE - GIRLS AND BOYS demo 1, Imagine: John Lennon Soundtrack LP, also #3, #37
WHAT YOU GOT extro

The Lost Lennon Tapes Part 216
Show #92-11, Broadcast the Week of March 9, 1992

WHAT YOU GOT intro
ROCK 'N' ROLL PEOPLE demo 1, also #17
'80 Peebles John interview re: Phil Spector's production
SOME OTHER GUY Ritchie Barrett, intro

INSTANT KARMA single 1970
'70 Wenner John interview re: Phil is great, doesn't fuss around
interview continued re: the Beatles inhibited each other
IMAGINE alternate take, no orchestra
interview continued re: Phil had a lot of energy
interview continued re: talking Phil into being producer
interview continued re: Rock 'N' Roll LP sessions
ANGEL BABY under dialogue
interview continued re: finishing the album by himself
AIN'T THAT A SHAME rough mix
BE MY BABY The Ronnettes, fragment
BE MY BABY rough mix, ROOTS LP mix, also #77, #158
STAND BY ME Old Grey Whistle Test, also #39
MOVE OVER MS. L outake
WHATEVER GETS YOU THROUGH THE NIGHT demo, intro longer, also #12, #165
WHATEVER GETS YOU THROUGH THE NIGHT rough mix, no Elton
I SAW HER STANDING THERE Madison Square Garden rehearsal, also #70
A HARD DAY'S NIGHT/HELP!/GLASS ONION/JUDE continued under dialogue
Elliot Mintz announcement re: end of show - 2 part finale
WHAT YOU GOT extro

The Lost Lennon Tapes Part 217
The Best Of The Lost Lennon Tapes Part I
Show #92-12, Broadcast the Week of March 16, 1992

WHAT YOU GOT intro
Yoko intro to The Lost Lennon Tapes
MEMORIES demo, under dialogue
MY LIFE demo, Starting Over, fragment
DON'T BE CRAZY demo, Starting Over, fragment
STARTING OVER - THE WORST IS OVER demo, fragment
STARTING OVER rough mix, cut into 1st verse
'80 Peebles John interview re: adding Just Like to title
Indian music under dialogue
Great WOK 1978 New Year's resolution, fragment, also #49, #50, #185
SERVE YOURSELF demo, fragment
'66 Chicago John press conference fragment re: Christ remark
GOD demo 4
interview re: I always suspected there was a God
HELP ME TO HELP MYSELF demo 1, takes 2, 3, also #150, #180
YOU SAVED MY SOUL demo 1, intro under dialogue, also #99, 213
NOBODY TOLD ME rough mix, under dialogue
MARCH OF THE MEANIES under dialogue
interview continued re: cleaning out apartment before bust
DRAGNET THEME under dialogue

interview continued re: picture on back of Life With The Lions
COLD TURKEY Live Peace In Toronto LP, under dialogue
'80 Sheff John interview re: Cold Turkey
'69 Toronto press conference John interview re: the drug problem
COLD TURKEY demo 1, take 1, also #72
CLEANUP TIME demo, under dialogue
'80 Peebles John interview re: Chinese acupuncturist
John interviews Sean fragment December 1975 re: New York
BEAUTIFUL BOY demo 4, also #<u>69</u> #3
John interviews Sean fragment re: good morning Sean
I PROMISE demo, fragment
MAKE LOVE NOT WAR demo, fragment
MIND GAMES under dialogue
'73 Mintz John interview re: word play
Elliot Mintz mind movie intro
TOO MANY PEOPLE Paul, under dialogue
interview re: How Do You Sleep?, used resentment to write song
How Do You Sleep? alternate take
OH YOKO! demo, under dialogue
interview cuts re: meeting Yoko at gallery
'70 Wenner John interview re: don't regret a thing since Yoko
interview continued re: they all sat there and judged us
'68 Christmas record fragment: Jock & Yono
GROW OLD WITH ME under dialogue
Yoko interview re: I think his spirit is still around
interview continued re: I do think we'll meet again in some form
OUT THE BLUE alternate mix
WHAT YOU GOT extro

The Lost Lennon Tapes Part 218
The Best Of The Lost Lennon Tapes Part II
Show #92-13, Broadcast the Week of March 23, 1992

WHAT YOU GOT intro
WATCHING THE WHEELS runthrough
studio dialogue re: feel of song into **I Am The Walrus** studio improv
WOMAN backing tracks, under dialogue
'80 Peebles John interview re: liking Woman, being romantic
studio dialogue re: feel like I'm in the fucking Beatles with this track
WOMAN runthrough
THE HAPPY RISHIKESH SONG demo, under dialogue
CHILD OF NATURE demo, fragment, child chord search
JEALOUS GUY Imagine LP
Maurice Dupont Part 2, mind movie, also #22
SHE'S A FRIEND OF DOROTHY'S demo, fragment

SALLY AND BILLY demo, fragment
TENNESSE demo, fragment
MEMORIES demo, fragment
I'M IN LOVE demo
I'M LOSING YOU rough mix, fragment also #71
'80 Peebles John interview re: couldn't get through
STRANGER'S ROOM demo, fragment
DOWN IN EASTERN AUSTRALIA I MET HER improv, fragment
'65 BBC TV: We Must Not Forget The General Erection
POWER TO THE PEOPLE under dialogue
'80 Sheff John interview re: I want maximum communication
GIVE PEACE A CHANCE fragment
'70 Wenner John interview re: hanger's on, I'm a genius
I'M THE GREATEST studio demo 2, John vocal, also #61
'80 Sheff John interview continued re: can't follow soap operas
soap opera excerpt
FALLING IN LOVE AGAIN improv in German
interview fragment re: I used to be pretty big in this business
SHE LOVES YOU/PPM/RAIN/COME TOGETHER/IN MY LIFE under dialogue
interview fragment re: Mimi, mother being killed, Quarry Men
interview fragment re: toppermost of the poppermost story
interview fragment re: Paul and I writing before George in the group
rattle your jewellery statement
interview fragment re: after Brian died we collapsed
interview fragment re: used Yoko as strength to leave
interview fragment re: point of bed-in is a commercial for peace
interview fragment re: getting green card
interview fragment re: couldn't deal with separation any other way
interview fragment re: torture writing
interview fragment re: didn't know Julian
interview fragment re: we want to do a record, public excepted it
STARTING OVER alternate mix
GET BACK outro: I hope we passed the audition
WATCHING THE WHEELS backing tracks, under dialogue
credits and thanks
Preview of The Beatle Years Series

CHRONOLOGY OF LOST LENNON TAPES TRACKS

1958		That'll Be The Day
1960-5	Quarrymen	Catswalk
		One After 909 - version one
		Moovin' And Groovin'
		Hello Little Girl
		One After 909 - version two
1962-01-02	Decca Audition	Hello Little Girl
1962-03-08	BBC	Dream Baby
1962-03-08	BBC	Memphis Tennessee
1962-08-22	Cavern	Some Other Guy
1962-09-04	Parlophone	How Do You Do It - 2 versions
1963-03-05	Parlophone	One After 909
1963-03-22	Please Please Me LP	I Saw Her Standing - alternate take
		Misery - take 1
		Misery - takes 2 to 6
		Do You Want To Know A Secret - alternate mix
		A Taste Of Honey - rough mix
		There's A Place - take 1
		There's A Place - take 3
		There's A Place - rough mix
1963-06-24 (1)	BBC	Monkey Business /
1963-05-13 (2)	BBC	Thank You Girl /
1963-04-07 (3)	BBC	From Me To You
1963-04-22	BBC	Side by Side
1963-05-31	demo	Bad To Me
1963-06-04 (1)	BBC	Pop Go the Beatles /
1963-06-18 (2)	BBC	A Shot of Rhythm and Blues
1963-06-11	BBC	I Got to Find My Baby
1963-06-11	BBC	Young Blood
1963-07-16	BBC	Carol / Soldier of Love / Lend Me Your Comb
1963-06-18 (1)	BBC	Sure to Fall /
1963-06-25 (2)	BBC	Anna /
1963-06-25 (3)	BBC	Twist and Shout
1963-06-23	BBC	Some Other Guy / A Taste of Honey
1963-06-24	BBC	I'll Be on My Way
1963-07-23	BBC	Sweet Little Sixteen
1963-07-23	BBC	Nothin' Shakin' (But the Leaves on the Trees)
1963-07-23	BBC	So How Come (No One Loves Me)
1963-07-30	BBC	Do You Want to Know a Secret
1963-07-30	BBC	Matchbox
1963-07-30	BBC	Please Mr. Postman
1963-07-30	BBC	Hippy Hippy Shake (The)
1963-08-06	BBC	Cryin', Waitin', Hopin'
1963-08-06	BBC	To Know Her Is to Love Her

1963-08-06	BBC	Honeymoon Song (The)
1963-08-13	BBC	Please Please Me
1963-08-13	BBC	I Got a Woman
1963-09-03	BBC	Honey Don't
1963-09-17	BBC	Chains
1963-09-17	BBC	You Really Got a Hold on Me
1963-10-05	BBC	I Saw Her Standing There
1963-10-05	BBC	Happy Birthday Saturday Club / I'll Get You
1963-10-10	BBC	Too Much Monkey Business
1963-10-17	7"	The Beatles Christmas Record (Crimble) recorded
1963-10-20	BBC	I Saw Her Standing There
1963-10-20	BBC	Love Me Do
1963-10-20	BBC	She Loves You
1963-10-23	POP '63	I Saw Her Standing There
		From Me To You
		Money (That's What I Want)
		Roll Over Beethoven
		You Really Got A Hold On Me
		She Loves You
		Twist And Shout
1963-11-04	Royal Variety Show	Twist And Shout
1963-11-04	7"	From Me To You - early mix
		From Me To You - count-in
1963-11-15	7"	I'm In Love - demo
1963-12-07	It's The Beatles	I Want To Hold Your Hand
		From Me To You
1963-12-21	BBC	This Boy
1963-12-21	BBC	Roll over Beethoven
1963-12-26	BBC	From Us to You
1963-12-26	BBC	Tie Me Kangaroo down Sport
1964-01-16/2-4	Paris	From Me To You
		This Boy
		I Want To Hold Your Hand
		She Loves You
1964-02-11	Washington	From Me To You
		This Boy
		Please Please Me
		She Loves You
1964-02-15	BBC	Johnny B. Goode
1964-02-15	BBC	I Want to Hold Your Hand
1964-02-19	Ed Sullivan	All My Loving / Till There Was You - She Loves You
		I Saw Her Standing There / I Want to Hold Your Hand
1964-02-16	Ed Sullivan	This Boy
1964-03-30	BBC	Roll over Beethoven / Beatles Crimble Medley
1964-03-30	BBC	Till There Was You
1964-03-30	BBC	I Wanna Be Your Man

Date	Source	Title
1964-03-30	BBC	All My Loving
1964-04-04	BBC	I Got a Woman
1964-04-04	BBC	You Can't Do That
1964-04-04	BBC	Sure to Fall
1964-04-26	Wembley	She Loves You
1964-05-06	Around The Beatles	Twist And Shout
		Roll Over Beethoven
		I Wanna Be Your Man
		Long Tall Sally
		Medley: Love Me Do / Please Please Me / From Me To You / She Loves You / I Wanna Hold Your Hand / Can't Buy Me Love
		Shout
1964-05-18	BBC	Whit Monday to You / I Forgot to Remember to Forget
1964-05-18	BBC	Honey Don't
1962-06-06	Parlophone	Besame Mucho
1964-06-12/13	Adelaide, Australia	I Saw Her Standing There
		I Want To Hold Your Hand
		All My Loving
		Twist And Shout
1964-06-15	Melbourne	You Can't Do That
		She Loves You / Twist And Shout / Long Tall Sally
1964-08-14	Parlophone	Leave My Kitten Alone
1964-09-02	Philadelphia	If I Fell - A Hard Day's Night
		You Can't Do That / She Loves You /
		Things We Said Today / Long Tall Sally
1964-07-10	A Hard Day's Night	A Hard Day's Night - alternate take
		Can't Buy Me Love - alternate take
1964-07-16	BBC	Long Tall Sally
1964-08-23	Hollywood Bowl	Twist and Shout
		If I Fell
		I Wanna Hold Your Hand
1964-11-26	BBC	I'm a Loser / She's a Woman / I Feel Fine
1964-11-27	7"	I Feel Fine - alternate take 6
		I Feel Fine - alternate take 9
1964-12-26	BBC	Rock and Roll Music
1964-12-26	BBC	Kansas City / Everybody's Trying to Be My Baby
1964-12-26	BBC	She's a Woman
1965-04-09	7"	Ticket To Ride - rough mix
		Yes It Is - take 1
		Yes It Is - take 2
		Yes It Is - take 8
		Yes It Is - take 14
1965-06-07	BBC	Honey Don't
1965-06-07	BBC	Dizzy Miss Lizzy
1965-06-07	BBC	Ticket to Ride

Date	Location/Source	Tracks
1965-06-20	PARIS - afternoon	I'm A Loser - Can't Buy Me Love / I Wanna Be Your Man / A Hard Day's Night / Rock And Roll Music / I Feel Fine / Ticket To Ride / Long Tall Sally
1965-06-20	PARIS -evening	I'm A Loser / A Hard Day's Night - evening / Can't Buy Me Love / Rock And Roll Music
1965-08-06	Help !	Help! - demo
		Help! - alternate take 1
		Help! - alternate take 5
		You're Going To Lose That Girl - rough mix
1965-08-14	ED Sullivan	I Feel Fine
		Ticket To Ride
		Yesterday
		Help!
1965-08-29	Hollywood Bowl	Twist and Shout / She's a Woman / Dizzy Miss Lizzy
1965-12-03	7"	Day Tripper - alternate takes 2 and 3
		We Can Work It Out - demo
		We Can Work It Out - alternate take 2
1965-12-03	Rubber Soul	Norwegian Wood - alternate take
		Norwegian Wood - alternate take 2
		Norwegian Wood - alternate take 4
		Michelle - guitar rehearsal
		Run For Your Life - alternate take 5
1966-06-30	Budokan, Japan	Rock And Roll Music
		She's A Woman
		If I Needed Someone
		Day Tripper
		Baby's In Black
		I Feel Fine
		Yesterday
		I Wanna Be Your Man
		Nowhere Man
		Paperback Writer
		I'm Down
1966-06-24	Munich, Gemany	Rock and Roll Music
		I Feel Fine
		Yesterday
		Nowhere Man
1966-06-10	7"	Paperback Writer - with count-in
		Rain - basic tracks
1966-08-05	Revolver	He Said He Said - demos 1 to 5
		She Said, She Said - demo
		Tomorrow Never Knows - reference mix
1966-08-29	Candlestick Park	Rock And Roll Music
1967-02-17	7"	Penny Lane - rough mix
		Penny Lane - playback and rehearsal
		Strawberry Fields Forever

		- 10 tracks of various versions and takes
1967-05-17	recording date	You Know My Name
1967-05-25	recording date	It's All Too Much
1967-06-01	Sgt. Pepper	Good Morning, Good Morning
		A Day In The Life
1967-06-25	Our World	All You Need Is Love
1967-11-24	7"	I Am The Walrus
1967-11-28	recording date	Christmas Time (Is Here Again)
1967-12-08	MMT EP	Flying
1967-12-15	7"	Christmas Message
1968-02-11	recording date	Hey Bulldog
1968-05-20 to29	Kinfauns	Cry Baby Cry
		Child Of Nature
		The Continuing Story Of Bungalow Bill
		I'm So Tired
		Everybody's Got Something To Hide Except Me And...
		What's The New Mary Jane
		Revolution
		Not Guilty
		Piggies
		Julia
		Back In The U.S.S.R.
		Mother Nature's Son
		Dear Prudence
		Sexy Sadie
1968-08-30	7"	Hey Jude - alternate take 9
1968	demo	The Maharishi Song
1968-08-26	7"	Revolution - single alternate mix
1968-09-04	filming date	Revolution - promo film soundtrack
1968-11-22	The White Album	Dear Prudence
		Julia
		Cry Baby Cry
1968-12-11/12	Rock And Roll Circus	Yer Blues - rehearsal take 1
		Yer Blues - rehearsal take 2
		Yer Blues - alternate mix
		Yer Blues
1969	demo	Everyone Had A Hard Year
1969-01-2 to 30	Get Back sessions	various rehearsal tracks
1969-03-25 to 31	Amsterdam bed-in	I Want You
1969-04-11	7"	Don't Let Me Down
1969-05-30	7"	Ballad Of John And Yoko
1969-05-26 to 1969-6-2	Montreal bed-in	Because
		Happiness Is A Warm Gun
1969-07-04	7"	Give Peace a Chance - 2 rehearsals - 2 takes
		Ballad of John & Yoko Crucify Capp improv
1969-09-26	Abbey Road	I Want You (She's So Heavy)

		Because
		You Never Give Me Your Money
		Mean Mr. Mustard
		Her Majesty
1969-10-24	7"	Cold Turkey - 3 demos - 1 take
1969-12-20	Toronto bed-in	Give Peace A Chance
1969-12	bed-in	Get It Together John & Yoko Christmas message
1970-05-08	Let it Be (Box Set)	Across The Universe
1970	POB sessions	Perkins jam
		Mystery Train
		Well Baby Please Don't Go
		That's Alright Mama
		jam
1970-12-11	POB	Mother - 1 demo - 1 take
		I Found Out - 2 demos - 1 mix
		Love - 1 demo
		Well Well Well - 1 demo 1 take
		Look At Me - 1 demo - 3 mixes
		God - 4 demos
		My Mummy's Dead - 1 take - 1 mix
		When A Boy Meets - 1 demo
1970-11	Tittenhurst	John and Yoko Christmas Message
1971-03-12	7"	Power to the People - 4 takes - 1 mix
1971-07-16		God Save Us - demo
		God Save Us - John vocal
		Keep Right On To The End Of The Road - flexi disc
1971-09	Clock Film	Shazam
		Honey Don't
		Glad All Over
		Lend Me Your Comb
		Heartbeat
		Peggy Sue Got Married
		Peggy Sue
		Maybe Baby
		Mailman, Bring Me No More Blues
		Rave On
	Imagine sessions	San Francisco Bay
1971-10-8	Imagine	Imagine - 6 takes - 1 mix
		Crippled Inside - 1 take
		Jealous Guy - 1 take - 1 mix
		It's So Hard - 3 takes - 1 mix - 1 overdub
		I Don't Wanna Be A Soldier - 2 takes - 1 mix
		Give Me Some Truth - 2 takes - 1 mix
		Oh My Love - 3 demos - 1 take - 2 mixes
		How Do You Sleep? - 2 rehearsals - 4 takes
		How? - 2 demos

		How? / Child of Nature / Oh Yoko! - demo
		How? - 2 takes
		Oh Yoko! - 3 demos - 2 mixes
1971-10-09	John Birthday	What'd I Say
		Goodnight Irene
		Blue Suede Shoes
		Crippled Inside
		Give Peace A Chance
		Imagine/Oh Yoko!
1971-12-10	John Sinclair Rally	Attica State
		The Luck Of The Irish
		John Sinclair
1971-12-16	David Frost	John Sinclair
		- broadcast with the following from Mike Douglas
1971-12	Attica State Rehearsal	Attica State
1971-12-17	Attica State Benefit	Imagine
1972-01-31	Mike Douglas	It's So Hard
1972-02-02		Memphis
1972-02-02		Johnny B. Goode
1972-02-04		Imagine
1972-05-05	Dick Cavett	Woman Is The Nigger Of The World
1972-08-22-26	One To One rehearsal	Come Together
		It's So Hard
		Woman Is The Nigger Of The World
		Give Peace A Chance
		Well Well Well
		Instant Karma
		jam
		Tequila jam
		Mother
		Come Together #2
		Cold Turkey
		Roll Over Beethoven
		Hound Dog/Long Tall Sally
		New York City - 3 radio ad backing tracks
	Some Time rehearsal	Not Fade Away
		Roll Over Beethoven
		Whole Lotta Shakin' Goin' On
		Rumble / Whole Lotta Love
		Send Me Some Lovin'
		Don't Be Cruel
		Ain't That A Shame
		Jam
1972-09-15	Some Time in NYC	Woman is the Nigger of the World - 2 demos - 1 take
		Attica State - 1 demo
		New York City - 2 demos

		The Luck of the Irish - 3 demos - 1 take
		Angela - 3 demos
1972-11-24	7"	Happy Xmas (War is Over) - demo - 3 takes
1971-1972	demo	Pill
	Mind Games demos	I Promise
1973-11-16	Mind Games	Mind Games - 1 demo - 1 take - 2 mixes
		Tight A$ - 1 demo - 2 mixes
		Aisumasen (I'm Sorry) - 2 demos - 2 mixes
		One Day (at a Time) - 2 mixes
		Bring on the Lucie (Freeda Peeple) - 1 demo - 1 mix
1973-11-16	Mind Games	Intuition - 2 demos - 2 mixes
		Out the Blue - 4 mixes
		Only People - 1 take - 3 mixes
		I Know (I Know) - 3 demos - 1 mix
		You Are Here - 1 mix
		Meat City - 3 demos - 2 mixes
1973-11-9	Ringo	I'm The Greatest
		- 2 demos - 3 studio demos - 4 takes - 1 mix
1974-08-30	Pussy Cats	Many Rivers To Cross - 1 mix
		Mucho Mungo - 3 demos
		- complete rehearsals from various fragments
1974	John Dawson Winter III	Rock & Roll People - 2 demos - 2 takes - 1 mix
1974	Mick Jagger	Too Many Cooks - 1 take
1974-10-4	Walls and Bridges	Going Down On Love - 1 demo - 1 rehearsal
		Whatever Gets You Through The Night - 2 demos
		- 2 rehearsal - 2 mixes
		Old Dirt Road - 1 mix
		What You Got - 1 demo
		Bless You - 1 rehearsal - 1 mix
		#9 Dream - 2 demos - 2 mixes
		Surprise, Surprise - 2 demos - 1 take
		Steel And Glass - 1 demo & rough mix - 1 rehearsal
		Beef Jerky - various piano and guitar outake extros
1973	Rock 'n' Roll rehearsal	Be-Bop-A-Lula - jam
		Peggy Sue - rehearsal
		That'll Be The Day - rehearsal
		Thirty Days - jam
1973-fall	Rock 'n' Roll recorded	Be-Bop-A-Lula
1974-10-21 to 25	Rock 'n' Roll recorded	Stand By Me - 1 take
		Medley: Rip It Up/Ready Teddy - 1 take - 1 mix
		You Can't Catch Me - 3 takes
		Ain't That A Shame - 1 mix
		Do You Want To Dance - 1 take
		Sweet Little Sixteen - 1 take - 1 mix
		Slippin' And Slidin' - 1 take
		Peggy Sue - 1 mix

		Bring It On Home To Me / Send Me Some Lovin' - 1 take
1974-10-21 to 25	Rock 'n' Roll recorded	Bony Morone - 1 mix
		Ya Ya - 1 take
		Just Because - 1 tale
		Be My Baby - 1 mix Roots LP
		Here We Go Again - demo
1974-11-15	7"	Only You - 1 take John vocal
1974-11-15	Goodnight Vienna	Goodnight Vienna - 1 mix John vocal
1974-11	Madison rehearsal	I Saw Her Standing There
1975-03-17	Old Grey Whistle Test	Stand By Me
1975-04-18	7"	Move Over Ms L - 2 demos - 2 rehearsals - 1 take - 1 mix
1975		Tennessee - 3 demos
1975		Nobody Told Me / Everybody's Talking Nobody's Talking - 2 demos
1975		Sally And Billy - 3 demos
1976		Mucho Mungo
1976		Cookin' - 3 demos
1977		She's A Friend of Dorothy - 2 demos
1977		Free As A Bird - 2 demos
1977		Whatever Happened To - 1 demo
1977		One Of The Boys - 2 demos
1977		Mirror Mirror - 3 demos
1977		Sea Ditties
1978		Too Much Monkey Business / Subterranean Homesick Blues
1978		Rock Island Line 2
1978		Brown Eyed Handsome Man / Get Back
1978		Beyond The Sea / Blue Moon / Young Love
1978		Knocking On Heaven's Door
1978		News Of The World
1978		Maggie Mae
1978		Falling In Love Again
1978		I'm A Man
1978		Twas A Night Like Ethel Merman
1979		I Don't Wanna Face It - part 83 demo 1 - demo 2 - demo 3
1979		I Watch Your Face - 1 demo
1979-10		Serve Yourself - demo 8 - demo 6
1979-10		Don't Be Crazy - demo 1 - demo 2
1979-10		Girls & Boys -part 115 demo 4 - part 180 early fragments demo 6
1979-10		Real Life - 7 demos
1979-10		Serve Yourself - demo 5 - demo 2
1979-10		Girls & Boys - part 115 demo 5 - part 3 demo 1
1979-10 to early 1980		Runs Them Round In Circles / Beautiful Boy - part 165 demo

Date	Location	Title
1979-10 to early 1980		Rock Island Line 1
1979-10 to early 1980		Many Rivers To Cross - part 201
1979-10 to early 1980		Beautiful Boy - part 90 demo 1
1979-10 to early 1980		Howling At The Moon - part 45 demo
1979-10 to early 1980		Beautiful Boy / Memories / Howling At The Moon / Across The River
1979-late		Help Me To Help Myself - part 180 demo 2
1979-late to early 1980		Life Begins At Forty
1979-late to early 1980		Girls And Boys - part 77 demo 2 take 4
1979-late to early 1980		Girls And Boys - part 91 demo 3 take 5
1980-early to April		Watching The Wheels - 1 demo - demo 3 - demo 6 - P1
1980-early to April		I'm Losing You (Stranger's Room) - part 30 demo 2
1980-early to April		John Henry - 3 demos
1980-early to April		Watching The Wheels - demo 4 - demo 5
1980-early to April		Corrina, Corrina
1980-early to April		I'm Losing You - Stranger's Room - demo 4 - demo 5
1980-early to April		My Life - demo 6 - demo 2 - demo 4
1980-early to April		Serve Yourself - demo 7 - demo 3
1980-early to April		Memories - demo 2
1980-early to April		Cathy's Clown
1980-early to April		You Send Me
1980-early to April		Memories - demo 1
1980-early to April		Memories / Watching The Wheels - demo 3
1980	Bermuda	Dear Yoko - part 72 - demo 2
1980	Bermuda	Borrowed Time - part 210 - demo 2
1980	Bermuda	I'm Stepping Out- part 120 demo 3 - demo 4
1980	Bermuda	Beautiful Boy - demo 2 - demo 3 - demo 4
1980	Bermuda	Borrowed Time - demo 1
1980	Bermuda	Dear Yoko - part 21 - demo 1
1980	Bermuda	Serve Yourself - demo 9
1980	Bermuda	Nobody Told Me - demo 1
1980	Bermuda	Memories - demo 4
1980	Bermuda	I'm Losing You - part 30 - demo 3
1980	Bermuda	I'm Losing You - p3 - demo 1
1980	Bermuda	I'm Stepping Out - part 17 - demo 1
1980	Bermuda	I'm Stepping Out - part 70 - demo 2
1980	Bermuda	Happy Rishikesh Song
1980	Bermuda	Real Love - part 58 demo 1 take 1
1980	Bermuda	Real Love - part 134 demo 2
1980	Bermuda	Grow Old With Me - demo
1980	Bermuda	Woman - demos 1 to 6
1980	Bermuda	Nobody Told Me - demo 2
1980	Bermuda	My Little Flower Princess - part 67 - demo
1980		The Worst Is Over - demo 1 - demo 2
1980		Help Me To Help Myself - part 150 demo 1
1980		My Life -demo 3 - demo 1 -demo 5

1980		Serve Yourself - demo 4 - demo 1
1980		Cleanup Time - 2 demos
1980		Starting Over - 2 demos
1980		Gone From This Place - 2 demos
1980-11		Dear John
1980-11-14		You Saved My Soul
1980-11-14		Pop Is The Name Of The Game
1976-1980	demos unknown date	I'll Make You Happy - 1 demo
		He Got The Blues - 1 demo
1976-1980	improvs	Eastern Australia
unknown date		The Best Things In Life Are Free
		Banana Song
		Case Of The Blues
		Send Me Some Lovin
		Mind Movie Tango
		We'll Meet Again
		Sailin' On The Carribean
		I Ain't Got Time
		Ants In My Pants
		Chords of Fame
		She'll Be Coming Round The Mountain
		Pedro The Fisherman
		The Boat Song
		Instrumental Diversion
		Let's Get Peculiar
		Little Jimmy Brown
		Only The Lonely / Crying / Gone From This Place
1980-11-17	Double Fantasy	She's A Woman - studio jam
		Starting Over - alternate mix - rough mix x 3
		- playback - booth
		Cleanup Time - rehearse - runthrough
		- alternate take x 2 - rough mix - remix
		I'm Losing You - rehearse - alternate take - studio
		- overdub - rough mix
		Beautiful Boy - runthrough - alternate take - early take
		- early mix - rough mix
		Watching The Wheels - runthrough x 2 - rough mix x 2
		Woman - runthru x 2 - alt take - overdub x 2 - guitar
		- early mix - rough mix x 3
		Dear Yoko - runthrough - basic tracks - rough mix x 2
1984-1-23	Milk and Honey	I'm Stepping Out - runthrough x 5
		I'm Stepping Out - outtake - alt take x 3 - rough mix x 2
		I Don't Wanna Face It - rough mix
		Nobody Told Me - runthrough - alternate take - rough mix
		Borrowed Time - runthrough x 3 - alternate take
		- alternate mix - rough mix x 2

TV - rehearsals - poetry & extras	My Little Flower Princess - alternate take
	Grow Old With Me - rough mix
	Waltzing Matilda
	Midsummer Night's Scream
	Good Dog Nigel
	I Sat Belonely
	National Health Cow
	The General Erection & Wumberlog
	The Clinic (Cynthia reads)
	Backwards Speak
	Grapefruit Reading
	The Pile
	Neville Club
	Wumberlog (Spaniard In The Works reading)
	BBC Top Gear promo
	BBC interview non-stop pop
	BBC interview Brian Matthew
	BBC goodbye
	KHJ complete
	KSAN complete
	WNEW complete
	nativity scene story
Yoko tracks	Remember Love - rough mix
	Poem Game
	I'm Not As Strong As You Think
	I'm Having A Baby
	Somewhwere In The Sky
	Happy Girl
	Kiss Kiss Kiss - rough mix
	Yes I'm Your Angel - rough mix
	Everyman Has A Woman
	Who Loves Him - studio dialogue - runthrough
	- double track vocal - rough mix x 2
	Hard Times Are Over - runthrough - choir practice
	- alternate mix - rough mix
	Walking On Thin Ice - studio dialogue - runthrough
	- vocal overdub
	No One Can See Me Like You Do - runthrough

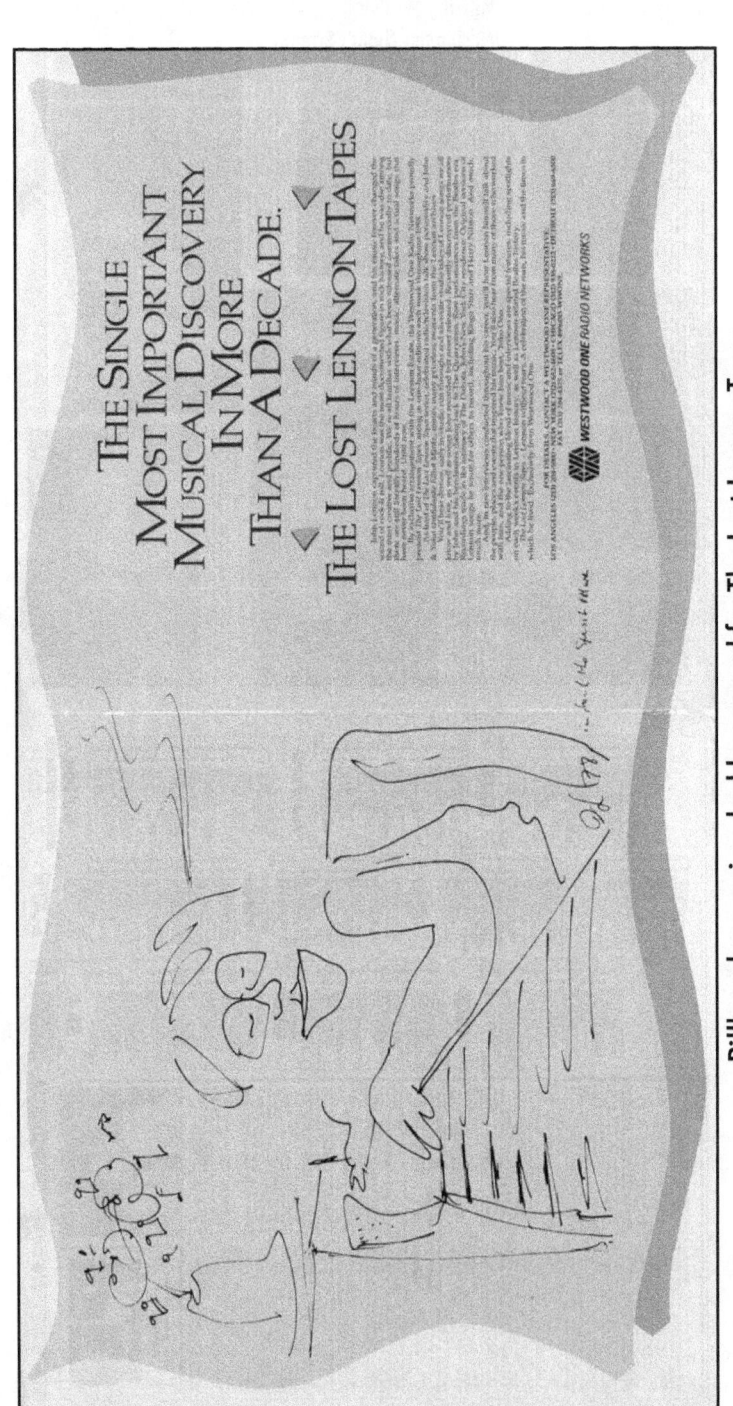

Billboard magazine double-page ad for The Lost Lennon Tapes

UNRELEASED TRACKS INDEX
IN SONG TITLE ORDER

Italicized text: tracks released on a Lost Lennon Bag Records bootleg.
Underlined text: tracks released on commercial versions only, not on a Lost Lennon Bag Records bootleg.
Bold text: unreleased, broadcast on The Lost Lennon Tapes only.

TITLE	SOURCE	TYPE	INSTRUMENT	VERSION	EPISODE
#9 DREAM - SO LONG AGO	HOME, NEW YORK 1974	DEMO 1	GUITAR	FULL	63
#9 DREAM - SO LONG AGO	HOME, NEW YORK 1974	DEMO 2, TAKE 2	GUITAR	FULL	81
#9 DREAM - SO LONG AGO	**WALLS AND BRIDGES LP**	**ROUGH MIX**	**BAND**	**FULL**	**81**
#9 DREAM - SO LONG AGO	**WALLS AND BRIDGES LP**	**ROUGH MIX**	**BAND**	**FULL**	**203**
A CASE OF THE BLUES	KENWOOD 1968	DEMO	GUITAR	FULL	204
A DAY IN THE LIFE	SGT. PEPPER'S LP	CLEAN INTRO	BAND	FULL	175
A HARD DAY'S NIGHT	PHILADELPHIA 1964	MASTER	BAND	FULL	52
A HARD DAY'S NIGHT	PARIS 1965	MASTER, AFTERNOON SHOW	BAND	FULL	74
A HARD DAY'S NIGHT	PARIS 1965	MASTER, EVENING SHOW	BAND	FULL	43
A SHOT OF RHYTHM AND BLUES	A HARD DAY'S NIGHT LP	OUTAKE	BAND	FULL	98
A TASTE OF HONEY	BBC, 18 JUNE 1963	MASTER	BAND	FULL	161
A TASTE OF HONEY	BBC, 23 JUNE 1963	MASTER	BAND	FULL	161
ACROSS THE UNIVERSE	PLEASE PLEASE ME LP	ROUGH MIX, TAKE 7	BAND	FULL	109
ACROSS THE UNIVERSE	NO ONE'S GONNA CHANGE OUR WORLD LP	ALTERNATE MONO MIX	BAND	FULL	13
ACROSS THE UNIVERSE	**NO ONE'S GONNA CHANGE OUR WORLD LP**	**DEMO**	**MELOTRON RIFF**	**FRAG.**	**179**
ACROSS THE UNIVERSE/ROCK 'N' ROLL MUSIC	GET BACK LP SESSION	REHEARSAL	BAND	FULL	68
AIN'T THAT A SHAME	GET BACK LP SESSION	REHEARSAL	BAND	FULL	68
AIN'T THAT A SHAME	**ROCK 'N' ROLL LP**	**JAM**	**BAND**	**FULL**	**67**
AISUMASEN	**MIND GAMES LP**	**ROUGH MIX**	**BAND**	**FULL**	**216**
AISUMASEN	MIND GAMES LP	ROUGH MIX	BAND	FULL	80
AISUMASEN - CALL MY NAME	HOME, NEW YORK 1971	DEMO 1	GUITAR	FULL	209
AISUMASEN - CALL MY NAME	HOME, NEW YORK 1971/1972	DEMO 2	GUITAR	FULL	80
ALL MY LOVING	ED SULLIVAN DEBUT 1964	MASTER	BAND	FULL	57
ALL MY LOVING	ADELAIDE 1964	MASTER	BAND	FULL	63
ALL MY LOVING	BBC, 30 MARCH 1964	MASTER	BAND	FULL	115
ALL YOU NEED IS LOVE	OUR WORLD TV BROADCAST	MASTER	BAND	FULL	29
ANGELA - J.J.	ST. REGIS HOTEL 1971	DEMO 1, TAKE 1	GUITAR	FULL	84
ANGELA - J.J.	ST. REGIS HOTEL 1971	DEMO 2, TAKE 1	GUITAR	FULL	186
ANGELA - PEOPLE	HOME, NEW YORK 1971	DEMO	GUITAR	FULL	65
ANNA	BBC, 25 JUNE 1963	MASTER	BAMD	FULL	161
AS TIME GOES BY	**IMPROV**	**IMPROV**	**A CAPPELLA**	**FRAG.**	**49**
AS TIME GOES BY	**EARTH NEWS RADIO 1976**	**IMPROV WITH YOKO**	**A CAPPELLA**	**FRAG.**	**92**
ATTICA STATE	HOME, NEW YORK 1971	DEMO 1, TAKES 2, 3	GUITAR	FULL	84
ATTICA STATE	JOHN SINCLAIR BENEFIT 1971	MASTER	BAND	FULL	16
ATTICA STATE	**REHEARSAL, ELEPHANT'S MEMORY**	**MASTER**	**BAND**	**FULL**	**168**

- 211 -

TITLE	SOURCE	TYPE	INSTRUMENT	VERSION	EPISODE
BABY'S IN BLACK	TOKYO, 30 JUNE 1966	MASTER	BAND	FULL	117
BACK IN THE U.S.S.R.	KINFAUNS 1968	DEMO, PAUL	GUITAR	FULL	105
BAD TO ME	HOME 1964	DEMO	GUITAR	FULL	17
BALLAD OF JOHN AND YOKO (THE)	SINGLE 1969	ALTERNATE MIX	BAND	FULL	114
BALLAD OF JOHN AND YOKO (THE) - CRUCIFY CAPP	UNKNOWN, MARCH 1969	IMPROV	A CAPPELLA	FRAG.	93
BANANA SONG	MONTREAL BED-IN 1969	IMPROV	A CAPPELLA	FRAG.	95
BE MY BABY	DAKOTA	IMPROV	VOCAL AND ORGAN	FULL	29
BEATLES CRIMBLE MEDLEY	ROCK 'N' ROLL LP SESSION	ROUGH MIX	BAND	FULL	77
BEAUTIFUL BOY	1963 XMAS FLEXI-DISC	MASTER	BAND	FULL	100
BEAUTIFUL BOY	DOUBLE FANTASY LP	ALTERNATE TAKE 1	BAND	FULL	92
BEAUTIFUL BOY	DAKOTA, SPRING 1980	DEMO 1	GUITAR	FULL	90
BEAUTIFUL BOY	BERMUDA 1980	DEMO 2	TAKE 1 DEMO 2	FULL	37
BEAUTIFUL BOY	BERMUDA 1980	DEMO 3	GUITAR	FULL	89
BEAUTIFUL BOY	DAKOTA 1980	DEMO 4	GUITAR	FULL	69
BEAUTIFUL BOY	DOUBLE FANTASY LP	EARLY MIX	BAND	FULL	37
BEAUTIFUL BOY	DOUBLE FANTASY LP	ROUGH MIX	BAND	FULL	83
BEAUTIFUL BOY	DOUBLE FANTASY LP	RUNTHROUGH	GUITAR	FULL	190
BEAUTIFUL BOY	DOUBLE FANTASY LP	DEMO	GUITAR	FULL	165
BEAUTIFUL BOY - SHE RUNS THEM ROUND IN CIRCLES/BEAUTIFUL BOY	DAKOTA	MEDLEY DEMO/IMPROV	GUITAR	FULL	87
BE-BOP-A-LULA	DOUBLE FANTASY LP	JAM	BAND	FULL	P3
BECAUSE	MONTREAL BED-IN 1969	DEMO	GUITAR	FRAG.	93
BECAUSE	ABBEY ROAD LP	EARLY REFERENCE MIX	BAND	FULL	58
BECAUSE	ABBEY ROAD LP	MASTER	A CAPPELLA	FULL	58
BEEF JERKY	WALLS AND BRIDGES LP	EXTRO WITH COUNT-IN	BAND	FULL	64
BESAME MUCHO	FIRST PARLOPHONE SESSION	MASTER	BAND	FULL	24
BEST THINGS IN LIFE ARE FREE (THE)	DAKOTA	IMPROV SATIRE	GUITAR	FRAG.	27
BLESS YOU	WALLS AND BRIDGES LP	ALTERNATE LONG MIX	BAND	FULL	91
BLESS YOU	WALLS AND BRIDGES LP	REHEARSAL	BAND	FULL	72
BLUE SUEDE SHOES	JOHN'S BIRTHDAY 1971	IMPROV	GUITAR	FULL	91
BLUE SUEDE SHOES	GET BACK LP SESSION	MASTER	BAND	FULL	116
BLUE SUEDE SHOES	GET BACK LP SESSION	REHEARSAL	BAND	FULL	59
BOAT SONG (THE)	DAKOTA	IMPROV	GUITAR	FULL	185
BONIE MARONIE	ROCK 'N' ROLL LP	ALTERNATE MIX	BAND	FULL	77
BORROWED TIME	DOUBLE FANTASY LP	ALTERNATE MIX	BAND	FULL	119
BORROWED TIME	DOUBLE FANTASY LP	ALTERNATE TAKE 3	BAND	FULL	74
BORROWED TIME	DAKOTA 1980	DEMO 1	GUITAR	FULL	31

TITLE	SOURCE	TYPE	INSTRUMENT	VERSION	EPISODE
BORROWED TIME	BERMUDA 1980	DEMO 2	GUITAR	FULL	210
BORROWED TIME	DOUBLE FANTASY LP	ROUGH MIX	BAND	FULL	48
BORROWED TIME	DOUBLE FANTASY LP	ROUGH MIX	BAND	FULL	173
BORROWED TIME	**DOUBLE FANTASY LP**	**RUNTHROUGH**	**BAND**	**FULL**	**190**
BORROWED TIME	DOUBLE FANTASY LP	RUNTHROUGH	BAND	FULL	215
BORROWED TIME	DOUBLE FANTASY LP	RUNTHROUGH	BAND	FULL	215
BRING IT ON HOME TO ME/SEND ME SOME LOVIN'	**ROCK 'N' ROLL LP**	**ALTERNATE TAKE**	**BAND**	**FULL**	**33**
BRING ON THE LUCIE (FREDA PEOPLE)	HOME, NEW YORK 1971/1972	DEMO	GUITAR	FRAG.	62
BRING ON THE LUCIE (FREDA PEOPLE)	MIND GAMES LP	ROUGH MIX	BAND	FULL	62
BROWN EYED HANDSOME MAN/GET BACK	DAKOTA	IMPROV	GUITAR	FULL	148
CAN YOU DIG IT	GET BACK LP SESSION	REHEARSAL, TAKE 1	BAND	FULL	71
CAN YOU DIG IT	GET BACK LP SESSION	REHEARSAL, TAKE 2	BAND	FULL	74
CAN'T BUY ME LOVE	PARIS 1965	MASTER, AFTERNOON SHOW	BAND	FULL	74
CAN'T BUY ME LOVE	PARIS 1965	MASTER, EVEVENING SHOW	BAND	FULL	45
CAN'T BUY ME LOVE	A HARD DAY'S NIGHT LP	OUTAKE	BAND	FULL	98
CAROL	BBC, 16 JULY 1963	MASTER	BAND	FULL	42
CATHY'S CLOWN	DAKOTA	IMPROV	PIANO	FULL	145
CATSWALK	1962 REHEARSALS	MASTER	BAND	FULL	110
CHAINS	BBC, 17 SEPTEMBER 1963	MASTER	BAND	FULL	166
CHORDS OF FAME	**PHIL OCHS, A. ARBOR 1971**	**MASTER**	**SLIDE GUITAR**	**FULL**	**148**
CHRISTMAS TIME IS HERE AGAIN	1967 CHRISTMAS RECORD	MASTER	BAND	FULL	101
CLEANUP TIME	DAKOTA	DEMO 1	PIANO	FULL	23
CLEANUP TIME	DAKOTA	DEMO 2	PIANO	FULL	69
CLEANUP TIME	DOUBLE FANTASY LP	OUTAKE, TAKE 1	BAND	FULL	86
CLEANUP TIME	DOUBLE FANTASY LP	REMIX	BAND	FULL	15
CLEANUP TIME	DOUBLE FANTASY LP	ROUGH MIX, REFERENCE VOCAL	BAND	FULL	89
CLEANUP TIME	DOUBLE FANTASY LP	RUNTHROUGH	BAND	FULL	188
COLD TURKEY	SINGLE 1969	TAKE 7, NO VOCALS	BAND	FULL	104
COLD TURKEY	KENWOOD 1969	ALTERNATE TAKE	BAND	FULL	23
COLD TURKEY	KENWOOD 1969	DEMO 1	GUITAR	FULL	217
COLD TURKEY	KENWOOD 1969	DEMO 2	GUITAR	FULL	23
COLD TURKEY	KENWOOD 1969	DEMO 3, TAKE 3	GUITAR	FULL	82
COLD TURKEY	**ONE TO ONE BENEFIT**	**REHEARSAL**	**BAND**	**FULL**	**20**
COME TOGETHER	ONE TO ONE BENEFIT	REHEARSAL TAKE 2	BAND	FULL	104
COME TOGETHER	**ONE TO ONE BENEFIT**	**REHEARSALS TAKE 1**	**BAND**	**FULL**	**78**
CONTINUING STORY OF BUNGALOW BILL (THE)	KINFAUNS 1968	DEMO	GUITAR	FULL	43

- 213 -

TITLE	SOURCE	TYPE	INSTRUMENT	VERSION	EPISODE
COOKIN' (IN THE KITCHEN OF LOVE)	DAKOTA	DEMO 1, TAKE 1	PIANO	FULL	78
COOKIN' (IN THE KITCHEN OF LOVE)	DAKOTA	DEMO 2, TAKE 8	PIANO	FULL	13
COOKIN' (IN THE KITCHEN OF LOVE)	DAKOTA 1976	DEMO 3	PIANO	FULL	86
CORRINA CORRINA	DAKOTA	IMPROV	PIANO	FULL	27
CRIPPLED INSIDE	IMAGINE LP	ALTERNATE TAKE	BAND	FULL	29
CRIPPLED INSIDE	JOHN'S BIRTHDAY 1971	MASTER	GUITAR	FRAG.	92
CRY BABY CRY	KINFAUNS 1968	DEMO 1	GUITAR	FULL	105
CRY BABY CRY	THE BEATLES LP	DEMO 2	PIANO	FULL	179
CRY BABY CRY	THE BEATLES LP	DEMO 3	PIANO	FRAG.	179
CRY BABY CRY	THE BEATLES LP	DEMO 4	GUITAR	FRAG.	179
CRYIN' WAITIN' HOPIN'	GET BACK LP SESSION	REHEARSAL	BAND	FULL	71
CRYIN', WAITIN', HOPIN'	BBC, 6 AUGUST 1963	MASTER	BAND	FULL	71
DAY TRIPPER	TOKYO, 30 JUNE 1966	MASTER	BAND	FULL	111
DAY TRIPPER	SINGLE 1965	ROUGH MIX	BAND	FULL	45
DEAR JOHN	DAKOTA, NOVEMBER 1980	DEMO, LAST SONG	GUITAR	FULL	12
DEAR PRUDENCE	KINFAUNS 1968	DEMO	GUITAR	FULL	20
DEAR PRUDENCE	THE BEATLES LP	REMIX	BAND	FULL	20
DEAR YOKO	IMAGINE LP	BASIC TRACKS	BAND	FULL	50
DEAR YOKO	BERMUDA 1980	DEMO 1	GUITAR	FULL	21
DEAR YOKO	DOUBLE FANTASY LP	DEMO 2, TAKES 2, 3	GUITAR	FULL	72
DEAR YOKO	DOUBLE FANTASY LP	ROUGH MIX	BAND	FULL	86
DEAR YOKO	DOUBLE FANTASY LP	ROUGH MIX	BAND	FULL	161
DEAR YOKO	DOUBLE FANTASY LP	RUNTHROUGH	BAND	FULL	189
DIG A PONY	GET BACK LP	MASTER	BAND	FULL	95
DIG IT	GET BACK LP SESSION	REHEARSAL 8'8'''	BAND	FULL	54
DIZZY MISS LIZZY	HOLLYWOOD BOWL 1965	MASTER	BAND	FULL	119
DIZZY MISS LIZZY	BBC, 7 JUNE 1965	MASTER	BAND	FULL	171
DO YOU WANNA DANCE	ROCK 'N' ROLL PEOPLE	ALTERNATE TAKE	BAND	FULL	119
DO YOU WANT TO KNOW A SECRET	PLEASE PLEASE ME LP	ALTERNATE MIX	BAND	FULL	28
DO YOU WANT TO KNOW A SECRET	BBC, 30 JULY 1963	MASTER	BAND	FULL	166
DON'T BE CRUEL / HOUNDDOG	SOMETIME IN NYC LP SESSION	JAM	BAND	FULL	42
DON'T LET ME DOWN	KENWOOD 1968	DEMO 1	GUITAR	FULL	73
DON'T LET ME DOWN	KENWOOD 1968	DEMO 2	GUITAR	FULL	75
DON'T LET ME DOWN	GET BACK LP SESSION	REHEARSAL	BAND	FULL	75
DOWN IN EASTERN AUSTRALIA I MET HER	DAKOTA	IMPROV	ORGAN	FRAG.	9
DREAM BABY	BBC, 8 MARCH 1962	MASTER	BAND	FULL	70

- 214 -

TITLE	SOURCE	TYPE	INSTRUMENT	VERSION	EPISODE
ELVIS MEDLEY	GET BACK LP SESSION	MASTER	BAND	FULL	116
EVERY MAN HAS A WOMAN	**YOKO, DOUBLE FANTASY LP**	**MASTER**	**VOCAL DOUBLE TRACK**	**FRAG.**	**184**
EVERY MAN HAS A WOMAN	**YOKO, DOUBLE FANTASY LP**	**MASTER**	**ROUGH MIX**	**FULL**	**184**
EVERYBODY'S GOT SOMETHING TO HIDE EXCEPT FOR ME AND MY MONKEY	KINFAUNS 1968	DEMO	GUITAR	FULL	15
EVERYBODY'S TRYING TO BE MY BABY	BBC, 26 DECEMBER 1964	MASTER	BAND	FULL	134
EVERYMAN HAS A WOMAN WHO LOVES HIM	**YOKO, DOUBLE FANTASY LP**	**ROUGH MIX**	**BAND**	**FRAG.**	**7**
EVERYMAN HAS A WOMAN WHO LOVES HIM	**DOUBLE FANTASY LP**	**RUNTHROUGH, YOKO & SEAN**	**BAND**	**FULL**	**190**
FALLING IN LOVE AGAIN	DAKOTA	IMPROV IN GERMAN	GUITAR	FULL	218
FLYING - AERIAL TOUR INSTRUMENTAL	MAGICAL MYSTERY TR EP	ALTERNATE MIX	BAND	FULL	32
FREE AS A BIRD	DAKOTA	DEMO 1, TAKE 1	PIANO	FULL	78
FREE AS A BIRD	DAKOTA	DEMO 2, TAKE 3	PIANO	FULL	128
FROM ME TO YOU	SINGLE 1963	EARLY MIX	BAND	FULL	55
FROM ME TO YOU	POP '63, RADIO 1963 SWEDEN	MASTER	BAND	FULL	31
FROM ME TO YOU	PARIS 1964	MASTER	BAND	FRAG.	56
FROM ME TO YOU	IT'S THE BEATLES 1963	MASTER	BAND	FRAG.	100
FROM ME TO YOU	WASHINGTON D.C. 1964	MASTER	BAND	FULL	107
FROM ME TO YOU	BBC, APRIL 1963	MASTER	BAND	FULL	161
FROM US TO YOU	SINGLE 1963	WITH COUNT-IN	BAND	FULL	28
GET BACK	BBC, VARIOUS DATES	MASTER	BAND	FULL	88
GET BACK	GET BACK LP SESSION	ALTERNATE LONG TK	BAND	FULL	114
GET BACK	GET BACK LP	MASTER	BAND	FULL	94
GET BACK	GET BACK LP SESSION	REHEARSAL	BAND	FULL	68
GET BACK	GET BACK LP SESSION	REHEARSAL	BAND	FULL	96
GET BACK REPRISE	GET BACK LP	MASTER	BAND	FULL	94
GET IT TOGETHER	**BED-IN**	**MASTER**	**GUITAR**	**FULL**	**164**
GIVE ME SOME TRUTH	**MIND GAMES LP**	**ALTERNATE MIX**	**BAND**	**FULL**	**128**
GIVE ME SOME TRUTH	IMAGINE LP	OUTAKE	BAND	FULL	52
GIVE ME SOME TRUTH	GET BACK LP SESSION	REHEARSAL	BAND	FRAG.	52
GIVE PEACE A CHANCE	MONTREAL BED-IN 1969	ALTERNATE TAKE	BAND	FULL	96
GIVE PEACE A CHANCE	TORONTO 1969	IMPROV	GUITAR	FULL	96
GIVE PEACE A CHANCE	JOHN'S BIRTHDAY 1971	MASTER	GUITAR	FRAG.	92
GIVE PEACE A CHANCE	MONTREAL 1969	ALTERNATE MIX	BAND	FULL	96
GIVE PEACE A CHANCE	**ONE TO ONE BENEFIT**	**REHEARSAL**	**BAND**	**FRAG.**	**19**
GIVE PEACE A CHANCE	**MONTREAL BED-IN 1969**	**REHEARSAL 1**	**GUITAR**	**FULL**	**93**
GIVE PEACE A CHANGE	MONTREAL BED-IN 1969	REHEARSAL 2	GUITAR	FULL	94
GLAD ALL OVER	CLOCK SOUNDTRACK 1971	MASTER	GUITAR	FULL	81

TITLE	SOURCE	TYPE	INSTRUMENT	VERSION	EPISODE
GOD	TITENHURST PARK 1970	DEMO 1	GUITAR	FULL	85
GOD	TITENHURST PARK 1970	DEMO 2	GUITAR	FULL	99
GOD	TITENHURST PARK 1970	DEMO 3	GUITAR	FULL	47
GOD	TITENHURST PARK 1970	DEMO 4	GUITAR	FULL	217
GOD SAVE US	HOME, NEW YORK	DEMO	GUITAR	FULL	186
GOD SAVE US	SINGLE 1971	REMIX, JOHN VOCAL	BAND	FULL	19
GOING DOWN ON LOVE	WALLS AND BRIDGES LP	REHEARSAL	GUITAR	FULL	138
GOING DOWN ON LOVE	WALLS AND BRIDGES LP		BAND	FULL	77
GONE FROM THIS PLACE	DAKOTA 1980	DEMO 1	GUITAR	FULL	48
GONE FROM THIS PLACE	DAKOTA 1980	DEMO 2	GUITAR	FULL	74
GOOD MORNING GOOD MORNING	KENWOOD 1967	DEMO	ORGAN	FRAG.	175
GOODNIGHT IRENE	JOHN'S BIRTHDAY 1971	IMPROV	GUITAR	FRAG.	37
GOODNIGHT VIENNA	GOODNIGHT VIENNA LP / ANTHOLOGY 1998	ROUGH MIX, JOHN VOCAL	BAND	FULL	201
GROW OLD WITH ME	DAKOTA	DEMO	PIANO	FULL	213
GROW OLD WITH ME	DOUBLE FANTASY LP	ROUGH MIX	BAND	FULL	184
HAPPINESS IS A WARM GUN	MONTREAL BED-IN 1969	DEMO	GUITAR	FRAG.	93
HAPPY BIRTHDAY SATURDAY CLUB	BBC, 5 OCTOBER 1963	MASTER	BAND	FULL	161
HAPPY XMAS	HOME, NEW YORK 1971	DEMO	GUITAR	FULL	48
HAPPY XMAS	SINGLE 1972	ROUGH MIX, NO CHOIR	BAND	FULL	202
HAPPY XMAS	SINGLE 1972	ROUGH MIX, NO STRINGS OR CHOIR	BAND	FULL	128
HAPPY XMAS	SINGLE 1972	ROUGH MIX, NO STRINGS OR CHOIR	BAND	FULL	205
HAPPY CHRISTMAS MESSAGE	TITENHURST PARK	IMPROV WITH YOKO	PIANO	FULL	48
HAPPY GIRL	HOME, NEW YORK	IMPROV, YOKO	A CAPPELLA	FULL	182
HAPPY RISHIKESH SONG (THE)	BERMUDA 1980	DEMO	GUITAR	FULL	4
HARD TIMES ARE OVER	DOUBLE FANTASY LP	ALTERNATE MIX	BAND	FRAG.	24
HARD TIMES ARE OVER	YOKO, DOUBLE FANTASY LP	REHEARSAL	CHOIR	FRAG.	104
HARD TIMES ARE OVER	YOKO, DOUBLE FANTASY LP	ROUGH MIX	BAND	FULL	184
HARD TIMES ARE OVER	YOKO, DOUBLE FANTASY LP	RUNTHROUGH	BAND	FULL	184
HE GOT THE BLUES	HOME, NEW YORK 1971/1972	DEMO	GUITAR	FULL	81
HE SAID HE SAID	HOME	DEMOS 1 TO 5	GUITAR	FRAG.	127
HEARTBEAT	CLOCK S/TRACK 1971	MASTER	GUITAR	FULL	26
HELLO LITTLE GIRL	DECCA AUDITION 1962	MASTER	BAND	FULL	71
HELLO LITTLE GIRL	THE QUARRY MEN 1960	REHEARSAL	BAND	FRAG.	71
HELP ME TO HELP MYSELF	DAKOTA 1980 / DOUBLE FANTASY 2000	DEMO 1	PIANO	FULL	150
HELP ME TO HELP MYSELF	DAKOTA 1980	DEMO 2	GUITAR	FULL	180
HELP!	TITENHURST PARK 1970	DEMO	PIANO	FRAG.	9

TITLE	SOURCE	TYPE	INSTRUMENT	VERSION	EPISODE
HELP!	ED SULLIVAN SHOW 1965	MASTER	BAND	FULL	80
HELP!	HELP! LP	TAKE 1	BAND	FULL	61
HELP!	HELP! LP	TAKE 5, BACK TRAX	BAND	FULL	61
HELP!/PLEASE PLEASE ME	GET BACK LP SESSION	REHEARSAL	BAND	FULL	74
HER MAJESTY	ABBEY ROAD LP	WITH LAST CHORD	GUITAR	FULL	82
HERE WE GO AGAIN	HOME, NEW YORK 1973	DEMO 2 1973	GUITAR	FULL	201
HEY BULLDOG - SHE CAN TALK TO ME	YELLOW SUBMARINE LP	DEMO	PIANO	FRAG.	179
HEY JUDE	OUTTAKE, TAKE 9,	MASTER	BAND	FULL	108
HIPPY HIPPY SHAKE (THE)	BBC, 30 JULY 1963	MASTER	BAND	FULL	166
HONEY DON'T	CLOCK SOUNDTRACK 1971	MASTER	GUITAR	FULL	81
HONEY DON'T	BBC, 7 JUNE 1965	MASTER	BAND	FULL	118
HONEY DON'T	BBC, 18 MAY 1964	MASTER	BAND	FULL	122
HONEY DON'T	BBC, 3 SEPTEMBER 1963	MASTER	BAND	FULL	166
HONEY DON'T / DON'T BE CRUEL / MATCHBOX	PLASTIC ONO BAND LP	JAM	BAND	FULL	22
HONEYMOON SONG (THE)	BBC, 6 AUGUST 1963	MASTER	BAND	FULL	166
HOUND DOG / LONG TALL SALLY	ONE TO ONE BENEFIT	REHEARSAL, NO BEG	BAND	FULL	51
HOW?	IMAGINE LP	ALTERNATE TAKE 1	BAND	FULL	39
HOW?	TITTENHURST PARK 1971	DEMO 1	PIANO	FRAG.	53
HOW?	TITTENHURST PARK 1970	DEMO 2	PIANO	FULL	85
HOW?	IMAGINE LP	EARLY TAKE	BAND	FULL	53
HOW DO YOU DO IT	LOVE ME DO SESSION 1962	ORIGINAL ENDING	BAND	FULL	24
HOW DO YOU SLEEP?	IMAGINE LP	ALTERNATE TAKE	BAND	FULL	217
HOW DO YOU SLEEP?	IMAGINE LP	ALTERNATE TAKE 1	BAND	FULL	9
HOW DO YOU SLEEP?	IMAGINE LP	ALTERNATE TAKE 2	BAND	FULL	53
HOW DO YOU SLEEP?	IMAGINE LP	ALTERNATE TAKE 3	BAND	FULL	75
HOW DO YOU SLEEP?	IMAGINE LP	REHEARSAL 1	BAND	FULL	87
HOW DO YOU SLEEP?	IMAGINE LP	REHEARSAL 2	BAND	FULL	118
HOW/CHILD OF NATURE/OH YOKO!	HOME, NEW YORK	REHEARSAL 2 INTRO	BAND	FULL	197
HOWLING AT THE MOON	DAKOTA	DEMO	PIANO	FULL	207
I AIN'T GOT TIME	DAKOTA	DEMO	PIANO	FULL	45
I AM THE WALRUS	SINGLE 1967	IMPROV, CROWD NOISE	GUITAR	FULL	79
I AM THE WALRUS	MAGICAL MYSTERY TR EP	ALTERNATE MIX	BAND	FULL	92
I AM THE WALRUS	MAGICAL MYSTERY TR EP	ROUGH MIX	BAND	FULL	10
I DON'T WANNA BE A SOLDIER	PLASTIC ONO BAND LP	TAKE 9, NO VOCALS	BAND	FULL	105
I DON'T WANNA BE A SOLDIER		ROUGH MIX SAX RUNTHROUGH	BAND	FRAG.	207
I DON'T WANNA FACE IT	DAKOTA, LATE 70s	DEMO 1	GUITAR	FULL	83

TITLE	SOURCE	TYPE	INSTRUMENT	VERSION	EPISODE
I DON'T WANNA FACE IT	DAKOTA 1980	DEMO 2	GUITAR	FULL	24
I DON'T WANNA FACE IT	DAKOTA	DEMO 3	GUITAR	FULL	105
I DON'T WANT TO FACE IT	DOUBLE FANTASY LP	ROUGH MIX	BAND	FULL	173
I DON'T WANT TO BE A SOLDIER	**IMAGINE LP**	**ALTERNATE TAKE 1**	**BAND**	**FULL**	**68**
I DON'T WANT TO BE A SOLDIER	**IMAGINE LP**	**ROUGH MIX**	**BAND**	**FULL**	**202**
I FEEL FINE	ED SULLIVAN 1965	MASTER	BAND	FULL	18
I FEEL FINE	BBC, 26 NOVEMBER 1964	MASTER	BAND	FULL	72
I FEEL FINE	MUNICH 1966	MASTER	BAND	FULL	116
I FEEL FINE	TOKYO, 30 JUNE 1966	MASTER	BAND	FULL	117
I FEEL FINE	PARIS 1965	MASTER, AFT. SHOW	BAND	FULL	98
I FEEL FINE	SINGLE 1965	OUTAKE, TAKE 9	BAND	FULL	98
I FEEL FINE	SINGLE 1966	TAKE 6, NO VOCALS	BAND	FULL	80
I FORGOT TO REMEMBER TO FORGET	BBC, 18 MAY 1964	MASTER	BAND	FULL	166
I FOUND OUT	PLASTIC ONO BAND LP	ALTERNATE MIX	BAND	FULL	43
I FOUND OUT	TITENHURST PARK 1970	DEMO 1	GUITAR	FULL	47
I FOUND OUT	TITENHURST PARK 1971	DEMO 2, TAKE 2	GUITAR	FULL	59
I GOT A WOMAN	BBC, 4 APRIL 1964	MASTER	BAND	FULL	60
I GOT A WOMAN	BBC, 13 AUGUST 1963	MASTER	BAND	FULL	166
I GOT TO FIND MY BABY	BBC, 11 JUNE 1963	MASTER	BAND	FULL	161
I KNOW (I KNOW)	HOME, NEW YORK 1973	DEMO 1, TAKE 2	GUITAR	FULL	75
I KNOW (I KNOW)	**HOME, NEW YORK 1973**	**DEMO 2, TAKE 3**	**GUITAR**	**FULL**	**104**
I KNOW (I KNOW)	HOME, NEW YORK 1973	DEMO 3, TAKE 4	GUITAR	FULL	121
I PROMISE	MIND GAMES LP	ROUGH MIX	BAND	FULL	75
I SAW HER STANDING THERE	TITENHURST PARK 1970	DEMO	PIANO	FULL	8
I SAW HER STANDING THERE	POP '63, RADIO 1963 SWEDEN	MASTER	BAND	FULL	31
I SAW HER STANDING THERE	ED SULLIVAN DEBUT 1964	MASTER	BAND	FULL	57
I SAW HER STANDING THERE	ADELAIDE 1964	MASTER	BAND	FULL	62
I SAW HER STANDING THERE	BBC, 5 OCTOBER 1963	MASTER	BAND	FULL	161
I SAW HER STANDING THERE	BBC, 20 OCTOBER 1963	MASTER	BAND	FULL	171
I SAW HER STANDING THERE	**MADISON SQUARE GARDEN**	**REHEARSAL**	**BAND**	**FULL**	**216**
I SAW HER STANDING THERE	PLEASE PLEASE ME LP	TAKE 2	BAND	FULL	55
I WANNA BE YOUR MAN	BBC, 30 MARCH 1964	MASTER	BAND	FULL	109
I WANNA BE YOUR MAN	AROUND THE BEATLES TV	MASTER	BAND	FULL	115
I WANNA BE YOUR MAN	TOKYO, 30 JUNE 1966	MASTER	BAND	FULL	117
I WANNA BE YOUR MAN	PARIS 1965	MASTER, AFT. SHOW	BAND	FULL	74
I WANT TO HOLD YOUR HAND	PHILADELPHIA 1964	MASTER	BAND	FULL	52

- 218 -

TITLE	SOURCE	TYPE	INSTRUMENT	VERSION	EPISODE
I WANT TO HOLD YOUR HAND	PARIS 1964	MASTER	BAND	FULL	56
I WANT TO HOLD YOUR HAND	ED SULLIVAN DEBUT 1964	MASTER	BAND	FULL	57
I WANT TO HOLD YOUR HAND	ADELAIDE 1964	MASTER	BAND	FULL	64
I WANT TO HOLD YOUR HAND	HOLLYWOOD BOWL 1964	MASTER	BAND	FULL	73
I WANT TO HOLD YOUR HAND	IT'S THE BEATLES 1963	MASTER	BAND	FULL	100
I WANT TO HOLD YOUR HAND	BBC, 15 FEBRUARY 1964	MASTER	BAND	FULL	171
I WANT YOU	GET BACK LP SESSION	REHEARSAL	BAND	FRAG.	79
I WANT YOU (NOT ABBEY ROAD VERSION)	KENWOOD 1968	IMPROV	GUITAR, OHN & YOKO VOCALS	FULL	157
I WANT YOU (SHE'S SO HEAVY)	AMSTERDAM 1969	IMPROV	GUITAR	FULL	79
I WANT YOU (SHE'S SO HEAVY)	ABBEY ROAD LP SESSION	REHEARSAL, PAUL VOCAL	BAND	FRAG.	79
I WATCH YOUR FACE	DAKOTA	DEMO	GUITAR	FULL	83
IF I FELL	PHILADELPHIA 1964	MASTER	BAND	FULL	52
IF I FELL	HOLLYWOOD BOWL 1964	MASTER	BAND	FULL	73
IF I NEEDED SOMEONE	TOKYO, 30 JUNE 1966	MASTER	BAND	FULL	117
I'LL BE ON MY WAY	BBC, 24 JUNE 1963	MASTER	BAND	FULL	161
I'LL GET YOU	BBC, 5 OCTOBER 1963	MASTER	BAND	FULL	161
I'LL MAKE YOU HAPPY	UNKNOWN	DEMO	PIANO	FULL	182
I'M A LOSER	BBC, 26 NOVEMBER 1964	MASTER	BAND	FULL	72
I'M A LOSER	PARIS 1965	MASTER, AFTERNOON SHOW	BAND	FULL	74
I'M A LOSER	PARIS 1965	MASTER, EVENING SHOW	BAND	FULL	43
I'M A MAN	DAKOTA	IMPROV	GUITAR	FULL	15
I'M DOWN	TOKYO 1966	MASTER	BAND	FULL	112
I'M HAVING A BABY	HOME, NEW YORK	DEMO	DEMO	FULL	183
I'M IN LOVE	HOME	DEMO	PIANO	FULL	218
I'M LOSING YOU	DOUBLE FANTASY LP	ALTERNATE MIX/CHEAP TRICK	BAND	FULL	158
I'M LOSING YOU	BERMUDA 1980	DEMO 1, INTRO	GUITAR	FRAG.	P3
I'M LOSING YOU	BERMUDA 1980	DEMO 3	GUITAR	FULL	30
I'M LOSING YOU	DOUBLE FANTASY LP	OVERDUBS	BRASS	FRAG.	189
I'M LOSING YOU	DOUBLE FANTASY LP	REHEARSAL	BAND	FRAG.	P3
I'M LOSING YOU	DOUBLE FANTASY LP	ROUGH MIX	BAND	FULL	71
I'M LOSING YOU	DOUBLE FANTASY LP	STUDIO EDITS PLAYBACK	BAND	FULL	193
I'M LOSING YOU - STRANGER'S ROOM	DAKOTA	DEMO 2	PIANO	FRAG.	30
I'M LOSING YOU - STRANGER'S ROOM	DAKOTA	DEMO 4	PIANO	FULL	122
I'M LOSING YOU - STRANGER'S ROOM	DAKOTA	DEMO 5, TAKE 3	PIANO	FULL	175
I'M NOT AS STRONG AS YOU THINK	HOME, NEW YORK	IMPROV, YOKO	A CAPPELLA	FULL	183
I'M SO TIRED	KINFAUNS 1968	DEMO	GUITAR	FULL	85

- 219 -

TITLE	SOURCE	TYPE	INSTRUMENT	VERSION	EPISODE
I'M STEPPING OUT	BERMUDA 1980	DEMO 1	GUITAR	FULL	17
I'M STEPPING OUT	BERMUDA 1980	DEMO 2	GUITAR	FULL	70
I'M STEPPING OUT	BERMUDA 1980	DEMO 3, TAKE 1	GUITAR	FULL	120
I'M STEPPING OUT	DAKOTA 1980	DEMO 4, TAKE 3	GUITAR	FULL	120
I'M STEPPING OUT	DOUBLE FANTASY LP	OUTAKE, TAKE 1	BAND	FULL	83
I'M STEPPING OUT	DOUBLE FANTASY LP	OUTAKE, TAKE 2	BAND	FULL	97
I'M STEPPING OUT	DOUBLE FANTASY LP	OUTAKE, TAKE 8	BAND	FULL	120
I'M STEPPING OUT	DOUBLE FANTASY LP	ROUGH MIX, EDITED	BAND	FULL	173
I'M STEPPING OUT	DOUBLE FANTASY LP	ROUGH MIX, UNEDITED	BAND	FULL	61
I'M STEPPING OUT	DOUBLE FANTASY LP	RUNTHROUGH	BAND	FULL	188
I'M STEPPING OUT	DOUBLE FANTASY LP	RUNTHROUGH 1 FIRST OF DAY	BAND	FULL	214
I'M STEPPING OUT	DOUBLE FANTASY LP	RUNTHROUGH 2	BAND	FULL	214
I'M STEPPING OUT	DOUBLE FANTASY LP	RUNTHROUGH 3	BAND	FULL	214
I'M STEPPING OUT	DOUBLE FANTASY LP	RUNTHROUGH 4 LAST OF DAY	BAND	FULL	214
I'M THE GREATEST	DOUBLE FANTASY LP	TAKE 2	BAND	FULL	61
I'M THE GREATEST	TITENHURST PARK	DEMO 1	PIANO	FULL	201
I'M THE GREATEST	TITENHURST PARK	DEMO 2	PIANO	FULL	201
I'M THE GREATEST	RINGO LP	ROUGH MIX	BAND	FULL	123
I'M THE GREATEST	IMAGINE LP, SESSION	STUDIO DEMO 1	BAND	FULL	8
I'M THE GREATEST	IMAGINE LP SESSION	STUDIO DEMO 2	BAND	FULL	61
I'M THE GREATEST	IMAGINE LP SESSION	STUDIO DEMO 3	BAND	FULL	75
I'M THE GREATEST	RINGO LP	TAKE 1	BAND	FULL	62
I'M THE GREATEST	RINGO LP	TAKE 2	BAND	FULL	66
I'M THE GREATEST	RINGO LP	TAKE 4	BAND	FULL	57
IMAGINE	IMAGINE LP	ALTERNATE TAKE	BAND	FULL	29
IMAGINE	IMAGINE LP	ALTERNATE TAKE, NO ORCHESTRA	BAND	FULL	216
IMAGINE	IMAGINE LP	EARLY TAKE	BAND	FULL	48
IMAGINE	IMAGINE LP	EARLY TAKE	BAND	FULL	54
IMAGINE	ATTICA STATE 1971 / ANTHOLOGY 1998	MASTER	GUITAR	FULL	2
IMAGINE	MIKE DOUGLAS SHOW 1972	MASTER	BAND	FULL	76
IMAGINE	JOHN'S BIRTHDAY 1971	MASTER	GUITAR	FRAG.	92
IMAGINE	IMAGINE LP	OUTAKE	BAND	FULL	121
IMAGINE	IMAGINE LP	ROUGH MIX	BAND	FULL	84
IMAGINE	ONE TO ONE BENEFIT	RUNTHROUGH	PIANO, LONGER THAN FILM	FULL	87
INSTANT KARMA		REHEARSAL	BAND	FULL	19
INSTRUMENTAL 42	GET BACK LP	MASTER	BAND	FULL	50

- 220 -

TITLE	SOURCE	TYPE	INSTRUMENT	VERSION	EPISODE
INSTRUMENTAL DIVERSION	DAKOTA	IMPROV	GUITAR	FRAG.	185
INTUITION	HOME, NEW YORK 1973	DEMO 1, TAKE 3	PIANO	FULL	123
INTUITION	HOME, NEW YORK 1973	DEMO 2 TAKE 4	PIANO	FULL	209
INTUITION	MIND GAMES LP	ROUGH MIX	BAND	FULL	79
INTUITION	MIND GAMES LP	ROUGH MIX	BAND	FULL	209
IT'S ALL TOO MUCH	YELLOW SUBMARINE SOUNDTRACK	MASTER	BAND	FULL	114
IT'S SO HARD	IMAGINE LP	ALTERNATE TAKE	BAND	FULL	30
IT'S SO HARD	DAVID FROST SHOW 1972	MASTER	BAND	FULL	45
IT'S SO HARD	MIKE DOUGLAS SHOW	MASTER	BAND	FULL	108
IT'S SO HARD	ONE TO ONE BENEFIT	MASTER	BAND	FULL	52
IT'S SO HARD	PLASTIC ONO BAND LP	REHEARSAL	BAND	FULL	207
IT'S SO HARD	PLASTIC ONO BAND LP	ROUGH MIX SAX RUNTHROUGH	BAND	FRAG.	207
IT'S SO HARD	IMAGINE LP	ROUGH MIX SAX RUNTHROUGH	BAND	FRAG.	107
I'VE GOT A FEELING	GET BACK LP	SAX OVERDUB	BAND	FULL	95
I'VE GOT A FEELING - EVERYONE HAD A HARD YEAR	KENWOOD 1968	DEMO	GUITAR	FULL	114
I'VE GOT ANTS IN MY PANTS	DOUBLE FANTASY LP SESSION	IMPROV	BAND	FULL	97
JEALOUS GUY	IMAGINE LP	ALTERNATE TAKE	BAND	FULL	20
JEALOUS GUY	IMAGINE LP	ROUGH MIX	BAND	FULL	73
JEALOUS GUY - CHILD OF NATURE	KINFAUNS 1968	DEMO	GUITAR	FULL	6
JOHN HENRY	DAKOTA	DEMO 1	PIANO	FULL	5
JOHN HENRY	DAKOTA	DEMO 2, CROWD NOISE	GUITAR	FULL	79
JOHN HENRY	DAKOTA	DEMO 2, FRAGMENT	GUITAR	FULL	50
JOHN SINCLAIR	JOHN SINCLAIR BENEFIT 1971	MASTER	BAND	FULL	16
JOHN SINCLAIR	DAVID FROST SHOW 1972	MASTER	BAND	FULL	45
JOHN, LET'S HOPE FOR PEACE	GET BACK LP SESSION	MASTER, YOKO	BAND	FRAG.	114
JOHNNY B. GOODE	MIKE DOUGLAS SHW 1972	MASTER	BAND	FULL	9
JOHNNY B. GOODE	BBC, 15 FEBRUARY 1964	MASTER	BAND	FULL	64
JULIA	KENWOOD 1968	DEMO 1	GUITAR	FULL	89
JULIA	KINFAUNS 1968	DEMO 2	GUITAR	FULL	105
JULIA	KENWOOD 1968	DEMO 3	GUITAR	FULL	113
JUST BECAUSE	ROCK N ROLL LP / ROCK N ROLL 2004	ALTERNATE TAKE	BAND	FULL	33
KANSAS CITY	BBC, 26 DECEMBER 1964	MASTER	BAND	FULL	134
KEEP RIGHT ON TO THE END OF THE ROAD	OZ FLEXI DISC 1971	IMPROV	GUITAR	FULL	69
KISS KISS KISS	DOUBLE FANTASY LP	ROUGH MIX, YOKO	BAND	FULL	202
KNOCKIN' ON HEAVEN'S DOOR	DAKOTA	IMPROV PARODY	GUITAR	FULL	14
LA MER/BLUE MOON/YOUNG LOVE	DAKOTA	IMPROV	GUITAR	FULL	150

- 221 -

TITLE	SOURCE	TYPE	INSTRUMENT	VERSION	EPISODE
LEAVE MY KITTEN ALONE	BEATLES FOR SALE LP SESSION	TAKE 5	BAND	FULL	42
LEND ME YOUR COMB	BBC, 16 JULY 1963	MASTER	BAND	FULL	42
LEND ME YOUR COMB	CLOCK SOUNDTRACK 1971	MASTER	GUITAR	FULL	81
LET IT BE	GET BACK LP	MASTER	BAND	FULL	94
LET'S GET PECULIAR	DOUBLE FANTASY LP	IMPROV	GUITAR	FRAG.	188
LIFE BEGINS AT 40	DAKOTA	DEMO	GUITAR	FULL	204
LITTLE JIMMY BROWN	DOUBLE FANTASY LP	IMPROV	GUITAR	FRAG.	214
LONG TALL SALLY	PHILADELPHIA 1964	MASTER	BAND	FULL	54
LONG TALL SALLY	MELBOURNE 1964	MASTER	BAND	FULL	66
LONG TALL SALLY	BBC, 16 JULY 1964	MASTER	BAND	FULL	69
LONG TALL SALLY	AROUND THE BEATLES TV	MASTER	BAND	FULL	115
LOOK AT ME	PARIS 1965	MASTER, AFTERNOON SHOW	BAND	FULL	98
LOOK AT ME	TITENHURST PARK 1970	DEMO	GUITAR	FULL	82
LOOK AT ME	PLASTIC ONO BAND LP	EARLY MIX	BAND	FULL	127
LOOK AT ME	PLASTIC ONO BAND LP	ROUGH MIX	BAND	FULL	88
LOOK AT ME	TITENHURST PARK 1970	ROUGH MIX	BAND	FULL	204
LOVE	BBC, 20 OCTOBER 1963	DEMO	GUITAR	FULL	77
LOVE ME DO	SOMETIME IN NY CITY LP	MASTER	BAND	FULL	171
LUCK OF THE IRISH (THE)	HOME, NEW YORK 1971	ALTERNATE TAKE	BAND	FULL	169
LUCK OF THE IRISH (THE)	HOME, NEW YORK 1971	DEMO 1 TAKES 1 & 2	GUITAR	FULL	7
LUCK OF THE IRISH (THE)	HOME, NEW YORK 1971	DEMO 2	GUITAR	FRAG.	63
LUCK OF THE IRISH (THE)	JOHN SINCLAIR BENEFIT 1971	DEMO 3	GUITAR	FRAG.	63
LUCK OF THE IRISH (THE)	DAVID FROST SHOW 1972	MASTER	BAND	FULL	16
MAGGIE MAE	DOUBLE FANTASY LP	MASTER	BAND	FULL	45
MAHARISHI SONG (THE)	KENWOOD 1968	IMPROV	GUITAR	FRAG.	22
MAILMAN, BRING ME NO MORE BLUES	CLOCK SOUNDTRACK 1971	DEMO	GUITAR	FULL	85
MAILMAN, BRING ME NO MORE BLUES	GET BACK LP SESSION	REHEARSAL	BAND	FULL	71
MANY RIVERS TO CROSS	DAKOTA MID-1970s	IMPROV	GUITAR	FULL	71
MANY RIVERS TO CROSS	PUSSY CATS LP	ROUGH MIX	BAND	FULL	201
MATCHBOX	BBC, 30 JULY 1963	MASTER	BAND	FULL	34
MAURICE DUPONT PART 1	DAKOTA	IMPROV	A CAPPELLA	FULL	166
MAURICE DUPONT PART 2	DAKOTA	IMPROV	A CAPPELLA	FULL	20
MAURICE DUPONT PART 3	DAKOTA	IMPROV	A CAPPELLA	FULL	22
MAYBE BABY	CLOCK S/TRACK 1971	MASTER	GUITAR	FULL	29
MAYBE BABY	GET BACK LP SESSION	REHEARSAL	BAND	FULL	22

- 222 -

TITLE	SOURCE	TYPE	INSTRUMENT	VERSION	EPISODE
MEAN MR. MUSTARD	KENWOOD 1969	DEMO	GUITAR	**FULL**	**8**
MEAN MR. MUSTARD	GET BACK LP SESSION	REHEARSAL	BAND	FRAG.	95
MEAT CITY	HOME, NEW YORK 1973	DEMO 2	GUITAR	FULL	123
MEAT CITY	HOME, NEW YORK 1973	DEMO 3, TAKE 2	GUITAR	*FULL*	*209*
MEAT CITY	MIND GAMES LP	ROUGH MIX	**BAND**	**FULL**	**125**
MEAT CITY	MIND GAMES LP	ROUGH MIX	**BAND**	**FULL**	**209**
MEAT CITY - JUST GOTTA GIVE ME SOME ROCK 'N' ROLL	HOME, NEW YORK 1971/1972	DEMO 1	GUITAR	*FULL*	*75*
MEDLEY	AROUND THE BEATLES	MASTER	BAND	FULL	65
MEDLEY OF BEATLE HITS	BBC, 21 DECEMBER 1963	MASTER	BAND	FULL	171
MEMORIES	DAKOTA	DEMO 1	GUITAR	*FULL*	*45*
MEMORIES	DAKOTA	DEMO 2	PIANO	FULL	108
MEMORIES - WATCHING THE WHEELS	DAKOTA	DEMO 3	PIANO	*FULL*	*163*
MEMORIES - WATCHING THE WHEELS	BERMUDA 1980	DEMO 4	GUITAR/PIANO	*FULL*	*201*
MEMPHIS TENNESSEE	MIKE DOUGLAS SHW 1972	MASTER	BAND	FULL	9
MEMPHIS TENNESSEE	BBC, 8 MARCH 1962	MASTER	BAND	FULL	62
MICHELLE	KENWOOD 1965	REHEARSAL	SOLO GUITAR	**FRAG**	**151**
MIND GAMES	MIND GAMES LP	ALTERNATE TAKE	MASTER	**FULL**	**164**
MIND GAMES	MIND GAMES LP	ROUGH - EARLY MIX	BAND	*FULL*	*24*
MIND GAMES	MIND GAMES LP	ROUGH MIX	**BAND**	**FULL**	**119**
MIND GAMES - MAKE LOVE NOT WAR	TITENHURST PARK 1970	DEMO	PIANO	*FULL*	*8*
MIND MOVIE - EL TANGO - COOCHIE FROM BRAZIL	DAKOTA	IMPROV WITH RINGO	ORGAN	FULL	44
MIRROR MIRROR ON THE WALL	DAKOTA 1977	DEMO 1, TAKE 5	PIANO	*FULL*	*20*
MIRROR MIRROR ON THE WALL	DAKOTA 1977	DEMO 2, TAKE 4	**PIANO**	**FULL**	**50**
MIRROR MIRROR ON THE WALL	DAKOTA 1977	DEMO 3, TAKE 1	PIANO	*FULL*	*212*
MISERY	PLEASE PLEASE ME LP	TAKE 1	BAND	FULL	78
MISERY	PLEASE PLEASE ME LP	TAKES 2 TO 6	BAND	FULL	78
MONEY	POP '63, RADIO 1963	MASTER	BAND	FULL	10
MOOVIN' AND GROOVIN'	THE QUARRY MEN 1960	REHEARSAL	BAND	FRAG.	P1
MOTHER	PLASTIC ONO BAND LP	ALTERNATE TAKE	BAND	*FULL*	*44*
MOTHER	TITENHURST PARK 1970	DEMO	GUITAR	FULL	70
MOTHER	ONE TO ONE BENEFIT	REHEARSAL	**BAND**	**FULL**	**186**
MOTHER NATURE'S SON	KINFAUNS 1968	DEMO, PAUL	GUITAR	FULL	113
MOVE OVER MS. L	HOME, NEW YORK 1974	DEMO 2	**GUITAR**	**FULL**	**64**
MOVE OVER MS. L	HOME, NEW YORK 1974	EARLIEST DEMO 1	GUITAR	*FULL*	*64*
MOVE OVER MS. L	WALLS AND BR. LP SESS. SESSION	OUTAKE	**BAND**	**FULL**	**216**
MOVE OVER MS. L	WALLS AND BRIDGES LP SESSION	REHEARSAL, TAKE 1	**BAND**	**FULL**	**26**

TITLE	SOURCE	TYPE	INSTRUMENT	VERSION	EPISODE
MOVE OVER MS. L	WALLS AND BRIDGES LP SESSION	REHEARSAL, TAKE 2	BAND	FULL	64
MOVE OVER MS. L	WALLS AND BRIDGES LP SESSION	REHEARSAL, TAKE 3	BAND	FULL	72
MT. ELGA	PUSSY CATS LP	REHEARSAL	BAND	FRAG.	34
MUCHO MUNGO	DAKOTA	DEMO 1	GUITAR	FULL	1
MUCHO MUNGO	HOME, NEW YORK 1974	DEMO 2	GUITAR	FULL	27
MUCHO MUNGO	HOME, NY, EARLY 1974	DEMOS 3, 4, TAKES 1, 2	GUITAR	FULL	81
MUCHO MUNGO	PUSSY CATS LP	REHEARSAL	BAND	FRAG.	173
MY LITTLE FLOWER PRINCESS	DOUBLE FANTASY LP	ALTERNATE TAKE 3	BAND	FULL	67
MY LITTLE FLOWER PRINCESS	BERMUDA 1980	DEMO, TAKE 3	GUITAR	FULL	67
MY MUMMY'S DEAD	PLASTIC ONO BAND LP	ROUGH MIX	GUITAR	FULL	92
MY MUMMY'S DEAD	PLASTIC ONO BAND LP	TAKE 2	GUITAR	FULL	187
MYSTERY TRAIN	DOUBLE FANTASY LP SESSION	REHEARSAL	BAND	FULL	60
NEW YORK CITY	HOME	DEMO 1	GUITAR	FULL	30
NEW YORK CITY	HOME	DEMO 2	GUITAR	FULL	30
NEW YORK CITY	ONE TO ONE BENEFIT	RADIO SPOT BACKING 1A	BAND	FULL	19
NEW YORK CITY	ONE TO ONE BENEFIT	RADIO SPOT BACKING 1B	BAND	FULL	213
NEW YORK CITY	ONE TO ONE BENEFIT	RADIO SPOT BACKING 2	BAND	FRAG	104
NEWS OF THE DAY FROM REUTERS (THE)	DAKOTA	IMPROV	GUITAR	FULL	14
NO ONE CAN SEE ME LIKE YOU DO	SEASON OF GLASS LP	RUNTHROUGH, YOKO	BAND	FULL	188
NOBODY TOLD ME	BERMUDA 1980	DEMO 1	GUITAR, DOUBLE TRACKED	FULL	105
NOBODY TOLD ME	BERMUDA 1980	DEMO 2	GUITAR, DOUBLE TRACKED	FULL	174
NOBODY TOLD ME	DOUBLE FANTASY LP	OUTAKE, TAKE 1	BAND	FULL	106
NOBODY TOLD ME	DOUBLE FANTASY LP	ROUGH MIX	BAND	FULL	41
NOBODY TOLD ME	DOUBLE FANTASY LP	RUNTHROUGH	BAND	FULL	188
NOBODY TOLD ME - EVERYBODY'S TALKIN', NOBODY'S TALKIN'	DAKOTA	DEMO 2	PIANO	FULL	200
NOBODY TOLD ME - EVERYBODY'S TALKIN', NOBODY'S TALKIN'	DAKOTA	DEMO 3	PIANO & GUITAR	FULL	200
NORWEGIAN WOOD	RUBBER SOUL LP	ALTERNATE TAKE	BAND	FRAG.	51
NORWEGIAN WOOD	RUBBER SOUL LP	OUTAKE, TAKE 2	BAND	FULL	73
NORWEGIAN WOOD	RUBBER SOUL LP	TAKE 4 WITH INTRO	BAND	FULL	51
NOT FADE AWAY	SOMETIME IN NYC LP SESSION	JAM	BAND	FULL	22
NOT FADE AWAY	CLOCK S/TRACK 1971	MASTER	GUITAR	FULL	22
NOT GUILTY	KINFAUNS 1968	DEMO	GUITAR	FRAG.	113
NOTHIN' SHAKIN' (BUT THE LEAVES ON THE TREES)	BBC, 23 JULY 1963	MASTER	BAND	FULL	166
NOW WE BE SAILIN' ON THE CARRIBEAN	SOMETIME IN NYC LP SESSION	IMPROV	BAND	FULL	67
NOWHERE MAN	MUNICH 1966	MASTER	BAND	FULL	113
NOWHERE MAN	TOKYO, 30 JUNE 1966	MASTER	BAND	FULL	117

TITLE	SOURCE	TYPE	INSTRUMENT	VERSION	EPISODE
OH MY LOVE	TITENHURST 1970	DEMO 1	GUITAR	FULL	113
OH MY LOVE	TITENHURST 1970	DEMO 2	GUITAR	FULL	113
OH MY LOVE	**TITENHURST 1970**	**DEMO 3 YOKO A CAPPELLA**	**A CAPPELLA**	**FULL**	**113**
OH MY LOVE	IMAGINE LP	EARLY TAKE	BAND	FULL	53
OH MY LOVE	IMAGINE LP	ROUGH MIX	BAND	FULL	73
OH MY LOVE	IMAGINE LP	ROUGH MIX	BAND	FULL	87
OH YOKO!	HOME 1970	DEMO 1	GUITAR	FULL	92
OH YOKO!	HOME, NEW YORK 1972	DEMO 1	PIANO	FULL	182
OH YOKO!	HOME, NEW YORK 1972	DEMO 2	PIANO	FULL	182
OH YOKO!	JOHN'S BIRTHDAY 1971	MASTER	GUITAR	FRAG.	92
OH YOKO!	IMAGINE LP	ROUGH MIX	BAND	FULL	52
OH YOKO!	IMAGINE LP	ROUGH MIX	BAND	FULL	77
OLD DIRT ROAD	WALLS AND BRIDGES LP	ROUGH MIX	BAND	FULL	173
ONE AFTER 909	THE QUARRYMEN 1962	MASTER	BAND	FULL	68
ONE AFTER 909	GET BACK LP	MASTER	BAND	FULL	110
ONE AFTER 909	FROM ME TO YOU SESSION 1963	OUTAKE	BAND	FULL	141
ONE AFTER 909	THE QUARRY MEN 1960	REHEARSAL	BAND	FULL	11
ONE DAY AT A TIME	MIND GAMES LP	EARLY MIX	BAND	FULL	123
ONE DAY AT A TIME	**MIND GAMES LP**	**ROUGH MIX**	**BAND**	**FULL**	**209**
ONE OF THE BOYS	DAKOTA 1977	DEMO 1, TAKE 1	GUITAR	FULL	211
ONE OF THE BOYS	DAKOTA 1980	DEMO 2, TAKE 2	GUITAR	FULL	24
ONLY PEOPLE	MIND GAMES LP	ALTERNATE TAKE	MASTER	FULL	164
ONLY PEOPLE	MIND GAMES LP	EARLY MIX	BAND	FULL	66
ONLY PEOPLE	MIND GAMES LP	EARLY MIX	BAND	FULL	121
ONLY PEOPLE	**MIND GAMES LP**	**ROUGH MIX**	**BAND**	**FULL**	**209**
ONLY THE LONELY / CRYING / GONE FROM THIS PLACE	DOUBLE FANTASY LP SESSION	IMPROV	GUITAR	FULL	70
ONLY YOU	GOODNIGHT VIENNA LP	MASTER	BAND	FULL	35
OUT THE BLUE	MIND GAMES LP	ROUGH MIX	BAND	FULL	48
OUT THE BLUE	MIND GAMES LP	ROUGH MIX	BAND	FULL	77
OUT THE BLUE	**MIND GAMES LP**	**ROUGH MIX**	**BAND**	**FULL**	**206**
OUT THE BLUE	MIND GAMES LP	ROUGH MIX	BAND	FULL	217
PAPERBACK WRITER	TOKYO 1966	MASTER	BAND	FULL	112
PAPERBACK WRITER	SINGLE 1966	WITH COUNT-IN	BAND	FRAG.	26
PEDRO THE FISHERMAN	DAKOTA	IMPROV	PIANO	FULL	185
PEGGY SUE	CLOCK S/TRACK 1971	MASTER	GUITAR	FULL	26
PEGGY SUE	**ROCK 'N' ROLL LP**	**REHEARSAL**	**BAND**	**FULL**	**33**

TITLE	SOURCE	TYPE	INSTRUMENT	VERSION	EPISODE
PEGGY SUE	ROCK 'N' ROLL LP	ROUGH MIX	BAND	FULL	71
PEGGY SUE GOT MARRIED	CLOCK S/TRACK 1971	MASTER	GUITAR	FULL	26
PENNY LANE	SGT. PEPPER'S LP SESSION	PLAYBACK & REHEARSAL	BAND	FRAGS.	112
PENNY LANE	SGT. PEPPER'S LP SESSION	ROUGH MIX	BAND	FULL	112
PIGGIES	KINFAUNS 1968	DEMO, GEORGE	GUITAR	FULL	104
PILL	BANK ST NY 1972	DEMO, ONLY TAKE	GUITAR	FULL	53
PLEASE MR. POSTMAN	BBC, 30 JULY 1963	MASTER	BAND	FULL	166
PLEASE PLEASE ME	WASHINGTON D.C. 1964	MASTER	BAND	FULL	107
PLEASE PLEASE ME	BBC, 13 AUGUST 1963	MASTER	BAND	FULL	166
POP GO THE BEATLES	BBC, VARIOUS DATES	MASTER	BAND	FULL	161
POP IS THE NAME OF THE GAME	DAKOTA	IMPROV	A CAPPELLA	FULL	213
POWER TO THE PEOPLE	SINGLE 1971	ALTERNATE TAKE	BAND	FULL	16
POWER TO THE PEOPLE	SINGLE 1971	ALTERNATE TAKE	MASTER	FULL	164
POWER TO THE PEOPLE	SINGLE 1971	ALTERNATE TAKE 2	BAND	FULL	76
POWER TO THE PEOPLE	SINGLE 1971	ALTERNATE TAKE 3	BAND	FULL	76
RAIN	SINGLE 1966	REMIX	BAND	FULL	2
RAIN	SINGLE 1966	BASIC TRACKS	BAND	FULL	44
RAVE ON	CLOCK S/TRACK 1971	MASTER	GUITAR	FULL	22
REAL LIFE	DAKOTA 1980	DEMO 1	PIANO	FRAG.	17
REAL LIFE	DAKOTA 1980	DEMO 2, TAKE 3	PIANO	FRAG.	17
REAL LIFE	DAKOTA 1980	DEMO 3	PIANO	FRAG.	17
REAL LIFE	DAKOTA 1980	DEMO 4	PIANO	FRAG.	17
REAL LIFE	DAKOTA, LATE 1970s	DEMO 5	PIANO	FRAG.	115
REAL LIFE	DAKOTA 1980	DEMO 6, TAKE 2	PIANO	FRAG.	215
REAL LIFE	DAKOTA LATE 1970s	DEMO 7	PIANO	FRAG.	215
REAL LOVE	BERMUDA 1980	DEMO 1, TAKE 1	PIANO	FULL	58
REAL LOVE	DAKOTA	DEMO 2	PIANO	FULL	134
REAL LOVE - GIRLS AND BOYS	DAKOTA	DEMO 1	GUITAR	FULL	3
REAL LOVE - GIRLS AND BOYS	BERMUDA 1980	DEMO 2, TAKE 4	GUITAR	FULL	77
REAL LOVE - GIRLS AND BOYS	BERMUDA 1980	DEMO 3, TAKE 5	GUITAR	FULL	91
REAL LOVE - GIRLS AND BOYS	DAKOTA	DEMO 4	PIANO	FULL	115
REAL LOVE - GIRLS AND BOYS	DAKOTA	DEMO 5	PIANO	FULL	169
REAL LOVE - GIRLS AND BOYS	SINGLE 1969	DEMO 6	PIANO	FRAGS.	180
REMEMBER LOVE - YOKO	KINFAUNS 1968	ROUGH MIX	BAND	FULL	95
REVOLUTION	KINFAUNS 1968	DEMO	GUITAR	FULL	85
REVOLUTION	PROMO FILM CLIP 1968	MASTER	BAND	FULL	47

TITLE	SOURCE	TYPE	INSTRUMENT	VERSION	EPISODE
REVOLUTION	SINGLE 1968	REMIX	BAND	FULL	16
RIP IT UP/READY TEDDY	**ROCK 'N' ROLL LP**	**ALTERNATE TAKE**	**BAND**	**FULL**	**33**
RIP IT UP/READY TEDDY	ROCK 'N' ROLL LP	ROUGH MIX	BAND	FULL	69
ROCK AND ROLL MEDLEY	GET BACK LP SESSION	REHEARSAL	BAND	FULL	68
ROCK AND ROLL MUSIC	CANDLESTICK PARK	MASTER	BAND	FRAG.	19
ROCK AND ROLL MUSIC	BBC, 26 DECEMBER 1964	MASTER	BAND	FULL	98
ROCK AND ROLL MUSIC	MUNICH 1966	MASTER	BAND	FULL	116
ROCK AND ROLL MUSIC	TOKYO, 30 JUNE 1966	MASTER	BAND	FULL	117
ROCK AND ROLL MUSIC	PARIS 1965	MASTER, AFT. SHOW	BAND	FULL	74
ROCK AND ROLL MUSIC	PARIS 1965	MASTER, EVE. SHOW	BAND	FULL	45
ROCK ISLAND LINE	DAKOTA	IMPROV 1	ELECTRIC GUITAR	FULL	18
ROCK ISLAND LINE	HOME 1970	IMPROV 2	GUITAR	FULL	148
ROCK 'N' ROLL PEOPLE	MENLOVE AVE LP	ALTERNATE MIX, TK 7	BAND	FULL	118
ROCK 'N' ROLL PEOPLE	MENLOVE AVE LP	ALTERNATE TAKE	BAND	FULL	17
ROCK 'N' ROLL PEOPLE	TITENHURST PARK 1970	DEMO 1	GUITAR	FULL	216
ROCK 'N' ROLL PEOPLE	TITENHURST PARK 1970	DEMO 2	PIANO	FULL	123
ROCK 'N' ROLL PEOPLE	MENLOVE AVENUE LP	OUTAKE	BAND	FULL	66
ROLL OVER BEETHOVEN	SOMETIME IN NYC LP SESSION	JAM	BAND	FULL	27
ROLL OVER BEETHOVEN	POP '63, RADIO 1963 SWEDEN	MASTER	BAND	FULL	31
ROLL OVER BEETHOVEN	AROUND THE BEATLES	MASTER	BAND	FULL	66
ROLL OVER BEETHOVEN	BBC, 30 MARCH 1964	MASTER	BAND	FULL	109
ROLL OVER BEETHOVEN	BBC, 21 DECEMBER 1963	MASTER	BAND	FULL	171
RUMBLE - WHOLE LOTTA LOVE	**SOMETIME IN NYC LP SESSION**	**JAM**	**BAND**	**FRAG.**	**41**
RUN FOR YOUR LIFE	RUBBER SOUL LP	ROUGH MIX, TAKE 5	BAND	FRAG.	89
SALLY AND BILLY	DAKOTA	DEMO 1	PIANO	FULL	30
SALLY AND BILLY	HOME 1970	DEMO 2	GUITAR	FULL	201
SALLY AND BILLY	DAKOTA MID/LATE 1970s	DEMO 3	PIANO	FULL	201
SAN FRANCISCO BAY BLUES	IMAGINE LP SESSION	IMPROV	GUITAR	FULL	53
SAVE THE LAST DANCE FOR ME / DON'T LET ME DOWN	GET BACK LP	MASTER	BAND	FULL	97
SEA DITTIES MEDLEY	DAKOTA 1980	IMPROV	GUITAR	FULL	185
SEND ME SOME LOVIN'	TITENHURST PARK 1971	IMPROV	GUITAR	FULL	30
SEND ME SOME LOVIN'	SOMETIME IN NYC LP SESSION	JAM	BAND	FULL	42
SERVE YOURSELF	DAKOTA	DEMO 1	PIANO	FULL	14
SERVE YOURSELF	DAKOTA	DEMO 2	PIANO	FULL	27
SERVE YOURSELF	DAKOTA	DEMO 3	PIANO	FULL	48
SERVE YOURSELF	DAKOTA	DEMO 4	PIANO	FRAG.	86

TITLE	SOURCE	TYPE	INSTRUMENT	VERSION	EPISODE
SERVE YOURSELF	DAKOTA	DEMO 5	PIANO	FULL	99
SERVE YOURSELF	DAKOTA	DEMO 6	PIANO	FULL	128
SERVE YOURSELF	**DAKOTA**	**DEMO 7**	**PIANO**	**FULL**	**135**
SERVE YOURSELF	DAKOTA	DEMO 8	PIANO	FULL	170
SERVE YOURSELF	DAKOTA 1979	DEMO 9	GUITAR	FULL	213
SEXY SADIE	KINFAUNS 1968	DEMO	GUITAR	FULL	85
SHAKIN' IN THE 60'S	GET BACK LP SESSION	REHEARSAL	BAND	FULL	68
SHAZAM!	CLOCK SOUNDTRACK 1971	MASTER	GUITAR	FULL	81
SHE LOVES YOU	POP '63, RADIO 1963	MASTER	BAND	FULL	10
SHE LOVES YOU	PHILADELPHIA 1964	MASTER	BAND	FULL	54
SHE LOVES YOU	ED SULLIVAN DEBUT 1964	MASTER	BAND	FULL	57
SHE LOVES YOU	MELBOURNE 1964	MASTER	BAND	FULL	66
SHE LOVES YOU	PARIS 1964	MASTER	BAND	FULL	73
SHE LOVES YOU	WASHINGTON D.C. 1964	MASTER	BAND	FULL	107
SHE LOVES YOU	WEMBLEY 1964	MASTER	BAND	FULL	115
SHE LOVES YOU	BBC, 20 OCTOBER 1963	MASTER	BAND	FULL	171
SHE SAID SHE SAID	KENWOOD 1966	DEMO	GUITAR	FULL	127
SHE'S A WOMAN	BBC, 26 DECEMBER 1964	MASTER	BAND	FULL	171
SHE'LL BE COMING ROUND THE MOUNTAIN	DAKOTA	IMPROV	GUITAR	FULL	167
SHE'S A FRIEND OF DOROTHY'S	DAKOTA 1975/1976	DEMO 1	PIANO	FULL	81
SHE'S A FRIEND OF DOROTHY'S	DAKOTA 1975/1976	DEMO 2	PIANO	FULL	201
SHE'S A WOMAN	**DOUBLE FANTASY LP SESSION**	**IMPROV**	**BAND**	**FRAG.**	**178**
SHE'S A WOMAN	BBC, 26 NOVEMBER 1964	MASTER	BAND	FULL	72
SHE'S A WOMAN	TOKYO, 30 JUNE 1966	MASTER	BAND	FULL	117
SHE'S A WOMAN	HOLLYWOOD BOWL 1965	MASTER	BAND	FULL	119
SHOUT	AROUND THE BEATLES	MASTER	BAND	FULL	66
SIDE BY SIDE	BBC, VARIOUS DATES	MASTER	BAND	FULL	161
SLIPPIN' AND SLIDIN'	**ROCK 'N' ROLL LP**	**ALTERNATE TAKE**	**BAND**	**FULL**	**33**
SO HOW COME (NO ONE LOVES ME)	BBC, 27 JULY 1963	MASTER	BAND	FULL	88
SOLDIER OF LOVE	BBC, 16 JULY 1963	MASTER	BAND	FULL	42
SOME OTHER GUY	CAVERN CLUB 1962	MASTER	BAND	FULL	13
SOME OTHER GUY	BBC, 23 JUNE 1963	MASTER	BAND	FULL	161
SOMEWHERE IN THE SKY	**HOME, NEW YORK**	**IMPROV, YOKO**	**A CAPPELLA**	**FULL**	**182**
STAND BY ME	**ROCK 'N' ROLL LP**	**ALTERNATE TAKE**	**BAND**	**FULL**	**33**
STAND BY ME	OLD GREY WHISTLE 1975	SINGLE, OVERDUBBED VOCAL	BAND	FULL	216
STARTING OVER	**DOUBLE FANTASY LP**	**CONTROL ROOM**	**BAND**	**FULL**	**21**

TITLE	SOURCE	TYPE	INSTRUMENT	VERSION	EPISODE
STARTING OVER	DAKOTA	DEMO 1	GUITAR	FULL	116
STARTING OVER	DAKOTA 1980	DEMO 2, TAKE 3	GUITAR	FULL	180
STARTING OVER	DOUBLE FANTASY LP	ROUGH MIX	BAND	FULL	21
STARTING OVER	DOUBLE FANTASY LP	ROUGH MIX	BAND	FULL	116
STARTING OVER	**DOUBLE FANTASY LP**	**ROUGH MIX**	**BAND**	**FULL**	**202**
STARTING OVER	**DOUBLE FANTASY LP**	**ROUGH MIX**	**BAND**	**FULL**	**218**
STARTING OVER	**DOUBLE FANTASY LP**	**STUDIO PLAYBACK**	**BAND**	**FULL**	**190**
STARTING OVER - DON'T BE CRAZY	DAKOTA 1980	DEMO 1	PIANO	FRAG.	21
STARTING OVER - DON'T BE CRAZY	DAKOTA	DEMO 2	PIANO	FULL	116
STARTING OVER - MY LIFE	DAKOTA	DEMO 1, TAKE 2	PIANO	FRAG.	21
STARTING OVER - MY LIFE	DAKOTA	DEMO 2, TAKE 3	GUITAR	FULL	21
STARTING OVER - MY LIFE	DAKOTA	DEMO 3, TAKE 1	PIANO	FULL	83
STARTING OVER - MY LIFE	**DAKOTA 1980**	**DEMO 4**	**GUITAR**	**FRAG.**	**134**
STARTING OVER - MY LIFE	DAKOTA 1980	DEMO 5	PIANO	FRAG.	180
STARTING OVER - MY LIFE	DAKOTA 1980	DEMO 6	GUITAR	FRAG.	180
STARTING OVER - THE WORST IS OVER NOW	DAKOTA	DEMO 1	GUITAR	FULL	90
STARTING OVER - THE WORST IS OVER NOW	DAKOTA	DEMO 2	GUITAR	FULL	180
STEEL AND GLASS	HOME, NEW YORK 1974	REHEARSAL	PIANO	FRAG.	197
STEEL AND GLASS	**WALLS AND BRIDGES LP**	**REHEARSAL**	**BAND**	**FULL**	**26**
STEEL AND GLASS	WALLS AND BRIDGES LP	ROUGH MIX	BAND	FULL	197
STRAWBERRY FIELDS FOREVER	KENWOOD 1967	DEMO 1	GUITAR	FULL	180
STRAWBERRY FIELDS FOREVER	**KENWOOD 1967**	**DEMO 1 - OVERDUB**	**MELOTRON**	**FRAG.**	**180**
STRAWBERRY FIELDS FOREVER	KENWOOD 1966	DEMO 2	GUITAR	FULL	11
STRAWBERRY FIELDS FOREVER	SGT. PEPPER'S LP SESSION	REMIX VERSION 2, TAKE 26	BAND	FULL	88
STRAWBERRY FIELDS FOREVER	SGT. PEPPER'S LP SESSION	TAKE 1	BAND	FULL	112
STRAWBERRY FIELDS FOREVER	SGT. PEPPER'S LP SESSION	TAKE 1, VERSION 7	BAND	FULL	79
STRAWBERRY FIELDS FOREVER	SGT. PEPPER'S LP SESSION	VERSION 1, TAKE 1	BAND	FULL	19
STRAWBERRY FIELDS FOREVER	SGT. PEPPER'S LP SESSION	VERSION 1, TAKE 4	BAND	FULL	61
STRAWBERRY FIELDS FOREVER	SGT. PEPPER'S LP SESSION	VERSION 1, TAKES 5,6	BAND	FULL	69
STRAWBERRY FIELDS FOREVER	SGT. PEPPER'S LP SESSION	VERRSION 2, TAKE 25, NO VOCALS	BAND	FULL	79
SUN KING	GET BACK LP SESSION	MASTER	BAND	FRAG.	97
SURE TO FALL	BBC, 18 JUNE 1963	MASTER	BAND	FULL	161
SURE TO FALL	BBC, 4 APRIL 1964	MASTER	BAND	FULL	166
SURPRISE SURPRISE	**WALLS AND BRIDGES LP**	**ALTERNATE TAKE**	**BAND**	**FULL**	**74**
SURPRISE SURPRISE	HOME, NEW YORK 1974	DEMO 1	GUITAR	FULL	35
SURPRISE SURPRISE	HOME, NEW YORK 1974	DEMO 2	GUITAR	FULL	74

TITLE	SOURCE	TYPE	INSTRUMENT	VERSION	EPISODE
SWEET LITTLE SIXTEEN	ROCK 'N' ROLL LP	ALTERNATE MIX	BAND	FULL	91
SWEET LITTLE SIXTEEN	ROCK 'N' ROLL LP	ALTERNATE TAKE	BAND	FULL	23
SWEET LITTLE SIXTEEN	BBC, 23 JULY 1963	MASTER	BAND	FULL	62
TENNESSEE	DAKOTA	DEMO 1	PIANO	FRAG.	5
TENNESSEE	DAKOTA	DEMO 2, TAKE 4	PIANO	FULL	5
TENNESSEE	DAKOTA	DEMO 3	PIANO	FULL	207
THANK YOU GIRL	BBC, 13 MAY 1963	MASTER	BAND	FULL	161
THAT'LL BE THE DAY	ROCK 'N' ROLL LP	REHEARSAL	BAND	**FULL**	**22**
THAT'LL BE THE DAY	THE QUARRY MEN 1960	REHEARSAL	BAND	FRAG.	71
THAT'LL BE THE DAY	GET BACK LP SESSION	REHEARSAL	BAND	FRAG.	71
THAT'S ALL RIGHT MAMA	PLASTIC ONO BAND LP SESSION	JAM	BAND	**FRAG.**	**116**
THERE'S A PLACE	PLEASE PLEASE ME LP	ALTERNATE TAKE	BAND	FULL	57
THERE'S A PLACE	PLEASE PLEASE ME LP	OUTAKE	BAND	FULL	46
THERE'S A PLACE	PLEASE PLEASE ME LP	ROUGH MIX, TAKE 11	BAND	FULL	98
PHILADELPHIA 1964	PHILADELPHIA 1964	MASTER	BAND	FULL	54
THINGS WE SAID TODAY	ROCK 'N' ROLL LP	REHEARSAL	BAND	FULL	33
THIRTY DAYS	PARIS 1964	MASTER	BAND	FULL	57
THIS BOY	WASHINGTON D.C 1964	MASTER	BAND	FULL	107
THIS BOY	ED SULLIVAN 1964	MASTER	BAND	FULL	160
THIS BOY	BBC, 21 DECEMBER 1963	MASTER	BAND	FULL	171
TICKET TO RIDE	ED SULLIVAN 1965	MASTER	BAND	FULL	18
TICKET TO RIDE	BBC, 7 JUNE 1965	MASTER	BAND	FULL	61
TICKET TO RIDE	PARIS 1965	MASTER, AFTERNOON SHOW	BAND	FULL	98
TIE ME KANGAROO DOWN SPORT	SINGLE 1965	ROUGH MIX, TAKE 2	BAND	FULL	105
TIGHT A$	BBC, 26 DECEMBER 1963	MASTER	BAND	FULL	171
TIGHT A$	HOME, NEW YORK 1973	DEMO	GUITAR	FULL	17
TIGHT A$	MIND GAMES LP	ROUGH MIX	MASTER	FULL	121
TIGHT A$	**MIND GAMES LP**	**ROUGH MIX**	**BAND**	**FULL**	**209**
TILL THERE WAS YOU	ED SULLIVAN DEBUT 1964	MASTER	BAND	FULL	57
TILL THERE WAS YOU	BBC, 30 MARCH 1964	MASTER	BAND	FULL	135
TO KNOW HER IS TO LOVE HER	BBC, 6 AUGUST 1963	MASTER	BAND	FULL	166
TOMORROW NEVER KNOWS	REVOLVER LP	REFERENCE MIX	BAND	FULL	26
TOO MANY COOKS	**1974 STUDIO SESSION**	**MASTER**	**R. J. PRODUCED**	**FULL**	**156**
TOO MUCH MONKEY BUSINESS	**DAKOTA**	**IMPROV**	**GUITAR**	**FULL**	**148**
TOO MUCH MONKEY BUSINESS	BBC, 10 SEPTEMBER 1963	MASTER	BAND	FULL	62
TOO MUCH MONKEY BUSINESS	BBC, 24 JUNE 1963	MASTER	BAND	FULL	161

TITLE	SOURCE	TYPE	INSTRUMENT	VERSION	EPISODE
TWAS A NIGHT LIKE ETHEL MERMAN	DAKOTA	IMPROV	A CAPPELLA	FULL	15
TWIST AND SHOUT	POP '63, RADIO 1963	MASTER	BAND	FULL	10
TWIST AND SHOUT	ROYAL VARIETY 1963	MASTER	BAND	FULL	56
TWIST AND SHOUT	ADELAIDE 1964	MASTER	BAND	FULL	63
TWIST AND SHOUT	MELBOURNE 1964	MASTER	BAND	FULL	66
TWIST AND SHOUT	HOLLYWOOD BOWL 1964	MASTER	BAND	FULL	89
TWIST AND SHOUT	AROUND THE BEATLES TV	MASTER	BAND	FULL	116
TWIST AND SHOUT	HOLLYWOOD BOWL 1965	MASTER	BAND	FULL	119
TWIST AND SHOUT	BBC, 25 JUNE 1963	MASTER	BAND	FULL	161
TWO OF US	GET BACK LP	MASTER	BAND	FULL	114
WALKING ON THIN ICE	SINGLE 1981	RUNTHROUGH, YOKO	BAND	FULL	184
WALKING ON THIN ICE	SINGLE 1981	VOCAL OVERDUB, YOKO	BAND	FULL	184
WATCHING THE WHEELS	DAKOTA 1980	DEMO 1	PIANO	FRAG.	P3
WATCHING THE WHEELS	DAKOTA 1980	DEMO 2	PIANO	FULL	21
WATCHING THE WHEELS	DAKOTA 1980	DEMO 3	GUITAR	FULL	29
WATCHING THE WHEELS	DAKOTA 1980	DEMO 5	GUITAR	FULL	84
WATCHING THE WHEELS	DAKOTA	DEMO 6, TAKE 1	PIANO	FULL	99
WATCHING THE WHEELS	DOUBLE FANTASY LP SESSION	ROUGH MIX	BAND	FULL	84
WATCHING THE WHEELS	DOUBLE FANTASY LP	ROUGH MIX	BAND	FULL	134
WATCHING THE WHEELS	DOUBLE FANTASY LP	RUNTHROUGH	BAND	FULL	188
WATCHING THE WHEELS	DOUBLE FANTASY LP	RUNTHROUGH	BAND	FULL	218
WATCHING THE WHEELS / I'M CRAZY	DAKOTA	DEMO 4, TAKE 1	PIANO	FULL	69
WE CAN WORK IT OUT	HOME 1966	DEMO, PAUL	GUITAR	FRAG.	45
WE CAN WORK IT OUT	SINGLE 1965	ROUGH MIX	BAND	FULL	45
WELL (BABY PLEASE DON'T GO)	IMAGINE SESSIONS	REHEARSAL	BAND	FULL	69
WELL MEET AGAIN	OLD GREY WHISTLE 1975	IMPROV	A CAPPELLA	FRAG.	44
WELL WELL WELL	TITENHURST PARK 1970	DEMO	GUITAR	FULL	82
WELL WELL WELL	PLASTIC ONO BAND LP	OUTAKE, TAKE 4	BAND	FULL	82
WELL WELL WELL	ONE TO ONE BENEFIT	REHEARSAL	BAND	FULL	78
WHAT YOU GOT	HOME, NEW YORK 1974	DEMO	GUITAR	FULL	77
WHAT'D I SAY	JOHN'S BIRTHDAY 1971	IMPROV	GUITAR	FRAG.	37
WHATEVER GETS YOU THROUGH THE NIGHT	WALLS AND BRIDGES LP	1ST STUDIO REHEARSAL	BAND	FULL	104
WHATEVER GETS YOU THROUGH THE NIGHT	HOME, NEW YORK 1974	DEMO 1	GUITAR	FULL	12
WHATEVER GETS YOU THROUGH THE NIGHT	HOME, NEW YORK 1974	DEMO 2	GUITAR	FULL	104
WHATEVER GETS YOU THROUGH THE NIGHT	WALLS AND BRIDGES LP	ROUGH MIX, NO ELTON VOCAL	BAND	FULL	216
WHATEVER GETS YOU THROUGH THE NIGHT	WALLS AND BRIDGES LP	REHEARSAL	BAND	FULL	35

TITLE	SOURCE	TYPE	INSTRUMENT	VERSION	EPISODE
WHATEVER GETS YOU THROUGH THE NIGHT	**WALLS AND BRIDGES LP**	**ROUGH MIX, NO ELTON VOCAL**	**BAND**	**FULL**	**202**
WHATEVER HAPPENED TO	DAKOTA	DEMO, TAKE 2	GUITAR	FULL	11
WHAT'S THE NEW MARY JANE	KINFAUNS 1968	DEMO	GUITAR	FULL	113
WHEN A BOY MEETS A GIRL	HOME 1970	DEMO	GUITAR	FULL	90
WHIT MONDAY TO YOU	BBC, 18 MAY 1964	MASTER	BAND	FULL	166
WHOLE LOTTA SHAKIN' GOIN' ON / IT'LL BE ME - MEDLEY	SOMETIME IN NYC LP SESSION	JAM	BAND	FULL	27
WOMAN	BERMUDA 1980	DEMO 1	GUITAR	FULL	99
WOMAN	BERMUDA 1980	DEMO 2	GUITAR	FULL	3
WOMAN	BERMUDA 1980	DEMO 3	GUITAR	FULL	22
WOMAN	**BERMUDA 1980**	**DEMO 4**	**GUITAR**	**FULL**	**22**
WOMAN	BERMUDA 1980	DEMO 5	GUITAR	FULL	70
WOMAN	BERMUDA 1980	DEMO 6, TAKE 1 & 7	GUITAR	FULL	122
WOMAN	DOUBLE FANTASY LP	EARLY MIX	BAND	FULL	77
WOMAN	DOUBLE FANTASY LP	GUITAR OVERDUB	GUITAR	FULL	188
WOMAN	DOUBLE FANTASY LP	MASTER	BAND	FULL	160
WOMAN	DOUBLE FANTASY LP	ROUGH MIX	BAND	FULL	22
WOMAN	DOUBLE FANTASY LP	ROUGH MIX	BAND	FULL	135
WOMAN	**DOUBLE FANTASY**	**ROUGH MIX**	**BAND**	**FULL**	**183**
WOMAN	**DOUBLE FANTASY LP**	**RUNTHROUGH**	**BAND**	**FULL**	**188**
WOMAN	**DOUBLE FANTASY LP**	**RUNTHROUGH**	**BAND**	**FULL**	**218**
WOMAN	DOUBLE FANTASY LP	VOCAL OVERDUB	BAND	FULL	22
WOMAN	DOUBLE FANTASY LP	VOCAL OVERDUB	BAND	FRAG.	189
WOMAN IS THE NIGGER OF THE WORLD	HOME, NEW YORK 1971 / ANTHOLOGY 1998	DEMO 1	GUITAR	FULL	31
WOMAN IS THE NIGGER OF THE WORLD	**HOME, NEW YORK 1972**	**DEMO 2**	**GUITAR**	**FULL**	**83**
WOMAN IS THE NIGGER OF THE WORLD	DICK CAVETT SHOW 1972	MASTER	BAND	FULL	146
WOMAN IS THE NIGGER OF THE WORLD	NEW YORK CITY LP	OUTAKE	BAND	FULL	83
WOMAN IS THE NIGGER OF THE WORLD	**ONE TO ONE BENEFIT**	**REHEARSAL**	**BAND**	**FULL**	**53**
YA YA	**ROCK 'N' ROLL LP**	**ALTERNATE TAKE**	**BAND**	**FULL**	**34**
YER BLUES	R 'N' R CIRCUS	ALTERNATE TAKE	BAND	FULL	114
YER BLUES	R 'N' R CIRCUS REHEARSAL 1	MASTER	BAND	FRAG.	50
YER BLUES	R 'N' R CIRCUS REHEARSAL 2	MASTER	BAND	FULL	75
YER BLUES	ROCK 'N' ROLL CIRCUS	MASTER	BAND	FRAG.	156
YES IT IS	OUTAKE, TAKE 8	BAND	BAND	FULL	140
YES IT IS	SINGLE 1965	OUTAKE, TAKE 2	BAND	FULL	105
YES IT IS	SINGLE 1965	ROUGH MIX, TAKE 14	BAND	FULL	105
YES IT IS	SINGLE 1965	TAKE 1	BAND	FULL	61

TITLE	SOURCE	TYPE	INSTRUMENT	VERSION	EPISODE
YES, I'M YOUR ANGEL	YOKO, DBLE FANTASY LP	BAND	ROUGH MIX	FULL	183
YESTERDAY	TOKYO, 30 JUNE 1966	MASTER	BAND	FULL	111
YESTERDAY	MUNICH 1966	MASTER	BAND	FULL	117
YESTERDAY	ED SULLIVAN 1965	MASTER	BAND	FULL	130
YOKO ONO POEM GAME	HOME, NEW YORK	IMPROV, YOKO	A CAPPELLA	FRAG.	183
YOU ARE HERE	MIND GAMES LP	ROUGH MIX	BAND	FULL	209
YOU CAN'T CATCH ME	ROCK 'N' ROLL LP	ALTERNATE TAKE	BAND	FULL	23
YOU CAN'T CATCH ME	ROCK 'N' ROLL LP	ALTERNATE TAKE	BAND	FULL	158
YOU CAN'T CATCH ME	ROCK 'N' ROLL LP	OUTAKE	BAND	FULL	128
YOU CAN'T DO THAT	PHILADELPHIA 1964	MASTER	BAND	FULL	54
YOU CAN'T DO THAT	MELBOURNE 1964	MASTER	BAND	FULL	65
YOU CAN'T DO THAT	BBC, 4 APRIL 1964	MASTER	BAND	FULL	166
YOU KNOW MY NAME	KENWOOD 1967	DEMO	PIANO	FRAG.	9
YOU NEVER GIVE ME YOUR MONEY	ABBEY ROAD LP	ALTERNATE TAKE	BAND	FULL	94
YOU REALLY GOT A HOLD ON ME	BBC, 17 SEPTEMBER 1963	MASTER	BAND	FULL	166
YOU SAVED MY SOUL	DAKOTA NOVEMBER 1980	DEMO 1, TAKE 1	GUITAR	FULL	99
YOU SAVED MY SOUL	DAKOTA NOVEMBER 1980	DEMO 2, TAKE 2	GUITAR	FULL	213
YOU SEND ME	DAKOTA	IMPROV	PIANO	FULL	145
YOU WIN AGAIN	GET BACK LP SESSION	MASTER	BAND	FULL	96
YOUNG BLOOD	BBC, 11 JUNE 1963	MASTER	BAND	FULL	161
YOU'RE GONNA LOSE THAT GIRL	HELP! LP	ROUGH MIX	BAND	FULL	82
YOU'VE REALLY GOT A HOLD ON ME	POP '63, RADIO 1963 SWEDEN	MASTER	BAND	FULL	31

BAG RECORDS BOOTLEGS TRACKS

Standard time abbreviations used are ' for minute and " for second.

CD/track	LP/track	TITLE	VERSION	BOOT USED	BEST LLT	LLT / BOOT LONGER BY	LLT / BOOT NOTES
1/1	1/1	Strawberry Fields Forever	demo 1	Part 4	Part 180	LLT: 0.5"	LLT: longer intro - more false starts -- BOOT: added intro comment - last chord missing
1/2	1/2	The Happy Rishikesh Song	demo	Part 4	Part 4	same	
1/3	1/3	Rock Island Line	improv 2	Part 5	Part 148	LLT: 5"	LLT: few extra strums at beginning
1/4	1/4	John Henry	demo 1	Part 5	Part 5	same	
1/5	1/5	Surprise Surprise	demo 1	Part 5	Part 35	LLT: 1.5"	LLT: longer - intro -- BOOT: also on boot #6
1/6	1/6	Keep Right On To The End Of The Road	improv	bootleg	Part 69	boot: 5"	LLT: better sound quality -- BOOT: extra dialogue at end
1/7	1/7	Goodnight Vienna	studio	bootleg	not on LLT	boot: 5"	LLT: better sound quality -- BOOT: poor sound quality
1/8	1/8	Tennessee	demo 1, 2	Part 5	Part 5	same	
1/9	1/9	God Save Oz	remix	Part 19	Part 19	same	BOOT: also on boot # 5
1/10	1/10	With A Little Help From My Friends	Sean	Part 3	Part 3	same	
1/11	1/11	Power To The People	alt mix	Part 2	Part 2	same	
1/12	1/12	Here We Go Again	demo	Part 23	Part 201	LLT: 2'	BOOT: bad sound with distortion
1/13	1/13	Mucho Mungo	demo 1	Part 1	Part 1	same	
1/14	1/14	God	demo 2	Part 2	Part 99	LLT: 2'	BOOT: ends at first of 2 runthroughs - cuts to CV - also on boot #14
1/15	1/15	Life Begins At Forty	demo 1	Part 2	Part 204	LLT: 14"	LLT: longer ending
1/16	1/16	Woman	demo 2	Part 3	Part 3	same	
1/17	1/17	Real Love (Girls And Boys)	demo 1	Part 3	Part 3	same	CV released later same year on Imagin Soundtrack LP
1/18	1/18	Cleanup Time	demo 2	Part 2	Part 69	LLT: 18"	LLT: has piano intro - longer ending
1/19	1/19	Beautiful Boy	demo 4	Part 4	Part 69	LLT: 2.5'	LLT: is this the correct time? -- BOOT: also on boot #10
1/20	1/20	Revolution	demo kinfauns	Part 6	Part 85	same	BOOT: also on boot # 6
1/21		Child Of Nature	demo kinfauns	Part 6	Part 6	LLT: 2'	BOOT: also on boot # 6
1/22	2/2	He Said He Said / She Said She Said	demo 1	Part 7	Part 127	LLT: 10"	LLT: She Said has intro chords -- BOOT: demo 1 plus She Said demo - also on boot #14
1/23	2/3	I'm The Greatest	demo 1	Part 8	Part 201	same	LLT: intro shouting and end piano chords
1/24	2/4	Make Love Not War	demo	Part 8	Part 8	same	
1/25	2/5	How Do You Sleep?	alt take	Part 9	Part 9	same	LLT: 1 extra second at beginning
1/26	2/6	Daddy's Little Sunshine Boy	improv	Part 8	Part 8	same	
2/1	2/7	I'm The Greatest	demo 1	Part 8		LLT: 30"	BOOT: starts with DOWN IN EASTERN AUSTRALIA I MET HER
2/2	2/8	The Luck Of The Irish	demo 1	Part 7		BOOT: intro not on LLT	BOOT: cuts off before end of song
2/3	2/9	Every Man Has A Woman Who Loves Him	rough mix	Part 7			BOOT: intro cut onto beginning
2/4	2/11	Starting Over	demo 2	Part 10	Part 180	same	BOOT: poor sound
2/5	2/11	I Promise (Love Is The Answer)	demo	Part 8			BOOT: poor sound - intro and end cut
2/6	2/12	Sea Ditties - medley	improv	Part 10	Part 185		LLT: clean ending on Part 213 - BOOT: Yoko interview re: John helping us over ending
2/7		Grow Old With Me	demo	Part 7	Part 213		BOOT: SATURDAY MORNING improv as intro - also on boot #16
2/8	3/1	Strawberry Fields Forever	demo 2	Part 11			LLT: count-in intro - also on boot #6
2/9	3/2	What's The New Mary Jane	demo kinfauns	Part 13	Part 113		

CD/track	LP/track	TITLE	VERSION	BOOT USED	BEST LLT	LLT / BOOT LONGER BY	LLT / BOOT NOTES
2/10	3/3	Julia	demo 2, kinfauns	Part 11	Part 105	same	LLT: proper intro - BOOT: count-in not from LLT - not on Part 11 - also on boot #6
2/11	3/4	Across The Universe	mono mix	Part 13		same	
2/12	3/5	You Know My Name	demo	Part 9		same	
2/13	3/6	Help!	demo	Part 9		same	
2/14	3/7	Whatever Gets You Thru The Night	demo 1	Part 12		same	
2/15	3/8	The General Erection	reading	Part 9		same	
2/16	3/9	The Wumberlog	reading	Part 12		same	
2/17	3/10	Dear John	demo	Part 11		same	
2/18	3/11	Whatever Happened To	demo 2	Part 13		same	BOOT: last chord missing in fade out
2/19	3/12	Cookin' (In The Kitchen Of Love)	clock s/track	Part 2 Preview		same	BOOT: uncut medley is in Part 26 - also on bootleg #5 and #22
2/20	3/13	Peggy Sue	demo 1	Part 3 Preview		1"	BOOT: also on boot #6
2/21	3/14	Watching The Wheels	demo 3	Part 3 Preview	Part 29	same	
2/22	3/15	Watching The Wheels	demo 1	Part 3 Preview		1 min 20"	LLT: complete - BOOT: cut to "that's the Bermuda tape" at 52 seconds - also on boot #7
2/23	3/16	I'm Losing You	demo 2	Part 3	Part 37	same	
2/24	3/17	Beautiful Boy	rehearsal dialogue	Part 3 Preview			unknown source
2/25	3/18	Cleanup Time					
2/26	3/19	One To One Radio Spots					
3/1	4/1	Revolution	remix	Part 16		LLT: 3"	BOOT: has clean intro unlike version broadcast on LLT
3/2	4/2	Power To The People	alt take	Part 16		same	
3/3	4/3	Attica State	John Sinclair	Part 16		same	
3/4	4/4	Luck Of The Irish	John Sinclair	Part 16		same	
3/5	4/5	John Sinclair	John Sinclair	Part 15		same	
3/6	4/6	I'm A Man	improv	Part 15		same	
3/7	4/7	'Twas A Night Like Ethel Merman	improv	Part 15		same	BOOT: ends with intro to La Mer
3/8	4/8	Medley: Lor Mer, Blue Moon, Young Love	improv	Part 15	Part 150	same	LLT: has "thank you" improv end
3/9	4/9	Cleanup Time	alt take	Part 15		BOOT: intro	BOOT: intro added from CV
3/10	4/10	Good Morning, Good Morning	demo	Part 15	Part 175	LLT: 3"	LLT: complete ending -- BOOT: cuts to Sgt. Pepper CV before ending
3/11	4/11	Everybody's Got Something To Hide..Monkey	demo Kinfauns	Part 15		same	BOOT: also on boot #6
3/12	4/12	Everyone Had A Hard Year	demo	Part 15	Part 114	LLT: 4"	LLT: complete ending -- BOOT: fades before end
3/13	4/13	Brown Eyed Handsome Man/Get Back	improv	Part 15	Part 148	LLT: 25"	LLT: intro and extro with John comment
3/14	4/14	Serve Yourself	demo 1	Part 14		same	
3/15	4/15	Knockin' On Heaven's Door	improv	Part 14		same	BOOT: first chord missing
3/16	4/16	The News Of The Day From Reuters	improv	Part 14		same	
3/17	5/1	Dear Prudence	demo Kinfauns	Part 20		same	BOOT: also on boot #5
3/18	5/2	Jealous Guy	alt take	Part 20		same	

CD/track	LP/track	TITLE	VERSION	BOOT USED	BEST LLT	LLT / BOOT LONGER BY	LLT / BOOT NOTES
3/19	5/3	God Save Oz	demo	Part 19	Part 186	same	LLT: Part 19 longer intro - ending fades -- BOOT: Part 186 eq'd with ending
3/20	5/4	Rock 'N' Roll People	demo 1	Part 17	Part 216	LLT: 25"	LLT: Part 216 extra verse at beginning
3/21	5/5	Rock Island Line	improv 1	Part 18		same	
3/22	5/6	Real Life	demos 1-4	Part 17		same	
3/23	5/7	My Life	demo 1	Part 21		same	
3/24	5/8	My Life	demo 2	Part 21			
3/25	5/9	Don't Be Crazy	demo 1	Part 21	Part 180	same	
3/26	5/10	The Worst Is Over	demo 2	Part 21		LLT: 45"	LLT: Part 180 longer ending -- BOOT: edited in Part 21 - different order to uncut Part 180
4/1	5/11	In The Studio	dialogue	Part 21		same	
4/2	5/12	Starting Over	rough mix	Part 21		same	
4/3	5/13	Starting Over	control room	Part 21		same	
4/4	6/1	Maggie Mae	improv	Part 22		same	
4/5	6/2	Honey Don't / Don't Be Cruel / Matchbox jam	improv	Part 20		BOOT: 15"	BOOT: CV intro cut onto beg
4/6	6/3	Dear Prudence	remix	Part 23		same	
4/7	6/4	Cold Turkey	demo 2	Part 22		LLT: 10"	BOOT: intro cough and notes cut - same version as bootleg 1 but longer and better quality
4/8	6/5	Here We Go Again	demo	Part 23		same	
4/9	6/6	Woman	demo 3	Part 18	Part 179	BOOT: 15"	BOOT: intro and extro missing - Part 18
4/10	6/7	Neville Club	poetry	Part 17		same	
4/11	6/8	Rock 'N' Roll People	alt take	Part 22		same	
4/12	6/9	Not Fade Away	nyc jam	Part 23		same	
4/13	6/10	Sweet Little Sixteen	alt take	Part 23		same	
4/14	6/11	You Can't Catch Me	alt take	Part 20	Part 212	LLT: 6'	BOOT: Part 20 end comment edited from middle of Part 212 - also on boot #18
4/15	6/12	Mirror Mirror On The Wall	demo 3 take 1	Part 20		same	
4/16	6/13	Mirror Mirror On The Wall	demo 1 take 5	Part 24		same	
4/17	7/1	Mind Games	early mix	Part 23		same	
4/18	7/2	Cold Turkey	alt take	Part 24		same	
4/19	7/3	One Of The Boys	demo 1	Part 17		same	
4/20	7/4	Tight AS	studio dialogue	Part 22		same	BOOT: has Donahue request call at beginning
4/21	7/5	Woman	vocal overdub	Part 22		same	LLT: double tracking comment is after take -- BOOT: double tracking comment- plus dialogue
4/22	7/6	Woman	demo 1	Part 21		same	
4/23	7/7	Dear Yoko	demo 2	Part 24		same	
4/24	7/8	I Don't Wanna Face It	demo 1				
5/1	7/9	Watching The Wheels	demo 2	Part 21		same	
5/2	7/10	I'm Stepping Out	demo 1	Part 17		same	BOOT: also boot #9

CD/track	LP/track	TITLE	VERSION	BOOT USED	BEST LLT	LLT / BOOT LONGER BY	LLT / BOOT NOTES
5/3	7/11	Cleanup Time	demo 1	Part 23		same	
5/4	7/12	Woman	rough mix	Part 22		same	
5/5	8/1	Roll Over Beethoven	NYC session	Part 27		same	
5/6	8/2	Whole Lotta Shakin' Goin' On / It'll Be Me	NYC session	Part 27		same	BOOT: 4 ads - Part 78, Part 53, first and last not broadcast on LLT
5/7	8/3	One-To-One Radio Spot Outtakes		several			BOOT: end of last radio spot - not on LLT
5/8	8/4	New York City					LLT: end drum roll not on boot -- BOOT: also on boot # 1
5/9	8/5	God Save Oz	john vocal	Part 19		LLT: 2"	
5/10	8/6	Introduction	Rock N Roll Circus	Part 27		same	
5/11	8/7	Dirty Mac Jam	Rock N Roll Circus	Part 27		LLT: 10"	BOOT: faded in late - faded out early
5/12	8/8	Maurice Dupont (Agent Provocateur)	improv	Part 29			BOOT: intro: "Maurice Dupont speaking to you from the hotel foyer"
5/13	8/9	Maurice Dupont (Agent Provocateur)	improv	Part 20			BOOT: Dupont part 1
5/14	8/10	Maurice Dupont (Agent Provocateur)	improv	Part 22			BOOT: Dupont part 2
5/15	8/11	That'll Be The Day	The Quarry Men				BOOT: not on LLT at this length
5/16	8/12	Rave On	clock s/track	Part 22		LLT: 2"	BOOT: last chord missing - also on boot #22
5/17	8/13	Not Fade Away	clock s/track	Part 22		same	BOOT: also on boot #22
5/18	8/14	Maybe Baby	clock s/track	Part 22		same	BOOT: also on boot #22
5/19	8/15	Heartbeat, Peggy Sue Got Married, Peggy Sue Medley	clock s/track		Part 26	same	BOOT: "Peggy Sue" also on bootleg #2 and #22
5/20	8/16	Corrina Corrina	improv	Part 27		same	
5/21	8/17	Serve Yourself	demo 2	Part 27		same	
5/22	8/18	Best Things In Life Are Free	improv	Part 27		same	
5/23	9/1	Eat The Document	film s/track				BOOT: not on LLT
5/24	9/2	A Nice Noise	improv	Part 18			BOOT: Sean bashing guitar - why is this on?
5/25	9/3	Revolution 9	CV				BOOT: 15" beginning of track from CV
5/26	9/4	Tomorrow Never Knows	reference mix	Part 26		same	
5/27	9/5	John backwards speaking	improv	Part 26		same	
5/28	9/6	Aerial Tour Instrumental (Flying)	alternate mix	Part 32		same	
5/29	9/7	Cry Baby Cry	demo 1 Kinfauns		Part 105	same	LLT: no organ intro -- BOOT: organ at beginning - from other source - also on boot #2
5/30	9/8	Dear Prudence	demo Kinfauns		Part 20	same	BOOT: last note not LLT - from other source
5/31	9/9	Sexy Sadie	demo Kinfauns		Part 85	same	
6/1	9/10	Julia	demo 2 Kinfauns		Part 105	same	BOOT: from other source - not LLT - also on boot #2
6/2	9/11	Child Of Nature	demo Kinfauns		Part 6	same	BOOT: from other source - not LLT - also on boot #1
6/3	9/12	Continuing Story Of Bungalow Bill	demo Kinfauns		Part 43	BOOT: 18"	BOOT: from other source - not LLT
6/4	9/13	I'm So Tired	demo 1 Kinfauns		Part 85	BOOT: 15"	BOOT: from other source - not LLT
6/5	9/14	Yer Blues					BOOT: from other source - not LLT
6/6	9/15	Everybody's Got Something To Hide	demo Kinfauns		Part 15	BOOT: 5"	BOOT: from other source - not LLT - also on boot #3

CD/track	LP/track	TITLE	VERSION	BOOT USED	BEST LLT	LLT / BOOT LONGER BY	LLT / BOOT NOTES
6/7	9/16	What's The New Mary Jane	demo Kinfauns		Part 113	BOOT: 2"	BOOT: from other source - not LLT - also on boot #2
6/8	9/17	Revolution	demo Kinfauns		Part 85	LLT: 2" end BOOT: 2" intro	BOOT: from other source - not LLT - also on boot #1
6/9	10/1	Imagine	alternate take	Part 29		same	
6/10	10/2	Crippled Inside	alternate take	Part 29		same	
6/11	10/3	It's So Hard	alternate take	Part 30		same	
6/12	10/4	A Case Of The Blues	improv	Part 30	Part 204	LLT: 1' 45"	
6/13	10/5	Sally And Billy	demo 2	Part 30	Part 201		
6/14	10/6	Sally And Billy	demo 1	Part 30			
6/15	10/7	Send Me Some Lovin'	improv	Part 31		same	
6/16	10/8	Woman Is The Nigger Of The World	demo 1	Part 30		same	BOOT: also on boot #12
6/17	10/9	New York City	john vocal	Part 35		same	
6/18	10/10	Only You	improv	Part 29		same	
6/19	10/11	Banana Song	demo 1	Part 35		same	BOOT: also on boot #1
6/20	10/12	Surprise Surprise	rehearsal	Part 35		same	
6/21	10/13	Whatever Gets You Thru The Night	demo 3	Part 29		same	BOOT: also on boot #2
6/22	10/14	Watching The Wheels	demo 1	Part 30		same	
6/23	10/15	I'm Losing You	radio commercial	Part 31		same	
6/24	10/16	Borrowed Time	improv	Part 29		same	
6/25	10/17	Tobias Casuals	demo 3	Part 37		LLT: 12"	BOOT: longer intro
6/26	11/1	Happy Birthday John		Part 44	Part 113		
6/27	11/2	Julia	alt take	Part 43	same	BOOT: 5"	BOOT: first missing chord added from CV
7/1	11/3	Mother	alt mix	Part 37	same		
7/2	11/4	I Found Out	birthday party	Part 39	same		
7/3	11/5	What'd I Say	take 1	Part 37	same		
7/4	11/6	How?	birthday party	Part 44	same		
7/5	11/7	Yellow Submarine	improvs	Part 37	same		BOOT: also on boot #2
7/6	11/8	Mind Movie - El Tango - Coochie From Brazil	demo 2	Part 45	same		
7/7	11/9	Beautiful Boy	demo	Part 45	same		
7/8	11/10	Howling At The Moon	demo 1	Part 30	same		
7/9	11/11	Memories	demo 3	Part 41	LLT: Part 200	LLT: 30"	LLT: longer intro and ending
7/10	11/12	I'm Losing You	demo 2	Part 41	same		
7/11	11/13	Nobody Told Me	rough mix	Part 37		BOOT: 10"	BOOT: Sean's Goodnight edited onto end
7/12	11/14	Nobody Told Me	early mix	Part 30		LLT: 2"	BOOT: last chord missing
7/13	11/15	Beautiful Boy	demo 2				
7/14	12/1	New York City					

CD/track	LP/track	TITLE	VERSION	BOOT USED	BEST LLT	LLT / BOOT LONGER BY	LLT / BOOT NOTES
7/15	12/2	Don't Be Cruel / Houndog	jam	Part 42	same		BOOT: also on boot #16
7/16	12/3	Send Me Some Lovin'	jam	Part 42	same	LLT: 2"	BOOT: intro comment missing
7/17	12/4	I Found Out	demo 1	Part 47	same		
7/18	12/5	Happy Xmas	demo	Part 48	same		
7/19	12/6	Christmas message with Yoko	improv	Part 48	same		
7/20	12/7	Tobias Casuals radio a	radio ad	Part 44	same		
7/21	12/8	Borrowed Time	rough mix	Part 48	same		
7/22	12/9	God	demo 3	Part 47	same		BOOT: last word "...no room service here" cut off
7/23	12/10	Serve Yourself	demo 3	Part 48	same	LLT: 2"	BOOT: last few notes cut off
7/24	12/11	Imagine	early take	Part 48	same		LLT: Part 173 different intro but longer
7/25	12/12	Mucho Mungo, Mount Elga	rehearsal	Part 34	LLT: Part 173		BOOT: interview re: magic in middle
7/26	12/13	Gone From This Place	demo 1	Part 48	same		BOOT: not on LLT - John and Paul jam - 31st March 1974
7/27	12/14	Stand By Me					
8/1	13/1	The Great Wok	improv	Part 50	same		
8/2	13/2	Yer Blues (Rock 'N' Roll Circus)	rehearsal	Part 50	same		
8/3	13/3	I Found Out	demo 2	Part 59	same		
8/4	13/4	Oh Yoko	demo 2	Part 52	LLT: Part 182	LLT: 2 1/2'	LLT: longer intro and ending
8/5	13/5	How?	demo 1	Part 53	same	LLT: 5"	BOOT: first chord missing - last chord added
8/6	13/6	Pill	demo	Part 53	same		
8/7	13/7	Out Of The Blue	rough mix	Part 48	same		
8/8	13/8	#9 Dream	demo 1	Part 63	same	LLT: 30"	LLT: longer ending -- BOOT: also on boot #9
8/9	13/9	Tobias Casuals ad	radio ad	Part 52	same		BOOT: "tired of jeans revolution" - with first 2 street interviews added to end
8/10	13/10	John Henry	demo 2	Part 50	same	LLT: 3"	BOOT: last chord cut off - same as crowd noise version which is longer
8/11	13/11	She's A Friend Of Dorothy's	demo 2	Part 50	LLT: Part 201	LLT: 5"	LLT: one more refrain on piano at end - eq'd with more bass
8/12	13/12	Real Love	demo 1	Part 58	same		
8/13	13/13	Dear Yoko	basic tracks	Part 50	same		BOOT: recites lyrics and dialogue intro
8/14	13/14	(Just Like) Starting Over	12" mix?		same		BOOT: long ending - not from LLT
8/15	13/15	Maurice Dupont 3	improv	Part 29	same		
8/16	13/16	Wedding Album Commercial	radio ad	Part 50	same		
8/17	14/1	Stay In Bed (Grow Your Hair)	Wedding LP				BOOT: not from LLT
8/18	14/2	Because	vocals only	Part 58	same		
8/19	14/3	Oh Yoko	rough mix	Part 52	same		
8/20	14/4	Grapefruit Excerpts	reading from book	Part 54	same		
8/21	14/5	Imagine	early take	Part 54	same		

CD/track	LP/track	TITLE	VERSION	BOOT USED	BEST LLT	LLT / BOOT LONGER BY	LLT / BOOT NOTES
8/22	14/6	Give Me Some Truth	alternate take	Part 52	same		BOOT: beep and cymbol at beginning - not from LLT
8/23	14/7	How?	alternate take	Part 53	same		BOOT: also on boot #11
8/24	14/8	San Francisco Bay Blues	improv	Part 53	same		
8/25	14/9	Oh My Love	alternate take	Part 53	same		BOOT: ends with phone ring and KHJ station theme
8/26	14/10	How Do You Sleep?	alternate take	Part 51	same		BOOT: not on LLT - John & Paul jam - 31st March 1974 - continued from boot #7
8/27	14/11	Tobias Casuals radio ad	radio ad				
8/28		Stand By Me					
9/1	15/1	I'm Stepping Out	rough mix	Part 61	same		
9/2	15/2	I'm The Greatest	demo 2	Part 61	same	BOOT: 1'	BOOT: begins with interview: re writing song for Ringo
9/3	15/3	Move Over Ms. L	demo 1	Part 64	same	BOOT: 2"	LLT: "well I mean, you know" at end not on bootleg
9/4	15/4	Bring On The Lucie (Freeda People)	demo	Part 62	same		
9/5	15/5	Bring On The Lucie (Freeda People)	rough mix	Part 63	same		BOOT: same version was cut short on boot #8
9/6	15/6	#9 Dream	demo 1	Part 65	same		
9/7	15/7	Angela (People)	demo 2	Part 63	same		
9/8	15/8	Luck Of The Irish	demo 3	Part 63	same		
9/9	15/9	Luck Of The Irish	early mix	Part 66	same		
9/10	15/10	Only People	alternate take	Part 66	same		
9/11	15/11	Rock 'N' Roll People	radio ad	Part 66	same		
9/12	15/12	Mind Games (Promo)	demo	Part 67	same		
9/13	15/13	Forgive Me (My Little Flower Princess)	radio ad	Part 67	same		
9/14	15/14	Tower Records Ad	alternate take 1	Part 68	same	LLT: 5"	BOOT: drum part at end cut off
9/15	15/15	I Don't Want To Be A Soldier Mama	rehearsal take 1	Part 69	same	LLT: 5"	BOOT: starts "mine are working" from 2nd dialogue fragment - first part of 2nd fragment missing
9/16	15/16	How Do You Sleep?	rehearsal	Part 69	same	BOOT: 2"	BOOT: has 2 sax notes at start from somewhere else - not part of this track
9/17	15/17	Well (Baby Please Don't Go)	demo 2	Part 64	same	LLT: 2"	BOOT: last chord missing
9/18	16/1	Move Over Ms. L	radio ad	Part 67	same		
9/19	16/2	Tobias Casuals (#5)	demo 2	Part 69	same	LLT: 2"	BOOT: intro chords missing - fades in
9/20	16/3	Clean-Up Time	alternate take	Part 67	same	LLT: 5"	BOOT: end John comment missing, "I think we'll quit now, while we're behind"
9/21	16/4	My Little Flower Princess	demo	Part 70	same		BOOT: missing John comment beginning "we never have to shut up for Dad..." - also boot #5
9/22	16/5	Mother	demo 1	Part 17	same		
9/23	16/6	I'm Stepping Out	improv	Part 70	same		
9/24	16/7	Only The Lonely/Crying/Gone From ... Place	flexi disc	Part 69	same		
9/25	16/8	Radio Free London/Oz Magazine Message	rough mix	Part 69	same	BOOT: 2"	BOOT: last chord missing
9/26	16/9	Rip It Up/Ready Teddy					
10/1	16/10	Watching The Wheels / I'm Crazy	demo 4	Part 69	same	LLT: 2"	BOOT: missing "take one of" at beginning

CD/track	LP/track	TITLE	VERSION	BOOT USED	BEST LLT	LLT / BOOT LONGER BY	LLT / BOOT NOTES
10/2	16/11	Beautiful Boy	demo 4	Part 69	same	BOOT: 2"	BOOT: intro chords added to beginning - also on boot #1
10/3	16/12	Walls And Bridges (Promo)	radio ad	Part 51	same		
10/4	16/13	Stranger's Room	demo 4	Part 71	Part 175	LLT: 30"	LLT: longer ending
10/5	16/14	Woman	demo 5	Part 70	same		BOOT: starts with Cott interview re: choosing only two people to work with with, Paul & Yoko
10/6	17/1	I'm Losing You	rough mix	Part 71	same		
10/7	17/2	Mailman, Bring Me No More Blues	clock struck	Part 71	same	LLT: 5"	BOOT: missing, "uh" at beginning, and end chord - also on boot #22
10/8	17/3	Peggy Sue	rough mix	Part 71	Part 217		
10/9	17/4	Cold Turkey	demo 1	Part 72	same	LLT: 5"	BOOT: starts with Toronto press conference re: the drug problem - intro longer
10/10	17/5	Dear Yoko	demo 2	Part 72	same		BOOT: also on boot #20
10/11	17/6	Bless You	rehearsal	Part 72	same	LLT: 5"	BOOT: missing "Yeah OK, let's do something else" at end
10/12	17/7	Move Over Ms. L.	rehearsal	Part 64	Part 210	LLT: 5"	BOOT: missing "OK at least its…" at end
10/13	17/8	Borrowed Time	demo 2	Part 72	same	LLT: 2"	BOOT: missing 2 intro chords
10/14	17/9	Don't Let Me Down	demo 1	Part 73	same	LLT: 2"	BOOT: missing tape turning on at start
10/15	17/9	Oh My Love	rough mix	Part 87	same	BOOT: 10"	BOOT: count-in and intro added - not from LLT
10/16	17/10	Jealous Guy	rough mix	Part 73	same	LLT: 2"	BOOT: missing bass note and "2" of count-in
10/17	17/11	Surprise Surprise	demo 2	Part 74	same		
10/18	17/12	Gone From This Place	demo 2	Part 74	same		
10/19	18/1	Borrowed Time	alternate take	Part 74	same		
10/20	18/2	Michael Lindsay-Hogg talks with John Lennon	interview	Part 75	same		
10/21	18/3	Yer Blues improv with Mick Jagger	dialogue	Part 75	same		
10/22	18/4	Yer Blues	rehears take 2	Part 75	same	LLT: 2"	BOOT: missing first count-in guitar note
10/23	18/5	Don't Let Me Down	demo	Part 75	same		
11/1	18/6	Meat City - … Give Me Some Rock 'n' Roll	demo 1	Part 75	same		
11/2	18/7	How Do You Sleep?	alt take	Part 53	same	LLT: 2"	BOOT: "OK" missing at beginning - also on boot #8
11/3	18/8	I Know	rough mix	Part 75	same		BOOT: also on boot #18
11/4	18/9	Power To The People	alt take 3	Part 76	same		
11/5	18/10	Love	demo	Part 77	same		
11/6	18/11	Out Of The Blue	rough mix	Part 77	same		
11/7	18/12	Bonie Maronie	rough mix	Part 77	same		
11/8	19/1	Be My Baby	alt take 2	Part 76	same	LLT: 2"	BOOT: missing "Ready?" at beginning - also on boot #16
11/9	19/2	Power To The People	rough mix	Part 77	same	LLT: 5"	BOOT: missing 2 bass notes - beginning - last "ko" or Yoko at end
11/10	19/3	Oh Yoko	demo	Part 77	same		
11/11	19/4	What You Got	demo 2	Part 77	same		
11/12	-19/5	Real Love - Girls And Boys	rough mix	Part 77	same		BOOT: beginning fades in
11/13	19/6	Woman	early mix	Part 77	same		

- 242 -

CD/track	LP/track	TITLE	VERSION	BOOT USED	BEST LLT	LLT / BOOT LONGER BY	LLT / BOOT NOTES
11/14	19/7	Cookin' (In The Kitchen Of Love)	demo 3	Part 86	same		BOOT: also on boot #13
11/15	19/8	Free As A Bird	demo 1	Part 78	same		
11/16	19/9	Intuition	demo 1	Part 79	Part 123	LLT: 2"	LLT: couple of noises at the end
11/17	19/10	Intuition	rough mix	Part 79		LLT: 5"	BOOT: beginning of "hey" missing in fade-in - runs 3" longer at end
11/18	19/11	Aisumasen - Call My Name	demo 1	Part 80	same		
11/19	19/12	Aisumasen - Call My Name	demo 2	Part 80	same		
11/20	19/13	Aisumasen	rough mix	Part 80	same		
11/21	19/14	One Of The Boys	demo 2	Part 81	Part 211	LLT: 10"	BOOT: missing "Hello hello hello" intro
11/22		Love	remix				BOOT: not on Lost Lennon Tapes
12/1	20/1	Honey Don't	clock struck	Part 81		LLT: 3"	BOOT: first few chords missing - fades-in - last chord missing - fades-out - also on boot #22
12/2	20/2	Glad All Over	clock struck	Part 81		LLT: 5"	BOOT: missing first note - few chords at end missing - also on boot #22
12/3	20/3	Lend Me Your Comb	clock struck	Part 81		LLT: 2"	BOOT: last note missing - also on boot #22
12/4	20/4	Shazam!		Part 81		LLT: 2"	BOOT: part of first note missing in fade-in - also on boot #22
12/5	20/5	#9 Dream	demo 2	Part 81		LLT: 2"	BOOT: part of first chord missing in fade-in - last chord missing
12/6	20/6	12 Bar Original	take 2	Part 82		BOOT: 3' 10"	BOOT: not on Lost Lennon Tapes - only fragment on Part 81
12/7	20/7	Well Well Well	demo	Part 82		LLT: 2"	BOOT: missing "what is it?" at end
12/8	20/8	Well Well Well	alternate take	Part 81	same		
12/9	20/9	He Got The Blues	demo	Part 82		LLT: 2"	BOOT: first note missing
12/10	20/10	Look At Me	take 2	Part 82		LLT: 4"	BOOT: extra seconds of tape recorder sounds at beg and end
12/11	20/11	My Mummy's Dead	demo 7	Part 83		LLT: 2"	BOOT: intro chords missing
12/12	20/12	Real Life	demo 1	Part 31		LLT: 2"	BOOT: first chord missing - last chord cut off - also on boot #6
12/13	20/13	Woman Is The Nigger Of The World	demo 3	Part 82	Part 187	LLT: 4"	BOOT: first chord missing
12/14	20/14	Cold Turkey	take 1	Part 83	Part 215	LLT: 2"	BOOT: "He never got to see the news..." missing at beginning
12/15	20/15	I'm Stepping Out	demo 5	Part 84			BOOT: lost chord missing - also on boot #13
12/16	20/16	Watching The Wheels	take 5	Part 89	same		
12/17	21/1	Run For Your Life	demo	Part 85		LLT: 2"	BOOT: first chord missing
12/18	21/2	The Maharishi Song	demo 1	Part 89		LLT: 5"	BOOT: beginning of first chord cut off - last chord slide missing
12/19	21/3	Julia	demo	Part 90		LLT: 2"	BOOT: intro chords missing
12/20	21/4	When A Boy Meets A Girl	demo 1	Part 85		LLT: 2"	BOOT: 2 chords missing intro
12/21	21/5	God	rough mix	Part 88		LLT: 5"	BOOT: echo on "hello" inaudible in fade-in - last fading notes missing
12/22	21/6	Look At Me	demo 1	Part 92		LLT: 10"	BOOT: missing live intro and "In the...." at beginning - missing chords at end
12/23	21/7	Oh Yoko	demo 2	Part 85		LLT: 2"	BOOT: missing first chord
12/24	21/8	How?	runthrough	Part 87		LLT: 1"	BOOT: missing start of first chord
12/25	21/9	Imagine	P.O.B. improv	Part 87		LLT: 2"	BOOT: missing start fades in -
12/26	21/10	Jam					

- 243 -

CD/track	LP/track	TITLE	VERSION	BOOT USED	BEST LLT	LLT / BOOT LONGER BY	LLT / BOOT NOTES
12/27	21/11	How Do You Sleep?	rehearsal 1	Part 87	same		BOOT: studio talk and count-in not from LLT
12/28	21/12	Oh My Love	rough mix	Part 73		BOOT: 3"	
13/1	21/13	Imagine	rough mix	Part 84	same	LLT: 2"	BOOT: first chord missing
13/2	21/14	Angela - J.J.	demo 1	Part 84			
13/3	21/15	Africa State	demo 1	Part 84		LLT: 2"	BOOT: extra chords at ending
13/4	21/16	Woman Is The Nigger Of The World	outtake	Part 83	same		
13/5	22/1	Sweet Little Sixteen	alternate mix	Part 91		LLT: 2"	BOOT: missing last symbol taps
13/6	22/2	Bless You	alternate mix	Part 84		LLT: 2' 25"	BOOT: missing intro - fades out early - also on boot #19
13/7	22/3	Many Rivers To Cross	demo	Part 86	Part 201	LLT: 3"	BOOT: repeating refrain at end faded - also on boot #11
13/8	22/4	Cookin' (In The Kitchen Of Love)	demo 3	Part 86	same		
13/9	22/5	My Life	demo 3	Part 83		LLT: 2"	BOOT: first chord missing
13/10	22/6	I Watch Your Face	demo	Part 86		LLT: 5"	BOOT: first chord missing - end chords missing
13/11	22/7	Serve Yourself	demo 4	Part 86		LLT: 3"	BOOT: first chord missing - couple end chords missing
13/12	22/8	Starting Over - The Worst Is Over	demo 1	Part 90		LLT: 2"	BOOT: couple of end chords missing at end - also on boot #12
13/13	22/9	Watching The Wheels	demo 5	Part 84		LLT: 3"	BOOT: 3 drums beats missing at end
13/14	22/10	Beautiful Boy	demo 1	Part 90		LLT: 2"	BOOT: first chord missing
13/15	23/1	I Don't Want To Face It	demo 1	Part 83		LLT: 5"	BOOT: intro chords missing - end descending guitar riff missing
13/16	23/2	Beautiful Boy / ... / Across The River - medley improv	demo 3	Part 87	same		
13/17	23/3	Real Love - Girls And Boys	demo 3	Part 91	same		
13/18	23/4	Beautiful Boy	demo 3	Part 89	same		
	23/5	Stepping Out	alternate take 2	Part 97			
14/1	23/6	Cleanup Time	runthrough	Part 86		LLT: 2"	BOOT: first few chords missing
14/2	23/7	Beautiful Boy	rough mix	Part 83		LLT: 4"	BOOT: "1'2" of count-in missing - few notes at end missing
14/3	23/8	Watching The Wheels	rough mix	Part 134	same		
14/4	23/9	Dear Yoko	rough mix	Part 86		LLT: 2"	BOOT: few chords missing in fade out
14/5	23/10	Cleanup Time	rough mix	Part 89		LLT: 4"	BOOT: first symbol crash missing - few chords missing in fade-out
14/6	23/11	You Saved My Soul	demo 2	Part 86	Part 213	LLT: 2"	BOOT: missing "something" at beginning
14/7	23/12	Pop Is The Name Of The Game	improv	Part 86	Part 213		
14/8	24/1	Serve Yourself	demo 9	Part 213		LLT: 4"	BOOT: notes missing at end
14/9	24/2	Illusions					BOOT: not on LLT
14/10	24/3	He Said He Said	demos 1 to 5	Part 127		LLT: 10"	BOOT: 5 separate segments - notes/chords missing from start of each one - also on boot #1
14/11	24/4	She Said She Said	demo	Part 127		LLT: 4"	BOOT: couple of chords missing from beginning and end
14/12	24/5	Yer Blues	alternate take	Part 114	same		
14/13	24/6	Oh My Love	demo 1	Part 113			BOOT: "John" missing from intro - (like) "that" missing from end

CD/track	LP/track	TITLE	VERSION	BOOT USED	BEST LLT	LLT / BOOT LONGER BY	LLT / BOOT NOTES
14/14	24/7	Oh My Love	demo 2	Part 113			BOOT: false start missing from intro - (un)"reasonable" inaudible in fade-out
14/15	24/8	Because	Toronto				BOOT: not on LLT
14/16	24/9	Happiness Is A Warm Gun	Toronto				BOOT: not on LLT
14/17	24/10	Give Peace A Chance	Toronto	Part 96		LLT: 2"	BOOT: couple of "mooshy mooshy" missing from fadeout
14/18	24/11	Give Peace A Chance - Montreal	rehearsal	Part 94	same		BOOT: not on LLT
14/19	24/12	Give Peace A Chance - Montreal	rehearsal 2	Part 96	same		
14/20	24/13	Give Peace A Chance -- film soundtrack	alternate mix	Part 96		LLT: 3"	BOOT: part of "All" missing in fade in - last note missing in fade out
14/21	24/14	Give Peace A Chance	alternate take	Part 99		LLT: 1"	BOOT: part of first chord missing in fade in - also on boot #1
14/22	24/15	God	demo 2	Part 92		LLT: 2"	BOOT: first two chords missing in fade in -
14/23	24/16	My Mummy's Dead	rough mix			LLT: 26"	
14/24	24/17	It's So Hard - sax overdub	dialogue/rehearsal	Part 107	& Part 207		BOOT: intro - ref to Jealous Guy after missing - sax notes at end missing - cuts to runthrough
14/25	24/18	Come Together - one to one	rehearsal	Part 118	same		BOOT: not on LLT
14/26	24/19	Honky Tonk Blues - one to one	rehearsal	Part 121			BOOT: not on LLT
14/27	24/20	I Know	demo 3	Part 121		LLT: 4"	BOOT: intro - missing "let's try from the intro to" (the end of 2 middle 8) - also on boot #16
14/28	24/21	Rock 'n' Roll People	alternate mix	Part 118		LLT: 7"	BOOT: intro chords missing - extra chords missing
14/29	24/22	Only People	early mix	Part 121		LLT: 4"	BOOT: intro - first chord missing from fade in - couple of chords missing from fade out
14/30	25/1	Whatever Gets You Thru The Night	demo 2	Part 104	same		
15/1	25/2	Steel And Glass	alternate mix				BOOT: not on LLT
15/2	25/3	Beef Jerky	alternate mix				BOOT: not on LLT
15/3	25/4	You Saved My Soul	demo 1	Part 99		LLT: 2"	BOOT: 2 chords missing at begining
15/4	25/5	Serve Yourself	demo 5	Part 108			BOOT: last chord cut off in fade
15/5	25/6	Memories	demo 2	Part 115	same		
15/6	25/7	Real Life	demo 5	Part 99		LLT: 2"	BOOT: couple of intro chords missing
15/7	25/8	Watching The Wheels	demo 6	Part 116		LLT: 10"	BOOT: "take 1" and couple chords at beginning - couple of chords at end
15/8	25/9	Don't Be Crazy	demo 2	Part 99		LLT: 4"	BOOT: drum machine and couple of chords at beg
15/9	25/10	Woman	demo 1	Part 116	same	LLT: 3"	BOOT: chord at beginning - drum beat at end
15/10	25/11	Starting Over	demo 1	Part 105		LLT: 2"	BOOT: 2 notes at end of fade out missing
15/11	26/1	I Don't Want To Face It	demo 3	Part 105		LLT: 35"	BOOT: intro dialogue longer 174 - end chord missing - also boot #20
15/12	26/2	Nobody Told Me	demo 1	Part 115	Part 174	LLT: 4"	BOOT: first chord attack missing - last chord missing
15/13	26/3	Real Love - Girls And Boys	demo 4		same		BOOT: not on LLT
15/14	26/4	I'm Losing You	alternate take dial & alt take	Part 92			
15/15	26/5	Beautiful Boy	alternate take	Part 106		LLT: 4"	BOOT: start of opening chord missing in fade-in - couple of end chords missing
15/16	26/6	Nobody Told Me	alternate take	Part 104		LLT: 2"	BOOT: couple of chords missing at end
15/17	26/7	Cleanup Time	rough mix	Part 116		LLT: 5"	BOOT: missing chords at end
15/18	26/8	Starting Over					

CD/track	LP/track	TITLE	VERSION	BOOT USED	BEST LLT	LLT / BOOT LONGER BY	LLT / BOOT NOTES
15/19	27/1	If I Fell	demo	Part 163	same		BOOT: not on LLT
15/20	27/2	I Sat Belonely	book reading	Part 163	same		
15/21	27/3	Foyle's Speech	speech				
16/1	27/4	National Health Cow	book reading	Part 113	same		
16/2	27/5	Strawberry Fields Forever	demo 2	Part 164		LLT: 5"	LLT: same version broadcast Part 11 -- BOOT: also on boot #2
16/3	27/6	Get It Together	peace message				LLT: "let's move, clear the air..." etc. missing from end
16/4	27/7	Happy Xmas	rough mix	Part 128	same		
16/5	27/8	Power To The People	alternate take 2	Part 118	Part 76	LLT: 2"	LLT: (we can't)"do anything" missing - from end -- BOOT: also on boot #7
16/6	27/9	Don't Be Cruel / Hound Dog	jam		Part 42		LLT: intro not on LLT - poor sound - 3" solo piano at end not on LLT -- BOOT: also on boot #11
16/7	27/10	I'm The Greatest	rough mix	Part 123		LLT: 3"	LLT: chords on LLT missing in fadeout at end
16/8	27/11	I Know	demo 3	Part 121	same		LLT: "try with" to end of 2nd mid 8 missing -- BOOT: poor snd - 3 sep tracks - also on boot #14
16/9	27/12	Rock 'N' Roll People	demo 2	Part 123		LLT: 2"	LLT: last chord cut in fadeout
16/10	27/13	Meat City	demo 2	Part 123		LLT: 2"	LLT: one vocal count in sound missing from intro
16/11	27/14	Meat City	demo 3	Part 125		LLT: 2"	LLT: first chord missing - longer ending
16/12	27/15	Meat City	alternate mix		Part 209		BOOT: not on LLT
16/13	27/16	One Day At A Time	early mix	Part 123		LLT: 3"	LLT: first 2 drum beats of countin missing
16/14	27/17	Only People	alternate take		Part 164	LLT: 3"	BOOT: same version poor quality mono - not from LLT
16/15	28/1	Tight A$	rough mix		Part 121	LLT: 4"	BOOT: same version poor quality mono - not from LLT
16/16	28/2	You Are Here	rough mix		Part 209	LLT: 2"	BOOT: same version poor quality mono - not from LLT
16/17	28/3	Going Down On Love	demo		Part 138	LLT: 2"	BOOT: same version poor quality mono - not from LLT
16/18	28/4	Whatever Gets You Thru The Night	alternate mix				BOOT: not on LLT
16/19	28/5	Surprise Surprise	alternate mix				BOOT: not on LLT
16/20	28/6	John on KHJ-AM Los Angeles	guest DJ	Part 124	same		
16/21	28/7	Do You Wanna Dance	alternate take	Part 119		LLT: 2"	BOOT: few chords missing in fade out - poor sound
16/22	28/8	You Can't Catch Me	alternate take	Part 158		LLT: 12"	BOOT: first drum beat missing - 10" of fade out missing - poor mono sound
16/23	28/9	Free As A Bird	demo 2	Part 128		LLT: 4"	BOOT: "hello hello free three" missing at start - last chord missing - poor sound

POOR SOUND THROUGHOUT THIS CD

CD/track	LP/track	TITLE	VERSION	BOOT USED	BEST LLT	LLT / BOOT LONGER BY	LLT / BOOT NOTES
17/1	28/10	Serve Yourself	demo 6	Part 128		LLT: 1"	BOOT: part of first "Well" cut off in fade in - poor sound
17/2	28/11	She'll Be Comin' Round The Mountain	improv	Part 167	same		
17/3	28/12	...Round In Circles / Beautiful Boy - medley	demo	Part 165		LLT: 3"	BOOT: first chord beat missing - key change to lost chords missing
17/4	29/1	Memories - Watching The Wheels	demo 3	Part 163		LLT: 1"	BOOT: first chord missing - LLT broadcast fades into CV at end
17/5	29/2	I'm Losing You - Stranger's Room	demo 4	Part 122		LLT: 4"	BOOT: first chord and "here in the" (afternoon) missing at start - couple end chords missing
17/6	29/3	Woman	demo 6	Part 122	same		
17/7	29/4	I'm Stepping Out	demo 3	Part 120		LLT: 4"	BOOT: "take one of the"(new one) missing at start - couple of chords missing at end

CD/track	LP/track	TITLE	VERSION	BOOT USED	BEST LLT	LLT / BOOT LONGER BY	LLT / BOOT NOTES
17/8	29/5	I'm Stepping Out	demo 4	Part 120		LLT: 2"	BOOT: chords missing at start
17/9	29/6	Starting Over	demo				BOOT: not on LLT
17/10	29/7	Dream Lover / Stay	jam			LLT: 30"	BOOT: not on LLT
17/11	29/8	Cleanup Time studio dialogue	dialogue	Part 136	same		
17/12	29/9	Beautiful Boy	dialogue	Part 135	same		
17/13	29/10	Watching The Wheels	rough mix	Part 134			BOOT: not on LLT - poor sound quality - different count-in than LLT rough mixes
17/14	29/11	Watching The Wheels	alternate mix	Part 119		LLT: 17"	BOOT: 15" of spoken words over echo missing at start - "gave it up" and last chord faded out
17/15	29/12	Borrowed Time	alternate take 8	Part 120			
17/16	29/13	I'm Stepping Out	rough mix	Part 135		LLT: 5"	BOOT: couple of start chords missing - "...woo hoo..." with end chords missing
17/17	29/14	Woman					BOOT: not on LLT
17/18	29/15	Lennon's Lost Diary Tape					
18/1	30/1	It's Not Too Bad	demo	Part 179	same		BOOT: not on LLT
18/2	30/2	Hey Bulldog - She Can Talk To Me	demos 2 - 4	Part 179	same		BOOT: 2 chords missing from end of 1 - has Universe mellotron riff in middle
18/3	30/3	Cry Baby Cry					BOOT: not on LLT
18/4	30/4	Two Virgins Outtake					BOOT: not on LLT
18/5	30/5	Plastic Ono Band Jam					
18/6	30/6	Look At Me	rough mix	Part 204	same		BOOT: not on LLT
18/7	30/7	I'm The Greatest	demo 2	Part 201	same		
18/8	30/8	How? / Child of Nature / Oh Yoko	demo 1	Part 182	same		
18/9	30/9	Oh Yoko	demo 2	Part 201	same		
18/10	30/10	Sally And Billy	rehearsal dialogue	Part 186	same		
18/11	30/11	Come Together	demo	Part 182	same		
18/12	30/12	Happy Girl	demo	Part 182			
18/13	30/13	I'll Make You Happy	rehearsal 2 and 1	Part 197		LLT: 2"	BOOT: "where would we put em" cut - repeated segment from 197 - 2nd runthru reh 1 at end
18/14	30/14	How Do You Sleep?	King Curtis overdubs				BOOT: not on LLT
18/15	30/15	It's So Hard	King Curtis overdubs				BOOT: not on LLT
18/16	30/16	I Don't Want To Be A Soldier					BOOT: missing chords at end
18/17	31/1	Intuition	demo 2	Part 209		LLT: 3"	
18/18	31/2	I Know	demo 1	Part 75	same		
18/19	31/3	I Know	rough mix	Part 75	same		BOOT: also on boot #11
18/20	31/4	Aisumasen	rough mix	Part 209	same		
18/22	31/5	Steel And Glass	demo	Part 197		LLT: 2'	BOOT: first chord missing - on LLT this fades to a 2' rough mix
18/23	31/6	Walls And Bridges Rundown	interview	Part 212			BOOT: not on LLT - '74 John Canada radio interview re: Walls And Bridges tracks
18/24	31/7	Mirror Mirror On The Wall	demo 3	Part 212		LLT: 5 1/2'	BOOT: last half of 9 + minute demo - also on boot #4
18/25	31/8	Memories - Watching The Wheels	demo 4	Part 201		LLT: 2"	BOOT: first chord missing - last note missing

CD/track	LP/track	TITLE	VERSION	BOOT USED	BEST LLT	LLT / BOOT LONGER BY	LLT / BOOT NOTES
19/1	31/9	Tennessee	demo 3	Part 201	same		
19/2	31/10	Sally And Billy	demo 3	Part 201	same		
19/3	31/11	She Is A Friend Of Dorothy's	demo 1	Part 201	Part 81	LLT: 10"	BOOT: spoken intro missing
19/4	31/12	The Boat Song	improv	Part 185	same		
19/5	31/13	Pedro The Fisherman	improv	Part 185	same		
19/6	31/14	Many Rivers To Cross	improv	Part 201	same	LLT: 3'	BOOT: starts 3' into take - also on boot #13
19/7	31/15	My Girl	improv	Part 185	same		BOOT: same track as "Many Rivers to Cross" cut into 2nd song
19/8	31/16	Unknown Instrumental 1979	runthrough 1	Part 214		LLT: 2"	BOOT: first chord and last missing
19/9	32/1	I'm Stepping Out	dialogue & runthru	Parts 161 & 189		LLT: 30"	BOOT: 15" of tuning at start is from somewhere else - cut out of middle of track
19/10	32/2	Dear Yoko	runthrough	Part 188	same		BOOT: 25" missing from start of dialogue - end of 161 cut to 189
19/11	32/3	Woman	overdub & dialogue	Part 189 and 160		same	BOOT: overdub from 189 is cut to dialogue from 160 and dialogue from 189
19/12	32/4	Woman	vocal overdub	Part 189	same		
19/13	32/5	Woman	runthrough	Part 188	same		
19/14	32/6	Cleanup Time	runthrough	Part 188	same		
19/15	32/6	Nobody Told Me	runthrough	Part 188	same		
19/16	32/7	Watching The Wheels	guitar overdub	Part 188	same		
19/17	32/8	Woman	alternate take	Part 160	same		
19/18	32/9	Woman	early take				BOOT: mostly guitar and vocals with reverb - not on LLT
19/19	32/10	Borrowed Time	alternate take				BOOT: not on LLT - fragment of Part 188 dialogue from Nobody Told me re: chocolate donuts
19/20	32/11	I'm Losing You	alternate take	Part 216	same		BOOT: couple of end chords missing
19/21	33/1	Imagine	alternate take	Part 217	same		BOOT: not on LLT
19/22	33/2	How Do You Sleep?	alternate take	Part 186	same		BOOT: not on LLT
19/23	33/3	J.J.	demo 2			BOOT: 9"	
19/24	33/4	Rock Island... / Maybe... Peggy... medley	TV footage			LLT: 1' 50"	
19/25	33/5	All You Need Is Love					
20/1	33/6	Out The Blue	alternate mix	Part 217	same		BOOT: CV intro cut onto missing intro from LLT
20/2	33/7	Old Dirt Road	alternate mix	Part 173	same		BOOT: first chord missing
20/3	33/8	Steel And Glass	rough mix	Part 197	same		BOOT: missing demo at start that fades to this mix
20/4	33/9	Whatever Gets You Through The Night	rough mix	Part 216	same		
20/5	33/10	Rock 'n' Roll Radio Spot	radio ad for LP				BOOT: not on LLT
20/6	33/11	Stand By Me	Old Grey Whistle...	Part 216	same		BOOT: not on LLT - similar to #39 ST mix - intro guitar & "more voice..." at end not on #39
20/7	33/12	Serve Yourself	demo 8	Part 170	same		
20/8	33/13	Nobody Told Me - Everybody's Talking	demo 2	Part 200	same		
20/9	33/14	Nobody Told Me - Everybody's Talking	demo 3	Part 200	same		BOOT: also boot #15
20/10	33/15	Nobody Told Me	demo 1	Part 174	same		

CD/track	LP/track	TITLE	VERSION	BOOT USED	BEST LLT	LLT / BOOT LONGER BY	LLT / BOOT NOTES
20/11	34/1	Falling In Love Again	improv	Part 218		LLT: 2"	BOOT: part of first word cut off
20/12	34/2	Cathy's Clown	improv	Part 145		LLT: 2"	BOOT: part of first chord missing
20/13	34/3	You Send Me	improv	Part 134	same		BOOT: 5"
20/14	34/4	Red Love	demo 2	Part 180		LLT: 2"	BOOT: clean intro is under dialogue in Part 134 - not on LLT
20/15	34/5	My Life	demo 5	Part 180		LLT: 2"	BOOT: last note missing in fade out
20/16	34/6	My Life	demo 6	Part 72			BOOT: 1" of intro chord fade-in missing - last chord missing
20/17	34/7	Dear Yoko	demo 2	Part 173	same		BOOT: also on boot #10
20/18	35/1	I'm Stepping Out	demo 2	Part 218		LLT: 2"	BOOT: couple of chords missing in end fade-out
20/19	35/2	I Don't Wanna Face It	rough mix	Part 190			BOOT: 2 extra beats in fade-out than on Part 173 - not on LLT
20/20	35/3	Watching The Wheels	runthu & dialogue		same		BOOT: runthrough from Part 218 edited to studio dialogue from Preview Part 3
20/21	35/4	Beautiful Boy	runthrough		same		
20/22		Jesus Apology Interview fragments					BOOT: not on LLT in with these edits
20/23		BBC Alan Freeman interview re: John's book					BOOT: not on LLT in complete form - edited in Part 115 as You Can't Do That intro
21/1		I'm Stepping Out - runthrough 1 - dialogue - runthrough 3		Part 214	same		BOOT: drum beat missing at start - dialogue up to and including Jimmy Brown
21/2		I'm Stepping Out - dialogue & runthrough 2		Part 214	same		BOOT: ordering dinner
21/3		I'm Stepping Out - dialogue & runthrough 4		Part 215			BOOT: check the tempo - "this was goo"(d) at end missing
21/4		Borrowed Time - dialogue - runthrough - dialogue		Part 215		LLT: 2"	BOOT: few tuning notes missing at start - latin rhythm - runthru distorted vocal - Bob Marley
21/5		Borrowed Time - runthrough 2		Part 173	same	LLT: 2"	
21/6		Borrowed Time - dialogue - runthrough	monitor mix				BOOT: local 802 I don't move mics - from mid, moved to beg. - followed by brief guitar runthru
21/7		(Just Like) Starting Over	rough mix	Part 45			BOOT: not on LLT
21/8		(Just Like) Starting Over		Part 45			BOOT: not on LLT
21/9		John Sinclair			same		BOOT: complete crowd clapping end - not on LLT
21/10		It's So Hard			same		BOOT: not on LLT
21/11		Luck Of The Irish					BOOT: not on LLT
21/12		Sisters O Sisters					BOOT: not on LLT
21/13		We're All Water					BOOT: not on LLT
21/14		Woman Is The Nigger Of The World					

SUPPOSEDLY COMPLETE BUT OTHER CLOCK TRACKS BROADCAST NOT HERE (ie. Not Fade Away)

CD/track	LP/track	TITLE	VERSION	BOOT USED	BEST LLT	LLT / BOOT LONGER BY	LLT / BOOT NOTES
22/1		Aisumasen					BOOT: not on LLT
22/2		Shazam		Part 81	same	BOOT: 20"	BOOT: also on boot #12
22/3		Honey Don't		Part 81			BOOT: whistling and "he lit a cigarette" comment at end - also on boot #12
22/4		Glad All Over		Part 81		BOOT: 14"	BOOT: 14" of intro missing - also on boot #12
22/5		Lend Me Your Comb		Part 81		BOOT: 18"	BOOT: end chords and "is that camera in the frame" missing from end - also on boot #12

CD/track	LP/track	TITLE	VERSION	BOOT USED	BEST LLT	LLT / BOOT LONGER BY	LLT / BOOT NOTES
22/6		Wake Up Little Susie					BOOT: not on LLT
22/7		Baby I don't Care					BOOT: not on LLT
22/8		Vacation Time					BOOT: not on LLT
22/9		Heartbeat				BOOT: 18"	BOOT: intro missing
22/10		Peggy Sue Got Married	Part 26	same			BOOT: also on boot #2 and #5
22/11		Peggy Sue	Part 26			BOOT: 13"	BOOT: "change the mood a little" comment missing at end - also on boot #2 and #5
22/12		Maybe Baby	Part 71			BOOT: 10"	BOOT: intro missing from start - "sorry" missing from end - also on boot #5
22/13		Mailman, Bring Me No More Blues	Part 71			BOOT: 10"	BOOT: guitar notes missing from end - also on boot #10
22/14		Rave On	Part 22			BOOT: 50"	BOOT: rock n roll guitar improv and "1 2 3 ah!" missing at end - also on boot #5
22/15		What'd I Say					BOOT: not on LLT
22/16		Yellow Submarine					BOOT: not on LLT
22/17		On Top Of Old Smokey					BOOT: not on LLT
22/18		Goodnight Irene	Part 37			LLT: 23" fragment	BOOT: not on LLT
22/19		He's Got The Whole World In His Hands					BOOT: not on LLT
22/20		Rolling Stone / Twist And Shout / Louie Louie / La Bamba - medley					BOOT: not on LLT
22/21		Bring It On Home To Me					BOOT: not on LLT
22/22		Yesterday					BOOT: not on LLT
22/23		Tandoori Chicken					BOOT: not on LLT
22/24		Power To The People					BOOT: not on LLT
22/25		Maybe Baby					BOOT: not on LLT
22/26		Peggy Sue					BOOT: not on LLT
22/27		My Baby Left Me					BOOT: not on LLT
22/28		Blue Suede Shoes					BOOT: not on LLT
22/29		Crippled Inside					BOOT: not on LLT
22/30		Give Peace A Chance					BOOT: not on LLT
22/31		Crippled Inside	Part 92			LLT: 30" fragment	BOOT: not on LLT
22/32		Uncle Albert/Admiral Halsey					BOOT: not on LLT
22/33		Happy Birthday					BOOT: not on LLT
22/34		Uncle Albert/Admiral Halsey					BOOT: not on LLT
22/35		My Sweet Lord					BOOT: not on LLT

COMMERCIAL VERSIONS OF LOST LENNON TRACKS

Tracks released on commercial version ("CV") CDs.
Standard time abbreviations used are ' for minute and " for second.

ANTHOLOGY
1998-11-02
UK Capitol 4 CDs

TITLE	SOURCE	TYPE	VERSION	BEST LLT	LLT / CD LONGER BY	NOTES
Working Class Hero	Plastic Ono Band sessions	alternate take	previously unreleased	not on LLT		
God	Plastic Ono Band sessions	alternate take	previously unreleased	not on LLT		
I Found Out	home	demo 1		Part 47		couple of extra strums on the intro
Hold On	Plastic Ono Band sessions	alternate take	previously unreleased	not on LLT		
Isolation	Plastic Ono Band sessions	alternate take	previously unreleased	not on LLT	ANTHOLOGY: 2"	
Love	Plastic Ono Band sessions	alternate take	previously unreleased	not on LLT		
Mother	Plastic Ono Band sessions	alternate take	previously unreleased	not on LLT		
Remember	Plastic Ono Band sessions	alt take take 1	previously unreleased	not on LLT		previously booted - diff mix, prominent organ
Imagine	Imagine sessions		bed-in from World of J&Yoko BBC	Part 29		
Fortunately	Imagine: John Lennon s/track			not on LLT		
Well Baby Please Don't Go	Imagine sessions	improv	rehearsal	Part 69	LLT: 1' 40"	Anthology fades out in solo
Oh My Love	Imagine sessions			not on LLT		previously booted, George messing up intro
Jealous Guy	Imagine sessions			not on LLT		previously booted
Maggie Mae	home	demo		not on LLT		
How Do You Sleep?	Imagine sessions		previously released	Part 19	ANTHOLOGY: 20"	take 4 breakdown, take 5 false start, take 6
God Save Oz		John vocal	previously released	not on LLT		intro dial & "that sounded all right" missing on LLT
Do The Oz		John vocal	previously unreleased	not on LLT		previously booted
I Don't Want To Be A Soldier	Imagine sessions	end of take 1, take 2		not on LLT		
Give Peace A Chance	Montreal rehearsal		previously unreleased	not on LLT		
Look At Me	Plastic Ono Band sessions		previously unreleased	not on LLT		
Long Lost John	Plastic Ono Band sessions		previously unreleased	Part 30		
New York City	home	demo 2		not on LLT	LLT: 1' ANTHOLOGY: first 56"	previously booted in longer form
Attica State	Attica State Benefit		live - previously unreleased	Part 2		
Imagine	Attica State Benefit		live	not on LLT	ANTHOLOGY: 17"	intro missing on LLT
Bring On The Lucie	Mind Games sessions	Mind Games sessions	previously unreleased	not on LLT		
Woman Is The Nigger Of The World	demo 1		Part 31	LLT: 1' 30"	tuning, 1st vrs, middle cut, 2nd vrs, middle cut, coda
Geraldo Rivera	One To One evening		One To One intro	not on LLT		
Woman Is The Nigger Of The World	One To One evening		live	not on LLT		
It's So Hard	One To One evening		live	not on LLT		
Come Together	rough mix with choir no strings		live	not on LLT		
Happy Xmas			previously unreleased	Part 16		
Luck of the Irish	John Sinclair Benefit		live		LLT: 10"	LLT: diff intro John speech, ANTH: "need a stool really"

TITLE	SOURCE	TYPE	VERSION	BEST LLT	LLT / CD LONGER BY	NOTES
John Sinclair	John Sinclair Benefit		live	Part 16	ANTHOLOGY: 25"	thank you MC speech at end and not on LLT
The David Frost Show	The David Frost Show		interview re: John Sinclair	Part 45	ANTHOLOGY: 25"	starts LLT "didn't want help", ANTH: beg of segment
Mind Games (I Promise)	home	demo		Part 8	LLT: 1'	1st min of demo, without "oh yeah" then verse
Mind Games (Make Love, Not War)	home	demo		Part 8	LLT: 2'	15" intro not LLT, cuts to "make love..." 53" in runs 1' alternate take no keyboards
One Day At A Time	Mind Games sessions		previously unreleased	not on LLT		
I Know	home	demo 3		Part 121	LLT: 2"	intro "let's try" missing, starts "to the end of 2 mid 8s"
I'm The Greatest	home	John vocal	previously unreleased	not on LLT		
Goodnight Vienna		John vocal		Part 201	ANTHOLOGY: 37" 18" intro 20" coda	LLT: diff mix, ANTH: LLT intro is cut onto end
Jerry Lewis Telethon	Jerry Lewis Telethon	improv	chant and Jerry Lewis talk	not on LLT		end of Give Peace..., crowd chant, thanks J&Y
A Kiss Is Just A Kiss	Earth News Radio	piano demo take 4		Part 92	LLT: 2"	LLT: one extra "hmm" from Yoko at the end
Real Love	home	demo	previously unreleased	not on LLT		
You Are Here	Mind Games sessions		previously unreleased	not on LLT		
What You Got	home		previously unreleased	not on LLT		
Nobody Loves You...	Walls And Bridges sessions		previously unreleased	not on LLT		
Whatever Gets You...	home	demo 1		Part 12	LLT: 4' 40" ANTH: starts 1' 46" in	middle is edit of 2 parts, ends 1' 13" before end
Whatever Gets You...	Walls And Bridges sessions		previously unreleased	not on LLT		
Yesterday (parody)	Walls And Bridges sessions		previously unreleased	not on LLT		
Be Bop A Lula	Rock N Roll sessions		previously unreleased	not on LLT		
Rip It Up/Ready Teddy	Walls And Bridges sessions	alt take with extra verse		not on LLT		
Scared	Walls And Bridges sessions		previously unreleased	not on LLT		
Steel And Glass	Walls And Bridges sessions		previously unreleased	not on LLT		
Surprise, Surprise	Walls And Bridges sessions		previously unreleased	not on LLT		
Bless You	Walls And Bridges sessions		previously unreleased	not on LLT		
Going Down On Love	Walls And Bridges sessions	dialogue		not on LLT		
Move Over Ms. L	Walls And Bridges sessions	improv		not on LLT		
Ain't She Sweet	Rock N Roll sessions		previously unreleased	not on LLT		
Slippin' And Slidin'	Rock N Roll sessions		previously unreleased	not on LLT		
Peggy Sue	Rock N Roll sessions		previously unreleased	not on LLT		
Bring It On Home To Me/Send...	Rock N Roll sessions		previously unreleased	not on LLT		
Phil and John 1	Rock N Roll sessions		previously unreleased	not on LLT		
Phil and John 2	Rock N Roll sessions		previously unreleased	not on LLT		
Phil and John 3	Rock N Roll sessions		previously unreleased	not on LLT		
When In Doubt, Fuck It	Rock N Roll sessions		previously unreleased	not on LLT		
Be My Baby	home	demo 5		Part 71, demo 4	LLT: 3' 20"	LLT Part 77 is Roots mix with talk over intro
Stranger's Room						cuts 4 times then to whistling, fades 1' before end
Old Dirt Road	Walls And Bridges sessions		previously unreleased	not on LLT		

TITLE	SOURCE	TYPE	VERSION	BEST LLT	LLT / CD LONGER BY	NOTES
I'm Losing You	Double Fantasy sessions	improv	previously bootlegged	not on LLT		
Sean's "Little Help"	home	demo take 2		Part 3	ANTHOLOGY: 20"	LLT starts on Sean singing 2nd "Do you need"
Serve Yourself	home	demo, sounds like take 2		not on LLT		takes 1 and 3 are on LLT
My Life	Double Fantasy sessions	demo	previously bootlegged	not on LLT		
Nobody Told Me	home	demo		Part 204	ANTHOLOGY: 10"	couple of more coda bars than on LLT
Life Begins At 40	Double Fantasy sessions	demo 3	previously unreleased	not on LLT		
I Don't Wanna Face It	Bermuda			Part 22, not on LLT		
Woman	Double Fantasy sessions	demo 3	previously unreleased	not on LLT		
Dear Yoko	home			Part 29	same	
Watching the Wheels	Double Fantasy sessions	alternate take 2		Part 97	LLT: 15" end - ANTH: 10" start	no 10" intro dial, LLT coda "ants..." twice with end chord
I'm Stepping Out	Bermuda	demo 1		Part 31	LLT: 50" end - ANTH: 11"start	11" intro dial before "welcome", fades 50" before end
Borrowed Time	home	demo		Part 4	LLT: 50" mid - ANTH: 1' 30"	2nd song cut on to ending, cut to coda after first 48"
The Rishi Kesh Song	home	improv		Part 18	LLT: 20"	starts 36" in with guitar, cuts to intro guitar for coda
Sean's "Loud"	Double Fantasy sessions			not on LLT		
Beautiful Boy	home	demo	previously unreleased	not on LLT		
Mr. Hyde's Gone (Don't Be Afraid)				not on LLT		
Only You	home	George Martin orchestra	John vocal	not on LLT		LLT Part 35 has different mix
Grow Old With Me	home	demo	previously unreleased	Part 12	LLT: 2' 6" cuts - ANTH: 14" end	cuts "September/November" cuts 20" guit ads 14" coda
Dear John	home	improv		Part 50	ANTHOLOGY: 1' 14"	music under not on LLT, 20" intro not on LLT
The Great Wok	home	demo 1		Part 1, LLT longer	LLE: 50" - ANTH: 12" start	intro 12" before LLT, ends 1' from end, missing middle 8
Mucho Mungo	improv			Part 14	same	
Satire 1 (...Heaven's Door)	improv			Part 14	ANTHOLOGY: 10" end	music under not on LLT, coda 10" longer, has final chord
Satire 2 (News of The Day)	improv			Part 27	ANTHOLOGY: 28"	music under not on LLT, 8" start, 20" end guitar not LLT
Satire 3 (Best Things In Life...)	home dialogue	improv	previously unreleased	not on LLT		
Sean's "In The Sky"	home dialogue	improv	previously unreleased	not on LLT		
It's Real				not on LLT		

MIND GAMES CD
2002-10-7
UK Parlophone CD

TITLE	SOURCE	TYPE	VERSION	BEST LLT	LLT / CD LONGER BY	NOTES
Aisumasen	home	demo 2		Part 80	LLT: 1' 20"	several false starts at beginning missing
Bring on the Lucie	home	demo		Part 62		5" of extra coda chords and "hello" at end
Meat City	home	demo 2		Part 123		same

TITLE	SOURCE	TYPE	VERSION	BEST LLT	LLT / CD LONGER BY	NOTES
Walls And Bridges 2005-7-11 UK Parlophone CD						
Whatever Gets You Thru The Night	Madison Square Garden single	demo	live	not on LLT		
Nobody Loves You			alternative version	not on LLT		
John Interviewed By Bob Mercer	B side of Whatever Gets You...		US promo 7"			
ROCK N ROLL 2004-9-27 UK Parlophone CD						
Angel Baby	Menlove Ave LP		previously unreleased	not on LLT		
To Know Her Is To Love Her			previously unreleased	Part 33		last 40" Part 33 end, "it hurts me" not LLT, rest is alt take
Since My Baby Left Me						
Just Because (Reprise)		alternate take			complete take	
DOUBLE FANTASY 2000-10-9 UK Parlophone CD						
Help Me To Help Myself	single	demo 1		Part 150	LLT: 2" no extra coda cords at end	1st vrs before dialogue missing, 5" of extra coda
Walking On Thin Ice	Walking On Thin Ice B-side		not on LLT	not on LLT		
Central Park Stroll (Dialogue)			17" fragment from single			only 17" fragment, complete track on 7"
MILK & MONEY 2001-10-1 UK Parlophone CD						
Every Man Has A Woman...	Every Man Has A Woman LP			not on LLT		
Stepping Out (Home Version)		John vocal demo		not on LLT		

- 255 -

TITLE	SOURCE	TYPE	VERSION	BEST LLT	LLT / CD LONGER BY	NOTES
REMEMBER						
2006						
US Starbucks exclusive CD						
Hold On	Imagine sessions	improv	fragment	not on LLT		same as on Anthology
Sean's "Little Help"		alternate take		Part 3		same as on Anthology, LLT starts on 2nd "Do you need"
I'm Losing You		studio dialogue		not on LLT	LLT: 20"	same as on Anthology
Going Down On Love			take 19	not on LLT		same as on Anthology, don't play in fills, take 6
Nobody Loves You				not on LLT		
THE U.S. VERSUS JOHN LENNON						
2006-9-25						
UK Capitol CD						
Bed Peace	Montreal Bed-In intro to CV	improv		not on LLT		John and Yoko improv with guitar
Give Peace A Chance	John Sinclair Benefit			not on LLT		22" of Bed-In dialogue clips before CV
Attica State	Bed-In			Part 16		not on LLT: 20" intro dialogue , 10" end dialogue
Happy Xmas			intro to commercial version	not on LLT		"War Is Over if you want it, peace" at start
How Do You Sleep?			instrumental backing tracks	not on LLT		
Instant Karma		interview fragment	intro to commercial version	not on LLT		"time wounds all heels"
ACOUSTIC						
2004-11-02						
EMI CD						
Phasing has been added to every track						
Working Class Hero	Anthology	unreleased take			ANTHOLOGY: 20"	ANTH: 10" more of intro - 10" Well Well Well end improv
Love	Anthology	unreleased take			ANTHOLOGY: 13"	ANTH: 13" false start
Well Well Well	home	demo		Part 82	LLT: 2"	LLT has "what is it?" at end
Look At Me	Anthology	unreleased take			ANTHOLOGY: same	
God	demo 3			Part 47	LLT: 6"	LLT has 2" extra guitar intro and 4" guitar coda
My Mummy's Dead	take 2			Part 82/187	LLT: same	
Cold Turkey	demo 2			Part 23	not on LLT	6" intro missing, same as Part 23 no harmony & overdubs
The Luck Of The Irish [Live]	Anthology John Sinclair Benefit			Part 16		different intro

TITLE	SOURCE	TYPE	VERSION	BEST LLT	LLT / CD LONGER BY	NOTES
John Sinclair [Live]	Anthology John Sinclair Benefit			Part 16		ANTHOLOGY: 19" doesn't have thank you speech at end
Woman Is The Nigger Of The World	Anthology	demo 2		Part 83		LLT: longer ANTH: same
What You Got		demo		Part 77		LLT: 50"
Watching The Wheels	Anthology	demo 3		Part 29		ANTHOLOGY: same
Dear Yoko		demo 2		Part 72		LLT: 1'
Real Love				Part 77		LLT: 4"
Imagine	Anthology	Attica State Benefit				ANTHOLOGY: same
It's Real	Anthology	dialogue unreleased				ANTHOLOGY: same

WORKING CLASS HERO - THE DEFINITIVE LENNON
2005-10-03
Parlophone 2 CDs

TITLE	SOURCE	TYPE	VERSION	BEST LLT	LLT / CD LONGER BY	NOTES
I'm Losing You	Anthology		previously bootlegged	not on LLT		
Real Love	Anthology	piano demo take 4	previously unreleased	not on LLT		starts after 1", John says "bloody ass hole" for screwing up
Grow Old With Me	Anthology	George Martin orchestra	previously unreleased	not on LLT		few fade in notes missing, out before Imagine [Live]

JOHN LENNON
2009-01-18
The Mail On Sunday U.K. newspaper free insert

TITLE	SOURCE	TYPE	VERSION	BEST LLT	LLT / CD LONGER BY	NOTES
Imagine	Anthology	alt take take 1		Part 29		

AFTERWARD

The never-ending flood of Beatles-related bootlegs did not letup since *The Lost Lennon Tapes* was broadcast. This material has been recycled many times since 1992, and it's possible that some of it may have been reissued in better or longer versions than on the original radio shows. I wouldn't know. As well, some of the material that was relatively scarce then (like some of the BBC tracks) are commonplace in the collectors' world today. It would be impossible to track what has become of every single rarity that was broadcast on *The Lost Lennon Tapes*. This book is a snapshot of what was new and what was previously bootlegged then and not now.

My personal connection with *The Lost Lennon Tapes* came when Fred McKie told me that they were looking for an audio tape of John on *The Tomorrow Show* with Tom Snyder. Of course, I had a copy, as I had dutifully recorded it from our television in 1975, using my favourite method of inserting two wires into the TV's speaker and running it to the "line in" on my reel-to-reel tape recorder (being careful not to electrocute myself in the process). I was amazed that they didn't have a copy of the interview themselves, and even more surprised that I was not credited on the show on which it was broadcast. Instead, I was given credit for a snippet of a bed-in interview that I sent along with it, which was broadcast on Show #96.

Looking back on it all, I would never have taken this on had I known the years of work that it was destined to take and had it not been for Belmo. It definitely was a "labour of love" as they say, and I certainly would not have begun a Beatles-related project of this scope today. All I can add now is thank goodness it's finished and to quote Johnny himself, "Good night to ya'z all and God bless ya'z."

www.ingramcontent.com/pod-product-compliance
Lightning Source LLC
Chambersburg PA
CBHW020747160426
43192CB00006B/273